EXCEPTIONAL STUDENTS IN THE MAINSTREAM

Lita Linzer Schwartz

The Pennsylvania State University
Ogontz Campus

Wadsworth Publishing Company
Belmont, California
A Division of Wadsworth, Inc.

Education Editor: *Bob Podstepny*
Production Editor: *Deborah M. Oren*
Designer: *Cynthia Bassett*
Copy Editor: *William T. Reynolds*
Technical Illustrator: *Mary Burkhardt*
Cover: *Grant Peterson*
Cover Photographs: *Elizabeth Crews*
Signing Representative: *Winston Beauchamp*

Part-Opening Photo Credits

Part 1 Elizabeth Crews

Part 2 Martine Franck/Magnum Photos, Inc.

Part 3 George Bellerose/Stock, Boston

Part 4 Paul Conklin

Part 5 James Motlow/Jeroboam

Part 6 Cheryl A. Traendly/Jeroboam

Printed in the United States of America

1 2 3 4 5 6 7 8 9 10—88 87 86 85 84

ISBN 0-534-02988-4

Library of Congress Cataloging in Publication Data

Schwartz, Lita Linzer.
  Exceptional students in the mainstream.

  Bibliography: p.
  Includes index.
    1. Exceptional children—Education—United States.
  2. Mainstreaming in education—United States.   I. Title.
  LC3981.S38   1984   371.9   83-12513
  ISBN 0-534-02988-4

CONTENTS

PART TWO / Physically Impaired Students / 105

Chapter 5 / The Orthopedically Disabled and Chronically Ill / 108

PART THREE / Students with Oral Communication Difficulties / 163

Chapter 9 / The Speech Impaired / 165

Chapter 10 / The Language Handicapped / 176

PREFACE

Both as a professional visitor to classrooms and as a parent, I'm well aware that there is no such thing as a class full of "average" children. One youngster has "lazy eye" and has to wear a patch over the "good" eye for several months, another student's parents have decided to get a divorce, and a third child is too shy to read aloud in class. In addition, a teacher may be confronted with students who have a temporary orthopedic handicap, or who are abused at home, or whose family lifestyle is different from that of the rest of the students. For all such youngsters, there are psychological ramifications that may affect their general behavior as well as their academic performance. Yet teachers do not ordinarily find these instances too unsettling or difficult to handle; they adapt to the situation.

However, once a student acquires an "exceptional" label, classroom teachers often feel ill equipped to help the children learn. It's been evident to me for years, as a result of witnessing such anxiety, that every teacher—general or special—can profit from learning about exceptional students in all their variety and about the techniques and skills that are helpful in teaching them. This book is the outcome, therefore, of experience, thought, and research applied to meeting these needs of preservice and in-service regular and special education teachers.

Special Features

Coverage   Exceptional students vary in age, grade level, personal characteristics, and degree of exceptionality. A comprehensive coverage of intellectual, physical, communicational, cultural, and psychosocial differences is therefore a key element of this book. Unique and useful are the chapters on the culturally and linguistically different, especially as more and more communities become home to Hispanics and Southeast Asians and to refugees from economic and political crises.

In addition, the effects on parents of students considered exceptional and their consequent interaction with school personnel are examined in an independent chapter. Too often the parents' role in their child's education is overlooked. Since parental support and cooperation are important for maintenance of student learning, particularly with intellectual or physical disabilities, it is equally important that the teacher recognize the impact of exceptionality on the family.

Controversial Issues   Several years of experience with the mainstreaming goal of the Education for All Handicapped Children Act (P.L. 94-142) have evoked controversy. The different positions are discussed in order to provide the reader with a fuller perspective on this critical issue. Although the emphasis in the book is on mainstreaming exceptional students, the reader is also informed of those instances where mainstreaming may not be appropriate and of what alternative placements are available.

Other controversial issues, such as education of the gifted and talented, bilingual education, preschool programs, educational philosophy and the culturally different, and the role of principals in special education, are similarly presented as food for thought. Awareness that there frequently are no pat answers is also educational.

Effects of P.L. 94-142   P.L. 94-142 has had a marked impact on preservice and in-service teacher education. We can no longer assume that exceptional students will be taught by special education teachers only; thus, innovations in teacher education generally are discussed, with ample attention paid to the needs of students with specific exceptionalities.

Also a result of P.L. 94-142 is the recognition that exceptional students are to be educated through age twenty-one. The chapters on exceptionalities therefore include discussions of secondary education programs, the problems of adolescence and young adulthood, and planning for adult roles and functioning.

Readability   Students and reviewers alike have commented that the text is highly readable and free of jargon. My favorite comment came from a student: "I can hear you talk as I read."

Format   Each chapter deals with a specific exceptionality, discussing the available options in educational modifications but focusing on practical techniques for teaching and working with students of that type. Stress is placed on the student's needs for today and tomorrow rather than on the causes of the condition (although these are discussed in introducing the exceptionality). Every chapter has a list of supplemental readings that provide a helpful addition to the references. The supplemental readings also permit the instructor to adapt the course requirements to the differing interests and levels of ability in the class.

General Philosophy

Like all people, students are unique individuals. That's what makes teaching them a challenging and exciting task. The students you will meet in this book are unique to a greater degree than so-called average students, but all of them can learn. It's all a matter of finding appropriate teaching techniques to help them learn. Teaching teachers to do this effectively is the goal of this book.

Acknowledgements

Photographs were taken especially for this book by Amy L. Birrittella, Wendy Bishop, G. Fred Rieman, Jr., and Marjorie Weintraub, for which I thank them. For permission to include other photographs, my thanks go to Gayle Carol Brygler, Norma Chein, Elizabeth Crews, and Larry F. McSwain. I also appreciate the thoughtful samples of IEPs provided by Michael Rothstein and Frances Schwartz.

For aid in obtaining articles and books that were frequently located in obscure places, I am really indebted to the staff of the Ogontz Campus Library of the Pennsylvania State University. The interest of the librarians in my areas of interest has truly made this project a shared enterprise.

Dr. Robert A. Bernoff and Dr. Sanford F. Nicol, Director and Assistant Director (Resident Instruction), respectively, of the Ogontz Campus, were most cooperative in arranging schedules so that there would be time to write this text. They also made possible my participation in on-campus programs for exceptionally able youngsters and in relevant professional conferences. All of their support is gratefully acknowledged.

Dennis J. Fahey, Western Oregon State College; Ted S. Hasselbring, North Carolina State University; Laura J. Jordan, University of Illinois; Ralph G. Leverett, Trevecca Nazarene College; Betty J. Malmstad, Whitworth College; Thomassine Sellers, San Francisco State University; Clyde Shepherd, Keene State College; Annette Shuck, West Virginia University; Douglas C. Smith, University of Illinois at Chicago Circle; and William W. Zimmerman, University of Tulsa were the critical and very helpful reviewers of early drafts of the book. Their suggestions were constructive and are much appreciated. Any weaknesses that remain, however, are strictly my responsibility.

Vera Heitzman has been a most careful and speedy typist as the manuscript went through its revisions. Her interest and efforts are much appreciated too.

Marshall Aronson and Bob Podstepny, education editors at Wadsworth during the book's preparation, and Debbie Oren, production editor, were supportive throughout the project and were of great assistance in unraveling assorted knotty problems. Thank you!

Finally, but never last in my thoughts, are my very patient sons— Arthur, Joshua, and Frederic—who closed their ears to the clacking of typewriter keys and their eyes to piles of books and articles. Without their patience and loving support, there would be no teacher in the family and certainly no new book. They are very special people.

CHAPTER 1 /
THE EXCEPTIONAL STUDENT: AN INTRODUCTION

When we describe someone as "exceptional," we set that person apart from the "average" or "normal" people we know with respect to one or more characteristics. For example, a person who is exceptionally thoughtful is viewed as much more considerate of other people's pleasures and pains than most people are. An exceptional teacher is one who is outstanding at transmitting information and helping students to comprehend and apply that information, conscientious and consistent in evaluating students' learning, and a model for colleagues. There are also people who are exceptional in negative ways, such as being unusually or extremely domineering, hostile, or anxious. So, too, there are students who are exceptional in one way or another. The students we will be considering here are exceptional primarily with respect to their ability to learn.

WHO ARE THE "EXCEPTIONAL STUDENTS"?

Most of us have personally experienced the average classroom, in which an entire class is taught a body of knowledge in a fairly standardized manner. Recent innovations in educational technology and practice have made it possible for each pupil to progress at his or her own pace through individualized instruction, either part or all of the time. When the learner's pace and/or abilities are markedly different from those in the "average" range, however, simply changing the size of the learning group may not adequately meet that student's needs.

Special education is the all-encompassing term that describes modifications in classroom placement, curriculum, and instruction that allow nonaverage learners to learn as effectively as possible. In general, special education comprises a variety of adjustments, ranging from small group sessions one hour per week to full-time programs in special residential or day schools.

Categories

There are various ways in which students may be considered exceptional with regard to learning ability, and thus in need of special educational services. The laws of most states recognize four *categories* of exceptional students: the intellectually different, those with physical impairments, those with difficulties in oral communication, and the psychosocially or emotionally troubled. In practice, there is also a category for the culturally different. Each category contains two or more *groups* or types of exceptional students:

- Intellectual Differences
  Mentally retarded
  Learning disabled

Exceptionally able

- Physical Impairments

  Orthopedically handicapped
  Chronically ill and health impaired
  Hearing impaired
  Visually impaired
  Multihandicapped

- Difficulties in Oral Communication

  Speech impaired
  Language handicapped (non-English-speaking)

- Psychosocial Problems

  Emotionally troubled
  Socially maladjusted

- Cultural Differences

  Learning disadvantaged
  Cultural minorities

In many cases, students are in two (or more) groups or categories because their exceptionalities are interrelated. For example, hearing impaired students (and adults) frequently have speech difficulties, while members of some cultural minorities may have language handicaps and also be among the learning disadvantaged. Each group of exceptional students has its particular needs with regard to teaching methods and content, and some may need modifications in the physical setting of the classroom and school.

Numbers

As shown in Table 1.1 (which does *not* include all of the groups just mentioned), almost 4 million exceptional students between five and seventeen received special education services in 1978–79, according to reports from the individual states; more than 3.5 million (aged six to seventeen) were served in 1980–81. Figure 1.1 illustrates how the groups of exceptional students compare in size. Reports to the Office of Gifted and Talented from forty-one of the states indicated that an additional 650,270+ in that group were being served in 1978–79. Statistics are not available for some of the other groups (although some of these students may be served in one of the listed areas). However, we do know that a larger percentage of exceptional students are receiving needed special education services today than a decade ago because of the passage of federal and state laws mandating such services for them.

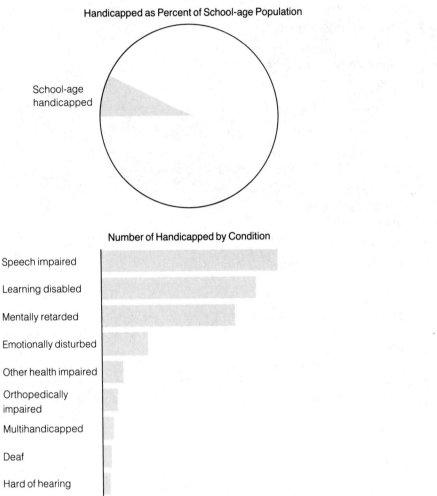

Handicapped as Percent of School-age Population

School-age
handicapped

Number of Handicapped by Condition

Speech impaired

Learning disabled

Mentally retarded

Emotionally disturbed

Other health impaired

Orthopedically
impaired

Multihandicapped

Deaf

Hard of hearing

Visually handicapped

Deaf-blind

0   1,000,000   2,000,000

Number

**Figure 1.1   School-age handicapped receiving special
education.** The handicapped who receive special education
through P.L. 94-142 and P.L. 89-313 represented almost 4 million
persons or about 8 percent of the total school-age population.
(Dearman & Plisko, 1980)

EDUCATION OF EXCEPTIONAL STUDENTS

There are three levels of government involved with special education and exceptional students: federal, state, and local. After looking briefly at the history of modern legislation leading to today's laws, and at the provisions of the Education for All Handicapped Children Act of 1975, we will examine the responsibilities assumed by each of these levels.

History of Federal Legislation

Although several states, beginning in the mid–nineteenth century, passed legislation providing for the education of mentally retarded, deaf, and/or blind children, federal action has been somewhat slower in coming. Congress did authorize the establishment of a school for the deaf, dumb, and blind in 1854, which subsequently became Gallaudet College for the education of the deaf. However, it took until 1931 for the U.S. Office of Education to develop a special unit for exceptional children (which became the Bureau for the Education of the Handicapped in 1966). In the past thirty years, though, the federal role has expanded much more rapidly.

Some educators view the 1954 *Brown* v. *Topeka Board of Education* decision (mandating desegregation of public school) as the critical event

Table 1.1 Handicapped Population Receiving Special Education and Related Services under P.L. 94-142

	School year		
	1978-79[a]	1979-80[b]	1980-81[b]
Total number served	3,709,054	3,446,168	3,560,695
Speech impaired	1,208,812	1,180,162	1,159,452
Learning disabled	1,141,202	1,265,872	1,452,738
Mentally retarded	801,813	768,840	732,940
Emotionally disturbed	269,629	295,811	310,137
Crippled/health impaired	163,840	158,554	141,230
Deaf and hard-of-hearing	58,897	56,580	54,473
Visually handicapped	22,965	22,659	23,044
Deaf-blind and multihandicapped	41,896	54,033	60,223

[a]Source: U.S. Department of Health, Education, and Welfare, Office of Education, Bureau for the Education of the Handicapped. Unpublished tabulations. Includes 5–17-year-old population.
[b]Source: Office of the Assistant Secretary for Special Education and Rehabilitative Services, U.S. Department of Education, April 1982. Includes 6–17-year-old population.

that led ultimately to Public Law 94-142, the Education for All Handicapped Children Act of 1975 (see Figure 1.2). There were by that time public school classes for all then-recognized groups of exceptional children in most states. Between 1958 and 1963, the focus of legislation and funding was on the preparation of teachers for exceptional children. The Civil Rights Act of 1964 and the Elementary and Secondary Education Act of 1965 (ESEA) were the bases for two other paths that led to P.L. 94-142. These two acts recognized that many groups in society had had unequal opportunities and set about to correct such inequities. Operation Head Start (part of the ESEA), for example, was a year-round early intervention program aimed at economically disadvantaged preschool children. Amendments to the ESEA in later years focused on early education programs for the handicapped (1968), technical assistance for educating the gifted and talented (1969), education of AmerIndian children (1972), teaching and research relevant to learning disabled children (1969), and bilingual education (1968).

Closely related to P.L. 94-142 as landmarks are court decisions such as *PARC* v. *Commonwealth of Pennsylvania* (1971) and *Mills* v. *District of Columbia Board of Education* (1972), which established the right of mentally retarded children and all handicapped children, respectively, to a "free, public program of education and training appropriate to the child's capacity. . . ." In addition, the *PARC* decision expressed a preference for regular class placement over special placement where possible and "established the right of parents to participate in major decisions affecting their children and in the observance of due process" (Reynolds & Birch, 1982, p. 33). These provisions are essential elements of P.L. 94-142. The Rehabilitation Act of 1973, Section 504, and later amendments specifically extended educational and other rights to handicapped individuals (including alcohol and drug addicts). Services to the gifted and talented, recognized as a national priority following the launch of Sputnik by the Soviet Union in 1957 (which led to the National Defense Education Act of 1958), were extended as a result of a special report by then-U.S. Commissioner of Education Sidney Marland (1971) and the passage of P.L. 95-561 (Title IX of the Education Amendments of 1978).

The pressure by parents, courts, and legislators came together in the Education for All Handicapped Children Act of 1975 (P.L. 94-142), which was signed into law by President Ford. For states to qualify for federal funds for their special education programs, they now must abide by the provisions of this law. Among these provisions are requirements that:

- All handicapped children (ages 3–21 years) are entitled to a free public education appropriate to their needs and abilities.
- There shall be no cost to the family, even if the child has to be sent to a nonpublic school to obtain an appropriate education.

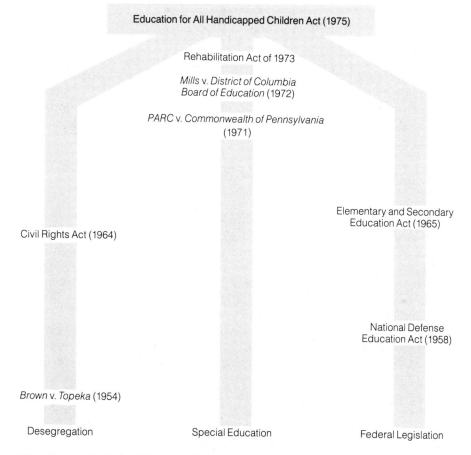

Figure 1.2   Paths leading to Public Law 94-142

- Each child to whom the Act applies must be evaluated in nondiscriminatory ways (by use of child's native or dominant language, valid tests, and knowledgeable examiners).
- Each child is to have a written Individualized Education Program (IEP) designed specifically for that child, with periodic evaluations and revision of the IEP.
- Education is to be provided in the least restrictive environment appropriate to the child's needs and abilities.
- Due process procedures are to be followed, meaning that parents have a right to all information regarding their child, to legal counsel if they feel it necessary, and to impartial hearings and appeals if they disagree with the plans for their child.

THE EDUCATION FOR ALL HANDICAPPED CHILDREN ACT

As already noted, the first step in providing services for exceptional students is to assess their abilities and needs. In fact, the Act mandates that states seek out all their handicapped children and do such assessments before designing IEPs. The goal is to match students and services as closely as possible.

Assessment

Psychological Tests   Exceptionalities may be observable at birth or soon after, as in cases of Down's syndrome (one form of mental retardation), vision or hearing impairments, and cerebral palsy. Other exceptional differences may not appear until the youngster approaches school age or is actually in school. Initial screening procedures often reveal areas in which these children have potential learning problems, but they are too unreliable to be effective diagnostic tools.

Thus, those who are identified by such screening measures as possibly in need of special services have to be evaluated further by individual tests. With regard to learning abilities, for example, children who score outside the average range on group intelligence tests (either above or below the average) are retested with individual intelligence tests such as the Stanford-Binet or the Wechsler Intelligence Scale for Children—Revised (WISC-R). In this one-to-one situation, the psychologist can observe behaviors and emotions that may affect responses that could not be observed by someone administering the test to a class of twenty-five to thirty-five children. Similarly, students identified as possibly having a hearing impairment during screening are referred to audiologists and physicians for further examination.

Educational diagnosis, using tests that are as unbiased as possible, indicates the skill levels at which the student is functioning in reading (or reading readiness), language usage, mathematics, and other academic areas. Typical diagnostic measures include phonics inventories, the Gates-McKillop Reading Diagnostic Test, the Durrell Analysis of Reading Difficulties, the Key Math Diagnostic Arithmetic Test, checklists, criterion-referenced tests, and achievement tests. Criterion-referenced tests have specific standards or criteria for a skill or content area that the student must meet in order to move on to the next level of instruction. The tasks within the test are so arranged that they can pinpoint weaknesses and strengths. These tests are also called "mastery tests," because they require that the student perform 80–90 percent of the task correctly in order to "pass," or show mastery.

FOR EXAMPLE . . .

The familiar Snellen eye chart, used by physicians and school nurses to test for vision problems, can lead to either false positive or false negative results sometimes. When too many children are incorrectly identified as being nearsighted, for instance, that is a false positive error. On the other hand, the chart may not pick up all vision problems; for example, a child might memorize the letters when reading with her better eye and simply repeat them when reading with the weaker or diseased eye. This would lead to a false negative error.

Patterns can be found in all of this testing that differentiate among exceptional students. Educable mentally retarded (EMR) students, for instance, tend to have low intelligence test scores that do not vary too much across types of tasks; they also tend to be from disadvantaged socioeconomic backgrounds. Learning disabled (LD) students (who, by definition, are of average or above-average intelligence) are distinguished by the variation of their scores on different tasks and by uneven patterns of achievement. Emotionally troubled (ED) students were differentiated from the preceding groups in one study primarily by their scores on a behavior checklist, for they had similarities to the other two in some academic areas: They resembled learning disabled students in intelligence test total scores and educable mentally retarded students in variability patterns (Gajar, 1980). Academically gifted students, on the other hand, tend to score well above average on intelligence and achievement tests.

Other Methods   Systematic observation by the teacher and/or school psychologist is often used to discover a student's work habits, preferred style of learning, emotional behavior, and interpersonal relationships. It is preferable to have two independent observers to reduce the chance of bias in the observations and also to guard against distractions while observing. Each observer watches the child in action for perhaps five minutes per hour several times a day for a few school days so that what is seen is truly representative of the child's behavior. (If observed on only one day, that may be the day that the child is upset, ill, or unusually quiet.)

Developmental, medical, social, and emotional case histories of the student also contribute to the assessment. The first two are often in checklist form, while the latter may be anecdotal (brief paragraphs describing specific incidents). These case histories sometimes reveal possible causes of learning difficulties, such as "Danny had meningitis at age two," or "Jill consistently has difficulty in following directions given to the group." Interviews with a youngster may also reveal strengths, weaknesses, and problems as he perceives them.

Designing the IEP

In order to determine what constitutes "appropriate education" for each exceptional student, the Act directed that an Individualized Education Program, or IEP, be designed (with the parents' participation) for each of these students. The IEP is based on a multifaceted assessment of each individual's academic, physical, and social abilities and needs. The written IEP spells out the nature of the personnel, resources, and learning environment that are expected to be most helpful to the student's progress and provides for changes in the program based on continuing evaluations of that progress toward specifically stated goals. Samples of IEPs are to be found in Appendix B of this book.

The total evaluation by the team of professionals is oriented to planning appropriate instruction rather than to pinning a diagnostic label on the student (although labels are often used as a convenient "shorthand"). In some cases, however, where a child has more than one area of exceptionality, it may be difficult to decide which exceptionality should have first priority in the planning.

The law requires that "all IEPs include statements of the child's present level of educational performance, annual goals, short-term instructional objectives, the extent to which the child will participate in regular programs, the dates during which the IEP will be applicable, and the criteria and procedures that will be used in evaluating the program's effectiveness" ("Implementing the IEP Concept," 1977, p. 7). The statements about performance are based on the assessment measures already described, and the criteria for evaluating the program's effectiveness will also include a variety of assessment tools. The effective dates of the IEP are usually inclusive of a calendar or school year, although there may also be intermediate dates by which short-term instructional goals are to be met. The specifications in the law are unusual in that they call for continuing evaluation and accountability (If the goals were not met, why weren't they?). The written IEP makes the teacher's task somewhat easier in the long run, as the content and format of instruction are spelled out in detail.

The IEP is developed not only by a student's teacher and a qualified special instructor, but also in consultation with the parents and possibly the student as well. Parents must be invited to participate (although they can choose not to accept) and must agree to the plans made; they can request a "due process" hearing if they feel that the program does not meet their child's needs. A due process hearing is held before an independent examiner who sees the IEP, hears the parental disagreement with it, and then determines whether the IEP meets the law's specifications with respect to the particular child.

It should be noted that the IEP includes items other than academic goals. It must also specify special services needed, such as transportation between home and school, rest periods for some health impaired students, provisions for an aide or sign language interpreter, adaptive physical education, and any kind of therapy needed (such as speech, physical, or occupational).

The Learning Environment

P.L. 94-142 requires that handicapped children be placed in the least restrictive environment appropriate to their needs and abilities. Initially, some educators interpreted this to mean that exceptional students were all to be "mainstreamed," that is, integrated into regular classes for part or all of the school day. The objective of mainstreaming is to remove students from a segregated environment so that they can be with "normal" children of their own age, gain a more positive self-concept, and improve their learning abilities. Certainly not all exceptional students can benefit from this practice, however, nor does the law expect that they could. (No educator, for example, would consider mainstreaming appropriate for a deaf-blind, moderately retarded student.) Therefore, in practice there are several levels of mainstreaming, as well as other alternatives. Examples of the former include placement in:

- Regular class with no special services
- Regular class with special educational materials
- Regular class with special education consultation for the teacher
- Regular class with itinerant teacher services

- Regular class plus resource room instruction
- Special class, integrated with regular class for some academic and social activities
- Special class, integrated with regular class for social benefits only (art, music, physical education, special events) (M. L. Hayes, 1981)

(As we come to these and other alternatives later in the text, their differences will become clearer.) Examples of placements that vary in degree of restrictiveness of environment but do not include mainstreaming are:

- Self-contained special class, full-time
- Self-contained special class, part-time (usually a half-day session)
- Special day school
- Homebound instruction
- Residential (custodial) placement (M. L. Hayes, 1981)

As you can see, there are many options from which to choose the "least restrictive environment" for exceptional students. In many cases, students may be moved from one type of environment to another as their needs and abilities change. For most exceptional students, this would mean moving toward placement in a regular class with no special services. However, for the exceptionally able, more appropriate movement might be toward regular class placement with supplementary services or a resource room, or even to a special day school. The continuing evaluation aspect of IEPs encourages such flexibility. As Meyen and Lehr (1981) point out, however, the assumed or real social benefits of mainstreaming should not outweigh the student's instructional needs when determining placement.

Impact on Teachers

The shifting views on educating exceptional children have also led to changes in preparing their teachers. Although teacher training in most states is oriented to specific certification (such as teacher of the mentally retarded or teacher of the blind), Pennsylvania, the District of Columbia, and a few other states now require that teachers of exceptional students be generalists in special education. There is some controversy about this change in policy. On the one hand, many exceptional students manifest more than one special condition (such as the learning disabled with emotional problems), so that the teacher needs to be competent in more than one area. On the other hand, critics of the policy question whether the generalist is sufficiently prepared to teach any of the exceptional children effectively. We will probably not have a definitive resolution to this conflict in views until we have had several years of experience with both generalist preparation and mainstreaming.

P.L. 94-142 has also had an effect on teachers already in the classroom. Those in special education are working with more students of different types as the number of recognized types of exceptional students increases. And those in regular classes are being asked more frequently to include students who often need special materials and attention to facilitate their learning. For this, most regular teachers are unprepared. They need information and support from their administrators and colleagues to reduce their anxiety about succeeding in these new situations (Harasymin & Horne, 1976) and, one hopes, to acquire positive attitudes toward their new students. One way that special education teachers can help to ensure a more beneficial and satisfying placement for both exceptional students and regular teachers is to use some variety of the checklist shown in Table 1.2 (Dardig, 1981). Thus, the special teacher is a key resource person both in preparing for mainstreaming and in implementing it.

Impact on Students

There are two groups of students to be considered here: the exceptional students and their nonexceptional peers. For the exceptional student, there are always the questions of self-esteem and peer acceptance to be answered: "Am I significant to anyone?" "Can I ever do anything right?" "Will the other kids like me?" Exceptional students need to feel good about themselves, just as other people do. They grow in many of the same ways as other children, but, because of the ways in which they differ from their peers, they may have a more difficult time achieving a positive self-concept or feeling of self-esteem. As Coopersmith (1967) has suggested, too often these (and other) young people look at themselves more in terms of their deficiencies than of their strengths and thereby develop a negative self-concept.

Although parents are the primary figures who can influence a child's feelings about himself, teachers and peers play an increasingly important role during the school years. Teachers therefore have to pay attention to the student's needs in this area as well as in academic matters. Teachers have to encourage their students to put forth effort in tasks where they can be successful, but also communicate to them that their worth as individuals is not dependent on any predetermined conditions (Battle, 1981).

After the parents and teachers, one must consider the effect of peer response to the exceptional child. As suggested in the checklist shown in Table 1.2, peers in the regular classroom should be prepared for their roles in the mainstreaming process. It has to be remembered that they will have preconceptions, brought from home or from their own experiences, that

Table 1.2   Preparing for Mainstreaming: A Special Teacher's Checklist

1. Handicapped student

Yes No
- ☐ ☐ Is familiar with rules and routine of the regular classroom?
- ☐ ☐ Follows verbal and written directions used in the regular classroom?
- ☐ ☐ Remains on-task for adequate time periods?
- ☐ ☐ Has expressed a desire to participate in the regular class setting?
- ☐ ☐ Reacts appropriately to teasing, questions, criticism, etc.?
- ☐ ☐ Student's IEP objectives match instructional objectives in regular class?

2. Regular class teacher

Yes No
- ☐ ☐ Has been given rationale for mainstreaming activities and asked to cooperate?
- ☐ ☐ Has information about handicapped student's needs, present skills, and current learning objectives?
- ☐ ☐ Has been provided with special materials and/or support services as needed?
- ☐ ☐ Has prepared class for mainstreaming activities?
- ☐ ☐ Has acquired special helping skills if necessary?
- ☐ ☐ Will be monitored regularly to identify any problems that arise?

3. Nonhandicapped peers

Yes No
- ☐ ☐ Have been informed about handicapped student's participation and about handicapping condition (if appropriate) with the opportunity to ask questions?
- ☐ ☐ Have been asked for their cooperation and friendship toward handicapped student?
- ☐ ☐ Have learned helping skills and praising behaviors?

4. Handicapped student's parents

Yes No
- ☐ ☐ Have received verbal or written information about mainstreaming situation?
- ☐ ☐ Have been asked to praise and encourage child's progress in regular as well as special class?

5. Nonhandicapped students' parents

Yes No
- ☐ ☐ Have been informed about mainstreaming activities at PTA meeting, conferences or through other vehicle and asked for their cooperation?

6. School administrator

Yes No
- ☐ ☐ Has been informed about specifics of mainstreaming activities?
- ☐ ☐ Has indicated specific steps she or he will take to encourage and support these activities?

Dardig, J. C. Helping teachers integrate handicapped students into the regular classroom. *Educational Horizons*, 1981, 59, 129. Reprinted by permission of the publisher.

can interfere with accepting their new classmate(s). Where mainstreaming is just being introduced, special programs might be arranged for regular classes so as to reduce such interference.

FOR EXAMPLE . . .

In one special program, the course content was adapted to the needs and interests of the regular students, rather than being a standardized presentation. One five-year-old, for example, was curious about how a blind student trained his guide dog. A fourth-grader, by contrast, wanted to learn to operate an optacon, which is an electronic scanner that enables the blind to read ordinary print by raising the individual letters so that they can be felt (Cleary, 1976).

An exceptional student who is integrated into a regular class for the first time will naturally have some anxiety along with the anticipation of more pleasant challenges. She should be prepared beforehand, too, so that she knows what to expect and what will be expected of her. Meeting the new teacher(s), visiting the new school or a different part of her home school, and being introduced to a few new classmates are all ways in which she can be reassured that she is expected and welcome. She should also be made to feel confident that if she needs special help or cannot quite "make it" after a reasonable trial period, there are other options available, and the special education teacher will be ready and willing to receive her.

Extension of the School Year

For many exceptional students (as well as some nonexceptional ones), the usual summer vacation from school leads to regression rather than progression. That is, the interruption in their education for such an extended period causes them to slip backward, to lose some of the gains made during the school year. Several parents took school systems to court about this, alleging that the usual 180-day school year did not meet their children's special needs and was therefore in violation of the requirements of P.L. 94-142. In 1980, the U.S. Third Circuit Court of Appeals supported a ruling of the U.S. District Court that agreed with this viewpoint. The court ordered that those exceptional children who would regress without year-round schooling, as determined on an individual basis, were to be provided with a lengthened school year to meet their needs (Reynolds & Birch, 1982). The impact of this decision on the nation's school districts in terms of costs and personnel contracts has yet to become known.

Criticism of the Act

The American ideal of providing education for as many as possible for as long as possible is being implemented through the Education for All Handicapped Children Act. The process of deciding who should have which services is a time-consuming one with many complications, but it is well worth it if students receive the education that best fits their abilities and needs. As we examine each of several exceptionalities in the following chapters, though, the conflict between idealism and practicality will become apparent.

Some voices have already been raised, in fact, questioning whether P.L. 94-142 (including its pressure for mainstreaming) actually accomplishes its goals. Vernon (1981), for example, points out that the Act, by placing the federal government in a position to dictate to local school districts how they will educate their handicapped children, may be in conflict with the Constitution. In addition, there are economic and moral problems in his view. Acknowledging that there is a moral obligation to provide for those who are most dependent, Vernon questions whether it is also morally justifiable to make the largest per capita educational investment in those least likely to profit from it or to become contributing members of society. Further, he questions the educational and economic feasibility of emphasizing local programs for handicapped students. He alleges that educational programs, especially in the areas where few exceptional students have similar needs, contradict what has been learned about teaching the handicapped over many decades. The costs of providing needed special services for each exceptional student, a factor that *cannot* be considered by local districts under the law, can be ten times the average per-pupil expenditure. Vernon considers this unreasonable and unrealistic.

Pittenger and Kuriloff (1982) echo several of these opinions, suggesting that the conditions to be met in conforming to the law place "onerous" burdens on states and local districts. While praising the requirement that parents be consulted about the education of their exceptional children, these educators are concerned with the resulting conflict on the merits of separate versus integrated schooling, the increases in administrative red tape and court suits, and the costs of the mandated programs, which "far outrun expectations" (p. 79).

Part of the purpose of mainstreaming, you will recall, is to integrate exceptional students socially with their peers. This practice is expected to increase social interaction between handicapped and nonhandicapped students, the social acceptance of the handicapped, and the social skills of handicapped persons. Gresham (1982), in his review of studies published in 1970–80, asserts that these assumptions are in error. He attributes some of the reported negative outcomes of mainstreaming to lack of adequate training of handicapped students in social skills. In his view, social skills assessment and training should be a continuing process before, during, and after the time that mainstreaming takes place. Battle and Blowers (1982) aver that exceptional children in special classes gain more positive self-esteem than their peers who are mainstreamed, possibly because they feel more accepted by peers like themselves than they would by non-handicapped peers.

These are serious criticisms of a law that is having so much impact on students, teachers, and taxpayers. Although many successful experiences are cited in the pages that follow, the points raised by these critics are likely to be continuing subjects of heated discussion as both perceived needs and the costs of meeting them increase.

GOVERNMENT RESPONSIBILITIES

Federal Responsibility

Although education is not mentioned anywhere in the United States Constitution, there is a clause in the Preamble to the Constitution that speaks of the government's responsibility for the "general welfare" of the people, and the Fourteenth Amendment guarantees "equal protection" under the law for everyone. This has meant that, unlike most countries, we do not have a centralized department of education that establishes a national curriculum or issues nationwide teacher certification. The existing U.S. Department of Education (established in 1980) is a descendant of the Office of Education established in 1867. Its main functions have been the collection and dissemination of information on education in and to the several states. A second area of functioning has been the administration of a variety of research projects and special programs.

Basing its action on the "general welfare" and "equal protection" clauses, however, the federal government, through Congress, has had a significant role in directing educational attention to specific needs and national priorities. In this century, for example, such efforts have included funding vocational, home economics, and adult education (Smith-Hughes Act of 1917); stimulating research and education in science and foreign languages (National Defense Education Act of 1958); teacher preparation; and education for exceptional children. These directions are encouraged primarily through the funding of research projects and special programs. President Johnson's massive "War on Poverty," for example, provided abundant funds for introducing programs that would enable economically disadvantaged children to have more equal *opportunity* for education, beginning with early intervention and remedial reading programs.

Such federally supported programs place a number of burdens on state and local educators, resulting in complaints that the federal government has intruded on the states' territory. President Reagan has proposed reducing the federal role, both by decreasing the funds appropriated in the national budget for educational purposes and by shifting the distribution of available funds to the states in lump sums or "block grants." Each state would then decide which programs would receive funds. (Note: The existing practice awards "categorical grants," which are funds given in specific amounts for educating specific groups or supporting specific programs. An example of a categorical grant would be $2 million for programs for the education of the moderately mentally retarded in vocational skills.)

State Responsibility

Since any governmental powers not specifically given to the federal government in the Constitution are left to the several states under Article X, education has been primarily a state responsibility throughout our history as a nation. Each state's legislature has passed laws that specify the number of days in the school year, which courses *must* be taught and which *may* be taught, pupil transportation policies, teacher qualifications, and so on. Each state's department of education is directly responsible for seeing that these requirements are met.

State laws vary in their specifications for programs for exceptional students (although presently they must conform to the Education for All Handicapped Children Act if federal funds are to be used for such programs). Generally, however, they affirm the "right to learn" for all children, describe the populations to be served under special education provisions, state administrative and financial responsibilities, and, in some cases, stipulate the number of children at varying age levels permitted in specified types of classes. The laws are intended to protect the rights of exceptional children, provide for their appropriate education, and protect special education teachers from such unrealistic teaching situations as overcrowded classes, too many types of exceptional children in a single class, and vague and limitless teacher functions.

Almost every state has special schools for specific handicaps, such as deafness and blindness. Others provide special schools within state institutions. The amount of financial support given to local school districts for special education services and facilities, however, varies widely. If the Elementary and Secondary Education Consolidation Act of 1981, which included the concept of block grants, had been passed, the ways in which the funding is handled would have changed. The bill would have effectively repealed P.L. 94-142 and related laws, reduced funding over a period of years, and in the opinion of the Council for Exceptional Children, undermined the progress made in special education in the past decade ("Block Grant Bill Submitted to Congress," 1981). Much more discretion would have been allowed on the part of the state and local school districts as to which special programs would be funded, leading to considerable conflict among parents and others concerned with the education of different groups of exceptional students.

Local Responsibility

The local school district acts as agent for the state in providing educational services. Through the school board, it raises the funds to operate local schools (in addition to those granted by the state), sets the budget (usually subject to state approval), hires and fires school personnel, decides what will be taught to meet state directives and local needs, and carries out all other education policies of the state. This responsibility in relation to special education specifically is examined in Chapter 16.

Part of the local board's job is to build and maintain school buildings. Because of federal legislation (both P.L. 94-142 and Sections 503 and 504 of the Rehabilitation Act of 1973), the board must now consider the needs of all children in planning a new school facility or renovating an old one. Architects and special education personnel should collaborate from early in the planning stage, carefully considering each other's needs and goals as they each translate their expertise into a physical environment comfortable for students and teachers.

It is at the local level that most teachers, students, and parents interact. It is here that the most complaints and compliments are heard about the ways in which exceptional students are or are not educated beneficially. It is also at this level that conflicts occur between taxpayers and school boards, as the cost of furnishing educational services for all children continues to rise. Because of the special education laws now in effect, the schools need more school psychologists to assess the special needs of exceptional children, more teachers to teach them as the law requires, and more special facilities and materials to meet their needs. Even taxpayers sympathetic to the needs of exceptional students, however, sometimes find it difficult to support tax increases in periods of inflation and a depressed economy. The resulting conflict in conscience is not an easy one to resolve.

MEETING THE TEXT

Overview of Contents

In preparing this text, I've tried to anticipate what questions might be asked by someone new to the world of special education and exceptional students. In developing answers to those questions, I have considered not

FOR EXAMPLE . . .

The McDonald Comprehensive Elementary School in Warminster, Pennsylvania, is one example of this type of preplanning. For the orthopedically handicapped, the designers have provided two classrooms and an adjacent therapy room, with ramps rather than stairs linking wings of the building, as well as a large swimming pool (used also for other purposes) and specially adapted lunchroom tables. The trainable retarded have a suite of small rooms approximating the major rooms in a home so that they may learn self-help and household routines by actually performing relevant tasks. The exceptionally able benefit from a well-stocked library and an instructional materials center. Each of these groups also has opportunities to interact with children in regular classes, either through mainstreaming or in the lunchroom, at school assemblies, and in other school-related activities.

only what is considered common knowledge in the field but also some of the controversies that surround policies and practices in this area of education. Pointing out the criticisms of P.L. 94-142 and the problems confronting local school districts are only two examples of such controversies. In this first chapter, I have also tried to give you a basis for understanding why modifications in regular classes are so often stressed in the chapters to come.

As indicated earlier in this chapter, there are five broad categories of exceptionalities, each comprising two or more groups of exceptional students. Accordingly, you will meet each of these groups in greater depth, chapter by chapter, following an introduction to each category of exceptionality. The three final chapters are focused on the teachers, administrators, and families of exceptional children. There is no way to understand the total picture of exceptional students without being aware of the interrelationships among these three groups and between each of them and the students. You should be aware, also, that many of the groups discussed are not included under P.L. 94-142 or any other special federal laws (although provisions for their special needs *may* be made at a state or local level).

Following the chapters, there are a number of appended sections. To illustrate the implementation of IEP goals, there is a brief section on lesson planning. Sample IEPs, designed by teachers of exceptional students, illustrate the details included in these documents. A list of organizations and resources relevant to the different exceptionalities is included, both for obtaining more detailed information now and for future use. There is then a list of literary works that focus on exceptional people. Often these books provide a new perspective on the people or their exceptionalities that goes beyond what is taught in a course.

A glossary defining new terms is also included so that you can better comprehend the special meanings of certain words or of technical language (although there isn't a great deal of the latter). Finally, of course, there is a reference list of all the authors cited in the text, alphabetized to make finding a specific reference easier for you.

Chapter Formats

In general, each chapter that deals with the students themselves (Chapters 2–14) begins by describing the characteristics of the group being discussed and the ways in which its members are identified. If there are controversies about how these students should be educated, the differing viewpoints are presented. The kinds of school settings, modifications to facilities (if needed), and teaching practices most appropriate to their exceptionalities form the "meat" of the chapter. If counseling and guidance are appropriate for a particular group, those aspects are also included.

Each chapter is introduced by an outline of its topics and ends with a summary of what was discussed. Specific examples are given to illustrate points, in the form of a brief case study, an anecdote, or perhaps a teaching strategy. Finally, each chapter has a list of suggested additional readings—articles and books that were not cited in the chaper but which can provide more information about matters that were included.

SUMMARY

Beginning with a broad description of exceptional students and their numbers in the school population, this introductory chapter has tried to "set the stage" for you as you begin your study of exceptional students. Five categories of exceptional students were identified who differ from the "average" student sufficiently to need special education to some degree. These are the intellectually different, the physically impaired, the psychosocially troubled, those with oral communication difficulties, and the culturally different.

Under the heading "Education of Exceptional Students," you became acquainted with the historical background that led to the Education for All Handicapped Children Act of 1975, and with both the provisions and the criticisms of that Act. Specifically, discussion of the Act dealt with assessment techniques (psychological tests and other means), the development of Individual Education Programs (IEPs), the concept of the "least restrictive environment" for the student's learning experiences, and the impact of the Act on both teachers and students. With several years of experience in implementing the Act behind us, some educators have found that the challenges it poses are creating new problems, and these, too, were discussed.

Each of the three levels of government—federal, state, and local—has responsibilities to the young people with whom we are concerned. The crucial question of whether the federal government should specify the programs to be funded or leave that decision to the states and local districts ("categorical" versus "block" grants) was examined in this section. The ways in which each level determines who is to be taught and how, as well as at what cost, were other issues discussed.

The final part of the chapter described the format of this book in terms of chapters and appended materials. Taken altogether, the chapter has introduced you to the complexities of educating exceptional students.

SUGGESTED ADDITIONAL READINGS

Abeson, A., and Blaklow, J. *Environmental design: New relevance for special education*. Arlington, Va.: Council for Exceptional Children, 1971.

Bernard, R., and Clarizio, H. Socioeconomic bias in special education placement decisions. *Psychology in the Schools*, 1981, *18*, 178–183.

Harmony, M., Ed. *Promise and performance: Children with specific needs: ACT's guide to TV programming for children*, Vol. 1. Cambridge, Mass.: Ballinger, 1977.

Hobbs, N. *The futures of children*. San Francisco: Jossey-Bass, 1976.

Joiner, L. M., and Sabatino, D. A. A policy study of P.L. 94-142. *Exceptional Children*, 1981, *48*, 24–33.

Kolucki, B. "Sesame Street" challenges secrets that shouldn't be. *The Directive Teacher*, 1980, *2* (5), 5–6, 29–30.

Landau, E., Epstein, S., and Stone, A. *The exceptional child through literature*. Englewood Cliffs, N.J.: Prentice-Hall, 1977.

Maddux, C. D., and Maddux, S. J. Peer relations: Key to mainstreaming. *Academic Therapy*, 1983, *18*, 261–266.

Merulla, E., and McKinnon, A. "Stuck" on Deno's cascade. *Journal of Learning Disabilities*, 1982, *15*, 94–96.

Miller, S. R. A crisis in appropriate education: The dearth of data on programs for secondary handicapped adolescents. *Journal of Special Education*, 1981, *15*, 351–360.

Powell, M. L. *Assessment and management of developmental changes and problems in children*. St. Louis: C. V. Mosby, 1981.

Ross, A. O. *The exceptional child in the family*. New York: Grune & Stratton, 1964.

Smart, R., Wilton, K., and Keeling, B. Teacher factors and special class placement. *Journal of Special Education*, 1980, 14, 217–230.

Tractenberg, P. L., and Jacoby, E. Pupil testing: A legal view. *Phi Delta Kappan*, 1977, 59, 249–254.

PART ONE/
INTELLECTUALLY
DIFFERENT
STUDENTS

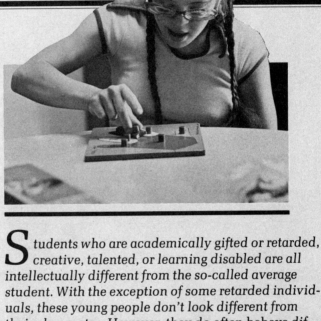

S tudents who are academically gifted or retarded, creative, talented, or learning disabled are all intellectually different from the so-called average student. With the exception of some retarded individuals, these young people don't look different from their classmates. However, they do often behave differently from the "normal" child as a result of their abilities, interests, and experiences. They also learn differently from the average student, in terms of pace, depth of comprehension, and ability to express and apply what they have learned. For these reasons, the intellectually different have a need for special attention from their parents and teachers, and for special educational services.

Educators usually distinguish the intellectually different student on the basis of standardized tests, observations of the child's behavior and rate of development, and other less formal measures. Intelligence test scores (usually referred to as intelligence quotient or "IQ" scores) can show how a person compares with

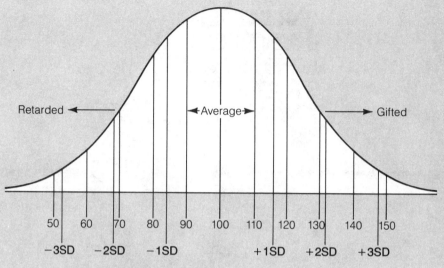

Retarded ←   ◄Average►   → Gifted

| 50 | 60 | 70 | 80 | 90 | 100 | 110 | 120 | 130 | 140 | 150 |

-3SD   -2SD   -1SD   +1SD   +2SD   +3SD

Distribution of intelligence test scores

others of the same chronological age on specific tasks. The mean IQ score
is 100, but scores in the range of roughly 90 to 110 are generally accepted
as average. Students performing markedly below or above that range are
frequently labeled exceptional students. The statistical normal curve
above illustrates the distribution of intelligence generally found in the
population.

A single test score, particularly if derived from a group test of intelligence, should not be accepted as the sole indicator of intellectual "difference," however. Group tests do not take into consideration whether an
individual's functioning was affected by ill health, a family problem, test
anxiety, language differences, or poor testing conditions. The score
merely indicates at what level the individual is functioning on a specific
day on a specific test. If available, scores and observations obtained over
a period of years are more helpful in identification of the intellectually
different.

Several years ago, Gallagher and Lucito (1961) compared groups of
gifted, average, and retarded people with regard to their high and low
subtest score areas on the Wechsler Intelligence Scale, summarizing the
results of several studies. Their results showed, among other things, that
the gifted and the retarded have almost completely opposite strengths
and weaknesses, while average students show a combination of the two
patterns (as shown in the following table). Those tests in which the gifted
score highly stress school-related learning and abstract reasoning abilities, while the retarded are strongest in areas that emphasize attention to
detail and nonverbal skills (presumably not school-related). Different

instructional techniques are therefore required to teach members of each group, since their strengths and needs are different.

A set of developmental norms has been derived from thousands of psychological and pediatric observations made in recent decades. These norms are especially useful for judging intellectual ability in preschool children. They indicate average age ranges for walking, size of vocabulary, other motor activities, varied types of interaction with family members and peers, self-care capabilities, and so on. According to developmental psychologists, for example, a child of two years should walk alone and have a vocabulary of 200–250 words, assuming normal physical conditions. A physically able three-year-old who does neither might be mentally retarded, or might have some other problem, perhaps a temporary lag or emotional troubles. A one-year-old who performs at the level of the average two-year-old, on the other hand, might be considered gifted. Finally, a two-year-old who is average or above in some areas but well below average in others might turn out to be among the learning disabled.

Combined with careful testing, a case history of the child's development, relevant medical information, and performance records, parents' or teachers' informal observations in play and work situations can help to fill out the picture of the child's intellectual abilities and suggest ways to help the child function appropriately in school and society. Whether gifted, retarded, or learning disabled, this means adapting education to the unique needs of the intellectually different individual.

Performance of Gifted, Average, and Retarded Children on the WISC

	Gifted	Average	Retarded
Number	43	565	52
Age	7–11 years	7–11 years	7–11 years
Three highest subtests	Vocabulary Information Similarities	Arithmetic Digit symbol Picture arrangement	Object assembly Digit span Picture completion
Three lowest subtests	Picture completion Digit span Digit symbol	Block design Information Similarities	Vocabulary Information Picture arrangement

Gallagher, J. J., and Lucito, L. J. Intellectual patterns of gifted compared with average and retarded. *Exceptional Children*, 1961, 27, 481. Copyright 1961 by The Council for Exceptional Children. Reprinted with permission.

CHAPTER 2/
THE MENTALLY RETARDED

Of all exceptional students, perhaps the most well publicized and most familiar to the general public are those known as the mentally retarded. Some of the publicity they have received is due to the increasing openness of public figures in discussing their familial experiences with retarded children, such as the sister of the late President Kennedy and the grandchild of the late Vice-President Humphrey.

Also, the media have increased their coverage of events like the special Olympics for retarded youth, outstanding accomplishments of retarded citizens, and investigations into the quality of services provided by institutions that house the retarded.

Beginning during the Kennedy administration in the early 1960s, a growing number of federal and state commissions have studied the specific needs of retarded citizens, and many laws have been passed to provide funding and facilities for programs to improve their lives. Among these are laws mandating special education and promoting vocational training for the retarded.

CHARACTERISTICS OF THE RETARDED POPULATION

A Definition of "Retarded"

According to the American Association for Mental Deficiency,

mental retardation refers to significantly subaverage general intellectual functioning existing concurrently with deficits in adaptive behavior, and manifested during the developmental period. (H. J. Grossman, 1973, p. 11)

The emphasis on the "developmental period" clearly focuses the definition on the first eighteen years of life, although individuals diagnosed as retarded can have a normal life span of several decades. This means also that although some people may function at a retarded level as a result of an injury or severe illness suffered in adulthood, they would not be included in the scope of the definition.

It should be noted that the definition refers to adaptive behavior as well as intellectual functioning. Adaptive behavior refers primarily to a person's ability levels in nonacademic areas such as self-care, taking responsibility, and personal independence. Direct observation, parental report, and standardized checklists are used to assess level of adaptive behavior. Subaverage intellectual functioning is usually indicated by a standardized intelligence test or other measure of an IQ score of 70–75 or below. Performance that is consistently and markedly below average in both areas is more typical of moderately to profoundly retarded persons than of the mildly retarded.

What Causes Mental Retardation?

The causes of mental retardation are generally considered to be either *endogenous* (genetic) or *exogenous* (external).

Genetic Defects   Among the endogenous causes of retardation are: (1) a dominant inheritance pattern, whereby a gene that causes a defect that results in retardation is transmitted from one generation to the next through several generations of a family; (2) a recessive inheritance pattern where neither parent is retarded but both contribute a recessive or hidden gene to a particular embryo; and (3) a genetic accident, such as a defective cell division or a genetic mutation (a sudden change in genetic structure). Examples of the first two are shown in Figures 2.1 and 2.2.

Most of the cases where inheritance is a factor are of the second type, where one or both parents are "carriers" (have the defective gene but do not exhibit signs of retardation). Examples of retardation caused by a recessive genetic factor are **phenylketonuria** (PKU), an enzyme disorder that leads to mental retardation if untreated; Down's syndrome, formerly called Mongolism; and Tay-Sachs disease, a brain disease that results in the child's early death.

In the case of PKU, there is now a diagnostic test that can be performed shortly after a baby's birth to determine whether the defect is present. If it is, the infant can be placed on a special diet immediately to prevent retardation from occurring. On the other hand, although screening tests can now identify whether a couple are carriers of Tay-Sachs disease, nothing can be done to prevent the retardation and death of a Tay-Sachs child once born. The infant's metabolism is affected, followed by degeneration of the brain and a gradual but progressive deterioration of the nervous tissue, until the child dies at age three or four. (There is a juvenile form of this condition that has its onset in early childhood rather than at birth, but death still follows within a few years.)

Down's syndrome, which is caused by the presence of extra genetic material (trisomy 21) on the twenty-first chromosome or by the location of a chromosome in the wrong place, is recognizable because of certain physical characteristics it produces: a lack of an eyelid fold (as in Asian

Figure 2.1   Transmission of dominant genes. Parent A is retarded, as are the two children who inherit the dominant gene for retardation. Parent B and the other two children are of normal intelligence, according to the laws of probability.

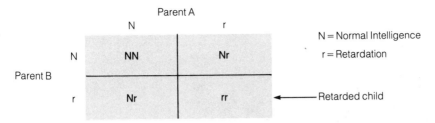

Figure 2.2 Transmission of recessive genes. If each parent is carrying a gene for normal intelligence and a recessive gene for retardation, both the parents and three of the four children (theoretically) will be normally intelligent. However, two of those three children will be carriers of the gene for retardation.

eyes), a flat face, a short broad neck, a tongue that appears large in proportion to the mouth, and fine, straight hair. This condition occurs in about one out of every 900–1,000 births. Down's syndrome was long thought to occur primarily in children born to women aged thirty-five and older and to be the result of defective cell division in the egg. More recent research, however, indicates that only about 20 percent of Down's syndrome babies are born to older mothers, and that in almost a quarter of these cases, the cause is traceable to a defective sperm fertilizing a normal egg (Holmes, 1978; *Mental Retardation*, 1981). Most Down's syndrome individuals function at a moderately retarded level (are *trainable*, in educational terms) and need supportive care throughout their lives (Koch & Koch, 1976).

External Factors   Among the exogenous or external causes of retardation are: (1) conditions affecting the mother during pregnancy (*prenatal*), such as acute illness (rubella or German measles, influenza, one of the herpes viruses), inadequate nutrition, radiation, toxemia (poisonous substance in the bloodstream), chronic illness (diabetes), chronic alcoholism, exposure to pollutants, and the use of certain drugs; (2) conditions that affect the infant at birth (**perinatal**), such as anoxia (oxygen deficiency), prematurity, low birth weight, difficulties experienced during labor or delivery, and blood incompatibility with the mother (different Rh factors); and (3) *postnatal* causes, such as nutritional deficiencies (lack of proteins, iodine, vitamins), head injuries, infection, exposure to various chemicals (carbon monoxide, lead, drugs, pesticides), and endocrine dysfunction.

A large portion of the retarded population, however, are victims of cultural-familial or psychological disadvantage. That is, the parents tend to be poorly educated and can offer their children little in the way of verbal or experiential stimulation. Because of their very limited range of experiences—not knowing one animal from another, never leaving the

Developing fine motor skills is often a major task for Down's syndrome children. (With permission of HDS/U.S. HHS.)

immediate home neighborhood, not being read to—these children are ill-prepared for formal schooling and consequently score poorly on tests and perform inadequately in the classroom. These are the mildly retarded youngsters most often found in regular classrooms.

Classifications and Abilities of the Retarded

There are four levels of retardation: mild, moderate, severe, and profound. Each level needs a different type of education and faces a different type of future. Although the regular classroom teacher will typically have only mildly (educable) retarded youngsters in class, some awareness of the characteristics and the educational requirements of the less able will provide the teachers with needed perspective. A breakdown of the different levels by IQ and expected adult performance ability is shown in Table 2.1.

If you think of the performance level of normal children at these different ages, then you will have a better idea of the maximum potential capabilities of the retarded as adults. College students visiting a school for the moderately retarded tend to be quite shaken, for example, when they observe youths of their own age learning to roll a ball to a target or barely able to read at a primer level. The students find the differences between chronological and mental ages difficult to reconcile. On the other hand, a mildly retarded adolescent could be as capable of handling a paper route

A Historical Perspective

Where several children in a family are retarded, it is sometimes difficult to determine whether the cause is a genetic one or the result of environmental deprivation. A classic study of this situation, replete with the prejudices and value judgments of the early 1900s, was Goddard's work on the Kallikak family (Goddard, 1912/1927). Tracing the family back through five generations (Figure 2.3), Goddard found that Martin Kallikak, Sr., had had, by a nameless "feebleminded" girl, a normal son who in turn sired five feebleminded children and was the ancestor of several hundred more retarded individuals, whom Goddard describes as "sexually loose," alcoholic, and criminal. Kallikak, Sr., later married a "normal" girl by whom he had normal children and hundreds of normal descendants. To Goddard, this seemed a clear case of genetic transmission, not only of feeblemindedness, but also of undesirable traits.

Today, we would question whether the descendants of Martin's first son were the victims of heredity or of culturally poor environments. As a son born out of wedlock to a poor, probably unschooled serving girl in the late eighteenth century, Martin Jr., probably had little stimulation at home, an inadequate diet, and a limited education. This socioeconomically and culturally poor environment was likely to be shared by his children and grandchildren as well. More recent research undertaken by Heber and his associates in Milwaukee (to be discussed in Chapter 11) stresses such environmental poverty as the key to familial retardation rather than heredity (Heber & Garber, 1975).

as any "normal" ten-year-old. Indeed, it is often impossible to identify an educable retarded youngster in a group of students, because they usually don't "look" different, they participate in peer activities, and their adaptation to daily life is reasonably appropriate.

Table 2.1   Characteristics of Various Levels of Retardation

Level	Educational label	IQ range[a]	Adult mental age
Mild	Educable	68–52	8–12 years
Moderate	Trainable	51–36	3–7 years
Severe	Custodial	35–20	Less than 3 years
Profound	Custodial	19 and below	Less than 2 years

[a]Hobbs (1976)

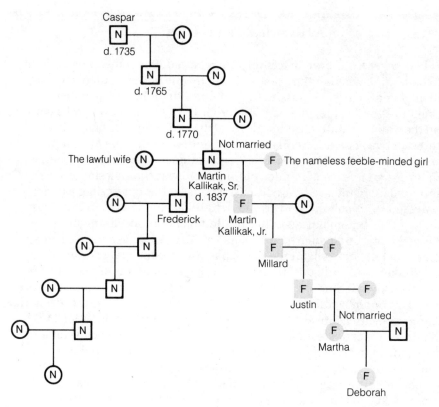

Figure 2.3   Goddard's tracing of the two branches of the Kallikaks

The Severely and Profoundly Retarded   For the severely and profoundly retarded, the future tends to be less hopeful than for those in the "higher" levels. Some never learn to use language, but most can learn certain minimal self-help skills by maturity, such as toileting, use of table flatware, dressing and undressing, and possibly some routine tasks done under direct supervision. Most severely and profoundly retarded youths do not profit from traditional education, even at the nursery school level, and cannot be expected to function independently as adults. These individuals are frequently placed in a custodial setting for long-term care.

More typical institutions, both state and privately operated, house up to several hundred retarded persons and can rarely provide more than basic custodial care because of budget and staff limitations.

The Moderately Retarded   The moderately or trainable retarded are able to do more than the custodial retarded: They can be taught to recog-

FOR EXAMPLE . . .

At the Mountainview School in Georgia, fifteen to twenty severely and moderately retarded young adults live on a large farm under the affectionate care and careful supervision of about ten teachers and houseparents. Taught to care for their personal needs, they also learn simple farming skills that enable them to help raise their own food. Rather than dully performing a single assembly line task day after day, they gain satisfaction from planting, nurturing, and harvesting vegetables and flowers.

Residents in their rural community have "adopted" some of the students, sitting with them as a family at church, having picnics with them, and exchanging gifts. To seventeen-year-old Sandy, whose IQ is about 20, these are merely familiar-looking and friendly people, but to nineteen-year-old Jonah (IQ 45), his "family" are friends who accept him as he is.

Every effort is made to help even the least able youth in the group have a measure of self-esteem and worth, even if he or she cannot read or sew or do more than set the table.

nize warning or danger signs, print their name, memorize their address and telephone number, care for their personal needs, dress themselves, and follow instructions for simple and routine tasks. Some may even master unskilled tasks that enable them to work as adults in a sheltered

FOR EXAMPLE . . .

Molly, aged seventeen and a Down's syndrome child, is the youngest of five children. She is also probably the happiest of the five, a characteristic of Down's syndrome youths. She smiles readily, greets family guests warmly, and generally tries to be helpful to her parents and older siblings. She can read at a third-grade level and do some very simple arithmetic, but her real talent is in arranging flowers. Through a work-study program at her school, after practice in the school's greenhouse, she is learning to be a florist's assistant. Molly's parents and counselor have drawn up a long-term program that has as its goal a job in a florist shop and living in a group home with three other young people and a supervisor. Her parents are aware that their other children have their own families and will be unable to take care of Molly in the future, although they do love her and welcome her in their homes.

workshop or under continuing close supervision. Full functional and economic independence is unlikely, however, for most moderately retarded adults. Indeed, the question of who will care for them after their parents die is a plaguing problem for their families. Some will be able to live in group homes in the community, but some will have to be institutionalized for lack of a caretaker within the family.

The Mildly Retarded   Mildly retarded people can function reasonably well among the general population if they have had the advantage of an appropriate education. In fact, some of them are called "six-hour retardates," because their performance level is relatively low only in the school setting. They are able to read (as adults) at an upper elementary level, can perform basic number operations, and have more adequate physical development and better motor coordination than the less capable retarded. With proper training, they can fill unskilled, semiskilled, and even some skilled jobs; in many cases, they can achieve a considerable measure of personal and economic independence. A significant increase in cooperation between employers and vocational counselors in the education and employment of the mildly retarded has opened up many new job opportunities for this group. Eventually, many individuals with mild retardation marry and have their own families and homes.

A study by Baller, Charles, and Miller (1967) of 109 men and women who had been classified as educable or mildly retarded in their school years, and who were in their mid-fifties at the time of the study, offers additional causes for optimism about this group of people. Apart from questions raised about the validity of the original diagnoses, three common factors emerged for the 65 percent of the sample who were self-supporting:

1. They tended to have middle-class habits, speech, and dress, making them more acceptable to society in general.
2. They either worked for a large paternalistic business or had learned and continued to use a single marketable skill.
3. As children, some significant adult had given them a sense of personal worth.

These factors suggest some specific practices to be incorporated into the education of the mildly retarded in regular or special classes, and also serve as a reminder that intellectual functioning is not the only criterion on which to base a diagnosis of retardation.

The mentally retarded are regarded with compassion, pity, concern, and sometimes even fear by the public at large. Their problem, while basically a learning one, also affects their behavior in other areas of life, thus causing these diverse (though not necessarily warranted) reactions. Since the educable retarded in particular can enjoy many facets of life,

Joe Taylor, now twenty-eight, is married to Doris and is the father of a six-month-old child. Joe's parents were poor and not well educated. There were few books in his home as a child. The school psychologist, on the basis of several tests, evaluated Joe as mildly or educable mentally re-tarded, with an IQ of 70. Accordingly, Joe was placed in special classes and was fortunate enough to have supportive teachers who found him very willing to learn and capable of following directions. The vocational counselor in high school helped Joe to obtain a job as a messenger for a local bank. Academically, Joe mastered the basics of arithmetic, could read on a sixth-grade level, and gained an understanding of simple business procedures through his part-time job.

After several years as a bank messenger, Joe, with the help of his wife and others, opened his own messenger service. Doris helps him with some of the paper work, and they agreed to hire as messengers other young people who had backgrounds similar to Joe's. After three years, the service is making a profit for Joe and providing employment for three others who are considered to be retarded.

even without a college diploma, and the less able retarded also may experience satisfaction and pleasure in their daily lives, such negative emotions are often inappropriate.

ASSESSMENT

How do you determine whether a child is "subaverage" in intellectual functioning and exhibits "deficits in adaptive behavior"? Generally speaking, you must use a variety of measures to assess the child's level of functioning in a variety of areas. Such evaluations are essential for plan-ning an appropriate educational program.

Approaches to Evaluation

We are accustomed to thinking of retarded students in terms of their IQs (a *psychometric* approach) or their deviation from the average score on intelligence and other achievement tests (a *statistical* approach). These are simply different ways of interpreting the same basic data. The psychometric approach is shown in Table 2.1; the statistical model, as shown in Figure 2.4, is a bell-shaped curve with emphasis on the area below the average or mean score. Here, one SD (**standard deviation**) is equal to fifteen IQ points. The educable mentally retarded (EMR) score two or more standard deviations below the mean, the trainable mentally retarded (TMR) are those in the range of about 3–4 SD below the mean, and the severely or profoundly mentally retarded (SPMR) are those scoring approximately 4.3 SD or more below the mean.

In addition to these two approaches, however, we must consider how well the youngster functions in daily life, that is, his/her adaptive behavior. This is a social or ecological approach to defining retardation. What demands are placed on the child in different situations and how well does he respond to them? Can the child care for herself in ways appropriate to her age? Can he accept responsibility such as, for example, running errands? Can she follow directions? How well does he interact with his "normal" age-peers? Can the child read, and at what level? What is her attention span? A major difference between EMR and TMR children, according to MacMillan, is that TMR children have deficits in all areas of performance, while the EMR child often has deficits only in academic areas (1982, p. 54).

Preschool evaluations

Down's syndrome children are usually diagnosed at birth, as the typical facial and other characteristics of this condition are immediately apparent. The severity of the retardation, however, is often not known for several months or even a few years. As with other infants, though, observations by parents, pediatricians, and social workers can provide clues to the rate of progress of a given child.

With very young children, marked developmental delays can be noted by anyone familiar with the average age ranges for acquisition of sensory-motor and communications skills. An unresponsive infant of, say,

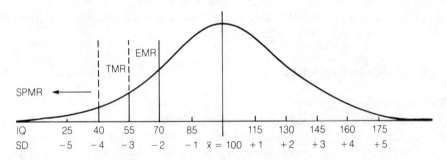

Figure 2.4   Relation of IQ scores to standard deviations from the mean

An Israeli psychologist, Reuven Feuerstein, has suggested that IQ tests can be used more effectively as **aptitude tests** (which measure ability to learn) than as **achievement tests** (which measure what has been learned). In his approach, the examiner/teacher presents a test task to the child. If the child cannot do it correctly, the examiner teaches her how to do it, then retests. This procedure is continued at more and more difficult levels.

Feuerstein found that youngsters performing at a retarded level had several weaknesses in cognitive processing that could be overcome with this type of training. These weaknesses included impulsiveness, failure to recognize inconsistencies in problems, viewing events and objects in isolation rather than in context, failure to make comparisons, and inadequate spatial orientation. There is also a self-image problem, according to Feuerstein, in that retarded children see themselves as passive receivers of information and not as being able to provide information (Chance, 1981).

Several studies testing Feuerstein's approach have been undertaken in the United States to see whether this view of plasticity of intelligence will ultimately have beneficial effects on retarded or learning disabled students in regular classroom settings. Meanwhile, findings from this test-train-test technique can be used diagnostically to direct the classroom teacher to specific needs for remedial work.

six months, who makes no effort toward turning over, smiling at familiar faces, or making cooing sounds, may be retarded (or have some other condition). One who does not sit alone by his first birthday and who appears neither to comprehend words nor to try to imitate them (assuming he has no hearing impairment) may be retarded. The Gesell Developmental Schedules (Gesell et al., 1940) and the Bayley Infant Scales (Bayley, 1969) are two measures commonly used to assess infant and toddler development. The Vineland Social Maturity Scale (Doll, 1965) and the American Association on Mental Deficiency's Adaptive Behavior Scale (Nihira et al., 1974) are used primarily to evaluate a child's progress in self-help skills and socialization.

IQ Tests

As the child approaches school age, intelligence tests often become the favored assessment tool. A child who earns a score two (or more) standard deviations below the mean IQ of 100 is considered to be retarded for educational purposes. Since these tests are largely dependent on verbal ability, the child who is slow to use and comprehend language, particularly the "standard English" of the tests, will likely earn a low score. The child who has had limited experiences also tends to score poorly; thus, a culturally different child is more likely to be labeled retarded than a white middle-class child. Children who have temporary problems that interfere with their functioning may score at a retarded level the first time they are tested, be labeled retarded, and be retained in special education classes for years despite later scores that take them out of this classification. (With the annual reviews of IEPs mandated under P.L. 94-142, this should not, of course, happen.) Possibilities such as these make it clear that IQ scores should never be the sole criterion for diagnosing retardation or for educational placement, even though they do indicate the child's functional academic level at the time of the specific test.

Observations of a child on a continuing basis, plus test scores over a period of time, are more reliable indicators of retardation than test scores alone. Similarly, Piaget's tasks can be used to provide information as to the child's level of cognitive functioning *and* to identify areas of deficit on which the teacher should focus effort (*Mental Retardation*, 1981). Work may be needed especially, for example, on memory skills and developing the ability to generalize from specifics. This would be particularly important for mildly retarded students who are to be mainstreamed in school. What type of educational placement and special services will ultimately be needed depends on knowing the magnitude of developmental lag in all areas of functioning, however, not just in cognitive abilities. What reasonable expectations can be held for the retarded individual as an adult are derived from this type of overall evaluation.

EDUCATIONAL MODIFICATIONS

In Pennsylvania, the state Association for Retarded Children successfully brought suit in 1971 to have all retarded children educated in the public schools beginning at age six. The association maintained that retarded children should not be forced to delay school entrance, nor should they be required to find private educational facilities. The state supreme court was instrumental in creating an agreement that mandated a free public education or training program for all retarded children between six and twenty-one; it also extended the right to have a public preschool program if a school district had one for nonretarded children. The school district has the option of placing these children in a classroom situation, a publicly supported training program, or homebound instruction, depending upon each child's needs. These provisions were later extended by the Federal Education for All Handicapped Children Act (P.L. 94-142).

Placement

There are a number of options for educational placement for the retarded student, depending upon the severity of the intellectual retardation and the availability of resources to serve him. Several of these options are shown in Table 2.2. They can be broadly grouped under three headings: custodial care, segregation, and mainstreaming.

Custodial Care   Custodial care is the placement alternative most commonly used for the severely and profoundly retarded because they need so much help throughout the day. If kept at home, the caretaker parent would have little time for the rest of the family, and the child would have limited opportunities for learning. (There are exceptions, of course, but they are truly rare.) Large institutions, however, tend to deindividualize the child, which is painful to the parents and not especially helpful to the child. Even with the training programs required by P.L. 94-142, relatively little learning occurs in large institutions, mainly because there are too few properly prepared teachers on the staff, and other personnel lack appropriate training. Small institutions with appropriate staff are hard to find and often expensive. Nevertheless, parents confronted with the reality that their child might outlive them turn to institutionalization as the only practical solution to care for this child who will behave as a very young person throughout his/her life span.

Segregation   Segregation in a separate building or in separate classes is most frequently the school district's response to the needs of the trainable (and some custodial) retarded. Too often, however, the provision of facilities and equipment for them has had a low priority in the district's budget. Thus, mentally retarded children have sometimes been assigned to old buildings with poor light, dingy surroundings, and inadequate equipment. By contrast, what all children need are color to bring warmth and stimulation to their lives, good lighting, and appropriate space for their

Table 2.2   Placement Options for Retarded Students

SPMR	TMR	EMR
Special day programs	Nonacademic	*Mainstreaming:*
Homebound instruction	mainstreaming	Full-time with aid
Institutionalization	Special classes	Part-time (half-day sessions)
	Special day school	plus resource rooms
		Special classes

learning experiences. Heated floors are also necessary for younger children, because they spend so much of their time on the floor in learning and play activities.

Three well-planned examples of segregated physical facilities in suburban Philadelphia can be cited. The first is a small wing in a public junior high school, with separate instruction rooms for the trainable and the educable retarded. These rooms are large and well lit and have bathroom facilities, sinks, cooking areas, and good storage space, in addition to the usual desks and chairs. Both rooms are located near the industrial arts, home economics, and physical education (regular and specially equipped) facilities, all of which the mentally retarded students use frequently. A second example is a suite for trainable mentally retarded youngsters at a comprehensive elementary school. In addition to spacious, bright classrooms, there is an "apartment without walls" to help familiarize the children with the basics of home care. They learn to make beds, wash dishes, and recognize the function of each part of a home. In the third example, a new one-story school was built to serve retarded and other exceptional students. In fact, the district's gifted elementary pupils are brought here for their enrichment classes, and there is some interaction with the neighboring elementary school population as well. Like the first two units, this facility uses color and space to provide a comfortable learning environment for the five- to twenty-one-year-old trainable mentally retarded students who are the full-time users of the building. An apartment without walls features a well-equipped kitchen that they use to prepare their own lunches. An industrial arts workshop and a greenhouse are also used for instruction.

Mainstreaming   Mainstreaming, or participating in regular classes for part or all of the school day, is possible only in limited ways for many retarded students. Some moderately retarded students may be able to handle nonacademic subjects such as music, art, shop, or physical education with nonretarded peers. There can also be integration in the lunchroom for many TMR students, as well as at school assembly programs that are primarily entertaining rather than informational. Since retarded youths differ in their individual strengths like anyone else, many of the upper-level EMR students may function well enough to take some or all academic subjects in regular classes, especially in the lower grades, but such placement is rarely appropriate for TMR children. Even the most cooperative teacher cannot hold back an entire class for one or two youngsters who learn *significantly* more slowly than the average student. (Indeed, in an analysis of various studies on mainstreaming, Gottlieb [1981] raises some serious doubts about the benefits of mainstreaming even for educable mentally retarded students.) In practice, teachers have reported that some EMR students can and do perform satisfactorily in

Moderately retarded students learn essential tasks living in this "apartment without walls." (Courtesy of Abington School District, Abington, Pa. Photo by G. Fred Reiman, Jr.)

regular classrooms, while some do not, depending on their individual strengths and weaknesses.

For those mildly retarded students who are mainstreamed, there are a variety of placement patterns at the elementary level. Least restrictive of all is full-time placement in regular classes, with in-class assistance as needed from teacher aides or peer tutors. In this setting, a consultant special education teacher often works with the classroom teacher, suggesting alternative teaching materials, content, and/or techniques as they are needed. A second option is to send the EMR student to a **resource room** for special instruction in specific skills such as reading comprehension, spelling, and multiplication. A third possibility, for those at the lower end of the EMR range, is part-time placement in a special class and part-time in a regular class, usually for less abstract subjects (MacMillan, 1982). According to Glass, Christiansen, and Christiansen (1982),

as the student progresses through the school program, the gap between his or her skills and those of the other students the same age usually grows increasingly

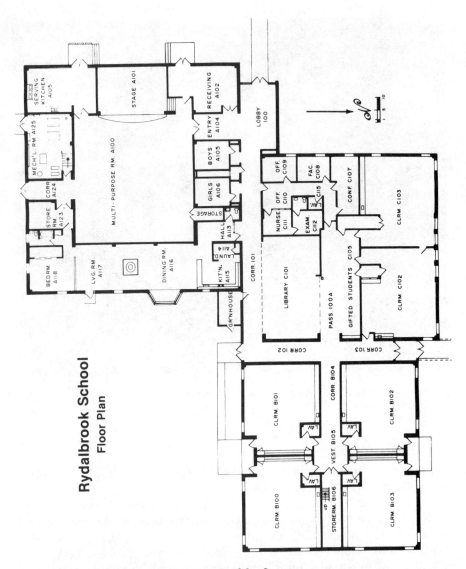

Rydalbrook School
Floor Plan

Rydalbrook school floor plan.   Designed for five- to twenty-one-year-old trainable mentally retarded students, this school enjoys interaction with neighboring elementary school students as well. (Courtesy of Abington School District, Abington, Pa.)

greater. This gap, particularly in reading, arithmetic, and language arts, makes it more difficult for mentally retarded students to participate in the classroom experiences designed for their age peers. There will be a gradual change, in most cases, to a somewhat differentiated curriculum; that is, retarded students may receive more instruction from a special instructor, and the instruction provided in

Music, woodworking, reading, and group discussion are all part of the curriculum for older TMR students. (Courtesy of Abington School District, Abington, Pa. Photo by G. Fred Reiman, Jr.)

the classroom will become more adapted to accommodate their skill level. While students may have initially received instruction from a special educator only in reading, arithmetic, and language arts, they will likely see the specialist for additional help in some content areas before the end of their elementary school program. (Glass et al., 1982, p. 65)

In secondary school, EMR students may be in regular (though somewhat homogeneously grouped) classes for required academic subjects and in regular ungrouped vocational subject classes. This, too, will vary with the specific student's skills and needs.

Caution must be exercised in mainstreaming retarded students, just as it should be in accelerating gifted students. Consideration must be given to each student's social skills, degree of peer acceptance, self-concept (which will vary with the achievement level of others in his class as well as with peer acceptance), and teacher's attitude, as well as to the number and adequacy of special services needed. Research findings suggest that successful social interaction requires preplanning and intervention by adults, such as teachers—a point to be remembered. Specific questions to ask include: Will the student be appreciably older than others in the class and therefore be uncomfortable? Do the student's problems extend beyond academic learning? Are there specific learning disabilities or emotional problems in addition to the slow learning rate? MacMillan (1982), after summarizing a number of studies with conflicting results that were done in the 1970s, cautioned educators not to exchange one set of problems (segregated education) for another (thoughtless mainstreaming). In other words, the successful placement of retarded students depends on truly examining the individual's strengths and needs rather than following a blanket policy of mainstreaming all educable retarded students. The idealism of P.L. 94-142 must be tempered by reality.

Content and Techniques

Controversy over how and what to teach all students has existed in the educational world for decades, if not for generations. In the early 1980s, however, the conflict has become more pronounced as regards the education of the retarded, as psychologists and special educators evaluate the effectiveness of recent practices. Although behavior modification is regarded as a proper approach for many tasks, there is renewed attention to Piagetian theory relevant to teaching retarded students (Weisz & Zigler, 1979); to such cognitive processes as symbolic discrimination, memory processes, and language development; and to the value of social learning theory, particularly with regard to the effect of motivation on learning in relation to these cognitive processes (Sabatino, Miller, & Schmidt, 1981). Needless to say, the benefit of training via any approach will vary with the severity of retardation, but Sabatino and his colleagues found that language training was especially important in helping all but the most severely retarded youngsters to reach higher levels of performance. Infant stimulation programs, for example, that emphasize sensory-motor activities, language, and human interaction are helpful in reducing (though they cannot overcome) many problems that severely and profoundly retarded children may have. Such programs are even more helpful to educable children who may eventually be mainstreamed.

How to Teach   Two techniques often used successfully with retarded youngsters are behavior modification and task analysis, frequently in combination. For the EMR student, these techniques may be used primarily by the resource teacher, although a willing classroom teacher might adapt assignments to a task analysis format and use positive reinforcement liberally as the youngster meets classroom goals.

Typically, trainable and educable retarded children in school can learn to read, write, work with numbers, and acquire other skills if the task is broken down into small steps arranged in sequence. This process in known as *task analysis*. As each new step is mastered, it is added to those already learned, so that task performance is the result of a sequential chain of subtasks. This is really no different in principle from teaching someone to drive a car with a standard transmission or to operate a sewing machine, except that the content is school oriented.

Behavior modification (or "operant conditioning") techniques have been used effectively to teach self-care habits, reading, and socialization skills for the past few decades. This approach is based on the principle that reinforcement of behavior will increase the probability that that behavior will occur again. The reinforcer (candy, points, play time) can be given at the completion of a task or assignment, for attending to the task for a stipulated time period, or for exhibiting other desired behaviors. If

FOR EXAMPLE . . .

Task analysis requires that the target skill be defined in behavioral terms, beginning with basic behavior patterns and working discretely step-by-step to the end result. This is similar to constructing a recipe for cooking. What ingredients (tools) are needed? What motor actions must be performed and in what sequence? What time span is appropriate for carrying out each step? In instances where there is difficulty in analyzing the sequence, several methods are possible: Slow-motion filming might be done; someone can verbalize the steps while performing the task and have the words taken down on tape or by an observer; or the analyst can work backward from the completed task to the start.

"Regardless of the method of analysis employed, teachers must ensure that every step involved in completion of the final task is described in specific behavioral terms. One way to avoid general, nonbehavioral statements (*know, understand, improve, learn,* and so forth) is to use only those verbs which denote concrete observable actions (*write, name, point, trace,* etc.). The task analysis should clearly indicate what the learner must do to perform the target skill" (Laycock, 1980, p. 289).

the task to be completed has several steps, the teacher may reinforce (or "shape") each step along the way. For example, in teaching a child to print her name, she can be reinforced for printing the first letter, then for printing the first and second letters, and so on until she succeeds in printing her full name. Modeling (demonstrating what has to be done) and prompting (giving clues to the desired behavior) are also helpful in teaching retarded and other students.

At whatever level, with respect to any theoretical approach and content, it must be remembered that mentally retarded students usually learn more slowly than average students. Their teachers must be realistic in terms of expectations and goals, as well as patient in working toward those goals. A stimulating environment that offers attractive opportunities for desirable learning experiences must also be provided.

What to Teach   The content of what is taught to retarded students can be divided into five areas: psychomotor, personal-social, language, academic, and vocational. Sometimes instruction in one of these areas also involves one or more of the other areas (physical education skills, for example).

In the *psychomotor* area, coordination is a major skill to be learned. For severely and profoundly retarded students, this may mean being able to reach out and grasp an object or a finger as the first step toward being able to feed oneself. Trainable and educable retarded students, however, tend to be beyond that stage, and ready to participate in music, art, and physical education lessons. All of these children are capable of learning to hum or sing songs, to play simple instruments, and to follow directions set to music. In fact, they may find it easier to follow directions set to music because of the rhythm that they can follow (true also of preschoolers). These activities are not only pleasurable but also offer the opportunity to increase hand-eye or mind-body coordination.

Physical education similarly strengthens coordination; it also reinforces the concept of following directions and is necessary to the youngsters' physical well-being. However, the physical education program needs to be adapted to the generally poor motor coordination of many TMR students, who often cannot catch a ball thrown to them from a few feet away. Exercises should have simple directions and involve only three or four steps in sequence for most of these children. In an extension of this program, many retarded students can participate in one or more events of the special Olympics for the retarded held throughout the country. (Educable retarded students, who typically do not have these physical and motor limitations, tend to participate more actively in playground activities with their peers.)

An arts and crafts program offers trainable retarded youths the opportunity for demonstrable achievement, as do the music and gym programs. The activities can range from the simplest cut-and-paste tasks (which may not be so simple for the TMR students) to woodworking, weaving, sewing and knitting, and other crafts. Finger painting and crayoning also provide chances for self-expression. The results are satisfying not only because there is a concrete product but also because such activities can become lifelong hobbies or even sources of income.

The adapted music, art, and physical education programs can also serve as a base from which the more able retarded students can move into parallel regular classes. If they have the needed coordination and other basic skills, they can participate in classes where most of their peers are also learning fundamentals. An added advantage to using these subjects as the first steps toward mainstreaming is that they don't have sophisticated vocabularies to be learned.

A second major area of instruction is *personal-social* skills, ranging from basic self-care in hygiene and dressing for SPMR and some TMR students to the acquisition of appropriate manners in social situations. For severely and profoundly retarded children, learning to brush their teeth properly will have to be taught as sequentially as a more able child is taught to print his name. They must learn very basic skills that are *not* characteristic of educable retarded children of school age.

Retarded youngsters who are not in a custodial setting will need to learn minimal social amenities so that other people will not be uncomfortable around them. A sample unit developed in Ohio for teaching moderately retarded adolescents some needed personal-social skills is shown in Table 2.3. Specific directions for teaching the unit are provided in an accompanying curriculum guide.

Among retarded teenagers, there are personal and social skills to learn, such as personal hygiene and sex education (a controversial issue), that might be taught more easily by a resource teacher than a regular classroom teacher. That sex education is especially important for these young people can be seen in the assertion that

people with disabilities—visual, auditory, physical, or intellectual impairments—have an even greater need than others for sex education because they have fewer opportunities to acquire sound information and to develop a personal identity and a sense of closeness with others. . . . Without proper sex education, individuals run the risk of being sexually exploited or sexually rejected by others. (Edmonson, 1980, pp.67–68)

Parents and teachers surveyed in several studies cited by Russell and Hardin (1980) agreed that retarded young people needed sex education to increase their understanding of bodily functions, intercourse, pregnancy, and childbirth, and to prevent them from being victimized. Many of the mildly retarded, particularly, may marry and will need to comprehend their responsibilities both in dating and in marriage itself. Professionals should reassure parents that teaching in this area will focus on information and the need for responsible sexual conduct and will not violate their moral code. (There is very limited literature on sex education for the severely and profoundly retarded individual. The few available articles tend to focus on the civil rights of institutionalized retarded persons with respect to sexual behavior.)

Retarded adolescents are also aware of and should be instructed in the social activities of their peers. They enjoy and respond to rock music and welcome the chance to learn dance steps. Swimming and ski instruction with other adolescents and young adults and escorted day trips in community recreation programs not only expand the world of the retarded youths but boost their self-image. Many local associations for retarded citizens sponsor programs that help educable retarded young adults to make new friends and have enjoyable leisure activities. It is important for them to acquire social and leisure skills that will allow them to be treated in accord with their chronological age, rather than their mental age, as often as possible. Regular classroom teachers need to be alert to opportunities to encourage peer acceptance of retarded classmates and to help the latter overcome feelings of rejection remaining from past experiences.

With regard to *language* learning, instruction may range from nonverbal communication to conversational skills. The type of instruction offered varies with physical abilities as well as degree of retardation.

Language learning for most trainable and all educable mentally re-

Table 2.3   Why Am I Afraid?

Pupils' problems	Pupils' needs	Pupils' interests	The unit topic
The students have demonstrated that they experience certain hesitations and fears concerning particular activities or actions.	The students need to understand that fear is a natural response and how controlling it can help them deal effectively with the situation. They need to be able to verbalize fear and to isolate the source. The students need to be able to differentiate between actual fear-producing situations and vicarious fear.	The students are interested in the various fears expressed by themselves and their peers. They enjoy putting themselves in controlled fearful situations such as movies or stories. They enjoy role playing, expressive art, films, etc.	The topic selected is "Why Am I Afraid?"

Objectives

Developing the ability to communicate	Managing one's body	Understanding one's self and others
1. Solves simple everyday problems by using suppositions, evaluations, predictions, and inferences.	1. Cautiously proceeds in potentially dangerous situations.	1. Remains calm in crisis situations.
2. Elaborates experiences using more detail and sentence complexity.		2. Recognizes limitations of physical existence.
3. Refers to events and experiences as happening in the past, present, and future.		3. Controls physical response in relation to emotional stress.
4. Rewords questions or statements for clarity when asked.		4. Contributes to the enrichment of the group by relating personal experiences.
5. Varies pitch, flow, and intensity of voice to add emphasis or emotion to verbal or signed utterances.		5. Shows interest in the affairs of others.
6. Relates experiences and ideas to small groups.		6. Expresses feelings in a socially acceptable way.
7. Discriminates relevant from irrelevant information in listening and speaking.		7. Helps others to remain calm in a crisis situation.
		8. Recognizes the need for and seeks to develop some form of protection for self.
		9. Offers and accepts criticism, suggestions and advice regarding personal matters.

From *State of Ohio Curriculum Guide for Moderately Mentally Retarded Learners*, 1977, p. 70. Reprinted by permission.

FOR EXAMPLE . . .

At the very simplest level, the nonverbal individual can be taught to signal "yes" by one eye-blink or a nod of the head and "no" by two blinks or some other motor signal. A second technique is to teach sounds and eventually words through imitation and reinforcement (typical of the behavior modification approach). Yet another option is to use abstract symbols, such as those Premack used to teach a chimpanzee to communicate (Anders, 1975; Deich & Hodges, 1975). A somewhat more complex device, using a computerized keyboard and symbols called "lexigrams," was developed by Rumbaugh at the Yerkes Regional Primate Research Center and has also been used to teach profoundly retarded children and adolescents to communicate (Rock, 1979). Some youngsters in this project, with mental ages of eighteen to thirty months, have been taught to make specific requests, to anticipate events, and to work with a few concepts. Other psychologists have used AMESLAN (American Sign Language) effectively with nonverbal retarded students. Still another approach to teaching language, also effective with trainable retarded students, is Tawney's highly structured *Programmed Environments Curriculum*, which uses a pretest-teach-posttest format that focuses on specific receptive, expressive, and cognitive skills (1980). This technique has some elements in common with Feuerstein's approach, mentioned earlier in this chapter.

tarded students is typically part of the school curriculum. As with other aspects of academic instruction, the content needs to be varied according to the capabilities of the individual student, not only because P.L. 94-142 requires it, but because such tailoring leads to the best results.

Reading is the basis for most *academic* instruction for all children. Whether or not they ever complete a first-grade reader, for example, trainable retarded students must be taught to recognize commonly used public signs and signals. This is necessary for their own safety. For both trainable and educable retarded students, programmed instruction materials, in print or on a computer, are useful in introducing reading readiness skills. These are similar to regular reading readiness workshops, except that they may be more receptive and use smaller "steps" to progress from one skill to another. Once the student has learned to discriminate and comprehend words, limited vocabulary readers with an interest level suitable for the social or chronological age of the students can be used, if needed, to teach or reinforce language and concepts. There is an increasing number of high-interest–low-skill readers available today, with themes ranging from biography to history to literature. Most such books have many illustrations (some are done in comic book style) and can be used by the regular or resource teacher to supplement classroom instruction.

For EMR students, teachers should provide pointed questions about content that will help these youngsters to direct their thinking. For example: What's missing in this picture? How are these words alike? How are they different? What is the beginning of a sequence? The middle? The end? Which flies, a dog or a duck? Is "big" always "best"?

In arithmetic, the teacher of TMR students might begin with a simple count of the number of children, chairs, or windows in the room. The count can be used to teach concepts of addition or subtraction. As the concept of number and the ability to manipulate numbers develop, practical arithmetic for daily use can be introduced using almost any concrete object in the classroom. Teachers usually have blocks, tokens, pennies, sticks, and other simple tools available to illustrate arithmetic problems. Cuisenaire rods, measuring from one to ten centimeters and color-coded, are also helpful in demonstrating basic mathematical relationships (such as one being "twice the size" of another) or teaching fractions. As the retarded students master basic concepts and any needed reading skills, they, too, can use printed workbooks that are available for the elementary grades.

Educable retarded students in the upper grade levels can apply their arithmetic skills to consumer math situations, in home economics and "shop" classes, and in general problem solving, although emphasis must be placed on moving from typical specific arithmetic examples to more general applications. Practical plane geometry (as in the measurement of area) is within the capabilities of some of the more capable EMR students.

Social studies can also be presented in concrete ways, such as visits to the local fire station, talks with understanding police officers, and field trips to local stores. Combining their arithmetic skills with trips to the stores, students can learn to count out money, to understand price tags, and to compare sizes or qualities to gain a sense of values. Older trainable and educable students can be taught to listen to radio news or to watch television newscasts so that they are aware of major events of the day. Discussing current events, even at a nonsophisticated level, gives the students practice in communication and helps them to understand the feelings of others. If, for example, a famous person dies, they can learn about what that person did in life and why people are sad because of the death.

Audiovisual equipment can often be used to increase the students' interest and comprehension. Some of the youngsters may be able to work better from tape-recorded instructions than from the printed page and should be taught how to operate a cassette player. Others, whose mechanical skills are relatively good, can be taught to assist with projectors, for example, thereby contributing to their self-esteem as useful individuals.

For the more capable retarded students, who are usually familiar with regularly broadcast television programs, guidance can be given so that they are encouraged to watch those programs that can help broaden their knowledge of the world, with discussion the next day in class to clarify misperceptions.

Finally, retarded adolescents need *vocational* preparation for their postschool years. Those who are able to carry responsibility can participate in work-study programs by working as messengers or in greenhouses, service stations, dry-cleaning shops, supermarkets, or factories. First in the classroom, and then in the work-study program, they learn how to obtain a job, plan a budget, manage money, and plan for the future. They also need instruction in using public transportation so that they can get to and from a job. Through direct instruction, modeling, and role playing, the students are taught how to fill out application forms and how to present positive information about themselves to prospective employers (Kelly, Wildman, & Berler, 1980). As more mildly and moderately retarded young adults live in the community rather than in institutions, it is also important to teach them personality and attitudinal behavior patterns that will contribute to their employability. These would include such traits as conscientiousness, assertiveness, cooperation, punctuality, regular attendance at work, perseverance, and the importance of maintaining quality of work (Mullins & Hays, 1980). Although the less able retarded students may be limited to work in sheltered workshops as adults, this is not true for all retarded young people, so marketable skills and proper work habits must be part of their curriculum. Educable retarded young people can function in "regular" jobs at semiskilled and sometimes skilled levels. With the necessary job and interpersonal skills, they can proudly take their place in society as reasonably independent, contributing citizens.

SUMMARY

Except for the speech impaired and learning disabled, mentally retarded students comprise the largest group of exceptional youth in the schools today. Whether they are retarded because of an inherited or prenatal problem, or whether their developmental lag is due to a postnatal injury or illness or other factors in their family environment, they either learn at a rate significantly slower than average students or reach their "ceiling" in education at a much lower level than their normal peers. Of the retarded student population, by far the largest number are educable.

After defining mental retardation and examining many of its causes, the classifications and ability levels of retarded children were discussed. Four levels of retardation are generally recognized: profound, severe, moderate, and mild. These are also called, in educational terms, severely/profoundly retarded (SPMR or custodial), trainable (TMR), and educable (EMR) and are usually differentiated by IQ scores. Methods of assessing the strengths, weaknesses, and probable learning abilities of retarded children include preschool observation and performance tests, standard IQ tests, informal assessments of adaptive behavior, and some modifications of intelligence tests designed to measure aptitude for learning.

With regard to educational modifications needed for retarded students, we looked at placement (custodial, segregation, and mainstreaming), teaching techniques such as behavior modification and task analysis, and content to be taught. Content includes instruction in the psychomotor, personal-social, language, academic, and vocational areas. Examples of types of content in each of these areas were given, with emphasis on maintaining interest and practicality. As with nonretarded students, many of the skills to be taught the retarded are directed toward their future as adults, for mentally retarded individuals are increasingly living and working in the community rather than being hidden at home or in institutions.

Although regular classroom teachers will work with the educable retarded students much more often than with those less able, information has been included here on trainable retarded students and, to a lesser extent, the severely/profoundly retarded in order to provide a better perspective. It is recognized that teachers will need to be more flexible in their teaching techniques in order to help EMR students who are mainstreamed, and that they will also benefit from the assistance of special education teachers and resource room personnel. Further, it is recognized that there is some conflict over the question of how long EMR students can profit from being mainstreamed and at what point their studies must be modified. However, it is also evident that many retarded students are more capable of accomplishment in regular classrooms than used to be thought, and that they, like all students, should be given the opportunity to "stretch" and to reach for higher goals.

SUGGESTED ADDITIONAL READINGS

Bricker, W. A., Macke, P. R., Levin, J. A., and Campbell, P. H. The modifiability of intelligent behavior. *Journal of Special Education*, 1981, 15, 145–163.

De la Cruz, F. F., and La Veck, G. D., Eds. *Human sexuality and the mentally retarded*. New York: Brunner/Mazel, 1973.

Elwood, S. Sex and the mentally handicapped. *Bulletin of the British Psychological Society*, 1981, 34, 169–171.

Horst, G., Wehman, P., Hill, J. W., and Bailey, C. Developing age-appropriate leisure skills in severely handicapped adolescents. *Teaching Exceptional Children*, 1981, *14* (1), 11–15.

Kempton, W. Sex education—A cooperative effort of parent and teacher. *Exceptional Children*, 1975, *41*, 531–535.

Kesselman-Turkel, J., and Peterson, F. Taking the tough route to fairness. *American Education*, 1981, *17* (1), 6–13.

Lambert, N. M. Psychological evidence in *Larry P.* v. *Wilson Riles*: An evaluation by a witness for the defense. *American Psychologist*, 1981, *36*, 937–952.

Margolis, J., and Charitonidis, T. Public reactions to housing for the mentally retarded. *Exceptional Children*, 1981, *48*, 68–70.

Piaget, J. [*The origins and intelligence in children*] (M. Cook, Trans.). New York: International Universities Press, 1952.

Simpson, H. M., and Meaney, C. Effects of learning to ski on the self-concept of mentally retarded children. *American Journal of Mental Deficiency*, 1979, *84*, 25–29.

Smith, T. E. C. Employer concerns in hiring mentally retarded persons. *Rehabilitation Counseling Bulletin*, 1981, *24*, 316–318.

Spreat, S. The AAMD Adaptive Behavior Scale. *Journal of School Psychology*, 1982, *20* (1), 45–56.

Sternberg, R. J. Cognitive-behavioral approaches to the training of intelligence in the retarded. *Journal of Special Education*, 1981, *15*, 165–183.

CHAPTER 3/
THE LEARNING DISABLED

S quare pegs in round holes" is one physician's apt description of learning disabled students (H. B. Levy, 1973). Others might call them "lazy," "hyperactive," or other even less pleasant names. They *are* intellectually handicapped because, despite average or above average intelligence, they learn and achieve in very uneven patterns and at a level below their capabilities in some areas. They are frequently a puzzle and a source of frustration to themselves, their parents, and their teachers.

WHO ARE THE LEARNING DISABLED?

These are youngsters who look like their peers, who constitute 1–10 percent of the public school population (depending on the criteria used), and who are diagnosed as minimally brain damaged, dyslexic, specifically learning disabled educationally handicapped, and even "the classroom menace." Most of these students are boys, although it is not clear why this should be. The causes of their problems may be prenatal, perinatal, or postnatal—there is no one explanation.

Description

The multiplicity of diagnostic labels does little to help pinpoint the source or nature of the student's difficulties, or to help plan appropriate instructional programs for him. Beginning with research in the 1940s, emphasis has been variously placed on brain damage, unexplained perceptual-motor dysfunctions, reading problems, hyperactivity, and (more recently) difficulty in sustaining **selective attention** (Ross, 1976). In fact, there is no single pattern indicative of learning disabilities, for each youngster so categorized displays a unique constellation of symptoms. The difficulty of describing the learning disabled is seen in *No Easy Answers*, a publication of the National Institute for Mental Health (S. L. Smith, 1978).

A more formal definition states that learning disabled children have average or better intelligence but also have specific learning deficits that are *not* "primarily the result of visual, hearing, or motor handicaps, of mental retardation, or of environmental, cultural, or economic disadvantages" (P.L. 94-142, Section 5[b][4]).

The consequences of defining learning disabilities and applying the label "learning disabled" to a student are many and varied. As Rist and Harrell (1982) pointed out, there are benefits to the child in that special learning problems and needs are recognized (and responded to appropriately, it is hoped). On the negative side are the stereotyped expectations, the rejection by peers and some teachers, and, "perhaps most devastating, the characteristic of 'learned helplessness' on the part of the child as a result of the self-attribution and internalization of the label first applied by others" (Rist & Harrell, 1982, p. 156). These conflicting outcomes of identifying a student as learning disabled should be apparent in the sections to follow.

Identification

Identification of the learning disabled is difficult despite the vast array of symptoms they may display. For example, if a child has problems focusing on one stimulus at a time (a phenomenon sometimes called *hyperdistractibility*) or, conversely, cannot shift attention from one stimulus to another (*perseveration*), she *may* have brain damage. Hyperactivity, im-

FOR EXAMPLE . . .

Who Is This Child?

Usually . . . This is an intelligent child who fails at school.

Usually . . . This is the child who at school age reads "on" for "no," writes 41 for 14, p for d or q or b, and can't remember the sequence of letters that make up a word.

Usually . . . This is the child who hears the dog barking, the truck honking, but barely hears his mother calling him . . . who hears the scratching of pencils, the sound of the air conditioner and footsteps outside, but does not hear what the teacher says.

Usually . . . This is the child who forgets names of people, places, things, his own address and telephone number, but does remember the ads on TV.

Usually . . . This is the child who loses her homework, misplaces her book, doesn't know what day it is, or what year, or what season.

Usually . . . This is the child with the messy room, the shirttail hanging out, the shoelaces undone, the child who attracts dirt to his person like a magnet.

Usually . . . This is the child who doesn't look where he's going, who bumps into the door, swings his lunch box into the nearest leg, who trips on his own feet and doesn't look at the person who is talking to him.

Usually . . . This is the child who has trouble lining up, who can't keep her hands off the child in front of her . . . who doesn't stop talking, who giggles too much and laughs the loudest.

Usually . . . This is the child who calls breakfast "lunch" . . . who is confused by "yesterday," "today," and "tomorrow," the child whose timing is always off.

Usually . . . This is the child who can't tolerate making the smallest mistake . . . who explodes at the slightest frustration . . . who tunes out in mid-conversation . . . who is happy one moment and tearful the next.

Usually . . . This is the child who is reluctant to try anything new, who is frightened by change.

Usually . . . This is the child who says "I don't care" or "I won't" when he or she really means "I can't" . . . who would rather be called *bad* than *dumb*.

Frequently . . . This is the child who can't picture things in his mind, who can't visualize or remember what he sees.

Frequently . . . This is the quiet child who bothers nobody in the classroom but does not learn.

Frequently . . . This is the older child whose language comes out jumbled, who stops and starts in the middle of a sentence or an idea . . . who talks about hopsitals, aminals, and emenies.

Frequently . . . This is the child who hugs the cat too tightly but can't hold his pencil . . . gets frostbite in the snow, and doesn't feel the hot water until it nearly burns him.

Frequently . . . This is the good swimmer . . . who stumbles up the stairs.

Frequently . . . This is the child who draws the same thing over and over . . . who asks constant questions but doesn't seem interested in the answers.

Frequently . . . This is the child who can't keep a friend . . . who prefers to play with children younger than herself.

Frequently . . . This is the child who wants everything done in a certain way . . . who tattletales . . . who picks on others for every little thing and bosses everyone around.

Frequently . . . This is the expert strategist in checkers or chess who can't understand a riddle or a joke.

Sometimes . . . This is the child who doesn't want to go to school, who develops stomach pains, fevers, headaches instead.

Sometimes . . . This is the child who lopes through life, slow to get up, slow to move or to think, but quick to play.

Sometimes . . . This is the child who rushes headlong into his work, is the first one finished and has done all the problems wrong.

Sometimes . . . This is the child who can add and multiply but not subtract or divide . . . who can do math in his head but can't write it down.

Sometimes . . . This is the child who skips words, omits them, or adds them when he is reading aloud.

Sometimes . . . This is the child who smiles at everyone, greets strangers with open arms, says "hello" to anyone he sees . . . whose good nature leads him into trouble as "the fall guy."

Occasionally . . . This is the child who tends to feel that life is unfair, who carries a big chip on her shoulder and refuses to try.

Occasionally . . . This is the child who can understand the *Odyssey* of Homer, but can't read the words "in," "the" or "if."

Smith, S. L. *No easy answers: The learning disabled child*. Rockville, Md.: National Institute for Mental Health, 1978, pp. xi–xii.

pulsiveness, overreaction to minimal stimulation, poor gross motor coordination, clumsiness, fine motor disturbances (such as the inability to draw a circle or copy simple patterns), eye-hand coordination difficulties, right-left discrimination problems, and letter reversals in word perception are other symptoms that may appear by the time a youngster enters kindergarten (see Figure 3.1). Some children, however, are not identified as learning disabled until second or third grade, when school tasks appear that call on specific areas of their previously unnoticed weaknesses.

In an effort to minimize later problems, many school districts have introduced group screening of kindergarten children. Because the validity of group-testing results is always open to some question, such results should be accepted with caution. Overzealousness in the application of screening standards can be as unfair and potentially damaging as the failure to provide any diagnostic programs or remedial courses. Too often, "learning disabled" becomes a catchall label for children who are nonconformist or otherwise troublesome to teachers.

Few learning disabled youngsters show gross neurological defects in diagnostic examinations and many, in fact, have normal examination results. Developmental optometrists and ophthalmologists may, however, detect visual perception problems that are related to the learning difficulty, and audiologists may similarly discover developmental lags in auditory acuity or perception through hearing tests. Psychoeducational tests, individually administered, also give clues to specific learning disabilities through comparison of IQ scores with achievement scores in reading, spelling, and arithmetic, or through study of the pattern of scores on subtests of an individual intelligence test. Psychologists use a variety of other diagnostic tools, too, such as the Illinois Test of Psycholinguistic Abilities, the Bender-Gestalt Visual Motor Test, and the Goodenough-Harris Draw-a-Man Test, to try to pinpoint specific problems.

A committee of school psychologists, under the auspices of their division of the American Psychological Association, have developed a teacher-completed rating scale in an attempt to provide another means of describing learning disabled elementary school students. Their emphasis was on the behavioral characteristics of these youngsters. The scale was used by teachers in 16 states for a multiethnic sample of 224 identified learning disabled (LD) children and 169 non-LD students in kindergarten through eighth grade. Of the forty-nine behavior patterns listed, eighteen were significantly different for the two groups of youngsters:

- Pays attention to instruction
- Sits still
- Concentrates well
- Good attention span
- Follows directions

What the book says   What the dyslexic student reads

Figure 3.1   Letter reversals in reading

- Neat written work
- Does his best on all assignments
- Frequently volunteers
- Cooperative with teacher
- A leader
- Appropriately competitive
- Poor awareness of time
- Bizarre statements or behavior
- Has trouble remembering
- Has trouble with comprehension
- Difficulty with oral reading
- Seems slow to learn new material
- Has "spotty" learning pattern; that is, good in some subjects, very poor in others (Telzrow & Hartlage, 1981)

Such an observation technique is an appropriate diagnostic tool, according to federal guidelines for assessing exceptional students.

In the perceptual and conceptual areas, the LD student may be unable to reproduce what she sees (and be unaware that what she draws is in error), to distinguish figures from a background, or to perceive things as a whole. Or she may suffer from perseverative perception, continuing to see a circle, for example, when shown other shapes. She may be bound to concrete objects and unable to cope with the abstract. These deficits can create problems in learning a variety of developmental and academic tasks and skills, including reading.

Examination may reveal, on the other hand, that the learning problems are due to receptive and/or expressive psychomotor dysfunctions. If receptive, the child has difficulty sorting out and interpreting incoming stimuli from one or more sensory modalities (visual, tactile, auditory, kinesthetic, olfactory). If the problem is expressive, he comprehends quite well but cannot effectively transmit his response to the hand, foot, or speech mechanisms involved. The result, in either case, is usually an inappropriate or inadequate response. Thus, emotional problems such as low self-concept, negativism, low frustration tolerance, and hypersensitivity are frequently secondary symptoms that result from the troubles that the learning disabled child experiences.

Nina's case (see Box) illustrates several points about learning disabilities. There is the gradual decrease in school functioning that finally alerts someone to the fact that she has a problem. There is uncertainty as to the source of the problem. There are difficulties in making a diagnosis, especially one specific enough to give direction to the remedial teachers. Through all of this, there are great emotional strains on Nina and her parents.

WHAT ARE THEIR PROBLEMS?

The previous sections have suggested a number of symptoms that are tied to the various academic and personal-social problems of learning disabled individuals. Here, we want to discuss the problems themselves.

Academic

Typically, the LD student has difficulty with some, but not necessarily all, areas of learning. For some, the problem may be rooted in short-term memory (impeding the ability to recall directions), deficits in auditory or visual discrimination, or some aspect of coordination. Each of these then leads to other learning problems. The memory deficit often means, apart from being criticized as disobedient or absentminded, that the youngster has trouble retrieving words (although he can recognize them), makes the wrong marks on tests, omits homework and other assignments, jumbles messages, and has more difficulty in spelling and writing than in reading. Discrimination deficits contribute to problems in distinguishing homonyms and sound-alike letter pairs (d/t, b/p), with resulting difficulties in learning phonics, disorganization of work, crowding of written work, and matching of shapes or symbols. These can affect the child's reading readiness and result in incomplete work. Poor eye-hand coordination frequently produces poor handwriting and an avoidance of activities requiring the use of tools (elementary crafts projects, industrial arts). Some slowly maturing children may exhibit these behaviors in kindergarten or first grade but not be learning disabled. The persistence of these behaviors and learning difficulties beyond that level is what often precipitates concern that the child *is* learning disabled and should be examined.

FOR EXAMPLE . . .

Nina, nine years old, was becoming more difficult to live with at home. She had difficulty controlling her temper; she complained of early morning stomachaches and headaches; and she seldom showed her usually warm smile anymore. Her schoolwork, too, was slipping. Her parents didn't know which was cause and which effect.

A general physical checkup showed no illness brewing. Talks with her teacher yielded little, other than that Nina's classroom performance was erratic. Her teacher reported that sometimes she knew an answer and sometimes she didn't; the level of the difficulty of the task didn't seem to matter. Tests by the school psychologist produced a similar erratic pattern. Neurological and ophthalmological examinations followed, and these test results pointed to minimal brain damage. Dismayed by this diagnosis, Nina's parents sought further information. Specific areas of dysfunction were delineated by psychiatrists (working out math problems on paper was one), and special school placement was recommended. By this time, Nina was academically a year or more behind her classmates and increasingly frustrated by her problems in school.

Because no public school program was available, Nina's parents enrolled her in a special private school that was ungraded and had a very low pupil-teacher ratio. Special techniques were used to remediate Nina's academic and coordination deficiencies, with frequent reinforcement for her successes. Family therapy, also part of the program, helped to reduce Nina's anger over frustrating experiences and her parents' tensions and anxiety.

After several years at the special school, Nina entered a small "regular" private boarding school as a transition to secondary education. (Again, no public, or even private, schools in the area had a program appropriate to Nina's needs.) Her new school, three hundred miles from her home, could supply the combination of ungraded, low-pressure academic and "life-preparation" courses from which Nina could profit. In her four years at the school, she learned to be more comfortable in social interaction, and she developed self-confidence in nonacademic affairs. She graduated with children her own age, and two junior colleges accepted Nina as a student in programs preparing preschool teaching assistants, a field compatible with her interests and abilities.

Perhaps the most difficult problem for Nina and her parents over the years was to accept the reality of the situation. Constant reevaluation of abilities, deficiencies, and expectations led to the realization, at last, that Nina would function successfully as an adult, except in a few relatively unimportant areas, and could have a high degree of social and economic independence. At twenty-four, she has a responsible job in a day-care center, lives and travels alone, goes out on dates, cooks, reads, and looks forward to a bright future.

FOR EXAMPLE . . .

Problems in thinking processes can affect an individual's functioning in a variety of situations and be a source of frustration to him as well as others. The result is often an exasperated "Why can't you see that?!" from a parent, teacher, or employer. S. L. Smith (1978, pp. 112–113) elaborates on some typical thinking problems of the learning disabled:

1. Has a hard time sticking to the main point; brings up irrelevant, extraneous points.

2. Doesn't grasp cause-effect relationships. Rarely uses the word *because*. Doesn't anticipate and evaluate.

3. Rigidity of thought. A word can have only one meaning. Or knows $5 + 7 = 12$ but can't answer $12 = 5 + x$; knows $8 \times 7 = 56$ but can't reverse gears and solve $56 \div 8 = x$.

4. Has trouble seeing similarities and differences. Has trouble understanding relationships.

5. Doesn't see patterns. All words have to be memorized, as he can't see spelling patterns; memorizes all multiplication facts one by one (that's why he gives up) instead of seeing patterns that simplify the task. He doesn't group ideas together to form patterns of thought.

6. Poor memory. Can't remember names of people or places. Also trouble with faces. Reasoning often gets sidetracked because of poor memory.

7. Doesn't organize the facts and concepts he does have and thus can't mobilize them to solve problems, to predict or foresee consequences.

8. Can't categorize or classify. Each experience is an isolated event. Doesn't summarize. Can't generalize from the concrete to the abstract.

9. Doesn't transfer learning from one lesson to another. Has to relearn each concept from scratch.

10. Understands concepts too narrowly or too broadly. All four-legged animals are dogs. Only black-and-white cats (like his own cat) are cats. Or he may call all cats Puff, the name of his own cat.

It's not difficult to see how such thinking problems represent an intellectual handicap. Even as an adult, a learning disabled person with only a few of these difficulties would have trouble on the job as well as at home.

Obviously, if a child has specific difficulties that affect reading ability, this condition will create learning problems throughout her school years. There are LD adults who have learned to hide their inability to read quite successfully but are bothered and embarrassed by it nevertheless. Deficits in eye-hand or gross motor coordination are inconvenient but do not have as great an overall impact on learning as do disabilities that affect reading.

Those LD youngsters who are hyperactive tend to have academic problems because of their limited ability to settle down, focus on a single task, and be persistent in their efforts. In a five-year longitudinal study, Minde, Lewin, Weiss, Lavigeur, Douglas, and Sykes found that such children have a high rate of cognitive disabilities, show little academic improvement over the years, lack motivation, and have a sense of failure (1971). Stimulant drug therapy may improve attention span temporarily but does not necessarily reduce academic problems and may result in drug dependence (Singh & Ling, 1980). (Note: It is not totally clear why caffeine and other stimulants reduce hyperactivity, even temporarily, but it appears to be akin to the mathematical principle that two negatives make a positive in multiplication.)

Personal-Social

Since school is the major activity of childhood and adolescence, failure or difficulty in this setting leads to frustration, negative feelings about the self, and behavioral problems (either attracting attention or covering up for poor academic performance). The child's frustration may cause her to display an explosive temper, often striking out at the closest available target, even if that is the teacher. If the disabilities are more in the coordination area, there may be poor peer relationships, for the ability to participate in games is also important to school-age youngsters and is basic to the formation of groups at that age. The clumsy child may become the butt of unkind remarks and pranks, further demoralizing her.

Developmentally, the LD student may behave like a much younger child—erratic, egocentric, yet unsure of his individuality; afraid of the unknown and therefore somewhat rigid and impulsive. He tends to be an embarrassment to his parents and siblings because of his strange ways. He is also a source of frustration and irritation to them at times, because in some ways he performs quite well and in others exhibits immature or obnoxious behavior. As the discrepancies in behavior become more obvious, he also becomes a source of anxiety, because the parents don't know whether he is emotionally disturbed, hearing impaired, retarded, or otherwise disabled. This can cause them to be overprotective, for example, rather than supportive and remedial.

Learning disabled children, as already noted, tend to have negative self-concepts because they experience so many failures. These tend to be reinforced by both parents and teachers before a proper diagnosis is made and can persist even when the problem is recognized. According to a survey of several studies by Bryan and Pearl (1979), the learning disabled tend to blame themselves for failure as a result of this negative self-concept, while attributing successes to luck or the intervention of others. The LD adolescent has particular difficulties in developing an identity, fitting in with her peers socially, and planning for the future.

EDUCATIONAL MODIFICATIONS

Placement

There are residential schools and camps especially geared to the needs of learning disabled youths, but they are not always the most appropriate setting for many of these youngsters, unless, as in Nina's case, no suitable program is available locally. For despite the passage of P.L. 94-142, there are still communities, especially in rural areas, where there are too few LD children of similar ages and/or achievement levels to enable the school district to arrange a proper program. In such cases, distasteful as sending a child to boarding school may be, it is a more desirable alternative than having a child be continually frustrated in school and beset by emotional problems and low self-esteem. The financial burden, under current laws, is shared by the local district, the state, and the federal government.

More often, the question is whether to place the child in a private day school, segregated classes, or the educational mainstream. Private schools, one of the alternatives for learning disabled students, are expensive ($5,000–$10,000 per year for tuition, transportation, and therapy). They have small staff-student ratios (possibly smaller than in the public school special classes) and may be oriented to a specific philosophy. Often, they are also the only option for educating LD adolescents, as there are still too few secondary-level special programs available for them in the public schools.

In the late 1960s, parent groups demanded special classes for their LD children; a decade later, they were confronted with federal insistence that the "least restrictive environment" principle be applied instead. Many parents were and are in conflict about which alternative might be more beneficial for their children, and they vacillate between segregated classes and mainstreaming with special attention in a resource room and with tutors. Weener (1981) analyzed forty-seven studies that compared normal and learning disabled children, focusing on the range of variability within each group and the amount of overlap between the groups. His conclusion was that segregating the groups did little to reduce the variability of performance in the classroom. Rather, he found that

the variability and overlap between LD and regular classroom groups . . . indicates that instructional treatments should be focused more narrowly on specific skills or cognitive processes rather than on broad categories of disability which are often used for grouping purposes in schools. (Weener, 1981, p. 231)

Much achievement would depend, clearly, on the individual teacher's ability to provide sufficient special guidance to the LD child and to integrate him into the class group.

As more learning disabled students have been identified, there has been a corresponding increase in the number of special classes for them, usually at the elementary level. Some of these are sponsored by a few school districts, especially in rural and suburban areas, because it is often difficult for a small district to support enough appropriate special classes. These special classes usually have a teacher-pupil ratio of about one to ten. Larger class sections may also have one or more aides to assist in demonstrating tasks, evaluating completed work, and other activities.

A transition program (moving learning disabled students from special classes to regular classes) that has been successful is the Madison Plan (Blum, 1971). An integral factor in this approach has been to change the regular teacher's feelings of being imposed upon when exceptional children are placed in his class. There are four levels in this plan, illustrated in Figure 3.2, that prepare the youngster for the mainstream, each having its own unique features. Preacademic I is highly structured, uses reinforcement schedules, and has separate "learning centers" scattered around the room. Preacademic II provides for more independent work, although there is intense academic remediation done in small groups, and reinforcement is still used liberally. Academic I is a large group setting with group instruction, independent study, supportive academic remediation, and regular report cards. The fourth level is actually the regular classroom setting, with access to the next lower level as needed. This type of transition program can also be used for upper-level educable mentally retarded students.

The mainstreaming plus resource room option usually involves the employment of a special education teacher, in a specific room with appropriate instructional materials, to whom the LD children are sent daily for remedial instruction. The teacher may be assigned to one building on a full-time basis, making it easier to work closely with the classroom teacher, or may be **itinerant**, that is, sent to two or more schools for part of each day. This can be an effective alternative if a child has only a few learning problems and is not a disruptive factor in the regular classroom. The special education teacher can suggest to the regular teacher ways in which to meet a youngster's specific needs and be a valuble source of support when frustrations overwhelm the child and/or the teacher.

Content and Techniques

The increased recognition of the variety of learning disabilities youngsters have and the mandate to educate all handicapped children have

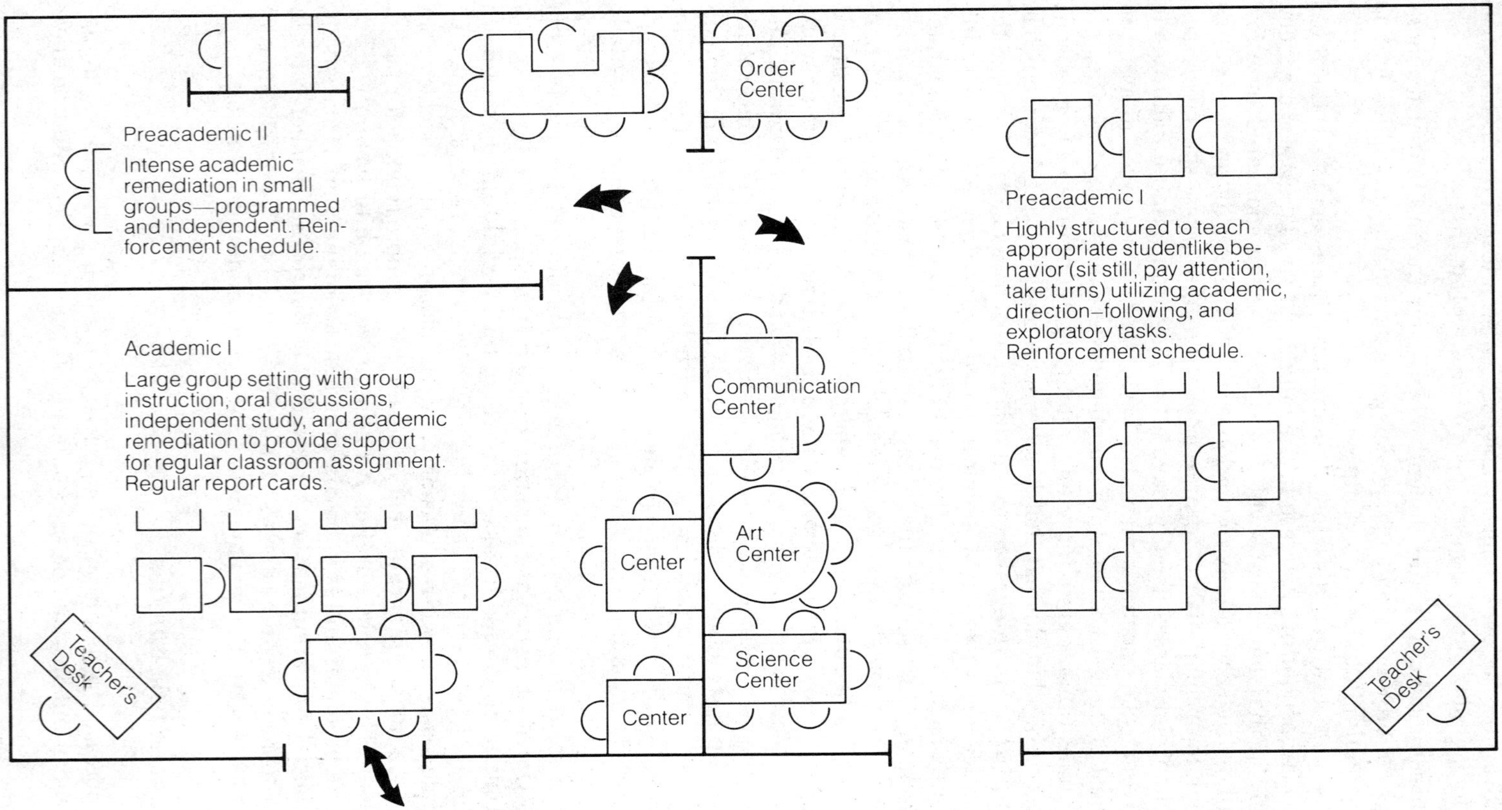
Order Center
Preacademic II
Intense academic remediation in small groups—programmed and independent. Reinforcement schedule.
Preacademic I
Highly structured to teach appropriate studentlike behavior (sit still, pay attention, take turns) utilizing academic, direction–following, and exploratory tasks. Reinforcement schedule.
Academic I
Large group setting with group instruction, oral discussions, independent study, and academic remediation to provide support for regular classroom assignment. Regular report cards.
Communication Center
Art Center
Center
Science Center
Center
Teacher's Desk
Teacher's Desk

Figure 3.2 **Two typical learning-center classrooms with connecting door.** (Used by permission of Frank D. Taylor)

resulted in the production of tremendous amounts of special instructional materials. Each publisher claims wondrous effects of its materials on achievement but does not necessarily supply good research data to support the claims. Hickman and Anderson (1979) urge teachers and others to be cautious in accepting these claims at face value. They suggest that task analysis principles be applied to evaluating the materials. This would include determining the instructional objectives and goals of the materials and the specific activities included that are directed toward each objective. The prerequisite skills needed for each activity and the level of difficulty should also be considered in the evaluation.

Perceptual-Motor Problems   Some LD youngsters have specific perceptual-motor problems that interfere with their learning in class and at play. For example, they may look at a geometric figure but be unable to copy it correctly (eye-hand coordination), or they may be unable to move correctly when given directions (laterality). For the first difficulty, sewing cards that depict different shapes can be used; the youngster outlines the shapes using thread or yarn. A second possibility is to outline a shape with glue, then sprinkle on some sand; when the glue dries, the child can run his finger over the shape and at the same time say the name of the shape.

For the second problem, adults working with the child will need to emphasize use of the preferred hand ("write with your right hand") or left-right progression in reading. Balance beam activities, with the teacher instructing the child to move "forward," "backward," "sideways to the left," and so on, are also helpful. Mazes, increasing in difficulty as the child makes progress, are also useful for narrowing the gap between perception and motor activity. Computer games, where the child must coordinate hand movement and perception of a moving target, will hardly seem like homework but will provide much-needed practice in visual tracking and eye-hand coordination. Manual dexterity, particularly fine motor coordination, can be improved through the use of peg boards, nuts-and-bolts sorting tasks, and construction materials such as Lego blocks and Erector sets.

Academic Deficits   Ultimately, the goal of special activities and materials is to enable the LD child to overcome her deficits and to achieve at a level consonant with her assumed potential. With the great variety of possible deficits and combinations of deficits, however, this means that the teacher must be very resourceful and very flexible. He often has to remedy underlying weaknesses, including coordination problems, before attempting to bring the youngster's achievement level up in content areas. Some general suggestions include blocking out or cutting up materials to reduce distractions, putting easy-to-follow directions on index cards in a file, using concrete objects (balls, buttons, chips) to aid the child who has trouble going from the concrete to the abstract, and using dictation to a teacher aide or a tape recorder for the child who can speak but not write (Wexler, 1980a). For hyperdistractible students, an individual learning carrel is often recommended (see Figure 3.3). This is not needed by *all* learning disabled students, however (as some educators used to think).

Some examples of activities directed toward remedying specific problems include:

Problems with Sound Discrimination:

1. Teach grossly different sounds such as thunder, rain, and wind; then horns, bells, and barks.
2. Progress to finer distinctions in sounds using various sound-making devices such as tuning forks and musical instruments.
3. Avoid teaching similar-sounding letters at the same time.
4. Introduce no more than one new sound a day to avoid overload.

Deficits in Visual Memory Sequencing:

1. Match and compare objects or symbols (letters, numerals) made of felt, wood, plastic, clay, or sandpaper.
2. Trace the letter or numeral with a finger over the textured model.
3. Reproduce the model with pen, pencil, clay, wet sand or finger paint.
4. Reproduce the object or symbol without the model.

This is known as the VTKA (Visual-Tactual-Kinesthetic Associations) approach to reinforcing visual memory. It is a teaching approach that was advocated by St. Jerome in his "Letter to Laeta" in the fourth century and reintroduced by Maria Montessori at the end of the nineteenth century (although some of the materials we have now, such as plastic, did not exist in their times).

Language Disorders in Arithmetic:

1. Have the student hold and compare objects of different weights (going from gross differences to finer differences) and then estimate which is heavier.
2. Obtain a concrete object and a container that can be used to teach concepts of space such as over, under, beside, inside, outside, below, above, near.
3. Use form boards to teach shape discrimination.

Figure 3.3   Reducing distractions while learning

As you can see from these very specific examples, each element in learning disabilities is distinctive and needs specialized remedial efforts.*

Thought patterns can be developed even through watching television programs. Parents can ask the child:

- "What was the show about?"
- "What happened—first, next, last?"
- "When did it happen? Where? How?"
- "What was the result?"
- "What was the main point, the theme?"

Over a period of time, such questioning can help the youngster to understand cause-and-effect relationships and the logic of sequences (S. L. Smith, 1978, p. 122). The same type of approach can be used to improve reading comprehension.

*Examples of activities adapted from Mann, P. H., and Suiter, P. *Handbook in diagnostic teaching: A learning disabilities approach.* Allyn & Bacon, 1974, pp. 70, 76, 142–144. Used by permission.

Walking on logs is one way of teaching balance and self-confidence. (Photo © by Elizabeth Crews)

Spelling is also a problem to many students, not just to those who have a learning disability in this subject. However, for the LD student, the VAKT (Visual/Auditory/Kinesthetic/Tactual) technique, using word families (such as -*at*, preceded by a variety of consonants: *c-at*, *f-at*), rhymes, and games (such as "Tongue Twisters," bingo, anagrams, and treasure hunts for words within words) may be helpful in improving spelling skills (Hammill, 1978). The spelling disability may reflect memory-sequencing, auditory discrimination, or coordination of problems, one or more of which may also be at the root of handwriting problems.

For learning disabled students entering secondary school, there is not nearly as much research available to suggest age-appropriate materials or techniques. Some of the literature recommends extending upward reading programs designed for the dyslexic population (J. D. Lindsey & Kerlin, 1979). High-interest, limited vocabulary reading materials may be useful for some but do not necessarily address all of the specific reading disabilities that may persist into adolescence. In addition, there are not enough teachers who are well trained in special remedial techniques for this age group, nor even in remedial reading techniques at the secondary level.

Reading affects progress in mathematics as well as in word oriented subjects like history, but LD adolescents may make errors that have little to do with the nature of the problem. Rather, they perform the incorrect operation (subtracting instead of dividing), reverse numerals, or simply misplace numbers. Suggested remedial strategies include the use of abaci, Cuisenaire rods, and calculators to reduce errors in the basic operations. Kutsick (1982) suggests having students use graph paper to reduce spatial and reversal errors (see Figure 3.4). Of course, they should be reminded to check their work upon completion or to review each other's work. It would be wise, at this level, to use math problems involving practical content, such as measurement, time, and consumer prices. This is another example of trying to match age-appropriate interests with low-level skills.

If there is a high school resource room, the teacher might encourage LD adolescents to take more responsibility for their learning by asking them to set learning goals for themselves (Gardner & Gardner, 1978). They should also contribute more to contractual arrangements with the teacher and be guided to increase their capacity for evaluating whether they have met their objectives satisfactorily. In the resource room there is also an opportunity for the teacher to help these older students improve their test-taking skills, a necessary competency if they are to function adequately in regular classrooms. Among the likely problems here are test anxiety, inability to ask for help with directions, inadequacy in solving problems, and lack of self-control when frustrated by a question or problem (Markel, 1981).

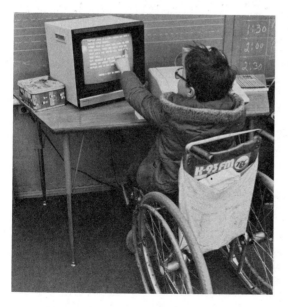

Computer programs are often better teaching tools for learning disabled students than are textbooks. (Photo by Evan Johnson/Jeroboam)

$$
\begin{array}{r}
672 \\
437 \\
796 \\
2934 \\
\hline
61314
\end{array}
$$

	6	7	2
	4	3	7
	7	9	6
2	9	3	4
4	8	3	9

Figure 3.4   Reducing misplacement of numbers (Based on Kutsick)

Personal-Social Disabilities   On the personal-social level, much can be done to help the learning disabled youngster get along better with peers and family. For one thing, the child surely has some abilities as well as deficits. The abilities tend to get lost in the efforts to remedy the weaknesses, so that the child begins to feel as if he has no redeeming qualities at all. Renewed attention to competencies will not only improve the child's self-esteem but also help him to gain respect from others. Emphasizing similarities in characteristics and interests among peers will also increase the acceptance of the LD youngster (Turnbull & Schulz, 1979). Reducing interpersonal competition in favor of competition with oneself (improving previous performance levels) would also reduce peer rejection.

Students with learning disabilities may also have problems with body image, spatial orientation, and expression of feelings that can affect not only their self-esteem and academic learning but their personal-social learning as well. Creative arts activities—music, art, dance, and drama—can be used therapeutically to

awaken and revitalize the body; afford opportunity for physical expression of feelings and impulses; foster nonverbal communication of repressed desires and affects and lead toward improved verbal communication; reestablish a sense of trust in oneself and others; aid in socialization and group participation; and provide an outlet for discharge of tension and hostility. (Kaslow, 1979, p. 182)

Dance and music are especially useful in helping the hyperactive youngster to be aware of and learn to control his movements.

Naturally, the degree of social acceptance an LD student attains will vary with her individual characteristics as well as the nature and severity of the learning disabilities she has. Nina, the young woman who served as an example earlier in this chapter, had a sunny personality and many friends. They were patient with her weaknesses, which were mostly academic, because they liked her as a person. Where amiability is not natural to the child because of past frustrations or rejections, the teacher should guide her in ways to become more acceptable to others. For example, learning disabled students can be taught to improve their conversational skills through modeling, coaching, and rehearsal with videotaped feedback (La Greca & Mesibov, 1979). Many of them will also have to develop an awareness of cause-and-effect relationships (for example, their behavior and the reactions of others), which may be difficult if they are unable to handle abstract concepts.

It may be effective, too, to develop a special unit on "the disabled in American culture" as an in-service course for teachers and then for high school students, as Hedberg (1981) did. After creating an awareness of attitudes toward the "different" and confronting stereotypes in an informational atmosphere, Hedberg reported a considerable increase in positive attitudes among the nondisabled. Learning disabled adults, still plagued with self-doubts and frustrations, have found that forming a mutual support group can not only relieve some of their stress but also help them in interpersonal interactions (C. Johnson, 1981). Both of these approaches can reduce the difficulties that the learning disabled must face in the nonacademic areas of their lives.

Vocational Placement   Gains in academic and social skills will ultimately contribute to an adolescent's *vocational* placement. To be employable, the learning disabled individual will need to be able to use public transportation independently, tell time and devise a schedule, fill out application forms, use a telephone, handle money appropriately, and interact satisfactorily with employers and co-workers. These are skills that can be developed in the high school program through direct instruction, modeling, and role playing. Counselors or special teachers will also need to match each student's weaknesses and strengths with demands of a work situation, whether in a senior work-study project (Wallbrown, 1979) or in a postgraduate placement. Vocational guidance or planning for postsecondary education involves more than the usual interest and aptitude testing when dealing with LD adolescents. They require more structured programs, with more specific task training, than most of their peers (even those who are exceptional in other ways).

Postsecondary Education   Postsecondary education for learning disabled students in the mid-1970s, when Nina graduated from secondary school, was obtainable only with great difficulty. Nina's parents visited several junior college admissions officers until they found those willing and flexible enough to permit Nina to work toward an Associate degree. Less than a decade later, there are several colleges, such as Curry and American International in Massachusetts, Southern Illinois University at Carbondale, and the College of the Ozarks in Arkansas, that not only accept learning disabled students but have programs specifically designed to meet their individual needs (Winslow, 1982). These programs stress the development of existing abilities and compensatory skills for weaknesses, provide a variety of individualized services, and solicit faculty support for both the LD students and the program itself.

SUMMARY

Of all groups of exceptional students, those who are learning disabled may be the most diverse in terms of behavioral characteristics and instructional needs. The challenges begin with the task of diagnosis—with not knowing whether a child's academic and/or personal difficulties are caused by retardation, brain damage, emotional disturbance, laziness, or specific auditory/visual/spatial/motor deficits. Even when the learning disabilities are identified, there are problems of appropriate school placement and instruction. Memory, coordination, and accuracy of perception are among the specific deficits that need remediation if the learning disabled student is to experience success in school and in life. The uniqueness of each learning disabled child's pattern of deficits calls for highly individualized instruction in some areas and may permit mainstreaming in others.

Theoretical differences regarding the nature and remediation of learning disabilities have led some special educators to focus on behavior modification techniques, others to stress reduction of distractions, and still others to experiment with variations of standard remedial techniques in an effort to improve performance. Most of the work in this area has been done at the elementary school level, leaving learning disabled adolescents somewhat more adrift than they can afford to be. There has also been more research and remediation in academic areas (for that is where the learning disabled individual is most disadvantaged) than in the personal-social and vocational preparation realms (which will probably be of greater importance in adulthood). Although learning disabilities have their primary impact on students' academic achievements, they affect all aspects of these youngsters' lives and frequently lead to secondary problems that may call for further modifications in teaching techniques.

SUGGESTED ADDITIONAL READINGS

Bireley, M., and Manley, E. The learning disabled student in a college environment: A report of Wright State University's program. *Journal of Learning Disabilities*, 1980, *13* (1), 12–15.

Bosco, J. J., and Robin, S. S., Eds. *The hyperactive child and stimulant drugs.* Chicago: University of Chicago Press, 1976.

Colewell, C. G. Humor as a motivational and remedial technique. *Journal of Reading*, 1981, *24*, 484–486.

Demers, L. A. Effective mainstreaming for the learning disabled student with behavioral problems. *Journal of Learning Disabilities*, 1981, *14*, 179–188, 203.

Houck, C., Todd, R. M., Barnes, D. H., and Englehard, J. B. LD and math: Is it the math or the child? *Academic Therapy*, 1980, *15*, 557–570.

Johnson, J. A. The etiology of hyperactivity. *Exceptional Children*, 1981, *47*, 348–354.

Koppitz, E. M. *The Bender Gestalt Test for young children.* New York. Grune & Stratton, 1964.

Larsen, S. C., Parker, R., and Jorjorian, S. Differences in self-concept of normal and learning disabled children. *Perceptual and Motor Skills*, 1973, *37*, 510.

Leonard, L. B. Language impairment in children. *Merrill-Palmer Quarterly*, 1979, *25*, 205–232.

Markel, G. Improving test-taking abilities of LD adolescents. *Academic Therapy*, 1981, *16*, 333–342.

Marsh, G. E. III, Gearheart, C. K., and Gearheart, B. R. *The learning disabled adolescent: Program alternatives in the secondary school.* St. Louis: Mosby, 1978.

McWhirter, J. J. *The learning disabled child: A school and family concern.* Champaign, Ill.: Research Press Co., 1977.

Myklebust, H. R. *The Pupil Rating Scale: Screening for learning disabilities.* New York: Grune & Stratton, 1971.

Otto, W., McMenemy, R. A., and Smith, R. J. *Corrective and remedial teaching.* Boston: Houghton Mifflin, 1973.

Reeves, W. H. Auditory learning disabilities and emotional disturbance: Diagnostic differences. *Journal of Learning Disabilities*, 1980, *13*, 199–203.

Reilly, S. S., and Barber-Smith, D. Expanded use of captioned films for learning disabled students. *Exceptional Children*, 1982, *48*, 361–363.

Sapir, S. G., and Nitzberg, A. C. *Children with learning problems: Reading in a developmental-interaction approach.* New York: Brunner/Mazel, 1973.

Schenck, S. J. An analysis of IEPs for LD youngsters. *Journal of Learning Disabilities*, 1981, *14*, 221–223.

Smith, B. K. *Learning disabilities in the future: LD in AD 2000.* Austin: The Hogg Foundation (University of Texas), 1977.

Thomson, M. E., and Hartley, G. M. Self-concept in dyslexic children. *Academic Therapy,* 1980, *16,* 19–36.

Thomson. P. An ounce of prevention. *American Education,* 1974, *10 (10),* 10–15.

Willner, S. K., and Crane, R. A parental dilemma: The child with a marginal handicap. *Social Casework,* 1979, *60,* 30–35.

CHAPTER 4/
THE EXCEPTIONALLY ABLE

When exceptional students are mentioned, people tend to think of handicaps and disabilities. Gifted, creative, and talented students, however, comprise a group that is abundantly endowed with abilities but frequently overlooked when provision is made for special education programming. They are not, for example, included in P.L. 94-142 (although some states, such as Pennsylvania and North Carolina, have passed separate parallel legislation to mandate programs for them).

The Gifted and Talented Children's Act of 1978 (Education Amendments of 1978, P.L. 95-561, Title IX) stipulated, but did not mandate, the development of new programs for these exceptionally able students. At that time, such students were characterized in the following way:

Gifted and talented children means children, and whenever applicable, youth, who are identified at the preschool, elementary, or secondary level as possessing demonstrated or potential abilities that give evidence of high performance capability in areas such as intellectual, creative, specific academic, or leadership ability, or in the performing and visual arts, and who by reason thereof require services or activities not ordinarily provided by the school. (Congressional Record, 1978)

It is more difficult to arrive at a succinct definition of a "creative" student. Creative students typically exhibit several of the following behavior patterns to an unusual degree: intellectual curiosity, problem-solving ability, flexibility in thinking, originality, independent effort, imaginativeness, nonconformity, and high rate of productivity.

The lack of strong statutory support for the exceptionally able at the national level reflects a public assumption that the intellectually gifted, the creative, and the talented can go forward by their own efforts and without public support. However, this is no more true for this group of exceptional students than for any other group.

IDENTIFICATION AND CHARACTERISTICS

The Gifted

Intellectually gifted children usually speak and read early, tend to have very good memories, are persistent, and seem quite mature for their years. They usually score well above the average range on intelligence tests or on other academic measures. For example, they have an IQ of 130 or above, which is two standard deviations above the average or mean score of 100. This places such students as far above the statistical mean as the retarded are below it. Their level of achievement is usually two or more grade levels above that of their peers (although some are underachievers for various reasons and may not even be identified as gifted). The intellectual ability of some gifted individuals may be high in most subject areas, but more often their interests lean toward a specific field, such as mathematics, physics, social sciences, or foreign languages.

Although the gifted have traditionally been identified by academic intelligence tests, there are other techniques that can be used for screening purposes, especially with underachievers and disadvantaged students. The Renzulli-Hartman scales (1971), completed by the teacher rather than the student, ask questions concerning the student's learning, motivational, creativity, and leadership characteristics. Unguided teacher judgment of who is gifted in a class, on the other hand, is not effective as a screening device (Pegnato & Birch, 1959; Nasca, 1979). The Goodenough Draw-a-Man Test is useful with preschool and first-grade children who may show unusual powers of observation for their age or unusual attention to detail. A vocabulary test, considered to be a good selection device for academic purposes, often reflects wide reading experience and comprehension but taps only a limited area of intellectual ability. However, the vocabulary test score may have more significance as a means of identifying the gifted if it is combined with careful observation of the student's elective activities, preferred topics of discussion, extracurricular interests, and peer relationships.

Alternatives to standard tests may also include nomination by specialist teachers, librarians, peers, and parents. Art and music teachers may pick up a student's skills in persistence, innovation, or background information that have not been observed by the classroom teacher. Librarians are often aware of which students borrow books for pleasure reading frequently or of who has read every book on particular shelves (Marland, 1971). This kind of informal observation can contribute to individualizing a student's assignments. For example, a teacher who sees a second grader reading *Little Women* can revise the reading assignments for that student to a higher level as soon as she confirms that the child understands what she reads.

Given descriptions of nameless students who exhibit specified behavior patterns in such areas as leadership, knowledge, and problem solving, peers can identify which classmate most closely matches each description. This technique might be especially effective with culturally different pupils who are gifted but do not test well or meet the school's academic standards because of language or other difficulties. Many gifted and creative students do not test well, whether because of test anxiety, boredom, the ability to see an unanticipated (and therefore uncredited) but superior answer, or for some other reason. In addition, most education-oriented tests are tied to a standard curriculum and may not tap the gifted student's area(s) of expertise or the specific abilities of creative and talented youngsters.

The Creative

To screen students for intellectual creativity, there are a number of tests, devised by Parnes, Guilford, Torrance, Mednick, and others. Most of these typically include a variety of verbal, and sometimes nonverbal, **divergent thinking** tasks designed to evoke questions, create pictures out of quarter-sized circles, find uses for objects, and suggest possible consequences if a particular event should occur. The Mednick Remote Associates Test, on the other hand, emphasizes **convergent thinking**; that is, the individual taking the test has to find the single answer that is the correct response.

Diagrammatically, we might represent the difference in these two types of productive thinking in this way:

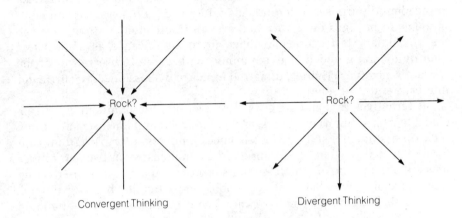

Convergent Thinking   Divergent Thinking

Other means of identifying the highly creative include looking for the student who not only solves problems but looks for them, who can work well independently, who uses her imagination in expanding ideas or adapting procedures, and who exhibits a high degree of curiosity. One teacher-generated list of creative behavior patterns in disadvantaged children, which might be equally applicable to nondisadvantaged creative students on some criteria, includes such additional items as:

- Shows that he/she sees hidden meanings, cause-and-effect relationships that are not obvious
- Builds and constructs things using unusual materials; uses ordinary materials in different ways
- Writes poems and stories in his/her spare time
- Finds new ways to get attention
- Goes beyond what is required in class assignments; makes his/her work "fancier" (Swenson, 1978)

Frequently the creative youngster is regarded as a daydreamer or a troublesome nonconformist by teachers. Both roles are characteristic of many creative students. Bored by routine or fascinated by a problem to solve, they may stare out the window as they mentally wrestle with more interesting ideas than those being presented in class. They also tend to challenge teachers on the whys and hows of directions and are thus perceived as difficult pupils.

FOR EXAMPLE . . .

Convergent Thinking:

In a crossword puzzle, there is only one "right" answer that will fit, although many associations and definitions may initially come to mind. For example:

1. Rock [ ][ ][ ][ ]

   stone   swing
   Hudson   candy
   crag   N'Roll
   agate   Gibraltar

Some possibilities are rejected because they have too many or too few letters, others because they don't mesh with other words in the puzzle.

Divergent Thinking:

Here there are many possible correct responses to the stimulus or problem. A typical task on creativity tests is to "find as many uses as possible for———" Using the same stimulus word *rock*, one might list the following uses:

- Weight—hold down papers
- Barrier—keep car from rolling
- Weapon—break glass; throw at attacker
- Ornament—decorate garden, floor of aquarium; paint
- Construction—build wall, steps, shelter, fireplace
- Heat to keep feet warm
- As a headrest

The Talented

Unusual artistic or musical talent may be apparent before the child reaches school age, although if the parents are not sensitive to it, the talent may remain undiscovered until an opportunity arises for its display in elementary school. Perfect pitch, an "eye" for color or design, and un-usual dance or other performance ability are demonstrable talents that can be ferreted out through special tests and/or keen observation. Talents in

Is Melissa a prima
ballerina-to-be?
(Photo by Amy L. Birrittella)

more mechanical areas that are traditionally associated with vocational education can often be discovered by asking questions such as, "Who in the class likes and is able to fix equipment?", "Who is a ham radio operator?", or "Who can build this needed apparatus?" These talents are often overlooked in the elementary grades, since they are not part of the typical curriculum, but students who possess them should not be ignored.

Other Characteristics

Students who are gifted, creative, or talented can be unusually mature in thought and behavior, or precocious and childishly obnoxious, or somewhere in between, depending on their past experiences. If they are not taught to have feelings of superiority, they interact comfortably with their peers as well as with adults. Despite prevalent stereotypes, gifted children are not necessarily physical, emotional, or social misfits. A fifty-five-year follow-up study on Terman's "geniuses" shows that his subjects tended to be physically and emotionally healthier, on the average, than their non-gifted age-peers (Goleman, 1980). The gifted and creative tend to be intellectually curious, self-motivated, and self-critical. These characteristics, as well as what they know and can do, are what make educational modifications necessary.

There are problems that can develop, however, for exceptionally able youngsters. The creative child, who is frequently a nonconformist in her thinking or behavior, may develop negative feelings of self-esteem if she focuses on the criticism she receives for not doing things the "right way." A gifted preschooler may be very good at expressing himself verbally and getting about on his own but feel frustrated because he is too young to exercise his growing abilities or desire for independence as much as he might like. Academically gifted elementary school children may feel the need to suppress their abilities so as not to be perceived as "different" by their classmates.

Gifted preadolescents, often judged to be more mature than they really are because of their verbal ability or grade placement, may need more social and emotional support from parents and teachers than they are given. They also can be in conflict with these adults, because their competence and their desire for power over their lives do not match the reality of their chronological age. An adolescent's mind in a child's body can be both overwhelming and threatening to some adults, often creating unnecessary impasses.

Many psychologists who work with the gifted believe the optimum group is in the 125–150 IQ range. At this level, the gifted person can excel without being eccentric, can understand the work of "geniuses," can make original contributions, and can also understand the inability of those less intellectually able to comprehend complex theories and procedures. Those with IQs above 150 allegedly have less interaction with "average" individuals and therefore less empathy with their lack of understanding. Some tend toward intellectual arrogance, even in their school years, although others make more of an effort to communicate in both social and academic settings.

SPECIAL GROUPS OF GIFTED STUDENTS

Gifted and Handicapped

What do Ludwig von Beethoven, Itzhak Perlman, and Ray Charles have in common? They were/are all gifted handicapped individuals. Beethoven composed some of his finest music when he was deaf; Perlman is an outstanding concert violinist who is orthopedically handicapped; and Charles is a highly regarded blind pianist. They and others like them have chosen to emphasize (and are lauded by others for) their talents rather than their handicaps. Gifted handicapped students who are now in school can be taught to do the same. The problem is to locate such youths.

FEIFFER

A program staffed by American University teachers at the Horace Mann Elementary School in Washington, D.C., was created to find gifted handicapped children through a series of specially designed observation measures. Students were evaluated in three major ways: "(1) reaction to a materials-centered approach to learning; (2) understanding specific science concepts; and (3) logical thinking skills" (Hadary, Cohen, & Haushalter, 1979, p. 40). The program, which was directed toward the visual and hearing impaired as well as to learning disabled children, proved to be an effective approach.

Gifted Delinquents

Although we tend to think of the gifted primarily in terms of intellectual or academic ability, the federal guidelines of recent years have also sought to identify the top 3–5 percent of school-age children in leadership ability (the socially gifted). In this group we are likely to find not only student government officers but also juvenile gang leaders. The latter, some of whom might be called "gifted delinquents," tend to have unusual abilities—in organizing ideas and materials, as well as people, and in problem solving—and are highly sensitive to experiences (Brooks, 1980). Due to their home environment, lowered expectations on the part of teachers, the irrelevance of the curriculum to daily life, their isolation from more "acceptable" peers, and/or social or emotional maladjustment, these gifted youths perform as academic underachievers and frequently drop out of high school before graduation. On the street, however, they are considered to be high achievers because of their exploits.

Locating school "ringleaders" early and developing programs that will foster their abilities in a constructive way is no easy task. They already have positive feelings of self-esteem due to their powers of leadership; thus, alternate sources of reinforcement must be sought that are equally (if not more) significant to the potential or actual delinquent. The curriculum must be made more meaningful, and not only to delinquents but to all those whose backgrounds are atypical, if these students are to benefit from their schooling and make a positive contribution to society.

Gifted and Disadvantaged

Gifted students who are disadvantaged—who come from minority or impoverished backgrounds and rarely score highly on traditional tests—

The 1981 PATS (Potentially Academically Talented Students) program at Pennsylvania State University, Ogontz Campus, placed gifted disadvantaged students in classes with other identified gifted students. Fifth and sixth graders are shown here in a physics class. (Photo by Marjorie Weintraub)

often suffer from the same meaninglessness of the curriculum as do gifted delinquents. They, too, are victims of lowered expectations—their own and those of their teachers. In recent years, considerable attention has been focused on identifying the gifted from disadvantaged and culturally different backgrounds (Gallagher, 1975; Torrance, 1977; Chambers & Barron, 1978). To locate these students, it is recommended that nonverbal as well as verbal tests be used and that nontraditional techniques be included in pupil assignments, as noted earlier. Experimental studies also suggest that the placement of gifted disadvantaged students in advanced classes (Tuckman & Bierman, 1971) or with identified gifted students results in improved self-concept and academic performance in a large number of the students so treated.

Exceptionally Gifted

A fourth special group of intellectually gifted are the exceptionally gifted, or "geniuses," youngsters who score four standard deviations or more

FOR EXAMPLE . . .

Alicia Witt said her first word when she was one month old, read college material at age two, and recited Juliet's balcony speech on nationwide television at five (with a typical kindergartener's lisp). Just before her third birthday, she was evaluated as having the intellectual ability of at least the average twelve-year-old (Lavallee, 1980).

Eugene Volokh, an immigrant from Russia at age seven, began taking extension courses from the University of California at Los Angeles when he was nine. He graduated from high school at twelve and entered UCLA as a sophomore, where he was also hired by a business firm to work part-time on computer programs. Early indicators of his precocity included an unusual vocabulary by age two, an aptitude for figures and maps before his fourth birthday, and competence with algebra and calculus by age seven (Mehren, 1981).

A third exceptionally gifted youngster is Jay Luo, who graduated from Boise State University in 1982 at age twelve. Unusually talented in mathematics, Jay began taking college courses at age nine ("At 12, He's Looking Forward to June and a College Degree," 1982).

above the mean (IQ 160+) or are precociously talented in music, mathematics, or some other specific area. When identified, they are extremely difficult to place within traditional school patterns.

Not all "geniuses" are identified early, or even once they are in school. Einstein, Edison, and Churchill are among those who were thought to be "dull" when they were students (Pang, 1968). Today, parents and educational researchers alike are trying to identify these children and find the most effective means of working with them for their optimal all-around development (Holden, 1980). As with all the exceptionally able, adjustments are necessary in their education to meet their unusual needs.

EDUCATIONAL MODIFICATIONS

A survey of state support for special education for the gifted in the early 1970s showed that of the thirty-seven states from which responses were received, only seventeen had laws providing special programs for this group (Laird, 1971). By 1979, forty-five states had such programs (B. M. Mitchell, 1980). In only a very few states (such as Pennsylvania and North Carolina) were measures required for the handicapped under P.L. 94-142 extended to support programs for the gifted and talented as well (Reynolds & Birch, 1977a), and recent changes in federal funding may reduce or eliminate these programs. The programs that are available vary widely in characteristics, quality, and the number of gifted they include.

Options

Basically, there are four options available for providing programs to meet the needs of gifted, talented, and creative students. These are:

1. Segregation
2. Acceleration
3. Mainstreaming
4. Enrichment (special programs)

Whether any of these options are to be exercised in a given school district is often the subject of heated debate. Some of the arguments are clearly presented by Cassivi (1979).

Segregation   Segregation can offer special opportunities for the gifted and talented, but it also evokes much controversy. On the positive side, supporters of "tracking" or homogeneous grouping (the most usual segregation technique) maintain that it is easier for the teacher to present material to students within a narrow range of ability than to students in heterogeneous classes, and that this increases the students' enjoyment of learning. Often, course material can be learned more rapidly and/or in greater depth than in traditional class arrangements. On the negative side, homogeneous grouping can evoke pressure from parents whose children are not included in the "gifted class," can stimulate inferiority feelings in those students who are not admitted, and can promote "busy work" for the gifted if the class is improperly handled. There is also a question as to whether gifted students should be homogeneously grouped for all classes, as even they tend not to be equally gifted in all areas.

Physical segregation in a separate building or wing is rarer than tracking, simply because of the number of students required to support such a special school. New York City has several schools that are, in effect, **magnet schools** (that is, special schools designed to attract students from an entire school district. These include Hunter College Elementary and High schools, the Bronx High School of Science, the High School of Music and Art, and the High School for Performing Arts (portrayed in the film *Fame*), among others. The admission process is highly competitive and is based on teacher recommendations, past achievement records, and special examinations or auditions. Philadelphia has one elementary school that houses both gifted and neighborhood youngsters, two special sex-ually segregated high schools for academically able students, and high schools for performing arts and for engineering and science. Other large urban centers have similar magnet schools, most of them at the secondary level. There are also two special state-wide segregated programs: North Carolina has a residential school for high school students gifted in science and mathematics, and Pennsylvania has a summer Governor's School for those talented in the performing arts and one for scientifically talented high school students.

At high schools for the talented (of which there were fifty-six in 1981), students carry a full load of academic courses plus classes in design, music theory and performance, dance, theater arts, photography, or other subjects appropriate to their special talent (Roth, 1981). They are also expected or required to participate in related extracurricular activities. At schools for the academically gifted, students frequently take more courses concurrently and pursue the subject matter more intensively than their peers in comprehensive or "regular" high schools.

Acceleration   Acceleration, also known as "skipping," was once a fairly common procedure for the gifted when schools had semiannual promotions. However, apart from the fact that the decision to accelerate was and is too often based on limited criteria (for example, IQ plus reading achievement scores), some research studies have shown that advanced grade placement can put an added strain on the gifted child's social and emotional development, particularly during early adolescence. This varies with the individual. Early admission to school, perhaps as early as age four, is often criticized for the same reason. Although intellec-tually gifted students do tend to be psychologically more mature than their peers, they are not always ready for the social activities and group interests of older students.

An alternative that some school districts have used is "rapid ad-vancement," whereby three years of work is compressed into two school years with no loss of content, only a more rapid learning pace. There is less social difficulty under this plan, since youngsters of the same age stay together in the program. In ungraded schools, students may progress at a more rapid pace on their own with teacher cooperation, but this system often fails to provide the social companionship about which so many people express concern.

Partial acceleration in advanced placement courses enables gifted students to acquire college credits while still in high school, without sacrificing social and emotional development. The most notable example of this practice is the Johns Hopkins University program for the mathe-matically talented (the Study of Mathematically and Scientifically Pre-cocious Youth, or SMSPY). Initially, most SMSPY participants take special

The Palcuzzi Ploy

Mr. Palcuzzi, principal of the Jefferson Elementary School, once got tired of hearing objections to special provisions for gifted children, so he decided to spice an otherwise mild PTA meeting with his proposal for gifted children. The elements of the Palcuzzi program were as follows:

1. Children should be grouped by ability.
2. Part of the school day should be given over to special instruction.
3. Talented students should be allowed time to share their talents with children of other schools in the area or even of other schools throughout the state. (We will pay the transportation cost.)
4. A child should be advanced according to his talents, rather than according to his age.
5. These children should have special teachers, specially trained and highly salaried.

As might be expected, the Palcuzzi program was subjected to a barrage of criticism. "What about the youngster who isn't able to fit into the special group; won't his ego be damaged?" "How about the special cost; how could you justify transportation costs that would have to be paid by moving a special group of students from one school to another?" "Mightn't we be endangering the child by having him interact with children who are much more mature than he is?" "Wouldn't the other teachers complain if we gave more money to the instructors of this group?"

After listening for ten or fifteen minutes, Mr. Palcuzzi dropped his bomb! He said that he wasn't describing a *new* program for the intellectually gifted but a program the school system had been enthusiastically supporting for a number of years—the program for gifted *basketball players*! Palcuzzi took advantage of the silence that followed to review his program again. Do we have ability grouping on our basketball team? Yes, we do. No doubt, the player who does not make the first team or the second team feels very bad about it and may even have some inferiority feelings. However, this will not likely cause the program to be changed.

Do we allow part of the school day to be given over to special work? Generally speaking, the last hour of the day can be used, by tradition, for practice of basketball talents.

Do we allow these children to share their talents with other students from other schools and other cities? Yes, we do, and, what is more, we pay the transportation costs involved without very many complaints being heard.

Do we allow gifted basketball players to advance by their talents rather than by their age? Indeed, we do. Any sophomore who can make the team on the basis of his talents gets the privilege of playing with seniors, and no one worries very much about it.

Finally, do we have special teachers who are specially trained and more highly salaried than the ordinary teacher? Yes, we do, and although there is some grumbling about it from the regular teachers, this does not materially affect the program.

What does this tell us? The culture and the community will support the kinds of activities that they find necessary, valuable, and/or enjoyable. If they feel that a program is sufficiently necessary or sufficiently enjoyable, all sorts of objections are put aside as being relatively inconsequential. If, on the other hand, the community is not fully interested or involved in supporting such a program, all kinds of objections can be raised as to why these things should not be done, or cannot be done.

Gallagher, J. J. *Teaching the gifted child* (2nd ed.). Boston: Allyn & Bacon, 1975, pp. 83–84. Reprinted by permission of the publisher.

math courses on Saturdays. Some attend college evening classes at Johns Hopkins, for which they earn full credit. Participating students are selected from among those scoring about 700 on the Scholastic Aptitude Tests while in the seventh grade (and occasionally earlier).

Many colleges and universities permit unusually well qualified students to enter as freshmen after completion of the eleventh grade. This encourages continued academic progress rather than intellectual stagnation during what would have been the student's twelfth-grade year. Nevertheless, the decision to accelerate here (as elsewhere) should be weighed carefully in terms of the individual's social and physical maturity and social interests as well as academic ability. To some, being the youngest person in a class is threatening, while to others it doesn't matter at all. Some gifted students prefer to build up college credits while remaining in high school, where they can participate in various extracurricular activities with their friends, rather than to accelerate their education at that point. It is important to consult the student about these factors when any decision about acceleration is to be made.

Mainstreaming Mainstreaming is a third option for placing gifted students. It, too, generates controversy. Advocates of mainstreaming, or heterogeneous grouping, maintain that it is a more democratic practice— it avoids elitism and feelings of inferiority (among the less able or unchosen)—and that it provides an environment more like the "real" world, where one mixes with all kinds of people. Opponents point out that it is unrealistic to expect students of varying abilities to proceed at the same

FOR EXAMPLE . . .

SMSPY research workers at Johns Hopkins have used a variety of acceleration techniques for exceptionally gifted children. A thirteen-year-old eighth grader was admitted to Hopkins as a freshman in 1969, received a B.A. degree in quantitative studies and an M.S.E. in computer science in 1973, and enrolled in a doctoral program at Cornell that same year—not yet eighteen years old.

Several of the students in this project have skipped two to four grades without experiencing personal or academic problems. Others have left high school early in order to become full-time college freshmen or taken college courses on a part-time basis. One fourth grader (age ten), for example, earned a B in college algebra and trigonometry at Johns Hopkins Evening College (Stanley, 1973).

pace, and that gifted students may become so bored that they become underachievers or acquire behavior problems.

Enrichment   An alternative that combines mainstreaming with special scheduling is assignment to a heterogeneous homeroom with flexible subject assignment or a part-time "pull-out" enrichment class. (Such a class typically meets once or twice a week for part of the day and provides learning opportunities not included in the regular curriculum.) Allowing fourth graders to attend sixth-grade math or social studies classes, for example, permits the intellectually gifted child to move ahead more rapidly in her areas of competence without skipping over weaker areas, as she would in a fully accelerated program. At the high school level, flexible programming would allow a student to take a fourth or fifth year of a foreign language or mathematics or, as suggested earlier, to take advanced placement or college courses.

Special programs may be designed on an individual or group basis. Enrichment programs for gifted and creative youngsters can include individualized, in-depth assignments; additional studies using different resource materials; seminar sessions with itinerant teachers of the gifted; field trips to special sites; and/or intensive lessons in music, art, or foreign languages (see Appendix B). Such activities should always be planned in keeping with the age, achievement level, maturity, special capabilities, and interests of the students. In relatively small or rural districts, this type of programming may require transporting students from more than one school to a central location. (And since transportation is costly, school board members may need to be convinced that such a program is beneficial to the students.)

In recent years, a number of colleges and universities have opened their doors to gifted students, on late afternoons, weekends, or during the summer, for noncredit enrichment classes, both academic and nonacademic. This type of program may or may not be arranged in cooperation with a local school district. Most of them charge a modest fee per course, as much to encourage commitment as to cover the expenses of faculty, materials, and space. There are also an increasing number of private summer camps that cater to the budding computer scientist, the precocious musician or dancer, and the prospective linguist.

Mainstreaming the Gifted

If the option chosen is mainstreaming, the teachers as well as the school district administration should be prepared to modify standard class assignments to accommodate the abilities of gifted, creative, and talented students, just as they do for other exceptional students. (Some of the modifications, in fact, may be applied to an entire class profitably.) At the same time, they should avoid exploiting the situation by using their gifted pupils as tutors (although some of them may welcome the opportunity to "teach" younger or less able children) or pointing them out as gifted "know-it-alls." There is a particular danger, also, of inhibiting gifted girls who are frequently (still!) taught to hide their brilliance with threats that otherwise they may never have a boyfriend (Schwartz, 1980a).

As teachers have become generally more cognizant of the desirability of encouraging nontraditional skills, they have provided more opportunities for creative expression at the elementary level for all children. Students are encouraged to write poetry, draw or write to varying musical themes, and create dances or skits. The more gifted and/or creative might develop plays related to class studies, writing the dialogue, designing and building the sets, and directing as well as acting in the production. Scientifically talented or creative students can work on local ecology problems. Artistic and musically talented youngsters can develop and present an arts festival. Research and writing topics can include futuristic visions and "second-guessing" history ("What if the colonists had failed in their revolution?").

Facilities at the elementary level for industrial arts projects, experimentation in the biological and physical sciences, learning to use and program computers, and filmmaking projects allow gifted and creative youngsters to explore new subject areas, develop new or budding skills, and have challenging learning experiences. Good writers also welcome the opportunity to prepare, assemble, and publish a newspaper or magazine periodically.

To stimulate interest in reading in the primary grades and demonstrate one way in which divergent thinking can operate, children might enjoy a series of books called "Choose Your Own Adventure" (Bantam

A "Futures" Project

The twenty-first century will soon be with us, and those now in school will shape its character. What better way for them to prepare for that responsibility than to design their own Utopia? As background, students might work with *Designs of Famous Utopias* (Gray & Orrick, 1959) and read *Looking Backward* (Bellamy, 1888), *Brave New World* (Huxley, 1932), and *1984* (Orwell, 1938/1961). C. Lewis (1979) has developed a unit for gifted elementary and junior high school students on the "city of the future" that not only incorporates a variety of disciplines and skills but also encourages thinking about the effects of decisions made in one sector of planning on decision making in other areas and about the implications of interrelated ideas. Suggestions for teachers can also be found in *Learning: The Magazine for Creative Teaching* ("Starting Points," 1974).

Books). Each of these provides the beginning of a story and then asks the reader to choose which of two or three events should occur next. There are several decisions to be made as the reader continues, so that each book has between thirty-five and forty-five possible endings. Not only does this maintain reader interest, but it also teaches the reader to think about the possible consequences of the decisions he makes.

Gifted youngsters are particularly concerned with the meaningfulness and purposefulness of their assignments and efforts. If they understand that they are learning a basic skill, they are likely to be happier learners than if they must perform seemingly isolated daily tasks. Even so, teachers should adapt the amount of drill to the pace of acquiring mastery, rather than mandating a common number of exercises for the whole class.

The unique needs of gifted students may be observed if one looks hard enough. P. S. Levy (1981) described five highly gifted seventh graders (IQ 140+) in a regular class who shared a few characteristics but differed in even more ways. Not only were their interests varied, but so were their peer relationships, thinking process skills, and personalities. Levy's efforts were directed toward developing and/or enhancing process skills in accord with each youngster's specific characteristics. Examples given include learning to organize time, identifying problems, playing the "school game" or "ways to interact with teachers," and communication and evaluation skills. In some cases, tutors or mentors were located to work with a youngster in a specialized way.

Independent study can provide the needed enrichment if there are only a few gifted students in a school. The students choose a topic in which they are interested (Greek mythology, history of sports, medical miracles) and proceed to survey the topic in terms of what the task involves, what resources (people or materials) are available, and whether it is too broad a topic or too narrow. With the aid of teachers, parents, and librarians, they then set to work, acquiring a host of research skills in the process.

The culmination of the project can be a presentation to the class, an exhibit, and/or a research report. Many educators believe that sharing the results of independent study is important for a student's social development, as well as providing an opportunity for recognition. Self-evaluation as to whether goals were met and what was learned (positive or negative) should be part of the final report (Cline, 1980; Cox, 1979).

Another form of independent study is student use of programmed materials. Well-written programs permit individual pacing as well as self-selection of content to be learned. In one relevant study, gifted and regular students used the Purdue Creativity Training Program to good effect, especially with regard to gains in verbal fluency for the gifted students (Huber, Treffinger, Tracy, & Rand, 1979). Mathematical and scientific topics can also be studied this way, as can recreational subjects like bridge and chess. "Branched" programming, as opposed to linear programming, tends to be more appropriate for gifted students, since larger bits of material are offered with less repetition of information.

Where available, the computer can be a valuable tool in the education of the gifted. It can be used for independent study, either for acceleration or for enrichment. Prepackaged computer games can be a motivational device or a reinforcer for completion of assignments. Some of the simulation "games" are especially good for teaching decision making. Creativity can also be stimulated as the student tries to solve puzzles using innovative logic, elaboration, and the computer's graphics capabilities. Responding to prepackaged software and writing new programs both require precision and attention to detail and thus help curb the impulsive behavior characteristic of many gifted youths. Finally, gifted students can use the computer for research, particularly in analyzing data (Landman, 1980). Fifth to eighth graders in an enrichment program (Project GO) at Penn State's Ogontz Campus during 1980–81 very quickly learned the rudiments of BASIC and PASCAL (two computer languages), played computer games with zest, and begged their families for personal computers so that they could continue developing their newly acquired skills (Schwartz, 1980b).

Where there are enough students to warrant having a teacher meet a group of perhaps ten, a "pull-out" enrichment program of one-half day to several hours each week can be appropriately combined with mainstreaming. Usually the teacher will initiate a unifying theme, with each group member contributing uniquely to the activities if the project is in the social sciences or literature. If the goal of the enrichment class is to teach a new skill or introduce a totally new subject area, on the other hand, allowance will have to be made for varying learning abilities even within a group of gifted students.

When the same students continue in the enrichment program for three or four years, the curriculum needs to be planned sequentially, just as "regular" subjects are. One program that has been used (in the Upper Moreland School District, Pa., during 1980–81) emphasizes discovery throughout grades one through five and stretches across the language arts, fine and performing arts, sciences, and social sciences. The gifted child moves from "discovering me" to "my immediate family," "my heritage," "my community," and finally "my country," paralleling the traditional social studies curriculum. Problem solving and decision making are integral parts of the science studies at every grade level, and writing is stressed in grades three through five. The content of this weekly half-day program complements rather than duplicates the standard classroom fare.

A final, though by no means unimportant, modification technique for the mainstreamed gifted student involves the cooperation of community residents. Individuals with special competencies or interests can be asked to serve as mentors to gifted youngsters with matching interests. Frequently they only need to guide the gifted rather than teach them. Another aspect of this approach involves internships, where the gifted student is able to gain actual working experience in a laboratory, law office, hospital, or other facility. This experience is likely to intensify interest in a field or, conversely, to direct the student toward some other career choice.

At all grade levels, mainstreaming plus enrichment seems to be the dominant mode of modifying education for gifted students. Even without enrichment programs, however, the gifted can be encouraged to work at higher levels of Bloom's "Taxonomy of Educational Objectives" (1956). They acquire information ("knowledge") and comprehend it rapidly. For primary grade gifted children, learning to apply what they know and to analyze relationships among discrete bits of information may be all that is appropriate. Slightly older or more intellectually able youngsters can work on "synthesis" and "evaluation" of their studies. They can also be taught, if they do not already know how, to develop systems of intrinsic (self-) reinforcement and resources to avoid dependence on extrinsic (parent or teacher) stimulation and rewards. These internal systems will help them cope with situations where there is little recognition for their giftedness of where they are less outstanding than in the typical heterogeneous class.

Special Programs

Programs such as Project GO, mentioned above, are becoming more common across the country, although few of them are free to students or offered during the school day, as this one is. Basically, the model comprises college faculty teaching gifted high school students on campus. Course content varies widely but typically includes a portion of a college-level course adapted to the ages and abilities of the youngsters attending. At the Ogontz Campus, eight-week sessions (at seventy-five to ninety minutes per week) have been presented in energy problems and solutions, computer science, reading and writing mystery stories, criminal justice (with a mock trial as the culminating activity), engineering drawing, and creative dramatics, among other subjects. Classes are small (ten to fifteen students), permitting a great deal of interaction between instructor and students and among the students. Critical to the success of the courses are the informal atmosphere, the lack of grades, and an abundance of "hands-on" experiences, such as laboratory experiments, surveys being developed, and the acquisition and practice of new skills.

As with other college-sponsored programs, there are extracurricular by-products. The gifted have an opportunity to meet and work with others like themselves from several communities; they have an opportunity to sample a different type of learning environment (the college setting) where they can meet and talk with college students; and they are recognized as individuals by a new group of significant adults (the college faculty). For some, this experience opens up new occupational goals; for some, it stimulates new aspirations to attend college.

At the College of Marin in California, tempting courses are offered to "Mentally Gifted Minors" such as "Dinosaurs" (kindergarten through third grade), "Allons en Français" (grades one through four), "Making Music with Pianos and Kids" (grades four through six), and "Calligraphy" (grades five through ten), along with more standard academic fare.

Classes are held weekdays, beginning at 3:30 p.m. At Purdue University, "Super Saturday" has given gifted children in grades two through nine an opportunity to select two six-week courses from foreign languages, math and computer science, "Humor and Creative Expression," and "Creative Thinking." Students, their parents, and the teachers have all evaluated the program, generally with strongly positive comments (Feldhusen & Wyman, 1980; Feldhusen & Sokol, 1982). Variations of these programs exist also at St. John's University in Brooklyn, at a consortium of colleges in the Wilkes-Barre, Pennsylvania, area, and at other colleges.

The majority of college programs for the precollege gifted, however, seem to be summer programs for high school students who can gain college credits while exploring their fields of interest. One of the more unusual programs in this category is LEAD, Inc. (Leadership Education and Development), which is held at the Wharton School of the University of Pennsylvania (Gould, 1981). Another was a series of summer workshops at Bard College in Annandale, New York, one of which was a music camp.

The opportunities afforded by special programs to attend classes with other students of varied ages, to reach for higher levels of achievement through self-competition, and to discover that there *are* challenges to one's learning abilities can be exciting to gifted youngsters who have previously always been at the top of their classes with relatively little effort. New interests stimulated through enrichment activities and special programs can lead to new career goals and, therefore, to a need for better academic and career counseling.

COUNSELING THE EXCEPTIONALLY ABLE

There are two major aspects to providing direct counseling services to the gifted: academic counseling and career guidance. Among the indirect services the counselor can offer, in addition, are consultations with parents of gifted youth and in-service workshops on education of the gifted with classroom teachers. The focus here, however, is on the direct services.

Academic Counseling

In cooperation with classroom teachers and the teacher of the gifted (if there is one), the counselor can plan an overall program that will attend to the social as well as the academic development of the gifted in a particular school. As a consultant to the teams that create IEPs for individual gifted children, the counselor can integrate the two programs. Zaffrann and

Colangelo (1977) have pointed out that some of the gifted need to work with each other in groups to enhance their social and communication skills. Others may need help with reading and study skills despite their advanced intellectual capabilities. Those who are creatively gifted may need to learn how to behave appropriately enough in class to avoid being regarded as having behavior problems, rather than as creative students. That is, they need to find a balance that will reduce friction between themselves and their teachers.

Counseling in the strictest academic sense requires identifying exceptionally able students as early as possible so that educational planning and programs can be implemented promptly. The counselor also needs to get acquainted with each gifted child in terms of her interests and aspirations, in order to seek appropriate role models and ease frustrations related to the child's special abilities (and weaknesses). Sometimes the counselor may have to intervene diplomatically with teachers on a youngster's behalf where conflict has occurred or where the necessary academic adjustments are not occurring. At the elementary level, youngsters should be carefully placed in enrichment activities or other modification options, but they should also be encouraged to acquire basic skills and a well-rounded fund of knowledge.

When planning for the secondary-level student, it would be wise to consider potential college majors and career goals as well as college admissions criteria. The problem here may be, as Gowan pointed out, that the gifted may be faced with an "embarrassment of riches" as they try to choose among several educational and career options (1960). Direct questioning and interest test scores can be helpful in suggesting potential directions for emphasis. Use of the *Dictionary of Occupational Titles* (U.S. Department of Labor, 1976) might lead to combining two or more of the student's interests and abilities into a single academic and career goal. In any event, the student should be encouraged to take both career-oriented and avocational (though still academic) courses and to acquire both library and computer skills in preparation for college work.

For the talented, the counselor should be familiar with school and community resources that can enhance their abilities—private teachers, scholarships to private music or art schools, appropriate competitions, and so on. If some adjustment is needed to the class schedule to allow for special lessons, the counselor can assist with this. In short, the counselor needs to be resourceful and to know what resources are available for these students.

Career Guidance

As the exceptionally able student progresses through secondary school, more and more attention must be focused on possible career goals and how to reach them. All students should have access to career information and guidance, but gifted students may be able to spare more of their school time for active investigation of the possibilities than the average student. If a student knows she wants to be an engineer, that's fine. If possible, the counselor should locate a female engineer in the community or at a local college with whom she can discuss the challenges and rewards of the field. For girls especially, a good role model is very important, as they are often discouraged from pursuing their goals by sexist advice given at home or in school (Schwartz, 1980a). Lacking a live role model, the counselor can suggest relevant articles in some of the magazines oriented to career women or ask the librarian to recommend appropriate biographies. If a boy's parents insist that he become a doctor, whereas he prefers the law or teaching, the counselor should take particular pains to find evidence from his past academic performance, interest tests, and extracurricular activities to suggest either support for a specific career direction or possibly a compromise (such as forensic medicine). Dettman and Colangelo (1980) have suggested that a "partnership approach" between parents and counselors should begin soon after a child is identified as gifted, creative, or talented. This would minimize potential career conflicts in the precollege years, since the parents would be well aware of their child's interests and strengths far in advance.

Mentorship and internship experiences can be valuable to the gifted, as indicated earlier. Less formally, guest speakers can be invited to meet with the gifted, and visits to colleges can be arranged. An experimental program tried at Texas A & M University along these lines was largely successful as a guidance mechanism and might serve as a stimulus to other schools seeking to improve their guidance program (Borman, Nash, & Colson, 1978). In some instances, college admissions officers will seek out not only the sports superstars but also the academic ones. Here, the counselor can help the student to weigh the advantages and disadvantages of offers, as well as the merits of particular departments in each college or university, and can generally bring a more objective perspective to the decision-making process. Ultimately, of course, the students must decide for themselves which path to follow.

SUMMARY

This chapter has examined gifted students and, to a lesser extent, creative and talented students in terms of their characteristics, how they are identified, which educational modifications they need and which may be available to them, and what their counseling needs are. It was emphasized that these students are not always readily identifiable. Some are hidden by other labels, such as handicapped, delinquent, or disadvantaged. They need to be located through nontraditional techniques that focus on behavior and interests rather than on test scores.

Specific attention has been paid here to mainstreaming plus enrichment opportunities, for this appears to be the dominant model of the 1980s. However, some of the major advantages and disadvantages of the segregation/homogeneous grouping, acceleration, and special program formats were also presented. It is not always easy to determine which is the best approach to modifying educational practices for a particular gifted student, nor may there be a variety of options to choose from. In such cases, resourceful teachers and counselors must adapt what is available to meet individual needs. Exceptionally able students cannot be left to wither on academic vines. They, like other exceptional children, need special education if they are to make the best possible use of their abilities as they mature. Neglecting them is not only an individual injury, it is a waste of a valuable, and possibly vital, social and national resource.

SUGGESTED ADDITIONAL READINGS

Alexander, P. J., and Skinner, M. E. The effects of early entrance on subsequent social and academic development: A follow-up study. *Journal for the Education of the Gifted*, 1980, *3*, 147–150.

Austin, A. B., and Draper, D. C. Peer relationships of the academically gifted: A review. *Gifted Child Quarterly*, 1981, *25*, 129–133.

Barbe, W. B., and Renzulli, J. S., Eds. *Psychology and education of the gifted* (2nd ed.). New York: Halsted Press/Irvington, 1975.

Carroll, K. L. Career decision-making and artistically gifted and talented students. *Roeper Review*, 1982, *4* (3), 14–15.

Feldhusen, J. F., and Treffinger, D. J. *Creative thinking and problem solving in gifted education*. Dubuque: Kendall/Hunt, 1980.

French, J. N. The gifted learning disabled child: A challenge and some suggestions. *Roeper Review*, 1982, *4* (3), 19–21.

George, W. C., Cohn, S. J., and Stanley, J. C. *Educating the gifted: Acceleration and enrichment*. Baltimore: Johns Hopkins University Press, 1979.

Getzels, J. W., and Dillon, J. T. The nature of giftedness and the education of the gifted. In R. M. W. Travers (Ed.), *Second handbook of research on teaching*. Chicago: Rand McNally, 1973.

The gifted and talented: Programs that work. Arlington, Va.: National School Public Relations Association, 1979.

Goleman, D. G., 1,528 little genuises and how they grew. *Psychology Today*, 1980, *13* (9), 28–53.

Maker, C. J. *Providing programs for the gifted handicapped*. Reston, Va.: Council for Exceptional Children, 1977.

Maker, C. J. The gifted hearing-impaired student. *American Annals of the Deaf*, 1981, *126*, 631–645.

Miller, A. *Prisoners of childhood*. New York: Basic Books, 1981.

Morgan, J. J., Tenneant, C. G., and Gold, M. J. *Elementary and secondary level programs for the gifted and talented*. New York: Teachers College Press, 1980.

Passow, A. H., Ed. *The gifted and the talented: Their education and development* (Part I). Chicago: National Society for the Study of Education, 1979.

Schwartz, L. L. Can we stimulate creativity in women? *Journal of Creative Behavior*, 1977, *11*, 264–267.

Sternberg, R. J. Lies we live by: Misapplication of tests in identifying the gifted. *Gifted Child Quarterly*, 1982, *26*, 157–161.

Szekeley, G. The artist and the child—A model program for the artistically gifted. *Gifted Child Quarterly*, 1981, *25*, 67–72.

Torrance, E. P. Future careers for gifted and talented students. *Gifted Child Quarterly*, 1976, *20*, 142–156.

Treffinger, D. J. Demythologizing gifted education: An editorial essay. *Gifted Child Quarterly*, 1982, *26*, 3–8.

Whitmore, J. R. Gifted children with handicapping conditions: A new frontier. *Exceptional Children*, 1981, *48*, 106–114.

Wittes, L. A., and Vasa, S. F. Programming alternatives for educating the gifted in rural schools. *Roeper Review*, 1981, *3* (4), 22–24.

Wolf, J., and Gygi, J. Learning disabled and gifted: Success or failure? *Journal for the Education of the Gifted*, 1981, *4*, 199–206.

Yadusky-Holahan, M., and Holohan, W. The effect of academic stress upon the anxiety and depression levels of gifted high school students. *Gifted Child Quarterly*, 1983, *27*, 42–46.

PART TWO/ PHYSICALLY IMPAIRED STUDENTS

I n 1981, the International Year of Disabled Persons, perhaps the most newsworthy event (and certainly an outstanding achievement) was the successful ascent of 14,410-foot Mount Rainier by a team of five blind climbers with Braille maps, an epileptic, a man with an artificial leg, and two hearing handicapped men. If anything could demonstrate that the handicapped "can do," this rugged climb was it. Two other climbers, both blind, had had to drop out en route, but the first accomplishment of all eleven was their preparation for and attempt to make the assault on the mountain. For the physically different, these people are first-class role models: They have shown that an impairment need not be an impediment to achievement.

Physically different students are those who have impairments that stem from prenatal or perinatal damage, genetic factors, or postnatal injuries or accidents (ranging from meningitis to auto accidents and shootings). With some youngsters, the problem is an obvious one, as when they use braces or wheelchairs; with others, the difficulty is hidden, particularly for those with cardiac damage or a hearing handicap. Professionals as well as lay persons tend to be uneasy in approaching the physically handicapped child or adult; some seem to believe that the physically handicapped automatically have an intellectual handicap as well. This, of course, is not the case.

Professional experiences with the victims of traumatic war injuries have given impetus to the development of diagnostic, educational, and vocational rehabilitation techniques and to effective methods of physical therapy. Biomedical engineers have created unique devices that permit the handicapped to function more independently. Environmental psychologists have teamed up with special educators to design modifications in the school environment that permit the handicapped to have easier access to regular classrooms. Although not all disabilities have been eradicated, more and more physically impaired but otherwise able students are enjoying a more normal life as a result of these varied innovations.

Since the early 1970s, federal legislation has established national advisory committees, bureaus within the Office (and Department) of Education, and regional resource centers that provide much valuable information to teachers working with exceptional children. The greatest impetus toward educational opportunities, of course, has come from the Rehabilitation Act of 1973 and the Education for All Handicapped Children Act of 1975. Provisions of the 1973 Act require that educational institutions receiving federal funds make all classrooms accessible to the handicapped. In practice, this means removing or reducing architectural barriers, supplying sign language interpreters for the deaf, and providing guides or other assistance to the blind. With these aids, plus those provided by the 1975 law, physically impaired students have a greater probability of having an educational experience that conforms to their abilities (as well as their disabilities) than ever before.

At the state level, bureaus of vocational rehabilitation offer services and support to those working with older handicapped adolescents who have finished school. Through offices in the various state departments of education, guidance and support are also furnished to local school districts so that they can meet the requirements of P.L. 94-142, and many state legislatures have passed laws that further enhance educational opportunities for the handicapped. There are also private organizations (the Easter Seal Society, the Lighthouse for the Blind, the March of Dimes), with memberships drawn from parents, professionals, and the general public, that contribute to the improvement of services to the physically handicapped through direct volunteer work or financial support of research and technical development.

The chapters included in Part Two focus on students with a variety of physical impairments: orthopedic disabilities, chronic illnesses, sensory disorders, and multiple problems. Within each of these groups, the degree of each youngster's educational and functional disabilities varies both with the nature and extent of physical damage and with the motivation of the individual. Calling a child "physically different" clearly tells only part of the story.

CHAPTER 5/
THE ORTHOPEDICALLY DISABLED AND CHRONICALLY ILL

In 1975–76, the estimated number of orthopedically disabled and health impaired children between the ages of one and nineteen, according to the National Advisory Committee on the Handicapped, was 328,000, with about 255,000 being served educationally. In 1978–79, including only those between five and seventeen, 175,900 students in this category were being served (according to the U.S. Department of Health, Education, and Welfare). Although this number is smaller than the total public school enrollment in a city the size of Houston, one must recognize that these students as a group require more classes, more teachers, and more physical facilities than the general school populations.

Physical disabilities, as we have seen, do not necessarily imply mental or intellectual handicaps.

Taking an acute rather than a chronic condition as an example, does the average student become intellectually impaired as a result of an accident that places her temporarily in a wheelchair or on crutches? Most children with orthopedic disabilities or chronic illnesses have learning abilities well within the normal range. Thus, the schools should provide them with every opportunity to use their intellectual (and physical) abilities as effectively as possible. Educational difficulties, apart from those allied to individual physical conditions, may stem more from psychosocial and personal adjustment factors than from the physical problems. This aspect of the disabled child's development is too often overlooked, however, by parents and teachers, resulting in slower than necessary educational and personal development.

For parents and teachers, the reactions to impairment and illnesses can vary from withdrawal to overprotection. For teachers, there may also be fear of the epileptic's seizure, the hemophiliac's bleeding, or the diabetic's insulin shock. The stereotypes they and others have concerning the orthopedically disabled and the chronically ill have been formed by literature and films to which they have been exposed since childhood. The same media can be used to correct these misperceptions.

TYPES OF PHYSICAL PROBLEMS

Orthopedic Disabilities

Images of children with limps, in wheelchairs, on crutches, or wearing leg braces are commonly brought to mind when reference is made to orthopedic disabilities. They may have missing or drastically shortened limbs (as was the case with most of the "thalidomide babies"), **muscular dystrophy** (a progressively degenerative disease that atrophies the skeletal muscles), paralysis of one or more limbs, a clubfoot, curvature of the spine, **cerebral palsy** (a paralytic condition caused by injury to the brain, usually during pregnancy), malformed hips, or **spina bifida** (a birth defect in which the spinal cord is not completely covered by vertebrae). Although the outward appearance of these children may be similar, the reasons for the appearance may differ. For example, a cerebral palsied youngster needs braces to control poor coordination or involuntary movements, while a child with a spinal condition needs braces for support.

Cerebral palsy, one of the more common physical problems, is primarily a disturbance of the voluntary motor functions that varies in severity from person to person and affects different functions, depending on the part of the brain affected. There are three major types of cerebral palsy: spasticity, athetosis, and ataxia. The spastic form is typified by abrupt and jerky movements; the athetoid form by slow repetitive motions, often accompanied by lack of control over facial and throat muscles, so that there may be drooling, sagging parts of the face, or difficulty in speaking; and the ataxic form by marked lack of coordination and a poor sense of balance (Reynolds & Birch, 1977a). Depending on the brain area(s) affected, the cerebral palsy victim may also be mentally retarded or gifted, learning disabled, visually or hearing impaired, or speech or language handicapped. The severity of the motor involvement does not have a direct correlation with any of these other impairments. That is, a youngster with cerebral palsy may be mildly ataxic and moderately mentally retarded, while another may be severely spastic yet have an average level of intellectual functioning.

Tragically, there are too many students who were born normal and became paralyzed or otherwise disabled because of gunshot wounds, injuries in auto accidents or sports, or the residual effects of diseases such as poliomyelitis or encephalitis. In most cases, their ability to learn has not been impaired, although their expressive abilities may have been affected—they may be unable to write or speak clearly or to turn pages, for instance. Such a disability becomes a handicap when the individual and others interpret it as such (Reynolds & Birch, 1977a, p. 415).

Chronic Illnesses

Some children have physical problems that cause them to tire easily, that restrict their physical activity despite a relatively healthy appearance, or that are life threatening. They may attend regular classes and be hospitalized in alternating cycles, which often interferes with their educational progress. About 4 million school-age children have chronic physical illnesses such as asthma, cystic fibrosis, leukemia, hemophilia, muscular dystrophy, cancer, sickle-cell anemia, diabetes, rheumatic fever, and epilepsy. A few of these conditions are invisible to the observer except when there is a complete loss of breath (asthma), a seizure (grand mal epilepsy), or other symptoms of an acute attack. Some chronically ill children are pale, tired, or weak much of the time, but most are able to participate in regular classes. However, teachers should be aware of students with these "invisible" illnesses and of any appropriate emergency measures they might need to take.

Children with epilepsy, a convulsive disorder, may suddenly have a glassy stare, wander aimlessly, appear not to hear a question, or act fidgety. These are symptoms of petit mal epilepsy, which involves a momentary loss of consciousness and which may occur frequently during the day (and sometimes be unobserved), or of psychomotor epilepsy, in which the child appears to be conscious but unaware of his inappropriate and aimless activity. With proper medication, these children usually have

fewer seizures and can function quite normally at other times. In cases of
grand mal epilepsy, however, there is often complete loss of consciousness, and there may be active convulsions.

Medication and occasional extended hospitalization for treatment are
necessary for many chronically ill children. Even as outpatients, they may
have to be excused from school for doctors' visits, or they may miss school
days because of a flareup of their illness. These absences, and sometimes
the side effects of their medication, tend to interrupt learning and also
interfere with building strong peer relationships. It is the interruptions,
however, rather than the illness itself, that may cause them to achieve
lower grades.

The impact of chronic illness tends to be related to the developmental stage at
which the child is first affected. A small child usually responds with vigorous
protest to restriction of movement or loss of recently gained skills. For the teenager, chronic illness imposes limitations that heighten the problems of identity
formation and may evoke a response of forceful rebellion. (Isaacs & McElroy, 1980,
p. 318)

EDUCATIONAL MODIFICATIONS

As long ago as 1861, New York City opened the nation's first hospital for
chronically ill children, and at the turn of the century it began public

school classes for children with heart diseases (Nazzaro, 1977). In New York and other large cities, because of the prevalence of tuberculosis at that time, many school buildings were constructed with roof areas designed for open-air classes. For more than a century, then, efforts have been made to include at least some of the orthopedically disabled and chronically ill within the realm of public school services. Too many, however, were turned away, even when it was evident that they could learn. Often this was because of facilities inadequate for the wheelchair-bound, or because of real or imagined fears of what would happen in an emergency, or because of too many steps for those on crutches or with heart impairments. Compliance with the Rehabilitation Act of 1973 has reduced (although not completely eliminated) the architectural barriers to education of the disabled. For example, the symbol for the handicapped (Figure 5.1) directs them to building entrances, parking spaces, and other facilities. Furthermore, compliance with the Education for All Handicapped Children Act has reduced the philosophical and policy barriers to inclusion of the disabled in the public education system.

Physical Facilities

For those not homebound or hospitalized, some practical problems arise when the time comes to enter school. How will the child get to school? (Transportation of the orthopedically disabled often requires a bus with hydraulic lifts as well as a driver who is cheerful, helpful, and sensitive to the needs of these special passengers.) Are there steps at the school entrance that the youngster cannot negotiate? Are doorways wide enough to permit wheelchairs to go through? Are there revolving doors? Are there ramps as well as stairs to permit easy transfer from one room to another? Are there elevators available for those who cannot climb stairs?

A school physical plant that will be used by orthopedically disabled and/or chronically ill students should be in a one-story building, with rest areas for those students who need rest periods, modified restroom facilities, drinking fountains that are adjustable in height to permit children with various disabling conditions to use them, and blackboards projected out from the wall to permit children in wheelchairs to take their turn at the board with a minimum of awkwardness. The sand and water tables for younger children in wheelchairs have to be shallow and of an appropriate height, allowing a chair to slide under them or into a niche. Cafeteria tables should similarly be modified so that children in wheelchairs can have lunch with their less disabled peers. If the physical facilities are properly arranged, many of the orthopedically disabled can attend classes in regular schools. This is most desirable for their self-esteem and learning progress and for the development of good peer relationships, *if* the supplementary aids and services they need are available.

Figure 5.1   International symbol for the handicapped

Placement

"Bedside" Instruction   The need for prolonged bed rest or intensive therapy mandates either in-hospital or at-home study for some disabled and ill students. Many of the special hospitals for these youngsters provide on-site "schools," with lessons scheduled in small groups or even at the bedside. Homebound students may be taught by itinerant teachers, furnished by the local school district, for one or more hours daily, or may be linked directly to their classrooms via special telephone hookups. In addition, books, films, tape recordings, educational and commercial television, and volunteer tutors can help the youngster to maintain educational progress.

Segregated Classes   For those not homebound or hospitalized, however, some consideration has to be given to the facilities available for them in the public schools, as just discussed. Occasionally these students are placed in segregated day schools rather than mainstreamed in regular classes.

Segregation may be the only option when the disability is so severe that the teacher in a regular class would have to devote too much time to the one student or when the available facilities are simply inadequate to meet the needs of the student and cannot be modified. Segregated schools usually have physical therapy rooms, an adapted gymnasium, and a swimming pool that is used more for therapy than for recreation. At the Widener Memorial School in Philadelphia, there are also a shop where braces are made and repaired, a mobility training room, and a workshop

The sink to the right allows ready access for a student in a
wheelchair. (Photo by G. Fred Rieman, Jr.)

where enabling implements are made for students with very special
problems. Segregated classes are often housed in a wing of a regular
school building (possibly with physical therapy rooms nearby), with
varying degrees of interaction with other students. Some orthopedically
disabled students have indicated, however, that they prefer not to have
physical therapy scheduled as part of their school day because it makes
them miss classes and fall behind in academic areas. The question of
whether the convenience of physical therapy should outweigh learning
sessions is one that should be decided on an individual rather than a
group basis.

Mainstreaming   Mainstreaming is possible in situations where the
child can move about conveniently, and it is usually more desirable than
segregation. Some adjustments may have to be made in time allotment to
move from one class to another, for the wheelchair-bound student obviously cannot race along a corridor filled with walking students, and
those with heart impairments or cystic fibrosis cannot walk too quickly.
Arrangements have to be made for getting these students out of the

building in case of fire drills or real emergencies. Other students have to be cautioned about running into the disabled or ill and may have to be prepared to give assistance as needed. Assignment of disabled and ill students to particular courses and sections should be based on their learning abilities primarily, but some realistic consideration should also be given to physical facilities, the nature of the impairment, and teacher attitudes.

In the classroom, the disabled child finds note taking an important but occasionally impossible task, due to paralysis or tremors in the hands or fingers. Electric typewriters are useful for some of these students. They should be provided and instruction in their use given so that assignments can be prepared. Tape recorders, possibly adapted for the youngster who cannot push the levers, can also be used for note taking and for oral fulfillment of assignments. An automatic page-turning device, operated by pushing a switch or button, will reduce the frustration or embarrassment caused by lack of manual dexterity. Youngsters who cannot use any of these tools may need a headband with a rubber-tipped stick attached that enables them to indicate letters and other symbols on a special board. Other helpful devices include push buttons or foot pedals rather than switches or levers, one-handed rolling pins, left-handed scissors, touch latches instead of handles on cabinet doors, nonslip bases on equipment, and lapboards.

Sometimes a student is so disabled that almost exotic means are necessary to help her use the abilities she has. Today's sophisticated

FOR EXAMPLE . . .

The LOGO system, developed at Massachusetts Institute of Technology, has helped one severely disabled student with cerebral palsy and superior intelligence to become an adept computer programmer, with a job looming in the future. The student, eighteen-year-old Michael Murphy, is so severely affected that he cannot walk or talk clearly or manipulate a pen or pencil (Wexler, 1980a). Other severely disabled youngsters can be similarly helped.

"Any motor signal a handicapped child can make can be harnessed, connected to a computer-based facility, and translated into electronic signals. Those signals allow the individual to communicate thoughts and answer questions. Powers are multiplied enormously as the person learns to issue commands—for example, to operate a wheelchair, to draw, to write, even to compose music. Under development is a system to generate voices for those with little or no speech" (Wexler, 1980a).

computers are one such means. Advances in engineering and electronics technology are similarly releasing the dammed-up abilities of other disabled students.

Content and Techniques

For the intellectually able but physically disabled student, few changes if any are needed in the content of most classroom instruction. Instead, adaptations may have to be made in the way assignments are carried out, with modifications of equipment such as those suggested above. In art courses, the child with impaired arms or hands can learn to paint or draw with the brush or pencil held in his mouth or toes. If his disability does not involve the upper limbs, there should be no problem other than having a work area appropriate in height and a surface area on which he can work comfortably. Similarly, industrial arts activities may have to be modified only in terms of work surface adaptability for those who can use their upper limbs; where there is an arm or hand impairment, the physical therapist, special educator, and art or industrial arts teacher should jointly plan appropriate activities that the youngster can handle. For the health impaired, sedentary art activities involving clay modeling, puppetry, craft projects, vegetable sculpture, and "picturing problems" would not be overtaxing (Milne, 1981).

Participation in group activities, according to the student's physical abilities, talents, and interests, is important to her psychological well-being. If her physical condition precludes playing a guitar or wind instrument, for example, playing the cymbals on cue may be within her capabilities and will have therapeutic value as well in the area of muscular control. If there is no appropriate role in the class play, the student can exercise certain muscles and have a part in the production by pulling curtain ropes, or she can be the prompter, director, or property person. The important thing is to involve the student in class activities in a meaningful way.

During physical education periods, disabled or ill students can participate in an adaptive program geared to their special needs. If there are enough youngsters in this category within a given school or district, they can have their own teams and "Olympics," as disabled adults do. Swimming offers therapeutic and recreational opportunities and is one sport in which the disabled youngster can relate to nondisabled peers on a fairly equal level. Cathey and Jansma offer specific suggestions on mainstreaming the orthopedically disabled person in several physical activities, including swimming and soccer (1980a, 1980b). Although such activities have merit, school personnel must remember that many of these youngsters have limited stamina and need ample chances to rest. If a particular child cannot participate actively because of impairments or ill health, perhaps he can act as team manager, scorekeeper, or timekeeper.

A volunteer provides a helping hand to a young woman with
severe coordination problems so that she can draw. (Courtesy of
New York Philanthropic League. Photo by Norma Chein.)

At the very least, he can be taught the fine points of a few sports so that he
will be an informed and more appreciative and enthused spectator, as
well as familiar with something that is important to many of his peers.

As mainstreaming of the disabled continues, literature dealing with
orthopedic disabilities and chronic illnesses can be incorporated into the
curriculum to increase the understanding of and promote more positive
attitudes in the healthier students. As Biklen and Bogdan (1977) have
pointed out, disabled persons have been stereotyped in books and films as
pitiful, burdensome, asexual, objects of charity, sources of ridicule, and/or
having supercompensatory powers. Some newer books for adolescents,
however, present a more realistic picture of the frustrations, need for
support, and latent abilities of the disabled (Stroud, 1981). The use of
literature in this way may be especially useful in cases where a local
football player has been permanently disabled in a game or a peer has
suddenly developed an illness diagnosed as imminently fatal.

Another aspect of mainstreaming is the need to modify test administration procedures for some students. Those with cerebral palsy may need
someone to write their answers or simply more time to complete a test

because of their coordination problem. Chronically ill students tend to attain better scores if they can rest between parts of a test (Fair & Birch, 1971). Special efforts are being made to adapt testing procedures to the needs of disabled and ill students, by the Educational Testing Service (1979), for example, with their large-scale standardized tests, as well as by classroom teachers. (The ETS has indicated, however, that there is still a problem in interpreting test scores obtained under such nonstandard conditions.)

In addition to their normal academic studies, disabled and ill students need other learning experiences. Sex education is important for them, both because it is a normal part of life and because all but the most severely impaired may at some time contemplate or engage in a close relationship with another person. Functional living skills must be taught so they can do more for themselves more effectively. The American Heart Association, for example, teaches the cardiac impaired how to cook without tiring as well as to perform other routine tasks. The academic program should also include special library privileges as needed and the use of the diagnostic and vocational guidance skills of rehabilitation specialists. As these counselors are sure to advise, vocational skills from typing to computer programming will be assets for those who will be able to work, either at home or elsewhere.

Socialization

Whether in a school or residential setting, disabled students need to learn to interact with other people in pairs or groups (Castle, 1980) and should have opportunities to do so. Extracurricular activities such as amateur radio clubs can bring the world to the disabled student (and perhaps allow the ham or "CB" operator to play an important role in an emergency, despite being chair-bound or housebound).

In New York City, the New York Philanthropic League, a volunteer organization, began over sixty years ago to provide recreational and physical therapy services for orthopedically disabled youngsters. During the school year, preschoolers through adolescents gather at a midtown clubhouse for a wide variety of recreational activities that include dancing lessons (!), writing a newspaper, putting on plays, and playing games.

Suzie J., aged six, had never been out of her home until she was brought into the program by the league. She was shy, overprotected, and very leery of the whole idea. At the end of her first Saturday, she was instead tired, smiling, and chattering away to her amazed parents. By the end of a month, Suzie was looking foward to attending school, and after a year, she was even willing to be seen in public places with her parents or with her friends on league outings.

Jeremy, who came to the league at age twelve, proved to be an aggressive and bright victim of cerebral palsy. With the new skills and self-confidence he gained in the recreation program, his schoolwork improved. When he completed high school, the League was able to help him obtain a scholarship to college. Today, he is a lawyer.

Varied recreational programs are important so that disabled adolescents can experience normal peer interaction and expand both their skills and their horizons (Haraguchi, 1981). The Variety Club, the Easter Seal Society, and other organizations devoted to the welfare of disabled and chronically ill youngsters often sponsor recreation programs during the year, as well as summer camps, specially equipped for their particular needs.

SUMMARY

Occasionally, the news media highlight the exploits of a one-legged skier, the poetry of an adolescent with muscular dystrophy, or the intellectual feats of a student severely affected with cerebral palsy. The stereotypes of the physically disabled and chronically ill then shrink just a notch. The disabled still have far to go, however, even though federal legislation has opened more of society to them and thereby made them more visible to society. Facilities have had to be modified to permit them to partake of the opportunities mandated in P.L. 94-142, from providing ramps for wheelchairs, wider lavoratory stalls, and rest areas to designing computer programs that will enable them to communicate and to learn.

Not all disabled and ill students can attend regular classes full time, partly because of secondary impairments (intellectual or emotional) and partly because their primary impairments make it too difficult for them to keep up without special assistance. Some of these students are hospitalized, some housebound, and some in segregated classes or schools. They may require special implements to enable them to use the limited abilities and physical resources they have, or they may be physically unable to sit and learn in a regular school setting. Some chronically ill children can be too weak to participate in regular classes and so need the help of an itinerant teacher for the homebound.

For those who can attend school, the adaptations needed tend to be less in the area of academic content than in physically dealing with the tools of learning and the normal activities of their peers. Modifications in schedule (to allow rest periods for those who need them), music, art, and physical education are often necessary to accommodate these exceptional students. Encouragement to participate in group activities is also highly desirable, for an increasing number of orthopedically disabled and chronically ill students will be in the work world when they mature, and they should be well prepared to act from their strengths rather than to be viewed in terms of their weaknesses.

SUGGESTED ADDITIONAL READINGS

Arundel, G. What is the least restrictive environment for physically handicapped students? *Educational Horizons*, 1982, *60*, 115–117.

Bloom, J. Sex education for handicapped adolescents. *Journal of School Health*, 1969, *39*, 363–367.

Cleary, M. E. Helping children understand the child with special needs. *Children Today*, 1976, *5* (4), 6–10.

Gliedman, J. The wheelchair rebellion. *Psychology Today*, 1979, *13* (3), 59–64, 101–102.

Gluckman, S., and Barling, J. Effects of a remedial program on visual-motor perception in spina bifida children. *Journal of Genetic Psychology*, 1980, *136*, 195–202.

Grady, D. Overcoming brain damage. *Discover*, 1981, *2* (6), 62–65.

Hamilton, A. The remarkable new prosthetics. *American Education*, 1975, *11* (1), 34–37.

Landon, C., Rosenfeld, R., Northcraft, G., and Lewiston, N. Self-image of adolescents with cystic fibrosis. *Journal of Youth and Adolescence*, 1980, *9*, 521–528.

Ottman, R. A. Before a handicapped student enters the classroom: What the special educator can do. *Teaching Exceptional Children*, 1981, 14 (1), 41–43.

Panides, W. C., and Ziller, R. C. The self-perceptions of children with asthma and asthma/enuresis. *Journal of Psychosomatic Research*, 1981, 25, 51–56.

Riffee, D. M. Self-esteem changes in hospitalized school-age children. *Nursing Research*, 1981, 30 (2), 94–97.

Sachs, M. B. Helping the child with cancer go back to school. *Journal of School Health*, 1980, 50, 328–331.

Smith, L. M. *The college student with a disability: A faculty handbook* (Report No. 8-327-505:QL4). Washington, D.C.: U.S. Government Printing Office, 1980.

CHAPTER 6/
THE HEARING IMPAIRED

Have you ever watched television with the sound off? Have you ever tried to figure out what the people across a crowded room were saying as they nodded in your direction? Have you ever tried to have a conversation when your ears were blocked by infection or excess wax? If your answer to any of these questions is affirmative, you have experienced some of the frustration of the hearing impaired. Theirs is generally a hidden disability unless they wear obvious hearing aids. Furthermore, awareness that an individual has a hearing problem may be delayed and the lack of responsiveness attributed to other causes, such as negativism, delayed development, or even anger.

THE NATURE OF HEARING IMPAIRMENT

Causes

Despite widespread belief in the nineteenth century that deafness was primarily inherited, particularly when both parents were deaf or when close relatives married, there is conflicting evidence today about this theory (Moores, 1978). In fact, in many cases the cause of hearing loss is unknown. The most commonly identified causes today are maternal rubella (German measles) during pregnancy, prematurity, Rh factor incompatibility, postnatal meningitis, and heredity.

A genetic cause may be presumed if one or both parents are deaf, but overlooked (possibly erroneously) if the parents and siblings of a child have normal hearing but there are other relatives who have a hearing impairment. Inherited or congenital deafness may be the result of a recessive gene carried by both parents, a dominant gene carried by one parent (who is, by definition, hearing impaired), or a sex-linked gene, which (like hemophilia) affects the male offspring and is only carried by female offspring. Figure 6.1 illustrates these possible combinations.

A more recently identified cause of deafness (as well as other physical problems) is maternal rubella. If a woman has German measles during

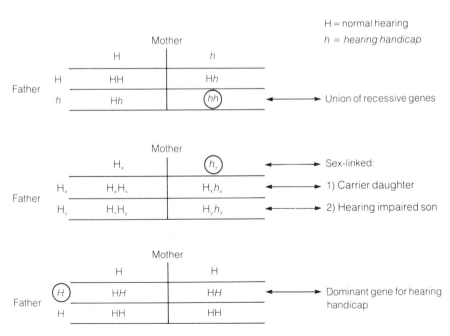

Figure 6.1   Inheritance of hearing handicaps

FOR EXAMPLE . . .

Colette is 4½ years old and profoundly deaf. . . . She was a premature baby, only weighing just over 3 lb. at birth, and her deafness is attributed to this. She was kept under observation for her first year, although deafness was not confirmed until she was 2 years old, as originally her slowness in speech and lack of response was thought to be due to mental retardation. She is now thought to be of average intelligence.

Gregory, S. *The deaf child and his family.* New York: Halsted Press, 1976, p. 32.

pregnancy, particularly during the first three months, the chances of her having a hearing impaired child are fairly high. Evidence of this is seen in the marked increase in the number of hearing impaired and multiply handicapped deaf children following the rubella epidemic of the mid-1960s. The risk is especially high because many of the internal structures, such as the inner ear, are differentiated in the first three months of prenatal development. (A vaccine to prevent German measles is available, and preventive inoculation is required by some school districts as a condition of admission. However, some parents still expose their daughters to the disease in childhood in hopes that they won't catch it as young women.)

Prematurity is a factor not only in hearing impairment but also in other physical difficulties. It is uncertain, though, whether premature birth is the cause or whether other conditions that stimulate premature birth have hearing impairment as a side effect. Moores has speculated that, because of medical advances that enable more premature babies to be "saved," there is likely to be an increase in the number of (possibly multihandicapped) deaf children in the future (1978, p. 91). As in other cases of hearing impairment, diagnosis may be delayed.

Ideally, of course, hearing tests should be administered shortly after birth, as they are in Luxembourg. There, infants are routinely tested at five days and again at six months, thus permitting early diagnosis and planning for those whose hearing is impaired. If a child is found to be deaf, the mother is brought to the school for the deaf (the Logopedics School) for a three-day training program in which she is taught how to speak and work with her child. Her efforts continue until the child enters the Logopedics School at age three (Polis, 1973). Early training programs are also available in the United States at the Johns Hopkins Clinic in Baltimore, the John Tracy Clinic in Los Angeles, and other locations, even though we do not have mandatory infant testing.

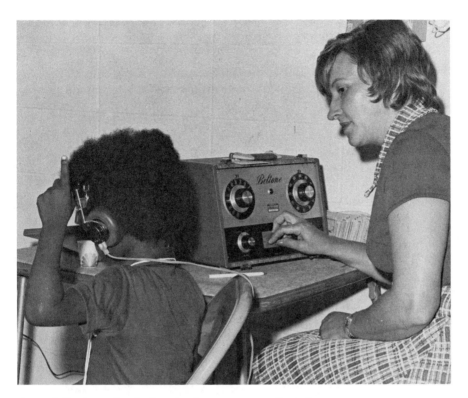

A specialist in testing for hearing loss uses an audiometer as well as other techniques. (With permission of HDS/U.S. HHS)

Degrees of Impairment

The hearing impaired category includes all of those who have difficulties in hearing, whether the loss is mild or profound. The Conference of Executives of American Schools for the Deaf has defined the deaf person (total hearing loss) as one with hearing loss of at least 70 **decibels** (or units of sound intensity), precluding the understanding of speech through the ear either with or without a hearing aid. The hard-of-hearing person, with a loss of 35−69 decibels (partial loss), has difficulty understanding speech through the ear alone, with or without a hearing aid. Since the average conversational level of sound is about 65 decibels, this difficulty is understandable.

For educational purposes, the hearing impaired are divided into four categories. They almost all need special speech and hearing assistance, but those with mild hearing loss (35−54 dB) do not usually require special class or school placement. Children with moderate loss (55−69 dB) occa-

FOR EXAMPLE . . .

The range of sound is 1–130 decibels (dB). Above 130 dB, sound is replaced by the sensation of pain. Continuous exposure to sounds above 90 dB (as on some factory assembly lines or working outdoors at a busy airport) has been shown to cause permanent damage to hearing. You should also note that prolonged exposure to the sound of a motorcycle or to loud rock music can be hazardous to hearing. By way of illustration, some commonly heard sounds and their decibel impact (taken singly rather than combined with other sounds, as they are typically in the environment) are:

- Rustle of leaves in a slight breeze   10 dB
- Average house sounds   45 dB
- Average conversational level   65 dB
- Telephone (medium ring)   85 dB
- Thunderclap   107 dB
- Motorcycle   110 dB
- Loud rock music   115 dB
- Turbojet engine   175 dB

The deaf would miss the first three sounds entirely, while the hard-of-hearing would not hear the leaves rustle and would have difficulty with the next two items. Those with profound hearing loss (90 dB or more) would also not hear the telephone ring and might notice thunder more as a vibration than as a noise.

sionally require special placement and usually need assistance with language development. Both the severely hearing impaired (70–89-dB loss) and the profoundly hearing impaired (90-dB loss and beyond) routinely need special class or school placement, language assistance, and educational assistance (Moores, 1978, pp. 5–7). It is also possible to view the hearing impaired youngster in terms of how much usable hearing he has and the quality of his language and speech skills. With great determination and sufficient residual (or aided) hearing and learning abilities, an occasional youngster has functioned well in regular classes despite a marked hearing disability.

Mark, a gifted boy with severe hearing loss, attended a special nursery school for hearing impaired children, partly to strengthen his language and communication skills and partly to give him normal preschool learning experiences. Since then, he has been in a private day school, the only hearing impaired child there. As a teenager, Mark attends only regular classes (except for math, where he is in an advanced section) and is studying two foreign languages. He has many hearing friends, communicates freely with them as well as with his family, and participates actively with others in extracurricular activities.

Author's case files.

Outcomes: Educational

Whether it is a congenital defect or one occurring in early childhood, hearing loss affects both learning and retention in speech, and this, in turn, affects most other areas of a child's functioning. The speech and, therefore, learning problems are somewhat reduced if the hearing impairment occurs after the child has learned to speak and develop language skills. Certainly the earlier the hearing loss occurs and the more severe it is, the greater the possibility of a learning disability (in the general sense). Much current research is focused on this specific relationship between restricted hearing and intellectual functioning. For example, since classroom and test performance is so dependent on language skills, the student's test scores may underestimate her intelligence level, and her classroom performance may be rated below average. Most of the intelligence tests commonly given in schools, such as the Lorge-Thorndike, Otis-Lennon, and California Mental Maturity Tests, are inappropriate measures for the hearing impaired student because of the way they are administered (instructions read aloud, for example) or scored (J. M. Davis, Shepard, Stelmachowicz, & Gorga, 1981). Although the average IQ of severely hearing impaired children on such standardized tests is about 90 (and therefore within the average range), their developmental lag in communication skills tends to retard their initial entrance to school and to keep them behind by two to five years academically. On the other hand, lowered test scores do not necessarily mean lowered abilities. Thomas Edison, inventor of the electric light bulb, the phonograph, and other devices, was hearing impaired.

Even when using nonverbal tests with deaf preschool children,

Brinich found that IQ scores were significantly related to the children's competence in communication (1981). A study of young Swedish children who had been taught total communication (gestures, signs, finger spelling, lipreading, reading, and writing) showed not only that their language development was accelerated but that some children developed speech spontaneously (Norden, 1981). It is logical and apparent that children who are taught communication skills early fare better on tests that are dependent on language development. Norden also noted that those children who had been taught sign communication early also seemed to have better emotional adjustments.

Outcomes: Personal-Social

In addition to the educational difficulties for hearing impaired students, there are a number of understandable personal and social adjustment problems with which they have to cope. The inability to hear in infancy and early childhood may prevent or delay the development of a good parent-child relationship and a positive self-concept. Parents may perceive chronic inattention and failure to respond when spoken to as behavioral symptoms of autism, retardation, or negativism and react to the child accordingly. On the child's part, frustrations arising from communication problems can lead to frequent temper tantrums, withdrawal, and inadequate or inappropriate behavior. Since hearing impairment is an invisible physical disability, others may view the child's "different" behavior, and therefore the child herself, negatively. Even a hearing impaired adolescent or adult, because of his lack of communication and understanding, may suspect that other people are talking about him and thus dislike him. In aggravated instances, this can lead to a paranoiac personality. Appropriate early diagnosis and subsequent instruction can reduce the probability of such unnecessary additional problems.

Socially, of course, the hearing impaired need to be able to communicate effectively with other people. Whether they ultimately choose to function primarily in the hearing world or in the hearing impaired community, they will have to be able to write if their speech is badly affected, use sign language with those who know it, lip-read, or use speech. On the one hand, the hearing impaired child should be raised in a speaking environment and encouraged to speak for herself as much as possible. On the other, deaf and hard-of-hearing individuals often form their own social groups, since they may be more comfortable with peers who have similar difficulties. Carefully chosen and well-designed summer camp programs can encourage peer interaction and ease personal and social adjustment problems. Exposure to total communication techniques also facilitates communication with both hearing impaired and nonimpaired people and reduces the defensive behavior of the hearing disabled person.

What appear to be behavioral traits characteristic of the deaf, according to Chess and Fernandez (1980), may be the result of stress stemming from communication problems rather than the impairment itself. Once again, it should be stressed that early identification and the prompt start of communication training are critical to the social-emotional as well as to the educational adjustment of hearing impaired youth.

EDUCATIONAL MODIFICATIONS

Facilities

The principal requirement of the hearing impaired, whether at home or at school, is the use of visual cues and/or amplifiers to supplement sound. For example, telephones can be equipped with amplifying devices and a blinker light to signal incoming calls. There is also the TTY, a combination telephone, teletypewriter, and computer that permits conversion of spoken messages into typed messages and vice versa, thereby allowing the severely and profoundly deaf to "talk" on the phone (see Figure 6.2). A blinking light can signal that the doorbell is ringing at home or that the fire gong is sounding at school.

The use of films and videotapes for the deaf, to promote their educational and cultural development, has been encouraged by several congressional laws. Many of these filmed materials are made with captions or

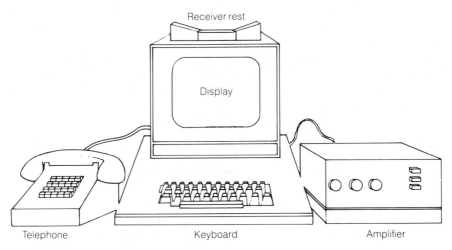

Figure 6.2   Model of telephone-typewriter for the hearing impaired

titles so that the non-lip-reader can follow the narrative. Captioned programs are also available on television (although they require an "unscrambler"), and some newscasts provide sign language presentations concurrently with regular reporting. The National Theater of the Deaf provides a fine opportunity for hearing impaired individuals to enjoy theatrical presentations.

In special classrooms, group hearing aids, which combine a central source of amplification with binaural earphones at listening stations, convey the teacher's or classmates' voices or sounds from other audio equipment. Hearing aid vests are available for children up to ten years old or so that enable them to wear bulky body hearing aids comfortably, and a device known as the Phonic Ear also amplifies sound comfortably.

In terms of special instructional equipment, tape recorders and Language Masters can allow children to hear prerecorded speech and thereby increase their own fluency. Acoustic puzzles, using tape-recorded sounds, can be used to teach mildly and moderately hearing impaired preschoolers to recognize human laughter, a dog's barking, the difference between scolding and crying sounds, and so on. This training helps children to interpret speech rhythms when they cannot hear the actual words. The

The Phonic Ear (Photo courtesy of Phonic Ear, Inc., Mill Valley, Ca.)

overhead projector, which the teacher can use while facing the class, is another helpful tool. Filmstrips, books, pictures, and symbols all provide supportive visual stimulation that, even without auditory accompaniment, is a valuable aid for communication and learning. Finally, family and/or school-sponsored field trips to stores, the zoo, even an amusement park, help hearing impaired children to expand their vocabularies and share in normal childhood experiences.

Placement

From Institutionalization to Segregation   Since ancient times, the hearing world has assumed that the deaf, especially those born deaf or who lost their hearing ability before they learned to speak (the prelingual deaf), were incompetent. As a result, they were rarely held responsible for some of their misdeeds, but they also lost most or all of their legal rights. At the same time (and even into the last century in America), they were viewed as a potential burden on the community. A state residential school for "deaf and dumb persons" was established as early as 1817 in Connecticut, followed by another sixteen schools before the Civil War and, in 1857, by the federally funded Columbia Institution for the Deaf and the Dumb and the Blind (Nazzaro, 1977). In 1894, the Columbia Institution was renamed Gallaudet College in tribute to Thomas Gallaudet, first principal of that early state school in Connecticut. The pattern of residence schools, or asylums, for the deaf persisted for many decades, although the first schools in New York, Philadelphia, Pittsburgh, and Boston also had some day pupils (Moores, 1978). Institutionalization is, however, the least preferred placement method for hearing impaired individuals.

Segregated day schools and classes appear to be desirable primarily as "stepping stones" to integrated education for young hearing disabled students. Infant programs for the deaf, such as those at John Tracy Clinic and the Lexington School for the Deaf in New York, emphasize the use of residual hearing to enhance language development, communication, and socialization. The approach is a functional, family-oriented one, teaching the mother to help both herself and her child in a healthy, affectionate relationship (Connor, 1976). Progression to a class of mixed hearing and hearing impaired preschool peers is one alternative for the next age level; continuing in a segregated class is another. Whether a hearing impaired student continues in special classes throughout the school years or at some point enters the regular school system depends on individual needs, available support services in regular classes, preparation of the child for mainstreaming, and the competence and attitudes of the receiving professional staff at regular schools.

Mainstreaming the Hearing Impaired   Frick has asserted that it is essential for teachers of hearing impaired students to know, through personal visits, what is expected of students in public schools. In this way they can prepare their students more effectively for regular classes (1973). Although hearing impaired youngsters may have better study habits than some of their hearing peers, for example, they also have to be able to lip-read and are more dependent on a hearing aid than they were in the special class. It should be noted that the hearing aid amplifies *all* sounds around the wearer, so the continuing noises in a regular classroom override the teacher's voice unless she is only a few feet in front of the child. According to Porter (1975), the selection of a regular teacher, his preparation, and his willingness to work cooperatively with the resource or liaison teacher are critical to successful integration of the hearing impaired student.

In special classes or schools for the deaf, the teaching methods are modified versions of those used for hearing students. In the regular classroom, however, the hearing impaired child is expected to adapt to the usual instructional techniques. As she progresses to higher grade levels, she *may* have difficulty keeping up with the pace of the regular teacher, especially where extensive new subject-oriented vocabulary and abstract concepts are introduced. For many of the more severely hearing disabled youngsters, therefore, complete mainstreaming may not be advisable. Like other exceptional children, however, they can profit from integrated art, music, and physical education classes. Art permits the expression of feelings and the development of talents for which sound is unnecessary. In music, hearing impaired children can respond to and learn rhythm, although they may not be able to hear the melody. The ability to detect

Painting is a pleasure—with or without hearing ability. (Photo by Elizabeth Crews)

rhythm can be combined effectively with language and speech therapy as well.

Although the hearing impaired child may not be able to hear a starter's gun, she can respond to a visual sign to begin a race. Through visual cues, in fact, she can learn a variety of sports, and the sense of rhythm can

AN ITEM OF INTEREST . . .

Involvement with music is not so strange as it might seem for hearing impaired students. Nanette Fabray and Florence Henderson, two stars of Broadway musicals, are hearing impaired, as is Johnny Ray, a singer of popular music. Beethoven, of course, was deaf for many of his most productive years.

be an aid in mastering physical fitness exercises. Given instruction in the fine points of a sport, deaf youngsters can become active and enthusiastic spectators along with their hearing peers and thus have a basis for positive interaction with them.

Content and Techniques

Communication Techniques: A Controversy   The major controversy in the field of education of the hearing impaired involves whether to teach them the oral method (lipreading and speech) only or whether to combine lipreading with finger spelling (manual alphabet) and/or signs (whole words expressed manually) and/or amplification. While there are philosophical differences in this controversy, the degree of functional hearing loss and the presence or absence of other abilities must also be considered. In general, the primary concern is to teach the child to communicate effectively. Total communication instruction, utilizing auditory training, lipreading, and cutaneous (touch), kinesthetic (movement), and visual cues is becoming the preferred method today. However, the child must also learn to attend to the communications of others through *their* use of speech, body language, gestures, sign language, finger spelling, and/or written cues. The controversy affects primarily the prelingual deaf and those who lost their hearing soon after acquiring language.

The manual alphabet used in finger spelling (see Figure 6.3) demands that every letter of every word be signed. Although the individual may learn to do this fairly rapidly with practice, it is more difficult for a young child to use as a means of conversation, and certainly more cumbersome, than the whole word signs. However, there are actually several sign languages that are not necessarily mutually intelligible. "Signed English" (as taught, for example, at Gallaudet College) is more formal than the American Sign Language (Ameslan), which is used in daily life by deaf people. The two are really different languages, each with its own grammatical style. There has been some attempt to standardize the signs used by many interpreters on public occasions or when seen on television. The use of sign language is more open today, too, whereas it used to be hidden from the eyes of the hearing public and its use forbidden in many of the special schools.

Lipreading, which was the sole method employed in some schools for the deaf for a century or more, also has its limitations. A deaf person can usually grasp only about 25 percent of the words said to him by a person speaking normally. This is partly because of the speed of speech, partly because some sounds look the same when said (p, b, and m; a and ka; t and d), and partly because of limited language development, which requires him to split his concentration between listening to what is being

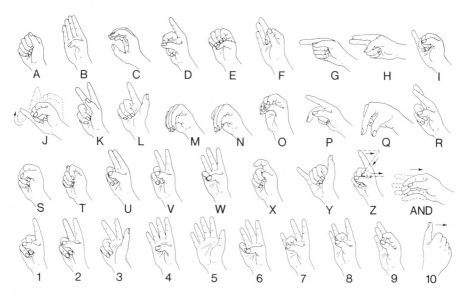

Figure 6.3   The manual alphabet

said now and attempting to comprehend the content of what has just been said. **Cued speech** augments lipreading with hand signals around the mouth area to indicate vowel sounds and groups of consonants. This combined manual-oral method has the advantage of using the same grammar as the spoken language, making it easier for children to communicate with hearing people and to learn to read. Phrases and short sentences, spoken clearly and slowly, can also aid and encourage lipreading. These should have meaningful content to enhance learning, rather than constitute dull, repetitive drills.

Obviously, it is important for the speaker to face a hearing impaired listener directly. In the classroom, face-to-face communication is made easier if the children's chairs are elevated enough to put them at eye level with the teacher's lips. (In some specially constructed facilities, chairs are mounted on a pole so they can be raised or lowered as needed.) Circular or semicircular classroom and mealtime seating arrangements also facilitate lipreading, since each person can see everyone else's face. When the hearing impaired child responds correctly to speech, he should be reinforced for his efforts.

Effective Teaching Strategies   The teaching of any content needs to be supplemented by pictures, diagrams, written key words and expressions, manipulation, and gestures. Hearing impaired children should be questioned to check on their comprehension, for such youngsters may be reluctant to indicate that they are "lost." Long- and short-term teaching objectives and assignments should be shared with the special resource teacher (if the students are mainstreamed) or with parents so that the students can be helped to maintain continuous progress. Having a dependable notetaker will be more valuable to most hearing impaired students than almost any other resource, particularly as they go into secondary and postsecondary education.

Whether a professional, paraprofessional, or volunteer, the following basic qualifications are vital for anyone taking notes or providing tutoring for hearing impaired students:

1. Knowledge of the subject matter of the class
2. Above average academic achievement
3. Sensitivity to the problems of hearing loss
4. Self-confidence in dealing with classroom teachers
5. Willingness to accept criticism or apparent ill will
6. Willingness to accept direction or management (Wilson, 1981)

An alternative to having a specific notetaker is to have two classmates take notes in carbon. As Reynolds and Birch (1977a) suggest, this reduces the chance of omissions of important information.

Special effort is needed to reduce the hearing impaired student's learning deficiencies, both oral and written. These deficiencies can include difficulties with small words like *the*, abstract words, words with multiple meanings (such as *run*), idiomatic expressions, and long or difficult words (Hardman, Egan, & Landau, 1981, pp. 172–173). Although the student may be able to write a paragraph, for instance, she is likely to omit small words or suffixes like -ing or to use wrong verb tenses. The teacher may need to prod the student a bit to help her develop correct language structure, by asking, for example: "Who is doing what?" "Who is it being done to?" "What is being done?" Appropriate questions can also be asked for math problems or in social studies classes.

In addition to these time-tested methods, the computer can be used in both testing and rehabilitation of the hearing impaired (Levitt, 1980) and for instruction (Goldberg, 1980). Computer Assisted Instruction (CAI) programs for hearing impaired students have been developed at Stanford University, the Model Secondary School for the Deaf at Gallaudet College, the National Technical Institute for the Deaf, and several other special schools. These programs not only offer academic content but also aid in speech instruction.

With the help of sign language interpreters, notetakers, and mechanical aids, academically able hearing impaired students can attend regular colleges. There are, however, some postsecondary institutions established especially for the deaf. Gallaudet College, which is federally funded, is the only liberal arts college for the deaf in the world. Technical programs for the deaf are available at the National Technical Institute for the Deaf at Rochester Institute of Technology and in three regional programs at post-secondary institutions in New Orleans, Seattle, and St. Paul, all of which are federally supported.

Vocational Planning and Guidance   This brings us to the question of how to plan for the future of hearing impaired students. For some, vocational goals will be the same as for hearing persons. For others, however, more realistic goals will be in skilled or semiskilled occupations that require minimal spoken communication. In either event, they will need to be taught skills that are assumed to be common knowledge in the nondisabled community—how to pay bus fare, what a "coffee break" is, where to seek information.

The printing trades used to be a major source of employment for hearing impaired people, but computer programming might be more appropriate today. Crafts such as carpentry, electronics, skilled repair and maintenance work, restaurant cooking and baking, and graphic arts are other fields where these youths can and do perform successfully. Academically able deaf students might choose to enter accounting or laboratory research positions or might themselves become educators of the deaf. Clearly the school or rehabilitation counselor, in advising hearing impaired students, will need to take into consideration not only interests and academic capabilities but also severity of hearing loss, ability to lip-read and/sign, and the kinds of communication skills required by a specific occupation. As with other exceptional groups, the opportunities for gainful employment are less restricted today than ever before.

SUMMARY

Although being aware of the causes of hearing impairment is important in learning about this group of exceptional students, it is more important to be cognizant of the severity of their hearing loss and how this is likely to affect their personal, social, and educational development. Degree of hearing impairment (and whether or not it occurred prelingually) is a major determinant in school placement and instructional techniques. For example, youngsters with a mild or moderate hearing loss may be able to function quite successfully in a regular classroom, with supplementary aid from a speech therapist and a resource teacher. On the other hand, children with a severe prelingual hearing loss might function better in a special class.

The major controversy in educating the hearing impaired has to do with teaching them communication skills. Despite the fact that they live in a hearing world, few are able to lip-read with total comprehension if they have a severe hearing deficit. Historically, the deaf have developed their own sign languages to express their needs and feelings, but it is only in recent years that the teaching of sign language has been encouraged as part of a total communication approach to language.

Also described in this chapter are the modifications of facilities necessary to accommodate the hearing impaired and helpful mechanical devices. The final section is concerned with postsecondary education and career planning. As in educational placement, the severity of hearing loss and the abilities available for communication must be considered, in addition to interests and learning abilities.

SUGGESTED ADDITIONAL READINGS

Bang, C. A world of sound and music: Music therapy and musical speech therapy with hearing impaired and multiply handicapped children. *The Teacher of the Deaf*, 1980, 4 (4), 106–115.

Benderly, B. L. Dialogue of the deaf. *Psychology Today*, 1980, 14 (5), 66–77.

Brissenden, B. The Rochester connection. *American Education*, 1981, 17 (1), 18–23.

Cayton, H. The contribution of drama to the education of deaf children. *The Teacher of the Deaf*, 1981, 5 (2), 49–54.

Cornett, R. O. What is cued speech? *Gallaudet Today*, 1974, 5 (2), 3–5.

Dale, D. M. C. *Deaf children at home and at school*. London: University of London Press, 1967.

Happ, D. A., and Altmaier, E. M. Counseling and the hearing impaired: Issues and recommendations. *Personnel and Guidance Journal*, 1982, 60, 556–559.

Higgins, P. C. *Outsiders in a hearing world: A sociology of deafness*. Beverly Hills: Sage Publications, 1980.

Messerly, C. L., and Aram, D. M. Academic achievement of hearing-impaired students of hearing parents and of hearing-impaired parents: Another look. *Volta Review*, 1980, 82, 25–32.

Neyhus, A. I., and Austin, G. F., Eds. Deafness and adolescence. *Volta Review*, 1978, 80, 263–377.

Quigley, S. P., Power, D. J., and Steinkamp, M. W. The language structure of deaf children. *Volta Review*, 1977, 79, 73–84.

Ross, M. Mainstreaming: Some social considerations. *Volta Review*, 1978, 80, 21–30.

Schwartz, A. V. Books mirror society: A study of children's materials. *Interracial Books for Children Bulletin*, 1980, *11* (1 & 2), 19–24.

Shepard, N. T., Davis, J. M., Gorga, M. P., and Stelmachowicz, P. G. Characteristics of hearing-impaired children in the public schools: Part I—Demographic data. *Journal of Speech and Hearing Disorders*, 1981, *46*, 123–129.

Stein, L. K., Mindel, E. D., and Jabaley, T., Eds. *Deafness and mental health*. New York: Grune & Stratton, 1981.

Stuckless, E. R. Projections for deaf students with maternal rubella: College and other alternatives. *American Annals of the Deaf*, 1980, *125*, 985–992.

Vandell, D. L., and George, L. B. Social interaction in hearing and deaf preschoolers: Successes and failures in interaction. *Child Development*, 1981, *52*, 627–635.

Whiting, S. A., Anderson, L., and Ward, J. Identification of the mentally gifted minor deaf child in the public school system. *American Annals of the Deaf*, 1980, *125*, 27–33.

Wiegersma, P. H., and Van der Velde, A. Motor development of deaf children. *Journal of Child Psychology and Psychiatry*, 1983, *24* (1), 103–111.

CHAPTER 7/
THE VISUALLY
IMPAIRED

To anyone who enjoys the colors of spring flowers and autumn leaves, or reading, or visual arts, or simply seeing the faces of loved ones, loss of sight is probably the most catastrophic impairment imaginable. Yet due to accidents or physical conditions, blindness strikes many people who started life as sighted individuals. Whether they are born blind or suffer the loss later, though, more visually impaired people function very well in society than commonly held stereotypes would lead us to believe.

VISUAL DISABILITIES

Types of Blindness

Legal Blindness   Legally, people are classified as blind when the corrected vision (that is, with glasses or contact lenses) in their better eye is no greater than 20/200 or when their visual field is no wider than 20° (tunnel vision). A vision rating of 20/200 means that a person can see at twenty feet what people with normal vision can see at two hundred feet. Although they may be able to differentiate between light and dark, see shadows, or see objects directly ahead of them, people who are legally blind cannot obtain a driver's license and are entitled to certain tax relief and social service benefits. Only a small percentage of the legally blind have total loss of vision and can literally see nothing.

Blindness for Educational Purposes   Educationally, the blind are those who must be educated primarily through auditory, cutaneous (touch), and kinesthetic (movement) senses—about one in three thousand school children. In addition, about one in every five hundred students is partially sighted (that is, has a corrected visual acuity of 20/70 to 20/200) and also needs special educational services.

Amblyopia   Amblyopia, or "lazy eye," is a fairly common condition that can be treated effectively if detected by physical examination of the eye before or at the time of entrance to school. This condition usually does not require special educational services, but it often means that the child will have monocular vision for a period of time while the "good" eye is patched and the "lazy" eye is forced to do the seeing. (The child might pretend to be a pirate or Moshe Dayan if that will help him feel better about looking different from his peers.) If not detected until middle childhood, however, only limited improvement from eye exercises can be expected in the functioning of the lazy eye. Then the disability can affect career opportunities; the youth will probably not be able to be a pilot, for example, or to work in any field that requires normal vision in both eyes.

Causes of Vision Loss

Heredity   Heredity is a leading cause of blindness, although the specific genetic factors cannot always be determined. Retinitis pigmentosa, for example, is a hereditary disease that leads to degeneration of the retina and consequent blindness, often by early adulthood.

Jeanne and Shirley M., two sisters in their early thirties, are blind as a result of retinitis pigmentosa, although you wouldn't know it if you met them. Both are employed in their city school district's program for visually handicapped students.

Jeanne is in charge of the Braille text library. No one in a group of twenty-five sighted students knew she was blind, nor did their instructor. Only when she moved over to a desk and groped in a drawer, with her back to it, to find a particular object did it suddenly dawn on the group that she groped, instead of looked, because she couldn't see. Her sister Shirley, meanwhile, was in a nearby classroom teaching blind students to use a Braille typewriter.

Neither woman "looks" blind. Their use of gestures, movements, and facial expressions are the same as those of sighted people, because they had sight until late adolescence. This early "normal" background, plus a good deal of training and guidance, helped them to adapt to their new lives as their world darkened.

Congenital Conditions   Congenital causes of blindness are conditions that occur during pregnancy and are present at birth. Women who have German measles or certain other diseases during pregnancy may have babies who are born blind. Some of the children born during the rubella epidemic of the mid-1960s are among the multihandicapped blind and deaf-blind. Congenital cataracts, which affect color and distance vision, can sometimes be corrected by surgery, reducing the amount of vision lost. Congenital syphilis, tumors, infections, and injuries are other causes of visual impairments in children.

Premature Birth   Birth in the seventh month of pregnancy can cause an incomplete development of visual structures. Prematurity often requires that oxygen be given the newborn to help them breathe and prevent diseases or brain damage. Unfortunately, this treatment can cause retrolental fibroplasia (RLF), which leaves the infant blind. Reducing the oxygen level in an attempt to avoid RLF was tried in the late 1950s, but the lower level of oxygen did not prevent brain damage or death, so the level had to be raised again despite the resulting damage to vision (Chase, 1974).

Other Causes   Other causes of blindness, such as glaucoma, diabetes, cataracts, and macular degeneration, occur most frequently among the elderly, so are not of primary concern here. However, vision impairment among the young can occur as a result of accidental injury (as from playing with firecrackers) or tumors pressing on the optic nerve, or as a side effect of other physical problems.

Outcomes: Social-Emotional

For blind children, the greatest threats to emotional well-being are over-protection and rejection. If they are permitted and encouraged to develop physical independence from early childhood, they can develop feelings of self-confidence. If, on the other hand, they are led everywhere, seated frequently to wait quietly while others are active, or perceived and treated as being retarded or deaf when they are not, they will have no feelings of competence, control, or significance to others. Frustrations may lead to aggressive behavior (tantrums, fighting, breaking objects), but this can occur with any children pushed beyond their ability to handle a particular situation.

The beginnings of a self-concept are found in the normal parent-child affectionate relationship. Blind babies, like any others, should be talked to, handled, reinforced for responding to voices, and encouraged to develop in all areas. They do smile less, vocalize less, and have less varied facial expressions, according to Fraiberg (1977), which often further upsets parents who already feel guilty about their infant's blindness. The parents must be even more persistent in stimulating and touching the baby, however, if bonds of attachment are to be formed. These bonds are needed if the baby is to develop a positive self-image, the concepts of person and object permanence, a sense of being a separate individual, and eventually the security to explore her environment (Cook-Clampert, 1981).

From early childhood on, the blind child needs to learn how to cope with social demands, his feelings of dependency, and other people's attitudes toward his disability. Many attitudes toward the blind seem to stem from ignorance and anxieties. Pity, cruelty, rejection, and even teasing are too often exhibited toward the blind child. When these behaviors are demonstrated by other children, they usually reflect family attitudes. The blind adolescent has a particularly difficult time in resolving the conflicts between her dependency and the rebellion against parents that is normal at this stage. Rebellion against those on whom the adolescent is so dependent creates quite normal feelings of guilt and resentment. Teachers or counselors can be helpful in giving the blind adolescent an opportunity to explore and express her feelings in this regard and about her impairment generally.

On the whole, however, the blind do not seem to have tendencies toward specific emotional problems, although these may develop if they are overprotected, strongly pressured to be "normal," pitied, or made to feel incompetent or inferior. They do have undeniable limitations as compared with sighted people in some activities, but they are usually capable of doing most of the same things their sighted peers can do.

Outcomes: Educational

Educationally, the blind need a variety of supportive services and mechanical aids, but their academic potential is limited only by their motivation and intellectual ability. The blind child has fairly normal growth patterns (with some understandable lag in independent mobility and other motor development), and there are few intellectual disabilities directly linked to blindness (except in cases of certain genetic problems or environmental deprivations). Speech development may be slower than for the sighted, due to poorer lip movements and fewer accompanying gestures. This merely reflects the lack of visual models by which most of us master these aspects of speech; there is no other language deficit peculiar to the blind. Although testing blind and partially sighted children is not easy, most studies indicate no significant difference in the measured intelligence of blind and sighted children (Hallahan & Kaufman, 1978).

EDUCATIONAL MODIFICATIONS

Facilities

For the partially sighted student in the classroom, lighting is probably the most important adjustment to be made. It is imperative that the student not have to look into the glare of direct light or at surfaces, such as desktops or chalkboards, that reflect glare. He may have to be close to a projection screen or a demonstration table, but for normal purposes he can sit anywhere in the classroom where the illumination is appropriate. An orientation visit to the school before classes open will help to familiarize the visually impaired child with corridors, classrooms, seating arrangements, and stairways. (In an emergency, of course, a teacher or classmate should be available to assist him to an exit speedily.) If seating arrangements are changed in a room, the youngster should be told in advance and reoriented so as to avoid injuries.

For the blind student, independent mobility is a key factor. A mobility specialist or the resource teacher should help the student to orient herself in and move about the school environment, inside as well as outside. Most students will be moving about without the aid of a cane, guide dog, or other means of assistance, so they must learn to depend on auditory

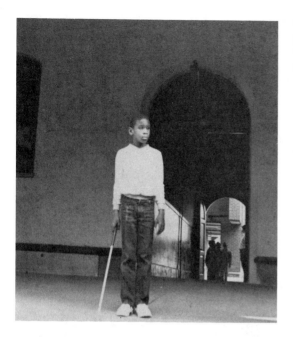

This blind boy is practicing independent mobility within the safety of his special school. (Photo by author)

cues and sometimes cutaneous cues to get about. (Note: These senses are *not* automatically improved to compensate for the vision loss; the blind person must be taught to be more attentive to stimuli.) Directions for finding objects and places must be clear and specific so that the visually impaired youngster neither damages things or herself accidentally nor gets lost (Gearheart & Weishahn, 1976).

In a special education setting, handrails along the walls as well as the stairways, easily reached and grasped door handles, and systematic storage facilities for books and other materials make it easier for the vision impaired student to function more independently. A textured tile path will help the blind child to find his way down corridors with minimal assistance and fewer bruises from bumping into walls. Corners may be curved rather than angled, again to reduce the possibility of injury. Any reduction in the need for help from others promotes the youngster's feelings of competence and independence.

Once settled in either a special or a regular classroom, visually impaired students can benefit from a variety of modified materials and equipment. Three-dimensional models, exaggerated bas-relief maps and globes, raised-line paper and guides, Braille or large-type typewriters and utensils, manipulable materials, equipment with audio signals, and tape recorders are all valuable aids. The Optacon, a miniature camera device that reproduces letter images that can be felt with a fingertip, enables the non-Braille user to read a wide range of printed materials.

The Optacon enables the blind individual to "read" normal print with his fingertips as the image of each letter is transformed into a vibrating pattern of that letter. (With permission of *Akron Beacon Journal*)

Braille reading materials (see Figure 7.1) and large (18- to 30-point) type books for the partially sighted (Figure 7.2) are available from the American Printing House for the Blind or may be printed locally by volunteers. The size of Braille texts, as a result of the heavy paper needed for the raised dots, makes their use difficult for young children and cumbersome even for adolescents. The **Cranmer Abacus**, a modified version of the one used in Japan, is helpful for basic mathematical calculations. "Talking Books," on records or audio tapes, are an alternative means of providing texts and pleasure "reading." Magnifying glasses or stands are useful for the partially sighted student, who should be encouraged to use whatever vision she has. Special equipment for sports activities will be discussed below in connection with educational content and techniques.

Assessment

Evaluating the educational ability of visually impaired students is a matter of continuing concern. As Heward and Orlansky correctly point out, intelligence tests are standardized for sighted children and include many questions dependent on vision or visual concepts (1980). As a result, the assessment of the blind child's abilities and needs is often inaccurate and his placement in school inappropriate. Furthermore, since the norms for these tests are based on standard conditions of test administration, they cannot really be applied to vision impaired youngsters for whom administration procedures have to be modified.

Many modifications of testing procedures are needed, ranging from extensions of time to substituting concrete objects for pictures to changing modes of response. Swallow's analysis includes a description of how intelligence, achievement, reading, mathematics, spelling, language,

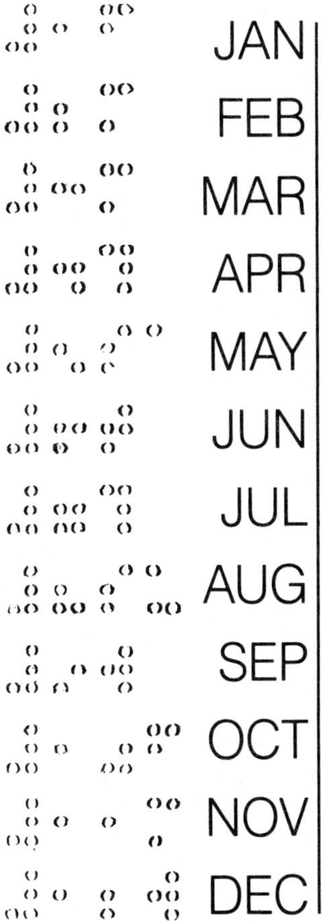

JAN
FEB
MAR
APR
MAY
JUN
JUL
AUG
SEP
OCT
NOV
DEC

Printing a complete calendar in Braille would take many times more space than a regular calendar. Therefore, the Braille calendar indicates only the day on which the first of each month falls.

The Braille calendar at left reads 1F, 2M, 3M, 4TH, and so on, indicating the first day of the first month is a Friday, the first day of the second month is a Monday, etc.

By knowing what day of the week the first day of a month is, all other days can then be determined.

Figure 7.1   The Braille calendar

This is regular size print used in most news publications. To read it is a strain for people who have poor vision.

This is the size print used in the Large Type Weekly. See how much easier it is to read.

Figure 7.2   Large print type

"Pictorial or graphical details may be lost for a low-vision student, or totally inappropriate in tactile form for a braille reader. If a test requires cross-referencing skills (e.g., column matching, visual-motor tasks), it may not be possible for a student to visually search and focus quickly" (Swallow, 1981, p. 65). Care must also be taken that the content of a reading test be within the experiential background of the blind student, for his reading problems may stem from lack of experience rather than reading ability deficits (Berger & Kautz, 1967).

perceptual-motor, early childhood development, and career education tests have been or can be adapted for assessing the abilities and interests of visually impaired youngsters (1981). Most of these tests have to be administered on an individual basis, either by original design or to adapt them for use with these students. Observations of the students' behavior in a variety of learning and leisure settings by teachers and parents help to round out the overall assessment of abilities that is necessary to plan an appropriate educational program.

Placement

Among the many educational accomplishments of Horace Mann, the first secretary of the Massachusetts State Board of Education, was the establishment of the New England Asylum for the Blind (later the Perkins School for the Blind) in 1829. For decades, residential schools such as this one were the only educational settings available for the blind unless they were taught at home. However, even the first director of the Perkins School, Dr. Samuel Gridley Howe, recognized that blind children really need to attend regular schools with their peers in order to maintain family contact and have opportunities for more normal social development (Maron & Martinez, 1980). Residential segregated facilities still exist, but there are also segregated day schools scattered across the country, like the Overbrook School in Philadelphia. Many large public school systems also have special facilities for the visually impaired, although they may serve a transitional purpose rather than as a permanent placement.

If a child has partial vision, he can usually function quite well in a regular classroom. The blind child, on the other hand, needs to learn to use Braille and/or other aids before being mainstreamed. For both types of disability, a resource vision teacher can provide substantial support for teachers and students in supplying materials and transcribing assignments. The vision teacher can also help the regular teachers develop techniques for prompt evaluation of the students' academic work, thereby monitoring progress and making any needed adjustments to the IEPs as quickly as possible.

Content and Techniques

At the nursery school level, in addition to the usual activities and routines, the blind child needs extra opportunities for tactual stimulation (books with variously textured fabric samples, simple puzzles of basic shapes, blocks, paste, finger paints), coordination exercises, outdoor recreation, and much individual attention. Whenever possible, she should be part of a group of both sighted and visually impaired children to enhance her self-confidence and social relationships. Early auditory training, to increase her attention to small cues and to facilitate her use of tape-recording and phonograph equipment, is also important. Listening skills are critical for learning and are an aid to mobility as well. Training in the use of Braille, in cases of total blindness, should begin early so that the child can have the benefit of it throughout the school years.

Once in elementary school, the vision impaired student can study any subject with the aid of mechanical devices and occasional extra assistance from teachers and classmates. Field trips provide further opportunities for stimulation and learning. Facilities designed especially for the blind, such as the Brooklyn Botanical Garden, the Krannert Art Museum of the University of Illinois, and other cultural institutions, arrange special tours and exhibits at which the blind can touch a variety of objects and experience their texture, weight, shape, and proportional relationships. They can also take art courses at one museum.

In the nonacademic realms of learning, adaptive physical education can lead to physical fitness, enable the blind youngster to participate in family and community recreation activities, help develop spatial orienta-

FOR EXAMPLE . . .

"Form in Art," a program started in 1972 at the Philadelphia Museum of Art, offers the visually disabled person a unique opportunity to explore the museum's collections through guided touch tours and to participate in studio sessions in which students experiment with clay, repoussé, papier-mâché, wire, and wood. These students incorporate more imagination into their art products than do many of their sighted peers.

tion and thereby improve mobility, and provide sports information that can be used as a social skill. Whenever possible, the blind child should participate in activities with sighted companions, as in scout troops for both boys and girls. There are also summer camps for visually limited youths, where they engage in activities normally associated with sight. These include archery (with balloons on the target and assistance in aiming the arrow), horseback riding, tumbling, swimming, and water-skiing. Every winter, ski instructors take groups of visually impaired youngsters out on the slopes and teach them the basics of that sport. Electronic devices embedded in baseballs even enable the youngster to play the national game.

Health and sex education are other aspects of the curriculum that are as important to visually impaired youths as they are to their peers. It is essential that teachers and parents work toward enabling visually limited children to have opportunities for understanding human sexuality through sex awareness training (Maron & Martinez, 1980). This means that they will have to learn that their dependence on the sense of touch may be misinterpreted and also that gender does make a difference in society. As part of this personal-social awareness, the blind need to be taught personal grooming, for others judge them by how they see them, even though these adolescents can't see themselves. Guidance toward a neat appearance ties in also with prevocational planning.

Postsecondary Counseling

Career and vocational planning have to be considered at the secondary school level for visually impaired as well as for sighted youths. If they are to be employed outside the home (a realistic possibility for many of them),

they will obviously have to learn mobility skills that permit them, for
instance, to make change, use public transportation, and orient themselves geographically. As noted earlier, if they have no intellectual impairments, blind individuals can do a wide variety of jobs and pursue
their education to obtain graduate and professional degrees. Broom
making and piano tuning, two occupations traditionally taught to the
blind, are not and should not be the upper limits of any blind youth's
aspirations.

Careers in law, teaching (where state certification laws or colleges
permit), social work, psychology, medicine, and many of the creative and
performing arts are all within reach of the vision impaired. For those who
have more modest aspirations, there are many clerical jobs that they can
handle. The Vision Foundation, a self-help support program in Massachusetts, is operated by people who are newly blind or who have a
progressive eye disease to provide services for people like themselves. In
the offices of the foundation, a wide variety of mechanical equipment is
used by the staff in their work as information gatherers, secretaries, grant
writers, group coordinators, administrators, and bookkeepers (Winer,

1980). There are also assembly-line jobs that depend on a keen sense of touch, at which visually impaired workers are found to be more proficient than sighted workers.

SUMMARY

For the visually impaired, whether blind or partially sighted, the major handicaps are those imposed by others—pessimism, pity, and prejudice. Youngsters who are blind from birth, due to heredity, congenital conditions, or prematurity, do have to learn in ways different from their sighted peers, but are just as capable of learning. Those who become blind after early childhood as a result of disease or injury, however, may remember enough experiences to transfer easily in learning techniques from regular print to Braille, to imagine shapes and objects, and to visualize mentally what people look like.

Visually impaired students can attend regular classes, if relatively modest modifications are made in the facilities, and, with the cooperation of their classroom teacher, resource teacher, and classmates, can function successfully. Many devices have been created to aid the blind in school and daily life, including Braille typewriters, the Optacon, audio-equipped sports equipment, and raised-line materials. The partially sighted can be helped by such simple expedients as large felt-tip pens, imaginative use of color, and large print books and typewriters. Teachers should emphasize sound presentations rather than visual ones in their lessons; these can easily be incorporated when planning the lessons. They should remember to tell a visually limited student if they are standing nearby or walking away and if classroom furniture has been moved, but they also have to recognize that they are working with students who are capable in other respects.

In this chapter, specific mention is made of the need for health and sex education, adaptive physical education, and realistic career and vocational planning. As the examples show, the blind or partially sighted student can aim high, as well as lead a quite "normal" life in most respects.

SUGGESTED ADDITIONAL READINGS

Barraga, N. Visual handicaps and learning: A developmental approach. Belmont, Calif.: Wadsworth, 1976.

Buell, C. E. Physical education for blind children. Springfield, Ill.: Charles C. Thomas, 1966.

Davidson, I. *Handbook for parents of preschool blind children.* Toronto: Ontario Ministry of Education, 1977. (Also available in French.)

Depauw, K. P. Physical education for the visually impaired. A review of the literature. *Visual Impairment and Blindness,* 1981, *75,* 162–164.

Foulke, E., Ed. *Education for the visually impaired.* Reston, Va.: Council for Exceptional Children, 1975.

Horovitz, E. G. Case study: Developing the body image of a visually handicapped child. *American Journal of Art Therapy,* 1980, *20* (1), 19–24.

Linn, M. C. An experiential science curriculum for the visually impaired. *Exceptional Children,* 1972, *39,* 37–43.

Locke, D. C., and Gerler, E. R., Jr. Psychological education for visually impaired children. *Education of the Visually Handicapped,* 1979–80, 11 (4), 118–120.

Scouting for the visually handicapped. New Brunswick, N.J.: Boy Scouts of America, 1968.

Shackleton, V. J., Wild, J. M., and Wolffe, M. Employment problems of partially sighted school-leavers: Methods of obtaining information. *Visual Impairment and Blindness,* 1981, *75,* 179–182.

Tisdall, W. J., Blackhurst, A. E., and Marks, C. H. Divergent thinking in blind children. *Journal of Educational Psychology,* 1971, *62,* 468–473.

Wexler, H. Books that talk. *American Education,* 1981, *17* (1), 14–18.

Young, P. S., Dickerson, L. R., and Jacobson, W. H. A study of the job responsibilities of the field rehabilitation teacher. *Visual Impairment and Blindness,* 1980, *74,* 386–390.

CHAPTER 8/
THE MULTIPLY HANDICAPPED

B y definition, multiply handicapped individuals have two or more disabilities that have to be considered in regard to their care, education, and planning for adult life. In 1975–76, the Office of Education estimated that there were forty thousand multihandicapped children in this country, of whom only sixteen thousand were being served by day-care programs or schools. The whereabouts and educational activities of the remaining children were unknown. However, many of these multihandicapped children were then only about ten years old and are now in late adolescence. Thanks to P.L. 94-142, more of them are being served educationally and plan to continue their education.

CHARACTERISTICS OF THE MULTIPLY HANDICAPPED

Examples of multiple handicaps include auditory and visual impairments (deaf-blind), cerebral palsy and mental retardation, aphasia and deafness (deaf-mute), spina bifida and partial sight, missing or shortened limbs and epilepsy, and almost any other combination of disabilities one can think of. Such difficulties may be present at birth as a result of maternal rubella, prenatal drug effects (especially those of thalidomide), Rh factor incompatibility, or other congenital conditions; they may also arise postnatally due to a traumatic injury or severe illness. Emotional problems are common additional complications, an outgrowth of the many frustrations suffered by the multiply handicapped.

Among the most difficult situations are those where a child has two or more sensory impairments, because the sources of stimulation to which that child can respond are so limited. A youngster whose development is severely hampered by cerebral palsy and who is also retarded and blind or deaf has a minimal chance of learning even the rudiments of self-help. If psychomotor damage is such that the speech apparatus is inoperative, it may be almost impossible to ascertain whether the child is or is not retarded, how much she can hear or what she comprehends. There are exceptions to this grim picture: Helen Keller, for instance, overcame severe auditory, visual, speech, and emotional handicaps (the result of an illness) and went on to lead a *relatively* independent and productive adult life. She was fortunate enough to have determined (and financially able) parents and devoted private teachers. For most multiply handicapped children, however, this is not the case.

EDUCATIONAL MODIFICATIONS

Facilities

Many of the modified facilities discussed in the previous chapters on disabled youngsters are also needed for the multiply handicapped. A complication, however, is that modifications appropriate for one disability are not necessarily practical when a second and third are also present. Flashing lights, used as signals for the severely hearing impaired, are obviously of no help to the deaf-blind. As another example, there is some evidence that color blindness occurs in the deaf with a disproportionately high frequency (Frey & Krause, 1971); thus, although color is generally a good educational tool, it may be of little value for some deaf children.

Modern technology has enhanced the receptive and expressive abilities of multiply handicapped people to a considerable degree, releasing them from the prison of total inability to communicate. The MIT LOGO program, cited earlier, is one example. Another is the work of a team in Seattle, consisting of a neurophysiologist, an electrical engineer, and an

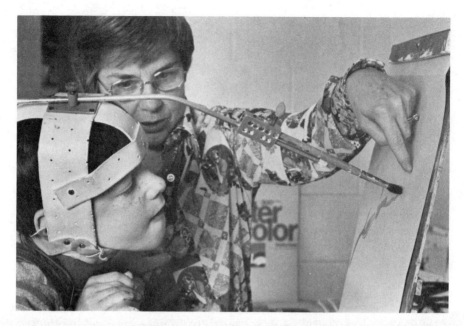

Head pointers are used by students who have little effective use of their hands. (George Bellerose/Stock, Boston)

electronics technician, who designed and built equipment that enables severely multihandicapped children to maintain head balance, develop muscle control, and convert auditory stimuli into visual patterns for communication (Hedrick, 1972). Specialists in biomedical engineering have also created innovative devices that permit a degree of communication and/or mobility for some of the multihandicapped that could not have been imagined a decade ago. Not everyone can be helped by such technology, but efforts are being made to increase the value of life and the ability to learn of multiply handicapped people, whether at home or in an institutional setting.

Placement

Segregation Most often, multiply handicapped students are in segregated classes or schools, either on a daily basis or permanently in residential facilities. The deaf-blind may be educated in one of the model centers established for them by Congress in 1960. These centers provide diagnostic and evaluative services for the students and effective consultation services for parents, teachers, and others involved with them. Special schools for multihandicapped children were also founded in the mid- to late 1960s, to meet the need created by the rubella epidemic of 1964–65.

One child who had several problems but attended regular classes on a full-time basis was a boy named Ned. When he was five, his parents were told that he should repeat kindergarten because he was "obviously unready" for first grade. Perhaps finding the teacher's reasons for this recommendation too vague, his parents resisted the advice, and he was promoted. In first grade, he was declared retarded because of his inability to read aloud clearly, lack of participation in class "show and tell" activities, and reluctance to play with his peers at recess. He also refused to draw, an activity common in the primary grades. The teacher commented on all of these behaviors in front of the class, adding intense embarrassment to the frustration Ned was already experiencing.

What were the facts? Due to prenatal injuries, Ned had a severe speech problem, an orthopedic handicap that made him unable to run, and poor hand-eye coordination. An independent psychological evaluation revealed that, far from being retarded, Ned had an IQ in the 135–145 range.

Because of the negative reactions of his early teachers, Ned viewed himself for several years as unacceptable to others. Fortunately, he *was* able to read well (silently) and with good comprehension, and he was strongly self-motivated to learn despite his physical impairments. He even practiced throwing a ball with a friend for hours at a stretch in an attempt to be accepted by his peers. Today, he is a gifted college graduate working in chemistry research; he is gregarious and reasonably self-confident in social as well as academic areas.

But what would have happened if his parents had believed those early teachers? Or if his later teachers had refused to accept the facts once they knew them?

Author's case files.

Several private organizations have also established preschool and day school centers for severely multihandicapped youngsters.

Mainstreaming   Mainstreaming is difficult for most multiply handicapped students, primarily because they need so much individual attention and may have very limited ability to respond. Although it is unlikely that many of today's multihandicapped children will be mainstreamed, it is possible. For example, if youngsters have two or more limited disabilities (such as an orthopedic handicap plus mild retardation or speech problems, or partial sight and a specific learning disability), they can be accommodated in regular classes with the support of resource teachers.

A psychologically therapeutic atmosphere of personal warmth, responsiveness, and acceptance of limitations is a requisite for all multiply handicapped children. Deaf-blind children whose mental abilities are unimpaired need much psychological support if they are to function intellectually and socially with any success despite their physical constraints. The minute responses of a mute cerebral palsied child—a smile or the voluntary movement of a limb—merit and usually receive excited reinforcement from the child's teachers in such an atmosphere. Constant encouragement is vital if these children are to learn at all.

Teaching

One of the difficulties to be faced in teaching multiply handicapped youngsters is that they often have communication problems. Therefore, one of the major tasks at the preschool level is to get them to attend to and then respond to external stimulation. Positive changes in behavior should also be encouraged in other areas of development at this level, such as: "(1) eating and drinking, (2) dressing, (3) toilet training, (4) muscle tone and posture, (5) locomotion, (6) play, . . . and (8) adaptive reactions" (Calvert, Reddell, Jacobs, & Baltzer, 1972, p. 419). In a preschool program for young retarded children who are orthopedically handicapped, sponsored by volunteers of the New York Philanthropic League, teachers have worked to develop self-help, social, mobility, and play skills. A few of these trainable and educable retarded children succeed well enough in the program to be transferred to special public school classes.

In a cerebral palsy center for severely multihandicapped school-age children, similar goals (with the exception of toilet training) were established. These children, aged six to ten years, look more as if they are six to ten *months* old, can rarely sit even when supported, and exhibit little voluntary control of any muscles. Clearly, they are among those for whom a residential setting and the acquisition of minimal skills would be most appropriate. On the other hand, at a school for multiply handicapped blind students, self-help, adaptability, mobility, and physical conditioning are stressed, and these students are exposed to as much academic learning as they can handle. Those whose learning potential is evaluated as normal are transferred to public school classes for the blind as soon as they are ready for the move, provided there are facilities at the receiving school adequate for their needs.

As already suggested, communication is a key problem for most of these exceptional students. Gold and Rittenhouse have provided detailed instructions for teaching eight manual signs to deaf-blind children that encompass eight basic daily needs: toilet, enough, more, sit, stand, eat, drink, and stay. They recommend that these eight signs (and all subsequent signs that might be taught using the same general format)

Lesson 4: Eat
(Trainer/expressive-learner/receptive)

Content

1. Form a *C* with the learner's preferred hand. The *C* should be formed so that all four fingers are together forming the top of the *C* and the thumb forming the bottom.
2. Keeping his fingers together, touch the learner's thumb to his index finger.
3. Bring the learner's preferred hand to his mouth so that his fingertips touch his lips.

Procedure

This sign should be taught immediately prior to eating. The trainer may wish to use food as a reinforcer for the development of the sign. However, care should be taken not to fall into the habit of using strong reinforcements for teaching signs. Wherever possible, the power gained by the communication should serve as the reinforcement for learning the sign.

Figure 8.1   Teaching a manual sign to a deaf-blind student.
(Gold, M. W., and Rittenhouse, R. K. Task analysis for teaching eight practical signs to deaf-blind individuals. *Teaching Exceptional Children*, 1978, *10*, p. 36. Copyright 1978 by The Council for Exceptional Children. Reprinted with permission.)

should be taught in a setting where the associations would be directly and normally related to the learner's interaction with his environment (1978). Figure 8.1 shows one such sign and the instructions for teaching it. Similarly, in speech and language therapy, it is often helpful to use those terms in practice sessions that are related to classroom language concepts, thus accomplishing two goals at once (Doob, 1968).

Because each child's combination of impairments is unique, a single program can hardly serve the needs of any group of multihandicapped children, nor can the same goals be set for all children. Taking one step alone may be a major achievement for one child, while moving a finger voluntarily may be the ultimate goal for another. (Note: When adults are felled by cerebro-vascular accidents, or "strokes," that finger movement may be the sole means of communication between patient and nurses.)

Extensive preparation and task analysis are vital elements of teaching multihandicapped students motor as well as intellectual tasks. Teaching a deaf-blind retarded child the concept of "sameness" is an example of the thoughtful preparation and analysis needed to teach abstract concepts to multiply and severely handicapped children (Yarnall, 1981). Some multiply handicapped youngsters may profit from instruction in reading and other academic subjects. Music can be used in many ways—to stimulate movement, to teach rhythm and concepts, for relaxation, and so on. Art is another acitivity in which many of these students can participate, if adaptations to their needs are made.

Vocational Planning

Some multihandicapped adolescents can look forward to living outside of an institution as adults, to working, and perhaps to postsecondary academic education. It is obviously important that they be able to take care of their personal needs independently, from toileting, dressing, and bathing to being able to communicate their needs and understand a variety of concepts. (Where there is a severe physical disability or weakness, an aide may be needed to assist in these and other tasks.) Those who are able to do so will need to take care of their living quarters to some extent and be able to prepare simple snacks. Then, to be employable, they will need to learn the skills most often involved in sheltered workshop tasks: placing items in a row, stacking, removing and putting on lids, screwing and unscrewing caps, sorting, inserting, folding, stapling, assembling, and gluing (Wencil, 1980). If multiply handicapped individuals are to be hired by regular industrial employers, some means of communication has to be established between employer and employee. One foundation in Florida sponsored a day of simulation exercises for prospective employers, during which they tried to carry out routine tasks with one or more limbs mobilized or vision or hearing blocked. After discovering the barriers and frustrations that confront multiply handicapped people constantly, they were then instructed as to appropriate communication and job-training methods (Dormady, 1980).

In academic settings, extensive guidance, counseling, and other support services are likely to be necessary (and perhaps simulation exercises for college personnel, too). Colleges that have programs or accommodations for multihandicapped students, particularly those who have hearing impairments, have already learned what kinds of services are needed. In 1982, they were preparing for a large increase in the number of young people to whom they would have to supply such services. These are the academically able members of the rubella epidemic generation. The influx of deaf and handicapped students, however, came at a time when funds for their postsecondary education were being cut by almost one-third (Karmel, 1982). That the programs are effective in individual cases can be seen in the next example.

Whether these needs will be met is questionable. In a survey of educators of the deaf-blind, the respondents expressed their views on future directions of education in this field. They were not too optimistic. Of those events they deemed both desirable and likely to occur, a greater emphasis on prevocational and vocational training and an increase in the early detection of deaf-blindness ranked highest (Tweedie & Baud, 1981). Among their more pessimistic visions of the future, however, were decreased federal funding of special workshops, programs, and support services and the likelihood that deaf-blind students would be assimilated into programs for the severely and profoundly retarded. The latter would generally not be an appropriate educational placement and could result in a reduction of abilities to function rather than an increase.

SUMMARY

In discussing people with multiple handicaps, it is apparent that there is considerable overlap with the needs of and programs for persons with a single physical impairment. It is also clear, however, that each combination of disabilities is unique and therefore requires a carefully tailored program that uses existing abilities to overcome impairments as much as possible. Few of the multihandicapped children with serious disabilities can be mainstreamed, but some of those with milder problems can and should be.

Specific content to be taught multihandicapped children begins with self-help skills, for without these, they have little chance for success in any other area. Depending on the nature and severity of their disabilities, multihandicapped youngsters can move on to academic and occupational skills instruction to prepare them for life after school. The importance of support services and empathetic attitudes from nonhandicapped teachers and employers cannot be emphasized enough if these students are to achieve some measure of the "good life" as adults.

Unfortunately, not all multihandicapped children can look forward to a semblance of "normal" adult life. Those who cannot will, with much help, be taught as much as they can accomplish. Even when they are not in public schools (and the most severely multihandicapped youngsters will not be), finding ways to reach them is a critical task for teachers.

SUGGESTED ADDITIONAL READINGS

Bishop, C. M. Hearing-impaired learner with special needs: The deaf-blind. *American Annals of the Deaf*, 1981, *126*, 654–661.

Bravin, P. W., and Smith, R. B. Deaf-blind computer training program at Ohlone Community College. *American Annals of the Deaf*, 1981, *126*, 731–735.

Duncan, E. A sense of hope. *Human Behavior*, 1978, *7* (5), 43–48.

Flathouse, V. E. Multiply handicapped deaf children and Public Law 94-142. *Exceptional Children*, 1979, *45*, 560–565.

Green, A. A preventive care guide for multihandicapped children: Dental care begins at home. *Rehabilitation Literature*, 1970, *31* (1), 10–12.

Griffing, B. L. Multihandicapped deaf students in postsecondary programs: Guidelines for planning services. *American Annals of the Deaf*, 1980, *125*, 1018–1021.

Mira, M., and Hoffman, S. Educational programming for multihandicapped deaf-blind children. *Exceptional Children*, 1974, *40*, 513–514.

Pawelski, C. E., and Groveman, A. B. The community-based model for life skills training. *The Pointer*, 1982, *26* (4), 21–24.

Petersen, G. A., Austin, G. J., and Lang, R. P. Use of teacher prompts to increase social behavior: Generalization effects with severely and profoundly retarded adolescents. *American Journal of Mental Deficiency*, 1979, *84*, 82–86.

Vernon, McC. *Multiply handicapped deaf children: Medical, educational, and psychological considerations.* Washington, D.C.: Council for Exceptional Children, 1969.

PART THREE/
STUDENTS WITH ORAL COMMUNICATION DIFFICULTIES

Two large groups of children have difficulties with oral communication. One group suffers from such speech impairments as stuttering, vocal disorders, or inadequately developed speech. The other group consists of those who are language handicapped. They speak little or no English and may also have a poor command of their native language.

Although the sources of their problems are quite different, the children in these groups share a common difficulty—they cannot make themselves understood easily. This not only frustrates them and those to whom they are trying to speak, but can also lead to the mistaken impression in some cases that they are slow, retarded, emotionally disturbed, or otherwise disabled. The inability to communicate effectively can have long-term negative effects on a child's personality, on his educational progress, and ultimately on his career plans.

There have been speech therapy programs in the schools for most of this century, and there has been judicial and legislative support for programs for the language handicapped in recent years. Both types of programs are necessary, because, as a result of right-to-education laws, more children in these two groups will enter and remain in the school population. Therefore, it should be evident that support for special education services in oral communication will have to be increased accordingly. One key to interpersonal, and even international, conflicts is ineffective communication. Since speech is the basis of much of our interaction with other people, and ineffective communication hinders learning as well as social activities, support services and effective remediation are crucial.

CHAPTER 9/
THE SPEECH IMPAIRED

A lisp is cute in a toddler or temporarily toothless six-year-old, and the stammer of a young child groping for a word is understandable, but the persistence of these speech characteristics in older children and adults is neither cute nor generally acceptable. There is a wide range of speech impairments, ranging from these relatively simple examples to more serious ones caused by organic dysfunctions or developmental lags. As a result, speech impairments are found more frequently in the schools than any other single exceptional condition.

Speech impairment and language disability are two quite different problems, as we shall see. In the first, the individual has difficulty with producing sounds clearly, smoothly, or at all. The language impaired person, on the other hand, can speak but has difficulty either with vocabulary or the grammatical flow of words. Speech impairments are the subject of this chapter; language handicaps will be dicussed in the next.

SPEECH DISORDERS

Speech impairments, because they are disturbing, distorted, and restrictive, handicap interpersonal communication and relationships. The inability to communicate clearly and freely inhibits emotional expression, a frustration that ultimately affects an individual's personality and behavior. It can also interfere with her learning.

Causes of Speech Problems

Speech dysfunctions can arise from emotional, physical, environmental, or intellectual factors. For example, delayed onset or inadequate development of speech can have emotional causes (anxiety about parental reaction to what is to be said), physical causes (delayed maturation of the speech apparatus or hearing loss), environmental causes (lack of response to early vocalizations), intellectual causes (mental retardation), or some combination of these. Articulation problems—creating inaccurate, incorrect, or unclear sounds—may be due to physical impairment or the lack of good speech models. (The absence of good speech models may also affect a child's spelling ability, as many teachers have discovered.) Vocal disorders—problems with volume, pitch, and quality of speech—are often caused by physical or emotional factors. Speaking too loudly, for example, might be an effect of poor hearing ability, but it might also result from growing up in a family with a hearing impaired or grossly inattentive parent. Fluency problems such as stuttering are frequently a response to anxiety, which increases along with the stuttering in a cyclical pattern. Some therapists assert that there may be a physical basis for stuttering, although its nature is unclear. The therapies used to try to overcome stuttering tend to be related to particular theories about its cause—coordination, behavioral, or emotional.

Some speech problems are self-correcting with maturation. The normal hesitancies of the three- to five-year-old usually fade by school age if the child does not develop other emotional problems. Disorders related to articulation are self-correcting by the time children are about ten years old, if they hear correct pronunciation. Organically based speech disorders, however, which stem from a **cleft palate** (a fissure or opening in the roof of the mouth), cerebral palsy, or hearing loss, are generally not self-corrective and require more varied therapeutic techniques for remediation. Usually, the earlier such conditions are discovered, the more the child can be helped to achieve effective speech. (Some of the therapeutic techniques, such as surgery to repair the cleft palate, are beyond the scope of this book.)

Problems of speech appear in approximately 1 out of 20 children. They occur with little regard to socioeconomic condition, family, sex, race, rate of cognitive devel-

FOR EXAMPLE . . .

Annie Glenn, wife of the United States senator from Ohio and former astronaut, John Glenn, and also the daughter of a stutterer, was classified as an 85 percent stutterer. Her disability was a real handicap, even in everyday life, in that she could not talk on the telephone, go to the market, or carry on the simplest conversation.

Mrs. Glenn, like other stutterers, tried a number of therapies over the years. In her late fifties, however, she finally overcame most of her problems through a three-week therapy program at Hollins College in Virginia. The program, directed by Dr. Ronald Webster, has three phases. In the first week, students speak at the rate of two seconds per syllable. (Try it!) The following week, they double the rate to a syllable per second. Finally, if they are ready, they make telephone calls and go shopping in the third week. Mrs. Glenn went through the program twice and continues to have therapy twice a month, but she now converses with others, talks on the telephone, and even makes speeches (Cuniberti, 1982).

Mrs. Glenn's case brings out an interesting alternative to the usual thinking about stuttering and its remediation. The behavior modification approach proved to be an appropriate therapy for Mrs. Glenn, as there was apparently a physical basis for her disability. Many stutterers like Mrs. Glenn have emotional difficulties as a *result* of their speech problem, rather than the other way around. This makes the need for speech therapy a higher priority than the need for psychotherapy. If, however, once greater fluency is attained, withdrawal behavior (for example) continues, then psychotherapy may be useful to relieve that problem.

opment, or the presence of other exceptionalities. The fact that they may crop up almost anywhere, coupled with their potentially devastating personal, social, and academic consequences, as well as their substantial numbers, make the prevention and correction of speech problems one of education's major challenges. (Reynolds & Birch, 1977a, p. 485)

To sum up, a person is considered to have a speech problem or impairment if, when speaking, the listener is distracted from *what* is being said by *how* it is said.

Types of Speech Problems

Articulation Difficulties   Articulation disorders are the most common type of speech impairment. For example, children may omit initial or final consonants ("ste" for *step*), substitute one sound for another ("wittle" for *little*), distort sounds through slurring or lisping, omit syllables ("winshiper" for *windshield wiper*), or add sounds to words. Some children have not been stimulated to modify, or are encouraged to maintain, their infantile speech by a parent who thinks it's cute ("misghetti" for *spaghetti*, "chicken" for *kitchen*). In other instances, these speech disorders reflect exposure to others' faulty articulation, as when the g is omitted from words that end in -*ing*. If other children in the class speak correctly, they may tease or ridicule the child who makes these errors. Some children will then emphasize the errors, rejoicing in the attention that this brings them, while others will hesitate to speak at all for fear of being laughed at.

Lack of Fluency   Lack of fluency in older children appears to be closely related to parental sensitivity to the child's speech (W. Johnson, 1958). If the parent perceives the child as a stutterer, she often becomes one, in line with the principles of the self-fulfilling prophecy. As the child begins to perceive herself in this way and is admonished for her dysfluencies, she often becomes more anxious. Blinking, tics, or extra vocalizations may be added to her speaking behavior as she tries to avoid, prevent, or release the distress-causing words.

Culatta and Culatta (1981) have suggested that children often use dysfluency (subconsciously) for one of three purposes: to secure attention, to express hostility, or to control the behavior of others. As we noted earlier, however, there can be other reasons for dysfluent speech.

Vocal Disorders   Vocal disorders are more frequently related to physical factors than are articulation or fluency difficulties. The child with cerebral palsy or a hearing impairment, for example, may speak too softly (because this is how she hears others), too loudly (because others shout to him), or with insufficient variation in pitch and volume. Disorders of the larynx can also cause problems with the volume of speech, as anyone who has ever had laryngitis can testify. At the extreme are individuals who have had a laryngectomy (removal of the larynx, usually because of cancer). These are more frequently older adults, however, than young students.

Other disorders of speech volume may be the result of inappropriate learning, for the appropriateness of volume varies with different settings and situations. Yelling is appropriate at sports events or to warn someone of an oncoming car, but certainly not in museums, offices, or normal conversation. Irregular changes in pitch are common in young adolescents, particularly males, but become troublesome and irritating if they persist. However, people whose pitch never changes (monotone speakers) also have a problem, one that troubles their hearers more than themselves. Quality of speech can also be considered a speech disorder. Nasality and harshness are examples of speech qualities that are considered to be in need of correction.

The Luick et al. study found that children with severe communication disorders typically could not respond correctly to analogies presented to them orally or to items in pictures. Given their chronological age of 6–8.3 years and normal intelligence potential, they should have been able to respond satisfactorily to tasks like these:

- "I cut with a saw; I pound with a _____."
- Shown a picture of one dog: "Here is a dog." Then shown a picture of two dogs: "Here are two _____."

Their scores on visual-motor tasks were much higher than those for auditory association or verbal response and may reflect a basic problem in organizational abilities (1982).

Severe Dysfunctions   Children with severe oral language disorders either are nonverbal or have very few words that they use. They also have normal intellectual potential and hearing ability and are not autistic. According to one major study, these children show severe deficits in auditory association and grammatic closure (filling in the correct word to complete a sentence) on the Illinois Test of Psycholinguistic Abilities, a commonly used diagnostic test (Luick, Kirk, Agranowitz, & Busby, 1982).

An interdisciplinary team of teachers, speech therapists, psychologists, and other professionals should assess the child's development in different settings—classroom, testing session, at play, at home—to determine whether the problem is environment-specific or comprehensive. Where the child has been known to use some words, linguistic analysis is used to evaluate not only the quality of existing speech but also the complexity level (grammatical structure, length of utterances) and functions of language used (Weber, Kushnir, & Weber, 1982). In severe oral language disorders, language development lags considerably behind cognitive development. For those children who are neither mentally retarded nor deaf, the cause of this lag may be difficult to determine. It is also difficult to correct, though not necessarily impossible.

EDUCATIONAL MODIFICATIONS

Resource Teachers

For children whose speech impairments are due primarily to emotional factors, learned behavior, or mild physical dysfunctions, remedial assistance usually consists of clinical therapy, once a week for an hour or so, with a speech therapist. The therapist often assigns exercises to practice at home that will reinforce the new speech habits being taught in the clinical session (see Figure 9.1).

Speech therapists are often itinerant personnel, assigned to a different

1. FIND WORDS FOR THESE PICTURES:

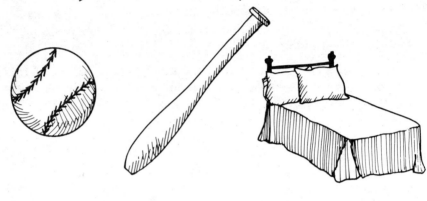

2. FIND PICTURES FOR THESE WORDS:
    PET
    PILLOW
    PARTY

3. WRITE A SENTENCE WITH EACH OF THESE WORDS:
    VERY
    TELEVISION
    VALLEY

SAY EACH WORD THREE TIMES BEFORE DINNER TO YOUR MOM, DAD, BIG BROTHER OR BIG SISTER. SAY THE SPECIAL LETTERS SLOWLY AND CLEARLY. DO THIS EVERY DAY UNTIL WE MEET AGAIN.

Joan Ashley
SPEECH THERAPIST

Figure 9.1   Exercises for pronouncing B, P, and V

school each day of the teaching week. In most mild cases of speech impairment, there is relatively casual contact between this therapist and the classroom teacher. Where the dysfunction is more severe, however, the therapist can suggest to the teacher specific modes of working with the student to make his speech clearer or to reduce his anxiety in speaking situations. Indeed, it may have been the classroom teacher who made the initial referral for speech therapy and who should thus be kept informed of progress for reasons of courtesy, at least.

Children with severe oral language disorders need much more attention, of course. They are usually assigned to a special class, where they are given speech and language therapy as well as aid in linguistic and cognitive development. It would be unrealistic to place them in regular classes with only part-time resource services, since they could not communicate with their teachers or peers, and since their lack of speech would create a variety of problems for the others in the room, as well as for themselves.

Although speech impairments rarely affect educational progress to the extent that some other exceptionalities do, the teacher may observe that a student's speech interferes with her communication, contributes to feelings of inadequacy on her part, or is alienating her from her peers (Charles & Malian, 1980). The resource teacher can help to remedy not only the student's speech impairment but also other problems that are speech related. In addition, speech therapists can work with classroom teachers to modify their attitudes toward speech impaired youngsters and gain their support in the therapeutic process (Crowe & Walton, 1981).

Remedial Techniques

What is to be done? The speech therapist must observe the student's speaking behavior, diagnose the disorder(s), and create an appropriate remedial program. There are a number of corrective methods and psychologically supportive techniques that the therapist can use to improve both speaking performance and peer relations in the classroom. Among these methods are teaching correct tongue placement and mouth movement, drill on sounds, and use of the Language Master, audiotapes, and modeling.

Although no drastic architectural changes are needed for the speech impaired, a number of aids should be available at school and, where possible and necessary, at home as well. A large mirror enables the child to see whether he is placing his tongue correctly or to observe and eventually eliminate the undesirable mannerisms that accompany his speech. The Language Master permits a student to hear both correct speech sounds and her delivery of the same sounds while she sees what she is to say (object, word, or situation). Tape cassettes and videotapes are also effective devices for teaching and recording speech.

For youngsters (or even adults) with speech disorders so severe that

Learning *how* to make sounds properly is important for speech impaired students. (Eileen Christelow/Jeroboam)

they cannot be understood by others, there are devices available that enable them to communicate on a functional level. For laryngectomy patients, for example, there is the electrolarynx, which is a substitute sound generator. Students with speech disorders due to severe hearing impairments, mental retardation, or neurological problems can use "Talking Pictures" to express their needs (Leff & Leff, 1982). Each of these pictures has an illustration appropriate to health, food, clothing, people, bathroom, or other categories, and they can be kept together by a metal ring or in a file box for ready use. Some pictures might show specific items, such as eyeglasses, a water faucet, a bathroom interior, a hat, or coins. With these, the "listener" can discover the speech impaired individual's specific need by asking questions, to which the "speaker" can respond with a nod or shake of the nead. Variations of this idea are also in use, such as a poster with sections appropriate to different categories. Other techniques for teaching communication to nonverbal mentally retarded or physically disabled youngsters include the use of symbols and computers, as mentioned in earlier chapters.

Stuttering, a fairly common fluency disorder, provides a good example of multifaceted approaches to remediation. First, the speech therapist observes carefully what types of behavior or situations precede or accompany stuttering and then works to replace them with behavior that will enhance fluent speech. The cooperation of the child's parents, his teachers, and even his classmates should be enlisted to help him change his self-image as a stutterer. These allies have to be taught how best to respond when stuttering occurs. Frequent injunctions to "speak more slowly," "hold your breath," "start again," and the like only tend to increase the child's self-consciousness and, therefore, his dysfluency. Positive reinforcement for improved speech, or for efforts to control the rate of speech, is more desirable. While the therapist is working directly with the student and his stuttering problem, the teacher can use com-

Puppets enable the child to speak without being seen, yet oblige her to speak fluently and clearly so that the puppet's story and actions can be understood by listeners.

Choral singing and speaking, where the stutterer is merely one of the group, tend to reduce dysfluency. Attention is focused on the words rather than on the individual singer or speaker, thus helping to eliminate self-consciousness.

Participation in debating is similarly helpful to the stutterer, according to Wingate (1976). Attention is centered on the ideas to be communicated, and debaters are urged to speak slowly and deliberately. This style gives the stutterer time to "face" troublesome words without emphasizing his special need for pausing or making a "dry run" to avoid dysfluency.

plementary techniques to reduce pressure on the student, even while encouraging oral participation in class activities.

Youngsters with speech impairments may or may not have related emotional problems. If there are such problems, psychotherapy can help to reduce the conflicts, decrease the anxieties, and improve the child's general emotional adjustment, all of which in turn can relieve the speech disorder. Cooperation among psychotherapist, speech therapist, teacher, and parents is essential if there is to be a consistent approach to remedying the speech problem(s).

It is interesting to note that the emotional factor is often revealed if the student is studying a foreign language, for the child's speech may be quite correct in the second language. On the other hand, speech problems with a physical basis will continue in the second language. The foreign language teacher must be aware of the student's difficulties in either case and respond to them diplomatically. (Whether or not to encourage or insist upon the child's participation in individual recitation must be decided on an individual basis; some children will be able to do this, while others will become more dysfluent or inarticulate.)

In the case of organically based speech disorders, additional techniques are often needed. The child with a cleft palate, for instance, needs both surgery and speech therapy to reduce nasalization of vowels and unclear consonants. The child with cerebral palsy frequently needs exercises in motor coordination and muscle control along with corrective speech exercises. Children with hearing impairments must have access to amplification equipment if they are to hear sounds correctly and then be able to reproduce them.

Classroom Support

The classroom teacher can help to reduce pressures on speech impaired students by neither constantly correcting them nor expecting "miraculous" improvement in the early stages of therapy, by not saying difficult words for the student, and by reinforcing correct speech production by praising it tactfully. The teacher should also see to it that other students don't tease a speech impaired peer but rather recognize improvements in her speech. Such teacher and peer behavior is of considerable importance, because the student with speech disorders will only be in regular classrooms as a matter of course, except for limited periods of time spent with a speech therapist.

It is critically important that all of the speech impaired children be accepted as worthwhile to themselves and others. Everyone who interacts with them should encourage their verbal participation without embarrassing them and give them nonspeaking responsibilities in other situations that will still allow them to contribute to group projects and to their own learning. In other words, a speech disorder should not be an excuse for avoiding contact with others. Emphasizing the child's assets and interests and encouraging him to share these with others can help provide him with access to normal social intercourse and learning progress.

SUMMARY

For most speech impaired students, the disorder more often distracts their listeners than themselves. Stuttering puts hearers "on edge," and echoing disturbs them. Infantile speech makes teachers and others look down on the youngster, questioning her intellectual competence. Poor voice quality or monotone speech irritates some people. The reactions of all these "significant others" to speech problems can contribute to secondary emotional problems or, conversely, to the reduction of the problems through clinical speech therapy and support.

The most severely handicapped are those youngsters who have a severe oral language dysfunction and use few or no words to communicate. While they are generally not mentally retarded, autistic, or hearing impaired, their language development lags markedly behind their cognitive development. A particular problem they seem to have is related to their ability to organize concepts linguistically.

Psychotherapy may be necessary where emotional rather than physical factors contribute to the speech disorder or are a result of it. In other cases of speech impairment, behavior modification, surgery, amplification, or specially designed devices may be necessary adjuncts to speech therapy.

There is little question regarding placement of speech impaired students in regular classes. They have always been there. For decades, they have spent an hour or two a week with speech therapists, slipping in and out of class with little attention from peers, because "going to speech clinic" has become so routine. Caution should be exercised, however, that the therapy is not habit-forming, or the routine will become a "rut" or a work-avoidance alibi. Speech impairment is a very common problem in school-age children, but in most cases it is far from insuperable.

SUGGESTED ADDITIONAL READINGS

Boone, D. *The voice and voice therapy.* Englewood Cliffs, N. J.: Prentice-Hall, 1971.

D'Angelo, K. Wordless picture books and the young language-disabled child. *Teaching Exceptional Children,* 1981, 14 (1), 34–37.

Deich, R. F., and Hodges, P. M. Teaching nonvocal communications to nonverbal retarded children. *Behavioral Modification,* 1982, 6, 200–228.

Geoffrion, L. D., and Goldenberg, E. P. Computer-based exploratory learning systems for communication-handicapped children. *Journal of Special Education,* 1981, 15, 325–332.

Greenberg, J. B. The effect of the metronome on the speech of young stutterers. *Behavior Therapy,* 1970, 1, 240–244.

Leonard, L. B. Language impairment in children. *Merrill-Palmer Quarterly,* 1979, 25, 205–232.

Lubert, N. Auditory perceptual impairments in children with specific language disorders. *Journal of Speech and Hearing Disorders,* 1981, 46, 3–9.

Phillips, P. P. Variables affecting classroom teachers' understanding of speech disorders. *Language, Speech, and Hearing Services in Schools,* 1976, 7, 132–149.

Van Riper, C. *Speech correction: Principles and methods* (6th ed.). Englewood Cliffs, N. J.: Prentice-Hall, 1978.

Wetherby. A. M., and Gaines, B. H. Cognition and language development. *Journal of Speech and Hearing Disorders,* 1982, 47, 63–70.

Williams, D. E. Stuttering therapy: Where are we going—and why? *Journal of Fluency Disorders,* 1982, 7, 159–170.

CHAPTER 10 /
THE LANGUAGE
HANDICAPPED

Language handicapped people (in the United States) are those who cannot communicate effectively in English for cognitive reasons rather than for physical or emotional ones. They either have come from a non-English-speaking environment or speak a nonstandard English dialect that is not accepted or not understood outside of their subgroup. With the current shift in attitudes toward immigrants and cultural minorities, as well as changes in school attendance laws and labor market needs, the language handicapped present a problem to today's educators that was not the case much earlier in this century (although nineteenth-century American schools regularly offered classes taught in German, French, Swedish, and other languages, depending on local needs).

During the great immigration period (1880–1920), immigrants settled in neighborhoods where their native language was spoken. Their shopping needs were met by people from their homeland in neighborhood stores, and the adults could get jobs either in the neighborhood or with compatriots in a steel mill, mine, or construction project. They thus had little need to achieve fluency in English. Similarly, women who worked in factories could do so with others like themselves, and those who entered domestic service could manage with a minimum of English competency. The children, who usually attended neighborhood schools, learned English by immersion in school and sometimes on the street with their peers. If they failed to learn readily, they often dropped out of school prematurely and entered the work force. They, too, could find unskilled jobs that did not require them to speak English fluently or to be well educated.

Today, there are fewer ethnic enclaves that can meet neighborhood needs completely, fewer unskilled jobs available, but at the same time fewer pressures for assimilation into the grand "melting pot." As one Black educator has said to the author, she tells her students that "the gatekeeper speaks standard English," so that if they want to get a job, they had better speak it, too. Another professional, who is of Creole background, spoke French and Creole until he was of school age, then learned English. If he had not, not only would his education have been limited, but his activities would of necessity have been restricted to the Creole settlements in Louisiana. America today, as a result of its combination of an acceptance of cultural pluralism, rather than assimilation, and a labor market that needs relatively few unskilled workers, presents mixed signals in terms of retaining one's cultural identity but also learning to communicate in the larger society with reasonable ease. These mixed signals are clearly seen in the handling of bilingual-bicultural education of the language handicapped.

BILINGUAL EDUCATION: A CONTROVERSY

The civil rights movement of the 1960s led to the passage in 1968 of Title VII, an amendment to the Elementary and Secondary Education Act of 1965, commonly known as the Bilingual Education Act. Although it did not refer specifically to bilingual instruction, it did mention the "special education needs" of non-English-speaking children (or those with limited speaking ability) and the fact that "new and imaginative programs" would have to be created to meet those needs. Federal support for such innovative programs became increasingly available, and hundreds came into being within a few years. The seeds of persistent controversy about them blossomed, however, as two key viewpoints emerged. On one side

were those who viewed bilingual education as a means of providing temporary shelter and a transition to competency in English; . . . [on the other] were those who saw it as a way of resisting assimilation by keeping children within the linguistic and cultural fold of another milieu. (Thernstrom, 1980, p. 12)

A few states passed laws to support bilingual education where there were twenty students with a common native tongue in need of special instruction in English as a Second Language (ESL); the *Lau v. Nichols* decision, handed down by the Supreme Court in 1974, supported this practice by affirming that Title VI of the Civil Rights Act of 1964 required such programs. A revision of the Bilingual Education Act in 1974 expanded these programs and created an Office of Bilingual Education within the U.S. Office of Education. The number of language groups served was seventy by 1978, and most of the programs were bicultural as well as bilingual. Although the legislation was designed to promote competency in English by children with little or no ability to speak it, many of the newer programs served students who *could* speak English but could not read or write it. Frequently, students stayed in the special classes through their high school years, in effect segregated from their English-speaking peers rather than being encouraged to move into the mainstream of regular classes.

In Texas, New Mexico, New York City, Dade County, Florida, Ann Arbor, Michigan, and other parts of the country, ethnic groups have brought successful suits to mandate bilingual instruction. In 1982, however, the U.S. Court of Appeals (Fifth Circuit) overturned a lower court decision that required bilingual education for all Mexican-American children in Texas public schools ("Spanish 'Not Needed,'" 1982). The consequences of this decision in other localities remain to be seen. An additional complication in the matter, however, is that the presidential proposals to Congress for fiscal year 1983 included limiting the eligibility of bilingual students for such instruction to one year and reducing funds allocated to bilingual education by several millions of dollars (*Newsnotes*, 1982).

The effect of the mandated programs has often been to maintain the child's proficiency in his native language at the expense of his gaining competency in English. On the other hand, there have been successful transition programs as well that are often overlooked by those opposed to bilingual education. These programs are designed to provide children with content instruction in their native language while they study English, so that when mainstreamed into English-speaking classes, they will not be too far behind. It was this opportunity for equal access to educational opportunity that was the basis for the Lau suit by Chinese Americans in San Francisco.

There are also less philosophical and more psychological aspects to this controversy. For many of the students (and their parents), being forced to learn standard English is perceived as a rejection of their family and cultural environment. The youngsters are caught up in a painful dilemma: They must either reject their families or be rejected by the

The Birney School in Philadelphia serves elementary school children from Portuguese, Korean, Vietnamese, and other national groups. It provides native language instruction, both for purposes of linguistic and cultural maintenance and to teach some school subjects; additionally, the students spend several hours per week in an ESL laboratory, learning to speak and read English. For the Asians, the task is made more difficult because of the difference in alphabets and the lack of common linguistic roots. However, as the children become more fluent in English, they spend more time in English-speaking classrooms and eventually move on to regular middle schools.

schools (and therefore by society at large). The pain and poignancy of the situation were expressed in an autobiography:

For my part, I felt that I had somehow committed a sin of betrayal by learning English. But betrayal against whom? Not against visitors to the house exactly. No, I felt that I had betrayed my immediate family. I *knew* that my parents had encouraged me to learn English. I *knew* that I had turned to English only with angry reluctance. But once I spoke English with ease, I came to *feel* guilty. (This guilt defied logic.) I felt that I had shattered the intimate bond that had once held the family close. This original sin against my family told whenever anyone addressed me in Spanish and I responded, confounded. (Rodriguez, 1981, p. 30)

Furthermore, when the parents and peers of such a child do not seek upward or outward mobility (for the student or for themselves), the child who tries to learn English becomes a social outcast and is seen as "uppity."

A second effect of the bilingual conflict may be anxiety and/or embarrassment when the youngster does try to speak English correctly. This frequently leads to speech impairments, particularly stuttering and stammering, a phenomenon familiar to English-speaking adolescents in their struggle to learn French or Spanish. Furthermore, as the child tries to listen to and hear English words correctly, he may focus so much on the individual words that the concept or procedure being discussed is lost. The lack of ability to communicate effectively also handicaps social relationships with English-speaking peers, devaluing the child's self-concept and often leading to social withdrawal.

Whether or not "the gatekeeper speaks standard English," it is certainly the case that the door to higher education, a better job, and a place of equality in American society will remain closed to those who don't speak English. Thus, it is difficult to readopt the position taken several

FOR EXAMPLE . . .

Pablo, aged five, was referred to a diagnostic facility because he spoke very little at his preschool center and appeared to be either retarded or emotionally disturbed. Small but sturdy, he was reluctant to take the examiner's hand on his first visit and shuffled his way along the corridor with his head down.

Pablo was given the Wechsler Preschool and Primary Scale of Intelligence (WPPSI) test in English, as well as several other tests. The WPPSI results were of particular interest because of his irregular performance on the subtests. For example, Pablo could not "name two animals" but knew that milk came from an animal called "a cow" and defined a donkey as "an animal." He did not know the days of the week in English or Spanish. He could subtract, although he failed easier addition problems. In fact, on almost every subtest, he passed several difficult tasks while failing easier ones. Was this variable performance the result of a language or an experience deficiency? Repetition of several of the questions in Spanish at a second testing session suggested the latter, for Pablo still missed the questions.

Despite errors, Pablo earned verbal subtest scores in the range of 7 to 10 (indicating a verbal scale IQ of 91) and performance subtest scores in the range of 8 (mazes) to 14 (geometric designs), for a performance scale IQ of 111 and a full-scale IQ of 101. As Pablo carefully printed his name (he knew about two-thirds of the alphabet), he said that his twelve-year-old brother had taught him letters and some arithmetic concepts.

Pablo's brother, mother, and father all speak some English, but apparently only his mother speaks to him regularly in English. Since she is employed, his primary caretaker is a Spanish-speaking grandmother. As a result, Pablo appears not to have a good command of either language. Despite his ability to function within the average range, he will become—first academically, then socially and vocationally—handicapped without English language instruction and an expansion of his experiences.

decades ago and tell these students that bilingual education programs will no longer be supported by government funds—that they must "sink or swim" as earlier immigrants did. The duration and extent of funding for these programs, however, is in doubt as of the early 1980s. The magnitude of the problem might be reduced if there were stronger support systems at home, as can be seen in the above example.

There is no simple solution to the bilingual controversy that is fair to all parties. There are not even enough unequivocal research findings to confirm that one teaching approach is superior to others in any bilingual program. However, it is apparent that some effort must be made to meet the special educational needs of students who cannot speak, read, or write English fluently enough to profit from regular instruction.

CHARACTERISTICS OF THE LANGUAGE HANDICAPPED

The differences between non-English-speaking and "bilingual" students can affect learning and therefore teaching techniques. For both groups, however, the age at which they are introduced to standard English is a factor that must be considered in planning how they are to be instructed. Some attention needs to be paid as well to individual differences in language-learning ability and motivation.

Non-English Speakers

A revision of the immigration laws in 1965, along with political upheavals in Southeast Asia, the Caribbean, and elsewhere, has brought us millions of new residents, few of whom speak English, in a relatively short span of years. Some of the adults have been well educated; many more have come from the illiterate and impoverished segments of their societies. Their children are similarly varied as to the amount and quality of their schooling. With the refugees from Cuba and Haiti in 1980–81 and the "boat people" of Southeast Asia, the policy has been to disperse them throughout the United States in the care of sponsors (usually families and religious institutions). This has resulted in their being isolated from relatives and others who speak their language and at the same time being too few in number in many small communities to warrant seeking and hiring a bilingual teacher for their children.

Frustration in the classroom tends to substantially reduce motivation for learning. This leads to a high dropout rate and a subsequent high unemployment rate for language handicapped youths. Even in Texas and New Mexico, where Mexican-Americans have gained some political power, there is little hope for employment outside the **barrio** (a principally Mexican-American neighborhood) or the migrant labor circuit for those who speak only Spanish.

For adults, inability to speak English increases both their dependence on the truly bilingual and their isolation from the larger community. Many are unwilling to attend adult ESL classes because of embarrassment, preoccupation with meeting survival needs, or a negative view of their ability to learn the new language.

"Bilingual" Speakers

Many who are commonly considered "bilingual" know some English but mix it with their native tongue to such an extent that they are, in effect, speaking an almost incomprehensible mixture. Often a local dialect is combined with English to form such a hybrid language, thereby adding to the confusion of the listener. Examples of this type of "bilingualism" can be found in isolated Appalachian communities, in the very rural South, and in Northern urban ghettos. There are also French-Canadian, Puerto Rican, and AmerIndian children, all of whom are taught in English at school, but who rarely use that language fluently in the classroom or at all the rest of the time.

All of these students present a challenge to the teacher, an "outsider" from their point of view, who speaks standard English and expects them to do so, too. The lack of communication, if allowed to continue, is a mutual problem. Even if the teacher can speak the second language or dialect, she is usually unfamiliar with the idioms or **patois** (dialect or jargon) unique to the children's reference group. A further complication is that such students may not even speak their native language fluently or at a "standard" level. Anastasi and Cordova called this **language bifurcation**, or inadequate mastery of either language (1953). The case of Pablo, cited earlier, is an example of this problem. When students and teachers do not understand each other adequately, traditional instruction is of little profit.

In the past, some school districts did not permit students to use their native language during school hours, even at recess. This increased the youths' resentment of the school and its authorities and struck a low blow at their sense of identity and self-esteem. Today, happily, there is increasing recognition of these effects and therefore a less restrictive atmosphere in nonacademic periods of the school day.

It should be noted that true bilingualism, by contrast, is an occupational asset in many fields: foreign service, law enforcement and corrections, social work, teaching, politics, and international commerce, to cite some examples. It is a social asset (and sometimes a necessity) in many communities, particularly in Canada, where bilingualism is the law of the land. Maintenance of fluency in the native tongue should, therefore, be a target of education. It may even have beneficial cognitive effects in other areas of learning (Garcia, 1980).

ASSESSMENT

It is highly probable that language handicapped youngsters comprehend English better than they can speak it (which is often true for all of us), yet become confused in school situations. A child who speaks nonstandard English, for example, may be familiar with an object or concept by an idiomatic label but not know how to respond when her teacher calls it by another name. Such confusion can lead to depressed scores on tests as well as to misinterpretations of teachers' directions. This can ultimately result in the child's being erroneously labeled as retarded. Assessment of language handicapped children, therefore, can be seen to have certain unique problems.

One problem is that on some tests, only standard English is used in asking questions and/or giving credit for responses. A little latitude in testing the language handicapped might be appropriate. The examiner might go back to missed items and rephrase the questions, using alternate terms, saying "Show me the stove" instead of "Show me the range," for instance. Any such substitutions should be noted in the summary of test results. This practice is often followed by clinical psychologists when they suspect the **validity** of test results (that is, whether it actually measures what it was designed to measure), but not often enough in academic settings. The use of alternate terms is also appropriate when testing in Spanish, because different Hispanic countries frequently use different words for the same object or idea.

A second problem has to do with test-taking attitudes. Although language handicapped students may want to please the examiner, some come from cultures in which competition and/or guessing are considered unacceptable behavior. They may have not been encouraged, as American schoolchildren are, to "try your best." Or the assessment process may be perceived as yet another intrusion by school authorities.

Sometimes language handicapped students are simply not "test-wise." For example, they don't understand the directions but are too embarrassed to admit it. (I can recall once testing several Puerto Rican preadolescents who insisted that they understood all the directions, given in Spanish, but did not follow them. It turned out that they were unfamiliar with many basic testing terms, such as subrayar, "to underline.") Or they don't understand the role of speed in some testing situations and therefore work at a leisurely pace, spending too much time on each question. Problems such as these are encountered not only in standardized testing (such as intelligence and achievement tests) but also in the classroom on tests written by the teacher. At the college level, for example, some Asian students who speak reasonably good English and who tend to be strongly motivated toward success have difficulty taking course exams. They are so anxious to avoid errors caused by misunderstanding that they puzzle over each multiple-choice question as if it were a life-and-death matter. As a result, if they are allowed the extra time by the instructor, they may take two or three times as long to complete a quiz as their classmates. This concession to the foreign-born student, though usually tolerated by others in the class, could cause feelings of resentment.

Still another problem is locating appropriate tests for assessing the abilities of language handicapped students. This is necessary for suitable grade placement, especially where the child has attended school in his native environment. The first question to consider is whether to test in English or the native language. If the latter, are well-standardized tests available?

The American Institutes for Research did a study for the National Institute of Education on available assessment tests in foreign languages. They examined specifically the adequacy of tests for children in kindergarten through sixth grade whose first language was Chinese, French, Italian, Navajo, Portuguese, Spanish, or Tagalog (which is spoken widely in the Philippines). They sought tests in the following categories:

- Language dominance
- (Native) language proficiency
- English language proficiency
- Mathematics achievement
- Science achievement
- Social studies and ethnic studies
- Multi-subject-area achievement
- Attitude and self-concept
- Learning-style assessment
- General ability and scholastic aptitude (Locks, Pletcher, & Reynolds, 1978)

Too often, for each of the seven languages, they reported "no instruments located," that technical information was not available, or that the tests were inadequate or inappropriate for use with subgroups of the language population (for example, tests written in standard French could not be used with French Canadians, Haitians, or Creole speakers). They did report, however, that many tests were then under development (there is no later report on these). The greatest availability of acceptable instruments was for Spanish speakers, but it was noted that there "are definite dialectical differences in the Spanish spoken by students living in the United States who are of Cuban, Mexican-American, and Puerto Rican heritage" (1978, p. 33). These students also differ from Central and South American students in vocabulary, as results of the Spanish language WISC (standardized in Puerto Rico and Venezuela) have shown.

Recognizing that the linguistic "norm" for most tests may be culturally limited and therefore inappropriate for evaluating and placing language handicapped students, Mercer and Lewis (1979) assembled a "System of Multicultural Pluralistic Assessment" (SOMPA). SOMPA includes a number of standardized tests, including the WISC-R, but is based on more pluralistic norms for Black, Anglo, and Hispanic populations. Other components include a parent interview (in which questions are asked about the child's adaptive behavior, health history, and sociocultural environment) and visual, motor, and auditory tests. An Estimated Learning Potential (ELP) score is derived; this forms the basis for determining the most beneficial program of educational instruction relative to the child's background and level of performance. This method does not, however, resolve all of the problems of intracultural differences noted in the preceding paragraph. Further, questions have been raised about the validity of SOMPA as a predictor of success in the majority culture (Duffey, Salvia, Tucker, & Ysseldyke, 1981).

A final problem in assessing language handicapped students is finding trained bilingual examiners. Although an examiner can administer a test in Spanish, for example, and note the responses accurately, she may not be aware of subtle idiomatic differences between the test's vocabulary and the child's vocabulary. Under such circumstances, it would be beneficial to have the local bilingual teacher (if there is one) sitting in to clarify differences in terms.

Clearly, the assessment of these students is a task rife with potential hazards, even under ideal conditions. With fewer staff members available now in most districts, assessment procedures tend to be speeded up in an attempt to evaluate all of the newcomers. This can obviously contribute to erroneous conclusions and unsuitable placements. It may be that a directed interview in the native language would be more fruitful than a battery of tests, if the examiner can encourage the youngster to give elaborated responses to questions. Asking if the student has studied mathematics, for example, will probably yield a positive, but not informative, answer. "Show me what kinds of math problems you can do" might be more revealing. This approach might also be useful as a "warm-up" for more traditional testing.

EDUCATIONAL MODIFICATIONS

There are two basic approaches to educating the non-English or nonstandard speaker: immersion and nonimmersion. In immersion programs, the learner is exposed only to English. In nonimmersion programs, both the native language and English are used for instruction, but with two possible goals: The native tongue may be used for instruction only until the learner makes the transition to English, or the emphasis may be on maintenance of the native language while learning English (Garcia, 1980). No single approach has been found to be best for all students.

Whether at the preschool or secondary level, it is essential that the standard English speaker working with language handicapped students articulate clearly and pronounce words correctly. Otherwise, the listener will simply exchange one kind of nonstandard language for another. When the learner has difficulty making a certain speech sound that doesn't exist in his native language, the speech teacher should be called in for assistance. Some students may be able to profit if taught via the phonetic alphabet. The main thing is to make progress, for a child who continues to flounder is apt to feel both frustrated and humiliated.

Bilingual Projects

A Learning Environment Responsive to All (ALERTA), a bilingual program for preschoolers prepared at Teachers College of Columbia University, teaches sizes, shapes, concepts, and cultures in both English and Spanish ("Bilingual Preschool Program," 1980). It was designed for use with children who speak Chinese, Vietnamese, or an American Indian language, as well as Spanish speakers, and is an example of the transition/ maintenance approach. The staff determines that the child understands a concept in her first language before introducing it in the second language. Both languages are then used in play as well as in learning activities. Exposure to "Sesame Street" segments that use Spanish and English can reinforce what is learned in a program like ALERTA.

The principles of behavior modification find ready application in working with the language handicapped, as they try to progress to better comprehension and fluent conversational ability in English. Positive reinforcement for attempts to use the new, desired vocabulary and grammatical structures helps to increase the frequency of attempts. Since the first efforts may not be wholly successful, the teacher can use "shaping" techniques to reinforce closer and closer approximations to the desired goal.

The desire to learn standard English will also be increased if language instruction is embedded in a functional context rather than in isolated and abstract situations. A girl interested in athletics, for example, might respond well initially in a sports setting, where her ability to comprehend and use the appropriate terminology will enable her to participate in the game. While playing, she is likely to acquire additional incidental vocabulary and begin to mix with her English-speaking peers. One of these new friends can be asked to serve as a "buddy," helping to acquaint her with general vocabulary as well as sports terms. The buddy system can be used effectively wherever the student body consists of standard and nonstandard English speakers. Rapport is generally strengthened when the buddies have similar ethnic backgrounds, despite differences in English fluency.

As a practical matter, the buddy (or a tutor or teacher) should first introduce the language handicapped youngster to the names of teachers

A bilingual class in a Dallas public school. (Photo by Stock, Boston)

and classmates, terms for parts of the classroom and school building (including the important gender distinction between the words on the restroom doors), titles of subjects, procedures in the school, and the words for various familial relationships. Oral instruction can be paired with the written form in many cases. (Just as a note in passing, in how many schools does someone take the time to do these sorts of things for any newcomer, let alone one who doesn't speak the language?)

Language aides can be classmates (as in the buddy system), bilingual teachers, volunteer student tutors, or adult members of the community. If at all possible, the extra instruction should be on a daily basis, outside of the ESL classroom. (When an American student studies a foreign language, one of the weaknesses of the curriculum is that the new language is used only in that classroom and therefore seems irrelevant to the rest of the student's life. The problem is no different when reversed.) Language aides need not necessarily be bilingual. In one informal project, college students who spoke only English worked with young Puerto Rican children, teaching them vocabulary, numbers, and eventually reading. Several of the students later reported that they had learned some Spanish during the tutoring sessions, and that their willingness to learn had increased their rapport with the youngsters.

Mainstreaming

If the goal is to mainstream the language handicapped child as quickly as possible, art and music classes are good places to begin. These are considered "universal" languages, and they are an important mechanism for integrating students into the school. A student's competence in these areas can be a social asset and reduce some of the problems of self-esteem that may arise from the lack of language competence. Physical education classes are also useful for mainstreaming, since they depend more on visual activity than verbal. Home economics and industrial arts classes, which can make abundant use of diagrams and pictures for instruction, are also good choices for the initial mixing of language handicapped and English-speaking students.

Mathematics might be the next stage in the transition process. Although there are vocabulary problems, math can be taught to children from varied language backgrounds with greater ease than more word-oriented subjects. Numerical symbols are the same in most Western languages, and the fundamental processes can be applied readily both in school and at home. If a bilingual teacher is available, instruction can be given (at least initially) in both English and the other language or dialect. The principal aim for the student is to be actively learning rather than passively sitting in a classroom and falling further behind his classmates. Any growing lag in academic progress strikes at the youngster's sense of competence and reduces both his self-esteem and the respect of his peers.

As the student begins to acquire an oral English vocabulary, reading and writing can be introduced. If these can be geared to the child's interests, so much the better. Many books are now available that combine high interest levels with a simple reading vocabulary. They can be read to younger children so that they hear and learn the sounds and structure of English before trying to read the words for themselves. If a child is a nonreader in her native language as well, bilingual editions of common fairy tales may help her want to learn to comprehend and read. Many languages (particularly those of the Romance and Germanic groups) have words with English counterparts; such pairs of words, or **cognates**, have a common derivation and are often pronounced and/or defined similarly (see Figure 10.1). These common roots can be stressed early in language instruction, both to gain students' interest and to promote rapid successes.

Another technique that helps language handicapped students work at the level of their classmates is to translate assignments into their native language and allow the assignments to be completed in that language in the early stages of a transition program. (A bilingual resource teacher can help the classroom teacher with this task.) A variation of the "experience chart" used with beginning readers is also useful. A child's story told by the child in his native idiom is written down with the English translation

Figure 10.1   Cognates in English and other languages

next to it. Matching words from the two versions can be part of vocabulary instruction. Above all, the teacher needs to remember that an inability to express oneself in standard English does not mean that a student has no thoughts to communicate.

Social studies, at any level, tends to be a difficult area for the language handicapped. Apart from the many new and extensively used vocabulary items, it involves concepts that may be foreign to the students' experiences. One example would be the concept of "democracy," as used in the United States, to someone from a Latin American country with a military dictatorship or from a Communist country. Very specific and fundamental examples will be needed to clarify such ideas. A flash card file, with drawings or pictures on one side and the appropriate English words on the other, may help younger children respond to questions. Teachers might also call on other children first, so that the language handicapped student can follow the drift of the class discussion before having to answer questions on the topic. Teachers should use visual supplements to verbal questions as much as possible to enhance comprehension. The newcomers can also contribute by serving as resource persons if class discussion centers on their national or subcultural heritage, geographic area of origin, or life-style.

Many of the foregoing ideas were demonstrated in a five-year program in several New York City high schools. The non-English speakers were given ESL courses while learning subject matter in their native language, but they were also encouraged to interact with English-speaking students in the school. From the time they arrived at the high school, they took music, art, and physical education with American-born students. As soon as they learned some English, they were moved into regular math classes (Luxenberg, 1981, p. 33). The complete transition to English-speaking or mainstream classes usually took two to three years; the greatest difficulty occurred in history classes, where note-taking skills and speed were needed.

Several factors came to light in this program. One was the need to develop listener skills, so that the learner not only understands words but can comprehend the ideas and evaluate their importance as a native English speaker would.

A second factor emerging from the program was the recognition that English may be more difficult to learn for those coming from a Chinese or Vietnamese language background, which uses characters for letters and often has monosyllabic words, than for Hispanics or others whose alphabet is the same as that used in English. Japanese students, or at least those from large cities, may have had more exposure to English, as there are many signs in public places in Japan that are in both languages, a heritage of the post–World War II occupation.

Five Listening Stages

1. Stream of sound (zero comprehension of content)
2. Word recognition within the stream (minimal comprehension)
3. Phrase/formula recognition (marginal comprehension)
4. Clause/sentence recognition (minimally functional comprehension)
5. Extended speech recognition (general comprehension) (Taylor, 1981)

These are listening-comprehension stages we all go through as babies. Infants hear sounds but respond more to intonations than to individual words. In the middle to late part of their first year, they respond to words such as their name, *Mommy, Daddy, yes,* and *no.* They quickly progress from that stage to one in which they can pick out phrases like *go bye-bye* and *want milk.* In their second year, they recognize and respond to whole sentences, and general comprehension of simple vocabulary words is acquired rapidly thereafter.

A third factor that became apparent was the need to locate appropriate textbooks and study guides at all levels. Luxenberg pointed out, and teachers have confirmed from their experience, that students from other countries have different experiential backgrounds; they often do not share references to American historical events and heroes that we take for granted, do not comprehend idiomatic English phrases, and are unacquainted with "Middle American" life-styles and values (1981). It has been suggested that supplementary materials in the native language be developed that could clarify text content and thereby aid learning. Some efforts are being made in this direction at the college level, mainly in Spanish, but student guides are also needed in precollege classrooms and in other languages.

Other Approaches

Transition/maintenance classes, composed usually of children who have a common native language, not only provide content instruction in that language but also tend more and more to include studies of the various ethnic subcultures in the curriculum, rather than to reject them as "substandard." This has been particularly crucial in schools for AmerIndian children in the Southwest. Their values, practices, and concepts of interpersonal behavior frequently differ considerably from those of Middle America. In years past, everything Indian was viewed negatively by the staffs at schools established to teach these children. Today, the language, legends, and practices of the various tribes are interwoven with those of the larger society to present a more rounded curriculum with which the youngsters can live comfortably. This is done in many schools today for other linguistic and cultural groups as well, with the result that the students are more strongly motivated to learn.

Respect for other cultures is also seen in services outside the school, where individuals, ethnic associations, and/or community workers have established community centers for new arrivals. Philadelphia has witnessed the rise of several Korean self-help programs, ranging from housing resettlement to English language instruction. Los Angeles has an Inner City Bookmobile that supplies books in five languages to ethnic neighborhoods (Wagner, 1980). Literacy in the native language is encouraged, and the multilingual librarians also try to supply interesting English books for adults that have a low level of reading difficulty. The bookmobile also serves students, who often bring their parents and grandparents with them. More importantly, perhaps, the informality of this mobile library appears to stimulate reading interest in youngsters and improvement in reading skill, as they borrow more and more books.

That children tend to behave one way at school and another way at home is an often observed, and often forgotten, fact. This applies to the use of language as well. The language handicap tends to be intensified in the students' dealings with school personnel and other authority figures. Usually, a youngster communicates quite effectively away from school in his native language. There is a need, however, to increase the overall frequency of communication with adults in the school setting, too. This may take some modification of attitudes on the part of school personnel, who need to show a willingness to listen to the student's concerns in his native language as well as in English.

SUMMARY

The controversy over bilingual education has been a heated one in the past few years. Much public resentment exists in situations where American-born students are graduated from high school still unable to express themselves effectively in English. In many cases, they had participated in bilingual education classes that stressed maintenance of the native language rather than transition to English and mainstreaming.

Among the questions raised in the controversy are these: Should money be spent on native language instruction and materials while the non-English speaker adapts to a new country and is being taught English as a second language? Should language handicapped speakers be placed immediately in an all English-speaking environment? Some historical background helps to place these questions in perspective, for there are precedents for both approaches. There are also psychological considerations involved, such as maintaining the students' self-esteem and motivation to learn English, interpersonal differences in language-learning ability, and concerns for potential conflict between the school and home settings.

For the schools, specifically, there are problems in assessing students' levels of achievement and potential for learning, because there are too few well-standardized, appropriate testing measures available. This results in too many language handicapped students being placed in classes for the retarded or being "pushed out" of school because of inappropriate or thoughtless placement.

If a school adopts a transition approach rather than immersion, careful plans must be made for programming. How much of the school day is to be spent in ESL instruction and how much in subject matter instruction in the native language? In what ways and at what pace are language handicapped students to be integrated into the school's mainstream? Where are enough bilingual teachers to be found? What instructional materials are available? How can the monolingual English-speaking teacher communicate more effectively with the students? Discussions of these questions, and some possible answers, are provided in this chapter, along with examples of programs that have been successful.

SUGGESTED ADDITIONAL READINGS

Benderly, B. L. The multilingual mind. *Psychology Today*, 1981, *15* (3), 9–12.

Burt, M., and Dulay, H. Some guidelines for the assessment of oral language proficiency and dominance. *TESOL Quarterly*, 1978, *12*, 177–192.

Foster, C. R. Defusing the issues in bilingualism and bilingual education. *Phi Delta Kappan*, 1982, *63*, 342–344.

Grittner, F. M., Ed. *Learning a second language.* Seventy-ninth Yearbook of the National Society for the Study of Education, Part II. Chicago: National Society for the Study of Education, 1980.

Hilliard, A.G., III. Psychological factors associated with language in the education of the African-American child. *Journal of Negro Education*, 1983, *52* (1), 24–34.

Hornby, P. A., Ed. *Bilingualism: Psychological, social, and educational implications.* New York: Academic Press, 1977.

Innis, H. R. *Bilingualism and biculturalism: An abridged version of the Royal Commission Report.* Ottawa: McClelland and Stewart, Ltd., 1973.

Kleinfeld, J. S. *Eskimo school on the Andreafsky: A study of effective bilingual education.* New York: Praeger, 1979.

Lambert, W. E., and Tucker, G. R. The benefits of bilingualism. *Psychology Today*, 1973, *7* (4), 89–92.

Light, R. L., Richard, D. P., and Bell, P. Development of children's attitudes toward speakers of standard and nonstandard English. *Child Study Journal*, 1978, *8*, 253–265.

Manuel, H. T. *Spanish-speaking children of the Southwest: Their education and the public welfare.* Austin: University of Texas Press, 1965.

McLaughlin, B. Second-language learning in children. *Psychological Bulletin*, 1977, *84*, 438–459.

Ovando, C. J. Bilingual/bicultural education: Its legacy and its future. *Phi Delta Kappan*, 1983, *64*, 564–568.

Parr, G. D., Baca, F., and Dixon, P. Individualized versus group instruction in bilingual education: A two-year study. *The Elementary School Journal*, 1981, *81*, 223–227.

Plata, M., and Santos, S. L. Bilingual special education: A challenge for the future. *Teaching Exceptional Children*, 1981, *14*, 97–100.

Ryan, E. B., and Carranza, M. A. Language attitudes and other cultural attitudes of bilingual Mexican-American adolescents. *Ethnicity*, 1980, *7*, 191–202.

Simoes, A., Jr., Ed. *The bilingual child: Research and analysis of existing educational themes.* New York: Academic Press, 1976.

Wallwork, J. F. *Language and people.* London: Heinemann Educational Books, 1978.

PART FOUR/
CULTURALLY DIFFERENT
STUDENTS

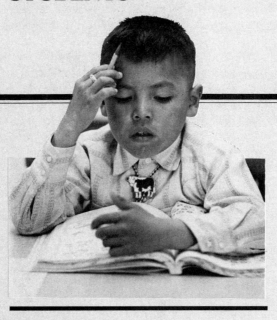

S ome cultural groups in the United States are at
an economic disadvantage because they cannot
compete effectively in the labor market. Others have a
linguistic disadvantage that inhibits their interaction
with the majority, as was seen in Chapter 10. Still
others must confront racial or national prejudice that
places them at a social as well as economic disadvantage. Almost all of these groups, because of their differences from the majority culture, are to some degree
at an educational disadvantage.

Several terms are used, almost interchangeably,
for groups that do not fit the white, Anglo-Saxon,
middle-class national self-image. The accuracy with
which the terms describe these groups is open to question. Calling them culturally deprived implies that
these are groups without a culture or ethos. Of course,
this is not the case, as each minority group has its
own set of attitudes, values, beliefs, and so on. Culturally disadvantaged poses similar difficulties. Great
differences between majority and minority cultures

may place the minority at a disadvantage in a number of areas, but the term implies that it is the culture, not the minority status, that is disadvantaged. A more appropriate term to describe these groups is culturally different.

A new spirit of pride in one's culture (whether it is the result of ethnic origin, religious beliefs, or isolation), without apology for its differences from the majority culture, has meant revision of textbooks and curricula. The effect on classroom atmosphere and teaching techniques has come more slowly. For the culturally different, whether the difference is racial, ethnic, or socioeconomic, special education can play an important role in reducing the gaps between the home and the larger society.

Respect for the child as an individual and for her family, home, and ethnic affiliation is important if she is to develop the self-image and self-confidence so vital to success in learning situations. We are belatedly realizing that diverse groups in the school population should be regarded by school personnel as a challenge rather than as a burden. Instead of condemnation to a marginal existence because of conditions into which they were born, these children surely have a right to equal opportunities in education. That they are disadvantaged initially in the learning situation should not mean that they are to become adults handicapped by conditions beyond their control.

CHAPTER 11 /
THE LEARNING
DISADVANTAGED

Learning disadvantaged children may or may not have physical or intellectual impairments, yet they are exceptional in one way. They are children who lack opportunities to learn the skills and have the experiences acquired by most young children in our society in the preschool years. A large number receive too little stimulation because of parental inadequacies. Their parents are not only the poor or undereducated, the "dropouts" from society in counterculture groups, the culturally different, the alcoholics, or the emotionally disturbed. Inadequate stimulation can also be found in middle-class homes where socially or professionally preoccupied parents delegate their child-raising responsibilities to persons whose primary job is housekeeping or baby-sitting, but not child rearing. Daily interaction with an inadequate parental surrogate, combined with benign neglect by the parents themselves, can be as great a disadvantage to a child's development as more obviously negative environmental situations.

A second group of learning disadvantaged youngsters are in residential institutions that provide essential housing, food, and general physical care but minimal intellectual stimulation. Often, these children have been abandoned, removed from their homes by welfare agencies (but not placed in foster homes), or incorrectly diagnosed as severely impaired in some way. There is also a third group of learning disadvantaged children, who are rarely identified at all. These are youngsters who live in communities so geographically isolated, and often so economically deprived, that their opportunities for learning are severely limited. Even Ibn Khaldoun, a great Islamic scholar of the Middle Ages, recognized that such isolation led to intellectual impairments and inequalities in terms of more urban societies.

PREVENTION AND/OR COMPENSATION
Sample Populations

Victims of Parental Inadequacies   As just noted, there are basically three groups of children who can be identified as learning disadvantaged even before they enter school. The first group consists of those who live in unstimulating and perhaps impoverished environments. They have no mobiles hanging over their cribs, no one handling and talking to them except as part of their routine physical care, and none of the experiences that teachers anticipate they have had. They are not read to, nor are there books in the home. Their parents may be poorly educated, both in the academic sense and in skills such as parenting and homemaking. Although some of these parents actually resent the intrusion of an infant into their lives, many of them neglect to foster the baby's development simply because they don't know any better. Lack of verbal stimulation from early infancy on impedes language development, and being kept in a crib or playpen all day inhibits their motor development and exploratory activities. These deficits grow through the preschool years, and the child arrives at school with an inadequate vocabulary, a passive cognitive style, and few interpersonal skills. (An excess of talking, where the baby is overwhelmed by words and voices, can also have negative effects.)

Institutionalized Children   The second group of children resides in institutions because of being abused, abandoned, or supposedly retarded. These facilities rarely have the funds to hire well-trained personnel, so that the children's caretakers are too often concerned only with routine care and avoiding problems with their supervisors that would be caused by noisy, curious toddlers. The physical environment may lack color, music, and other sources of stimulation that children in the average family take for granted.

Children in Isolated Areas   Finally, although it seems inconceivable in an era of instant mass communication, there are communities that teachers avoid because of isolation, living conditions, and sometimes extreme poverty. Conroy (1972) described one such community. The children he taught on an island off the Georgia coast were already school-aged, yet they lacked even the most fundamental knowledge expected of a preschooler. They functioned quite adequately in nonacademic areas such as fishing and hunting, however. In rural Alaska, educators at the Northwest Regional Educational Laboratory discovered that the children could not relate to traditional basic readers or other elementary texts because they had not had experience with many of the objects or concepts the texts included. Isolation, rather than neglect, makes such youngsters learning disadvantaged in the typical American school.

Children of migrant workers have some problems similar to those faced by children in isolated areas and some similar to those who are members of cultural minorities (see Chapter 12). Primarily as a result of their mobility, they suffer educational disadvantages because of unequal access to schools, appropriate educational services, and continuity of such services (Hunter, 1982). If the migrant student is handicapped in addition (and many of them do have health problems), the availability of appropriate services is reduced even more.

For all these children, there is a question of how to reduce the learning deficits that will probably make them early dropouts from school. In what ways can this problem be handled?

The Controversy

The principal approach to remedying these inequities is by means of compensatory educational programs, such as Project Head Start. These programs help to provide the rudimentary cognitive and social skills needed in school and to expose preschoolers to a variety of experiences that middle-class "advantaged" youngsters normally have. Research studies on the Get Set and Head Start programs have yielded conflicting results; several have indicated that the effects of the programs fade by the end of first grade. The funds and efforts invested are therefore perceived as wasted. Supporters of compensatory education, however, question whether the nature and quality of typical kindergarten and first-grade instruction are appropriate for these children. They want to see enrichment and support programs (such as "Operation Follow Through") continued through at least third grade, to give the children a solid basis for learning and self-esteem.

Preschool programs provide stimulating new experiences in
social and cognitive learning areas—and fun, too! (Hank
Lebo/Jeroboam)

The Kamehameha Early Education Project (KEEP), designed to teach
disadvantaged children of Hawaiian ancestry to read, had several features
that contributed to its success. KEEP had stable funding over a ten-year
period. Its researchers not only developed the research program but also
were in charge of the school. Multidisciplinary in conception and operation, KEEP also considered the Hawaiian culture in developing its teaching techniques (McNett, 1981). With these advantages, the project was
able to achieve, through continuing evaluation, what supporters of
compensatory education would like to see programs on the mainland
accomplish.

Many psychologists and educators, on the other hand, believe that
early, "preventive" educational methods are highly desirable, just as in
medicine: Better preparation for parenthood, plus intensive and extensive
programs during infancy and early childhood, seems to these professionals to be a wiser financial investment than prolonged remedial and rehabilitation programs in later years. This is a philosophy practiced widely
in Scandinavian countries, where children—perceived as the nation's
future—are considered a worthwhile investment of money, time, and
effort from early infancy on.

Child development specialists consider the first years of life crucial to
overall development. They point to certain periods in infancy and early
childhood when, if what should be learned is not learned, the pace of
development and learning may be permanently altered. The preventive

approach is based in part on these theories. It is also an attempt at positive intervention in infants' and young children's exposure to family attitudes and cognitive styles, linguistic experiences, home conditions, and nutrition. Many children evaluated as intellectually retarded in school might have the potential to perform at above average levels but are handicapped by negative situations in the home. According to Bronfenbrenner,

the family seems to be the most effective and economical system for fostering and sustaining the child's development. Without family involvement, intervention is likely to be unsuccessful, and what few effects are achieved are likely to disappear once the intervention is discontinued. (1975, p. 470)

Two examples of early intervention exemplify the heat that the prevention-compensation controversy has generated. Skeels reported on a thirty-year follow-up of two groups of institutionalized mentally retarded children. Thirteen children, in one group, were moved at an early age from an orphanage to an institution for the retarded. There they were cared for by some of the older female inmates until they showed normal intellectual development. Eleven of the children were subsequently placed for adoption, one was returned to the orphanage, and one remained in the institution. As adults, Skeels found that the adopted subjects were all self-supporting and reasonably well educated. By contrast, the group who remained in the orphanage suffered declines in ability, with the exception of one individual who apparently became a normal adult (1966). Although the study was highly praised by most psychologists after its publication for its laudable demonstration of the effects of early intervention, Longstreth criticized Skeels's work, alleging questionable selectivity of both subjects and test score data (1981). He found that the study offered "no convincing support for the malleability of early IQ" (1981, p. 624).

The second study was of an infant intervention program known as the Milwaukee Project, directed by Rick Heber. The mothers of the children involved were measurably and functionally retarded. Trained specialists went daily to the homes of the subjects, from the time the babies were about six weeks old, to provide stimulating experiences. Beginning at age three to four months, the babies were taken to a special center for several hours daily, where for the next few years they were instructed in language, visual and motor skills, music, art, science, and creative thinking. They moved gradually from individual instruction to very small groups. At the same time, the mothers of the children were encouraged, but not required, to participate in a center-run homemaking program.

With the program beyond its fifth year, Heber and his associates reported that the first groups of children with whom they worked measured and functioned at average or higher levels of academic achievement (Heber & Garber, 1975). In 1976, Heber reported that the experimental group, after three years in regular schools, was still maintaining an IQ

FOR EXAMPLE . . .

"When Carol came to the Center for Preschool Services in Special Education from an inner-city Get Set program she was 3 years old, but she could neither talk nor recognize herself in the mirror. Her mental development was that of an 18-month-old.

"After seven months at the Center she talked and did appropriate preschool work. Now, at age 5, Carol has outgrown the Center and is ready for a special kindergarten program in a private school that offers a strong program in language development. This all sounds encouraging, but the school for Carol is 30 minutes away by train, and she is too young to travel there alone. Her mother works, so Carol needs not only a scholarship but free transportation. . . .

"Preschool day care programs serve many thousands of city children from disadvantaged families. Hundreds of these children are presently failing to develop adequately and hundreds more will fail in future educational situations" (*Franklin Institute News*, 1972).

The Center for Preschool Services (since moved from the Franklin Institute Research Laboratories in Philadelphia) is a demonstration program that has a multidisciplinary approach. It stresses interventive psychoeducational procedures for preschool children who, left untreated, may become failures in school and society in only a few years. Using appropriate therapeutic techniques as well as nursery school stimulation experiences, it aims to prevent serious emotional disorders and enhance learning ability. The program also trains teachers from Get Set day-care centers to recognize children who might benefit from participation in its long-term therapy.

advantage over control group children in excess of twenty points (Trotter, 1976). However, Page, a critic of the project for several years, found that

on the broad intellectual skills of school achievement, there appears to have been much less transfer than hoped—indeed, a decline to the level of the C[ontrol] group in reading. Also, the Milwaukee Project seems to have raised IQ scores by intensive training, but not to have produced improvements in real and lasting intelligence. (Page & Grandon, 1981, p. 254)

Meanwhile, Bonfenbrenner asserted that both the Skeels experiment and the Milwaukee Project demonstrated the effectiveness of early environmental intervention (1975).

The people doing the research and those who criticize their claims are all well-respected psychologists. Which view can one believe? Are the intervention programs, which are very expensive to operate, effective enough to warrant their continuation? Are they being properly designed and appropriately evaluated? A closer examination of some of the projects may help you to decide.

EDUCATIONAL PROGRAMS

Get Set and Head Start, the federally funded projects begun in the 1960s, are familiar compensatory programs. They take youngsters of nursery school age and offer them educational toys and activities, field trips, and concerned teachers in an effort to provide experiences and skills that have long been assumed to constitute part of "school readiness." The staff members are alert to characteristics that would place a child "at risk" at school entrance and try to get help for the child before that situation arises. Carol's case illustrates the interaction between one of these programs and an intervention program.

A similar program, Project EARLY (Early Assessment and Remediation Laboratory), is operated by the Chicago Board of Education for preschoolers aged three to five years. In their assessment procedure, children are evaluated in five areas of functioning: gross motor, fine motor, language, visual discrimination, and memory. If a child is found to have weaknesses in one or more of these areas, teachers and parents work with the youngster to improve skills appropriately (Reed, 1982). Other intervention programs, especially for retarded and some physically disabled children, start even earlier.

Intervention Projects

A few programs for the learning disadvantaged begin with infants or their mothers rather than with preschoolers. The Milwaukee Project is one such program. McCandless, as another example, directed a parent-child development program at Emory University in Atlanta. Its emphasis was on training the mothers of babies aged three months to three years in all areas of child development. In addition to the principles of child development, the mothers were taught reinforcement techniques, the value of play experiences, nutrition, and homemaking skills (see Figure 11.1). (Mothers of subjects in the Milwaukee Project were given opportunities to participate in a similar program.)

Many of the intervention projects were started in response to the civil rights movement of the early 1960s, President Johnson's "War on Poverty," and equal opportunities programs in the middle and late 1960s. The Perry Preschool Project in the Detroit area, for example, focused on disadvantaged Black preschoolers with IQs in the 50–85 range. Daily half-day classes were combined with weekly home visits by staff members (from

Figure 11.1   Early sources of infant stimulation

October to May) to stimulate the children's learning abilities and skills (Weikart, 1967). In Florida, child development workers went into the homes of rural Blacks to teach family members techniques of infant stimulation (Gordon, 1972). Children from the Florida program were found to be more likely to profit than those in the Perry Project, because, as D. Hayes and Grether have argued, children from noninvolved families tended to lose ground during the summer months, when the programs were not in operation (1969).

Preschool programs range from several months to a few years in duration, and from a traditional playschool format to aggressive drill (see Bereiter & Engelmann, 1966) in character. Some stress personal-social development; others, such as the Montessori schools, emphasize sensory-motor training; and a few focus on cognitive concepts. A difficulty in evaluating the relative merit of the programs is that too often the evaluations are done after only one year of a project. Spaulding pointed out, in his report of a five-year compensatory education program, that the one-year projects are less effective than two- to four-year programs. He cited evidence that greater success is obtained when children are enrolled at a younger age, continue in the project for two or more years, and participate in programs designed to maximize their problem-solving and self-management skills—that is, to give them feelings of competence and power (1972). However, it must be recognized that the active stimulation and increased attention found in *any* intervention program are bound to cause some improvement in intellectual functioning.

For institutionalized children, the Scandinavian model, in which trained pediatric nurses and early childhood teachers are the primary caretakers, gives an indication of what is needed. Instead of hiring attendants at minimum wage levels, a common practice that leads to little stimulation of the children, trained paraprofessionals can provide care, nurturing, and stimulation beyond the bare necessities of survival. The preparation of such workers was the goal of the Child Development Associate Consortium, begun in the 1970s in the U.S. Foster grandparent programs, either paid or volunteer, offer another opportunity for the personal interaction so acutely needed in the development of infants and toddlers. Foster grandparents can also help slightly older children to learn a variety of skills. (Note: In addition to giving, these older volunteers also gain a sense of being needed.)

In the case of geographically isolated youngsters who have no access to preschool programs, compensatory education techniques are more difficult to employ. Although preschool training is what these children require, it is hardly appropriate to use preschool materials once they have reached school age. Conroy used the students' existing life skills as the basis for remedial instruction and supplemented available texts with audio and visual materials to enlarge their experiences (1972). Educators working with Aleut, AmerIndian, and rural Appalachian children have similarly had to develop books and other means to demonstrate the similarities (such as survival needs) and differences (such as life-styles) between these groups and the larger society, in order to reduce the experience gap of these students.

Parental Education

As Bronfenbrenner (1975) concluded, the programs most effective in reducing or preventing learning disadvantages are those in which there is direct parent involvement. Parenthood is a profession for which virtually no training is offered in schools. Nevertheless, being inadequately prepared for the role or functioning poorly in it should not excuse parents' allowing a child to become learning disadvantaged. With changing attitudes toward day care, an increasing financial need for both parents to work, and a recognition that biological motherhood does not automatically make a woman the best possible caretaker of a child, more and more children will experience time away from home in the preschool years. The stimulation they experience in these other environments needs to be reinforced at home if the effects are to be lasting. This means that there is a real need for parental education during late pregnancy and continuing after the child's birth.

The implementation of intervention projects requires extensive reorientation and reeducation. Parental cooperation can be sought through outpatient maternity and well-baby clinics, welfare agencies, and private obstetricians and pediatricians. Ideally, impoverished mothers could be required to attend weekly sessions on child care and development in order to receive Aid to Dependent Children benefits. Realistically, however, course attendance, even if required, cannot guarantee a true modification of attitudes and practices.

Concerted efforts by community resource agencies could lead to the development of effective alternative intervention programs for future and current parents. When the children are admitted to public schools, these agencies could offer after-school programs that continue to provide a supportive environment where the children can obtain a snack, tutoring assistance, and a learning atmosphere free of their home difficulties. The agencies can also provide lecture and counseling services for the parents so that they continue to be involved with their children's development. In the best of all possible worlds, the funding for such programs would be increased, not reduced (as is the current government policy).

SUMMARY

Children become learning disadvantaged through circumstances beyond their control. They live in unstimulating homes, have neglectful or inadequate parents, are institutionalized, or are isolated from the larger society and its experiences. Without the exposure to experiences assumed to be common to preschoolers, they enter kindergarten or first grade "behind" almost before they begin. For many of these children, lack of prereading skills is the problem (vocabulary, basic concepts, visual discrimination ability). For others, there may be a lack of preparation for the classroom as a social unit (teacher-pupil or peer relationships, appropriate behavior). And for some, there are physical and/or emotional anomalies that place them "at risk."

Since there is general agreement among psychologists and educators that the early years of childhood are very significant for future learning performance and personality development, it seems to make good sense to invest in preventive programs rather than to have to try to undo or remedy longstanding deficits in the school years. As is the case with diseases, the price of a single inoculation is far less than the cost of a cure. Intervention programs such as those described in this chapter have, despite mixed evaluations, the potential to minimize the risk of children being learning disadvantaged. Their design and implementation can be improved and their impact heightened by starting them earlier and operating them for longer periods, and their net effect can be to reduce the number of people ill prepared to function in society as well as in school.

SUGGESTED ADDITIONAL READINGS

Caldwell, B. M. The rationale for early intervention. *Exceptional Children*, 1970, *36*, 717–726.

Cartwright, C. A., and Cartwright, G. P. Competencies for prevention of learning problems in early childhood education. *Educational Horizons*, 1975, *53*, 151–157.

Day, B. *Early childhood education: Creative learning activities* (2nd ed.). New York: Macmillan, 1983.

Eckerson, L. O. Following through with "Follow Through." *American Education*, 1973, *9* (10), 10–16.

Frechtling, J. *Compensatory education study: Final report to Congress from the National Institute of Education*. Washington, D.C.: National Institute of Education, September 1978.

Gotts, E. E. The training of intelligence as a component of early interventions: Past, present, and future. *Journal of Special Education*, 1981, *15*, 257–268.

Hunt, J. McV. *The challenge of incompetence and poverty: Papers on the role of early education*. Urbana: University of Illinois Press, 1971.

Ryan, T. J. Poverty and early education in Canada. In B. Z. Friedlander, G. M. Steritt, and G. E. Kirk (Eds.), *Exceptional Infant* (Vol. 3). New York: Brunner/Mazel, 1975, pp. 304–322.

Stanley, J. C., Ed. *Compensatory education for children ages two to eight: Recent studies of intervention*. Baltimore: Johns Hopkins University Press, 1973.

Tjossen, T. D. *Intervention strategies for high risk infants and young children*. Baltimore: University Park Press, 1976.

Zigler, E. Project Head Start: Success or failure? *Learning*, 1973, *1* (7), 43–47.

Zigler, E., Butterfield, E. C., and Capobianco, F. Institutionalization and the effectiveness of social reinforcement: A five- and eight-year follow-up study. *Developmental Psychology*, 1970, *3*, 255–263.

CHAPTER 12/
CULTURAL MINORITIES

We tend to think fondly of the United States as the great "melting pot," in which ethnic and racial heritages are submerged (except on holidays) to enrich the population stew as flavors assimilate. The "average" American, despite some recent changes in curricula and textbook content, is thought to emerge from the educational process melted down into a white, English-speaking, middle-class person. This point of view has often been an expedient justification for ignoring cultural differences, particularly in the schools. In reality, however, we have a growing number of Hispanic, Asian, and Caribbean refugees whose values and life-styles are in many respects inimicable to this projected outcome of the melting pot process. Not only do they differ from the traditional majority, but, as Baca stresses, it is "difficult, if not impossible, to generalize within a single majority group because of the regional, cultural, linguistic, and other types of differences that prevail" (1980, p. 583). The question confronting educators, and others, thus becomes: Do we want a bland (well-assimilated) population stew or one with zest (culturally pluralistic)?

WHO ARE CULTURAL MINORITIES?

The term *cultural minorities* encompasses a wide variety of immigrant and native-born peoples. Among them are Mexican-Americans, Puerto Ricans, the French Canadians in New England, Asian Americans, AmerIndians, Eskimos, Blacks, residents of Appalachia, migrant workers, and the ghettoized third- and fourth-generation descendants of European immigrants. Since the expansion of immigration privileges in 1965, we have also had an influx of refugees from various parts of the world where political and economic upheavals have made hundreds of thousands of people want to escape from their own countries. Much of this refugee population needs medical care, food, jobs, housing, schooling, and English lessons for the adults as well as the children. In California alone, the estimated cost of these services for Haitian, Indo-Chinese, and Cuban refugees in 1981–82 was $391 million (Fremstad, 1981).

It is not the difference in heritage alone that creates problems in school for the children of these diverse groups. For many, it is the cultural difference plus economic disadvantage, plus geographic isolation (even within a large city), plus social isolation. The children's families tend to be deeply enmeshed in a neighborhood or local cultural subgroup, attending to "outsiders" only when they must. Many of the parents, if they wished to locate helpful resources for their children, would have no idea where to being their search and would be reluctant to ask authority figures for assistance. Among both the native-born and the more impoverished immigrants, there tends to be a sense of powerlessness as well as disorientation, often because they are accustomed to a rural way of life that serves them poorly in an urban setting.

CONFLICTING PHILOSOPHIES

In educating the children of these diverse cultural minorities, there is a basic conflict: Do we want to "Americanize" the children to the extent that they lose identification with their heritage, or do we want to preserve that identification at the risk of keeping the children on the fringes of the larger society? There is a point of balance between these extremes, although we have yet to achieve it. As part of that balance, children should be able to develop and retain feelings of self-respect and ethnic pride. Without such feelings, they have little motivation to learn either academic content or skills that are needed to function effectively in the larger society.

Although there is a long history of unsuccessful attempts to develop nonbiased tests for the culturally different (Bailey & Harbin, 1980), educators need to realize that what students are capable of is ultimately more important than what questions they can answer on a test. However (and with some justification), many professionals assert that using special criteria for the evaluation of culturally different students (such as local or special group norms) reduces their chances for mobility. Referrals for special education services, as a result of current testing programs, have typically resulted in disproportionate numbers of minority students being locked into special education classes (Mercer, 1973). (They have also resulted in a number of lawsuits, particularly in California, New York City, and other areas of high minority enrollment.)

Too many research studies of AmerIndian, Black, and Hispanic students have indicated that the longer many of these children are in school, the less progress they make. Part of the problem seems to lie in their placement, which has, in turn, been determined by tests that are acknowledged to be biased in language and to assume common experiences and values (see Chapter 10). Also, these students are often in schools that have the least access to financial support or student personnel services. If they are erroneously placed in classes for the retarded or viewed in a stereotyped fashion, these youngsters lack the opportunity to acquire the techniques needed for self-advancement. If they lack the appropriate techniques, the open-enrollment policies and special programs available for them in higher education are meaningless. For too many minority group members, the result of attempts to take advantage of these programs with inadequate preparation is a mixed bag of frustration, anger, feelings of rejection, recurrent failure, and finally, withdrawal and return to the security of the cultural group. When this happens, the youth, the cultural group, and society at large are all losers.

If a minority student does succeed in school, she needs to have access to information about options for the future and the possible impact that deciding among them will have on her relations with her family and other ethnic group members. Certain questions have to be asked: Do I want to move out of the inner-city ghetto or the barrio? If so, what other life-styles are available to me? Is it possible to acquire a good education, perhaps enter a profession, and then return to the old neighborhood comfortably? At what point does my personal success or acquisition of middle-class goals begin to have a negative value for me? What is the cost of assimilation, in terms of family relationships, friendships, and self-esteem? A lack of sensitivity to these concerns (and there are educators who would prefer to ignore them) will lead to professional mistakes and personal tragedies. Oriented to middle-class values as our schools are, we must consider whether we have the right to impose such values on others. If the response is that morally we do not have the right, then we must ask whether we are

These AmerIndian students seem enthused about a classroom event. (© Paul Conklin)

perpetuating discrimination and segregation. In fact, most schools today *do* assume this right, although they are seeking to accommodate more diversity within the school population.

EDUCATIONAL MODIFICATIONS

Expectations

Although the Rosenthal and Jacobson study *Pygmalion in the Classroom* has been criticized because of its methodology, the authors stressed two related points that are generally accepted, concerning the role of the self-fulfilling prophecy in achievement and the effects of teacher expectations on achievement (1968). If teachers expect little learning on the part of students whom they perceive as poor, "non-American," or otherwise culturally different, few of these students seem to be satisfactory achievers. On the other hand, if the students are placed in a high-achievement section (Tuckman & Bierman, 1971) or a special enrichment program (such as Project PATS; see Chapter 4), they and their teachers assume that the placement is appropriate, and the students' self-esteem and achievement tend to match these higher expectations.

In other words, children tend to perform as they are expected to

Many schools have culturally diverse populations. (Photo by Elizabeth Crews)

perform by their teachers. The expectations come through in tone of voice, gestures, the way in which a student's papers are handled, smiles or lack of them, and other nonverbal behavior. Teachers with middle-class values frequently abhor dirt, dislike casual attitudes toward routines and rules, and often resist understanding alternative value systems and lifestyles. Culturally different students frequently have characteristics and come from home environments that make such teachers uncomfortable, and therefore they are less than positive in their attitudes toward such youngsters. This is especially true when a child lives in poverty. Even if the child and his clothing are well scrubbed, the teacher perceives his poverty as an unpleasant "difference" and consequently has low expectations for his success in the classroom. (Note: Some teachers' aversion to poverty may reflect anxiety about their own "escape" from a similar background.)

Differing values between teachers and their culturally diverse students also affect interpersonal relationships. The Asian-American child who is taught at home to lower her eyes in respect to an older person may be perceived as lying or disrespectful by the teacher, who was taught to look a person straight in the eye. Stress on competition and independent effort, as another example, often conflicts with the group orientation and mutual dependence of Hispanics and AmerIndians (Bryant & Meadow, 1976). And certainly, if the students speak a language that the teacher does not understand, rapport and respect as well as communication are adversely affected.

Some changes are clearly needed and are already evident in some classrooms. Teachers have to learn to accept these children, with all their cultural "baggage," and build on their strengths and existing skills rather than focus on deficits and differences. Teachers should reinforce all desirable behavior, pay (and mean) compliments (on a pretty smile, a helpful hand, a sweet singing voice), respond to the children's questions, ask them each day what's important in their lives, and attempt to discover each child's strengths and needs.

Many culturally different children are aware by school age that authority figures in the larger society perceive them as lazy, incompetent, and inadequate. Already accustomed to receiving the leftovers and hand-me-downs of society, they can hardly believe that they have much significance in that society. Manipulated by the unscrupulous, even as preschoolers, they also see themselves as powerless. Given that sordid assortment of feelings, it is no wonder that they have low expectations for themselves of positive experiences in school. Encouraging competence in such children is therefore a difficult task unless they have some motivation and see a purpose to classroom activities.

Content of Instruction

For many cultural minority children, the curriculum has little relationship to their past learning experiences and present home environment. For some Alaskan children, and other groups as well, the introduction of cultural awareness and native language instruction into the curriculum has contributed to higher self-esteem and greater interest in traditional school subjects that can be used as tools in learning about their own traditions.

Most poor and many other cultural minority youngsters have seen or used few of the appliances and accessories taken for granted in their textbooks. They can't conceive of buying three pounds of meat at any price or a dozen oranges at one time, so that what are supposed to be practical arithmetic examples are really meaningless to them. The niceties of syntax in standard English contribute little to the child's functional language (but could be taught in relation to the structure of their home language). The theoretical bases of science offer little to the student who can't read or pronounce the terms, is aware of "chemicals" only as explo-

FOR EXAMPLE . . .

Until schools external to the native culture came along, Tlingit and Haida families [in Alaska] had a highly sophisticated system for educating their children. Grandparents, aunts, and uncles each had a clear role in teaching the language and the basics of family culture and tradition. Responsibility for educating the older boys . . . rested with the maternal uncle, while the girls were taught by mothers and grandmothers. But the custom went by the board when schools were built and an alien culture was introduced by white teachers using white-oriented textbooks. Increasingly, native parents waited for the schools to teach their children the skills formerly handled within the family unit. As a result, many native children were entering school totally unprepared.

Moorefield, S. Alaskan journal. *American Education*, 1976, 12 (7), 17.

sives or drugs, knows the facts of life from direct experience, and connects electricity and gas with hard-earned money. History texts, even today, rarely mention minority groups and the poor, unless negatively or with a simple statement of their existence in certain centuries or during depressions. A few texts do devote some paragraphs to the great immigration period of 1880–1920, but not necessarily constructively.

Compared with elementary textbooks published until the early 1970s, today's readers and social studies texts show more awareness of diverse cultural groups, although they may still include distortions, stereotypes, and an imbalance of content (Schwartz & Isser, 1978). Secondary school texts, especially histories, are still guilty of ethnocentric views and content, omitting mention of Blacks, for instance, between the Reconstruction Period after the Civil War and the Supreme Court decision of 1954 that ordered school desegregation, or viewing all immigrants as poor, illiterate, and content to live in slums. The role of people from countries other than England, Germany, and France (except for the explorers who followed Columbus) in our colonial period is still minimized, if not entirely overlooked, in many texts.

When studying the community, it is generally more profitable to ask children about their experiences with police officers and firemen than to present the usual view of these "community helpers." The children of the urban poor have learned that these are powerful (though sometimes friendly) authority figures who are not always as altruistic in the ghetto as they are in more affluent neighborhoods. Children of migrant laborers may have had quite negative experiences with community authority figures, as the migrant families are not often welcomed in the small towns near the farms where they work. The opportunity to share and describe

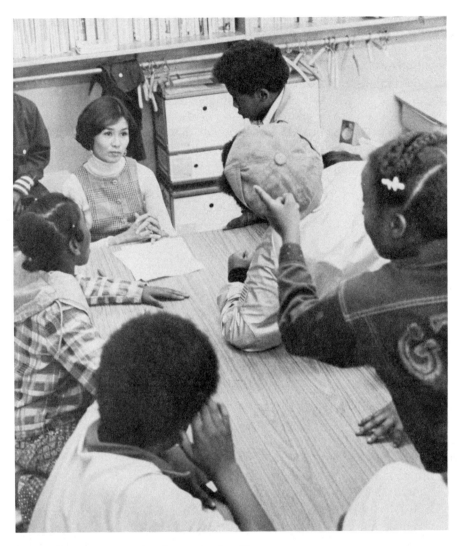

Integration in action in the classroom should accompany
an integrated approach to curriculum content. (Photo by
Elizabeth Crews)

their experiences encourages verbal expression and the development of
recall ability. With delicate handling by the teacher, the narrations can
become lessons (on both sides of the desk) in cause-and-effect relationships, sociology, and organization of thoughts and can permit the release
of feelings of hostility and rejection in a potentially constructive manner.
In secondary school, minority students might become involved in community services for the aged and less able, perhaps in conjunction with

FOR EXAMPLE . . .

Reading for pleasure or to meet a class requirement can contribute to the broadening of students' awareness of cultural diversity. Lists of books appropriate for different age and reading levels can and should include well-written and nonstereotyped works dealing with a variety of peoples. A reading list for the middle grades, which may also be useful for younger and older children might include:

The Leopard (Cecil Bodker), for grades 4–7; Focus: Rural Ethiopia

Paul Robeson (Eloise Greenfield), for grades 1–5; Focus: Biography of the Black singer (emphasis on his music)

Patrick Des Jarlait (Neva Williams), for grades 3–5; Focus: AmerIndian artist

Last Night I Saw Andromeda (Charlotte Anker), for grades 5–8; Focus: Blacks, whites, and science

Song of the Trees (Mildred D. Taylor), for grades 2–5; Focus: Rural Blacks

An Eskimo Birthday (Tom D. Robinson), for grades 2–5; Focus: Eskimo life

Sing to the Dawn (Minfong Ho), for grades 3–8; Focus: Thai village life

The Chichi Hoohoo Bogeyman (Virginia Driving Hawk Sneve), for grades 4–9; Focus: Sioux legends and life

Wingman (Manus Pinkwater), for grades 2–6; Focus: AmerIndian children

Sod-House Winter (Clara I. Judson), for grades 5–8; Focus: Swedish immigrants in the 1800s

Black Folktales (Julius Lester), for all grades; Focus: African and Afro-American folktales

Cultures in Conflict: Problems of the Mexican American (Rudy Acunna), for grades 5–8; Focus: Mexican-Americans

The Sea of Gold and Other Tales of Japan (Yoshiko Uchida), for all grades; Focus: Japanese folktales

Hawaii, the Aloha State (Helen Bauer), for grades 5–8; Focus: Hawaiian history

Once I Was A Plum Tree (Johanna Hurwitz), for grades 4–8; Focus: Jewish-American identity

These books have all been recommended by Professor James Banks, an authority on ethnic studies, or by the Council on Interracial Books for Children as being nonracist, nonstereotyped, constructive, and well-written reading matter. As the council stresses in its publications, native authorship or the use of a specific cultural background does not guarantee the value of a book, so each must be evaluated for the information and illustrations it includes, its biases, and what it omits.

local government agencies, so that all parties have the opportunity to interact in positive ways.

In recent years, there have been increasing demands for ethnic studies in the curriculum. There has been a movement away from more extreme programs (such as holding classes in Black history every Friday after lunch) to a more integrated, multicultural curriculum in many schools. This approach, which is generally more effective than isolated experiences with ethnicity, utilizes literature by non-Western authors in readers, comparative studies of myths and legends in two or more cultures, the history of different groups of people as it fits into the time period or geographical area being studied, and common and unique social problems of different peoples. Projects, field trips, and films can enhance such studies.

Music, art, and physical education offer ample opportunities to integrate diverse cultural patterns into school life. Songs and crafts usually reflect cultural histories, values, materials, and life-styles, thus providing additional bases for multicultural studies. Through concerts, art exhibits, and dance performances, the entire community can gain an appreciation of the ways in which people from a variety of cultural backgrounds traditionally express their emotions and view events significant to them. While cultural differences and similarities are being pointed out, whether in the classroom or on stage, there should never be an implication that minority ways are "quaint" or somehow inferior to any other group's ways. Care should be taken also that the different cultures are seen in context—that is, in terms of their economic life (agricultural or industrial), access to other cultures, political structure, legends, and so on.

Respect for cultural differences and the teaching of an intellectually honest multicultural curriculum must permeate the classroom walls on a daily basis if self-concept is to be enhanced and motivation for learning increased. These practices, if effected in the elementary grades, can have positive results at the most malleable stage of the child's school life. It is also in these years that there is the last real opportunity to modify children's attitudes toward peoples of a variety of backgrounds. Ethnic studies first introduced at the ninth-grade level or above suffer from being "too little too late." (Schwartz & Isser, 1978, p. 189)

Future Planning

Much of the attention paid to culturally different students has been focused on their dropout rate. If we believe that it is important to educate all individuals to their fullest potential, this rate must be reduced. Students stay in school only when they believe that this choice holds positive consequences for them and that, when continued, education is the most desirable option open to them. What is learned in the classroom must be coordinated with the student's life and aspirations and with an eye to reality. If a student is capable of college-level studies, she should be made aware of this, given appropriate counseling, and encouraged to follow this path. Less academically capable students should be encouraged to learn a skilled trade or marketable skills. (Adolescents from cultural minority groups should *not*, however, be routinely placed in vocational schools. Are all middle-class whites equally successful in college?)

Visits to high schools by minority group members who have "made it" in the larger society serve as a vivid example of the fact that one need not always be among the poor or powerless. Successful group members in the community might also be willing to serve as mentors for students thinking of jobs in the business world or professions. Bolstering pride in the ethnic group through these and similar programs can also raise the level of student aspirations.

Studies of the career aspirations and expectations of students in different ethnic groups are frequently contradictory in their findings, contrary to popular opinion. The differences found among Puerto Rican, Anglo, and Black students, for example, suggest that although they may have varying aspirations, their career expectations are more closely related to socioeconomic status than to ethnic identification (Dillard & Perrin, 1980). Among Chicana high school seniors, socioeconomic status was also found to be one of three factors discriminating between those who are college-bound and those who are not (Buriel & Saenz, 1980). (The other two factors were degree of "masculinity" and extent of bicultural orientation.) As noted in the latter study, the traditional role of females in a given cultural group may preclude high school graduation, let alone any aspirations that would take a young woman out of the traditional role of wife and mother. Counselors need to keep this in mind when advising these female students on future plans.

According to 1980 census data, educational levels among members of minority groups have improved considerably since 1960 and earlier decades. For the first time, more than half (50.6 percent) of the Black population aged twenty-five years and older were high school graduates. This was in comparison with 20 percent in the 1960 census and 33.3 percent in 1970. Among Asian Americans, 74 percent of this age group were high school graduates, and so were 43 percent of Hispanic Americans (Herbers, 1982). However, there is great variation from one state to another in educational level, both for minorities and the population as a whole, due to differences in educational opportunities.

Children of migrant workers present a special problem in terms of planning for the future. They tend to lose time from the classroom, both because they move about so much and because they often work in the fields to help increase the family's income, even during the school year. Despite attempts to keep track of their academic standing through a computerized network, the lost school time tends to reduce their motivation and achievement. Lacking roots and identification with peers in a single stable community, they do not have much opportunity to interact with those who might have career goals other than being low-paid agricultural workers. School counselors, frequently overloaded with students to advise, may not place a high priority on guiding these migrant students. A possible alternative to this barrier might be a program of itinerant counselors who would visit the migrant labor camps on a regular basis, working with the parents and young people to point out the potential value of continued education to the student and the family.

Whether a student leaves school before high school graduation or continues on to postsecondary education, he must be prepared to function effectively in both his group of origin and the larger society. Whenever he concludes his formal education, it should be with a sense of having profited from the years of school attendance. He should have some marketable skills and problem-solving abilities, as well as the information considered to be appropriate for good citizenship. And he should have the self-esteem that comes from social acceptance of his cultural diversity.

SUMMARY

There is some question as to whether money alone will reduce the educational problems of cultural minority students. Can new paint and carpets reduce the rate of failure? Can new textbooks change the fact that a child's background is perceived as inferior by teachers and peers? Can higher salaries for teachers alter their attitudes toward cultural minorities?

The primary need for minority students is a new orientation in education. Education, as an institution, has long regarded children in much the same way as some psychiatrists regard their patients: namely, that the patient's problem should be fitted to the therapeutic technique. We should, as educators, be more like the tailor, cutting the cloth and fitting the garment to the wearer. Much of this tailoring has to be done in the area of building students' self-esteem, which will in turn increase their motivation, learning, and aspirations.

The appropriate integration of multicultural content into the curriculum is seen as an effective mechanism for raising self-esteem, motivation, and interest in learning among cultural minority students. It is also a means of increasing awareness and respect in nonminority students, who must also live in a culturally pluralistic society. We can no longer expect automatic assimilation, nor can we impose a single set of values on all students. We can, however, provide information about different life-styles and options and make it possible for students to grow into adults who are at home both in their cultural group and in the larger society. We can make it possible for all students to leave school sharing a common pool of information and greater mutual respect.

SUGGESTED ADDITIONAL READINGS

Banks, J. A. *Teaching strategies for ethnic studies*. Boston: Allyn & Bacon, 1975.

Cheyney, A. B. *Teaching children of different cultures in the classroom: A language approach*. Columbus, Ohio: Charles E. Merrill, 1976.

Chinn, P. Curriculum development for culturally different exceptional children. *Teacher Education and Special Education*, 1979, *2* (4), 49–58.

Clifton, R. A. Ethnicity, teachers' expectations, and the academic achievement process in Canada. *Sociology of Education*, 1981, *54*, 291–301.

Council on Interracial Books for Children. *Human—and anti-human—values in children's books: A content rating instrument for educators and concerned parents*. New York: Racism and Sexism Resource Center for Educators, 1976.

Drury, D. W. Black self-esteem and desegregated schools. *Sociology of Education*, 1980, *53*, 88–103.

Fair, G. W., and Sullivan, A. R. Career opportunities for culturally diverse handicapped youth. *Exceptional Children*, 1980, *46*, 626–631.

Jensen, G. F., White, C. S., and Galliher, J. M. Ethnic status and adolescent self-esteem: An extension of research on minority self-esteem. *Social Problems*, 1982, *30*, 226–239.

Jones, M. L., Ed. *Mainstreaming and the minority child*. Reston, Va.: Council for Exceptional Children, 1976.

Larry P. v. Riles. Civil Action No. C-71-2270, 343 F.Supp. 1306 (N.D. Cal., 1972).

Maehr, M. L., and Stallings, W. M. *Culture, child, and school: Sociocultural influences on learning*. Monterey, Calif.: Brooks/Cole, 1975.

McShane, D. A., and Plas, J. M. Wechsler Scale performance patterns of American Indian children. *Psychology in the Schools*, 1982, *19*, 8–17.

Nurcombe, B. *Children of the dispossessed*. Honolulu: University Press of Hawaii (East-West Center), 1976.

Perry, J. The ECS Interstate Migrant Education Project. *Exceptional Children*, 1982, *48*, 496–500.

Richardson, E. A. *Islamic cultures in North America*. New York: The Pilgrim Press, 1981.

PART FIVE/
PSYCHOSOCIALLY
TROUBLED STUDENTS

*I*f a student is troubled and anxious, it is very difficult for him to learn. If a youngster is in trouble
with society, she may not be given an opportunity to
learn, or at least not to learn socially acceptable ideas
and skills. The education of psychosocially troubled
children and youth involves both reducing emotional
problems and/or inappropriate behavior and making
learning a palatable and positive experience. If both
goals are reached, the student will function more
successfully in and out of school.

The emotionally troubled student tends to have
problems in expressing or managing his feelings,
thereby creating difficulties for himself and others.
The socially maladjusted youth, who may also have
emotional problems, tends to have difficulties more
related to society and its laws. Both types of youngsters are found in the schools in greater profusion
than statistics indicate, for many cases are unre-
ported. This suggests that regular classroom teachers
should be better prepared to handle the emotional

and behavioral crises of all their pupils, and not only those who have been assigned "labels."

The teacher is not the only person involved with these learners, however. Psychologists and psychiatrists try to reduce their problems to a manageable level and to increase their ability to cope with the ones that are insolvable; social workers frequently intervene in the family situation to try to alleviate stresses there; and other persons (such as probation officers and art or occupational therapists) are called upon as needed. Ideally, all of these professionals, including teachers, should coordinate their efforts to provide the best possible educational opportunities for students with psychosocial problems. It is essential to their success that youngsters classified as psychosocially different be regarded not as problem children but as children who have problems. It is from this perspective that the next two chapters are presented.

CHAPTER 13/
THE EMOTIONALLY
TROUBLED

Whether one uses the term *emotionally disturbed*, *emotionally handicapped*, or *emotionally troubled*, the group being discussed here has emotional problems that interfere with learning. Not all of these students need or are entitled to special education under P.L. 94-142, but almost all of them need special attention of one kind or another from their teachers. How can one characterize such a group, however, when frequently the problem, like beauty, lies in the eye of the beholder? What one teacher or principal or parent perceives as emotional disturbance may be regarded by another as normal behavior or mere excess of energy, shyness, or exuberance. A longitudinal study of almost sixteen hundred elementary school students, typical of the general population, confirms this observation (Rubin & Balow, 1978). There is some truth to Rubin and Balow's assertion that "while emotional disturbance may not be synonymous with behavior problems, the functional definition of emotional disturbance in schools is most commonly that the pupil has been disruptive and disturbing—in short, a behavior problem" (1978, p. 109). This should alert educators and others to question the validity of statistics involving the emotionally troubled.

THEORETICAL MODELS

The causes of emotional problems are many and varied. At one end of the spectrum are persons with mental health problems that *may* have a physical basis. It is thought, for example, that schizophrenia, a mental illness, may be the result of a biochemical imbalance that predisposes the individual to that condition (plus an environment that nourishes the imbalance). At the other end are difficulties resulting principally from the student's environment—death or divorce of parents, abuse by parents, inadequate or ineffective parenting, poor peer relationships, or inadequate rest or diet.

There are several theoretical models that seek to explain emotional problems. The medical, biophysical, and sociological models are exemplified in the previous paragraph. Another model, the behavioral or psychological, focuses on the individual's behavior (the symptoms) and treats them rather than trying to dig out their underlying causes, as one would do in the medical model. A fifth model is concerned with the interaction between the child and her environment. In this ecological model, disturbances are frequently seen as the result of "a lack of mutual adaptation between child and setting or an inconsistency of expectations across settings" (Swap, Prieto, & Harth, 1982, p. 74).

As you read this chapter and the next one, try to fit the types of problems described to one of the models. Where does school phobia fit? Or depression? Does a particular emotional problem cut across two or more theoretical models?

With some youngsters, the fact that they are deeply troubled will be quickly apparent to even the casual observer. If you see a child with a vacant stare, hugging himself and rocking on his heels in the corner of the room, you would certainly suspect that he is troubled. If you see a student constantly fighting with other students, you would at least wonder why she feels the need to be physically aggressive so often. If a student's classroom behavior or grades change suddenly in a negative direction, you would surely question the reason for the change. In other cases, however, the disturbed or disturbing behavior is not so obvious and needs a sensitive observer to detect it.

WHO ARE THE EMOTIONALLY TROUBLED?

Those with Personality Disorders

People with personality disorders are frequently out of touch with reality. That is, their behavior is so strange as to be considered bizarre, or they respond with apparent inconsistency or incongruity to events and situations.

Autistic Children   If a child seems to daydream a great deal, living in a world of her own even when spoken to directly, it may be because the real world is so unpleasant and painful to her that she finds comfort only in a fantasy world. Children who live entirely in a world of their own making, who either refuse to communicate at all or use their own idiom as language, and who exhibit bizarre language and gestures (twirling their hands by the hour) are diagnosed as **autistic**. They seem to have rejected the real world completely.

Many psychologists and psychiatrists believe that autistic behavior is caused by a combination of genetic and experiential factors. The condition often becomes evident before nursery school age when the child does not respond to parents' verbal or physical approaches, has no speech or is echolalic (repeating verbatim what is said to him), rocks interminably,

What is troubling this girl? Is she fearful because of "misbehavior" or because she suddenly found herself alone? Is she hostile or autistic? (Photo by Elizabeth Crews)

appears to look through people, and indulges in making meaningless repetitive gestures and/or sounds. After ruling out hearing, vision, and intellectual deficiencies as the cause of such behavior, the parents are left with a diagnosis of autism and recommendations for the child's institutionalization or intensive special education. Autistic children are not commonly found in the public schools unless there is a special class for them. Unfortunately, there is little hope that most autistic children will ever function well enough to be considered "normal."

Schizophrenics Schizophrenic students are found in the schools, however. These young people may be characterized by an absence of emotional responses or inappropriate ones, excessive daydreaming that may include living in a fantasy world rather than the real one, delusions of one kind or another, or some combination of these. Of the most severely disturbed, some are violently aggressive, while others are completely withdrawn; some are mute (by choice, as part of their illness) and others speak in a garbled fashion known as "schizophrenic word salad" (a meaningless jumble of words). In one published case, a boy thought of himself as a machine, a mechanical boy (Bettelheim, 1967).

A behavior common to both autistic and schizophrenic children, but neither characteristic of all of them nor limited to these conditions, is elective mutism. Kolvin and Fundudis suggest that this psychological condition appears in children who have had normal speech development and then become unusually shy outside the immediate family group. The onset of the condition, in their experience, is between the ages of five and seven, or about the time of entrance to school (1981).

These mute youngsters tend to be bed wetters or soilers, to have a high rate of speech abnormalities and developmental immaturity, to have been shy as very young children, and to be sulky with strangers but stubbornly aggressive at home.

Although one might expect elective mutes to be more withdrawn with adults, Kolvin and Fundudis found that they tend to withdraw more from their peers. This behavior may be learned from a parent with a personality abnormality (at least 42 percent of the subjects had one such parent).

Mute children have nonverbal intelligence scores that range from the retarded to the average level. They do not speak at all in school (unlike other schizophrenic children), which certainly poses problems for the teacher. When reexamined five to ten years later, more than half the subjects were still mute, despite treatment.

Depressed Children   Mild to severe depression is seen in some students, most of whom can be found in regular schools. This depression, however, is not the temporary one of a student who has just failed an exam or a course; rather (as in the case of most of those classified as emotionally troubled), it is chronic and inappropriate. In more severe cases, the youngster is virtually unable to do anything because he feels hopeless and helpless. In mild cases, the child may occasionally show a spark of interest or enthusiasm but quickly relapses into lethargy and what seems to be a permanent downcast appearance.

Depression often masks feelings of anxiety or anger: anxiety about possible failure to meet expectations; anger at an inability to cope with a situation that threatens the individual in some way. A sense of powerlessness, experienced by overdominated youngsters as well as the poor and culturally different, can also lead to depression (Charnofsky, 1971). This may also be seen in children (and adults) who "learn from repeated experience that, no matter how hard they try, they are helpless and overwhelmed by life, and consequently are chronically depressed" (Highland, 1979, p. 581). Such learned helplessness increases the dependence of students on teachers or on anyone else who will help them cope with even a mild threat to their academic performance.

Suicidal Students   At the extreme of depression and other personality disorders are the suicidal students. Suicide is among the top five causes of adolescent deaths in the United States and is attempted in thousands of other cases. The adolescent who attempts suicide may do so for a number of reasons, some of which a careful observer may be able to detect early enough to provide intervention:

1. Feelings of worthlessness, negative self-esteem
2. Feelings of being rejected by parents, peers, or others
3. "Doing his/her own thing"—rejection of others
4. Homosexuality—guilt, panic, inability to find a comfortable sexual identity
5. Fascination with death—as an adventure, a chance for rebirth (as a "better person"), or the ultimate answer to the existential questions of youth
6. Bid for attention—sometimes combined with expressions of anger, such as "Now you'll have to notice me!" and "You'll be sorry when I'm gone"
7. Feelings of hopelessness (Rabkin, 1978)

Teachers may be able to spot preoccupations with death or hopelessness in a student's writings or artwork, or to observe her isolation or withdrawal from peers, and try to talk to the student directly or refer her to a counselor in the school or community. There are so many suicide attempts among adolescents that D. F. Smith recommends including the theory and study of suicide in teacher education programs. His goal is to sensitize educators to the signals given by, and possible on-the-spot counseling techniques for dealing with, potentially suicidal students (1976).

Anorexics and Bulimorexics   Somewhat related to both depression and suicide, yet technically a physical disorder rather than one of personality, anorexia nervosa is a condition seen mostly in female adolescents and young women. Anorexics are not only painfully thin but are morbidly afraid of gaining even an ounce. As a result, they resist eating even when hungry. The severe weight loss affects their physiological functioning (marked by cessation of menstrual periods, lowered body temperature, and physical weakness that is sometimes combined with hyperactivity) and intellectual functioning (marked by preoccupation with weight loss and consequent inability to concentrate on studies, depression, and even withdrawal from school).

FOR EXAMPLE . . .

I throw myself more vigorously into dieting. My weight has dropped to 105, and my latest scheme is the yogurt lunch. Each morning I mix up a different flavor. Plain yogurt has many fewer calories than the fruit brands, so I experiment using saccharine, extracts, and fresh or water-packed fruits to make my own dietetic variations. I convince myself that they taste delicious. At lunch my classmates laugh at me for my eccentric eating habits. It takes me nearly half an hour to eat a cup of yogurt while, during the same period, the others plow through platefuls of spaghetti and salad, chocolate cake and milk. I lick my spoon at each miniscule bite and, reaching the bottom of the container, insist that I feel full. It is worth it. It wins me notoriety. I'm becoming famous around school for my display of self-discipline. My audience stands in awe of me, and I love it. Here's my chance to surpass Kimmy, my way of earning social stature. In this one respect, I'm the best, but if I let it go, all is lost, and so I cling to my diet tenaciously.

There are other desirable side effects as well that help me remain faithful. My periods have stopped! I don't suppose the reprieve will last forever, but for the moment it delights me. And the more weight I lose, the flatter I become. It's wonderful, like crawling back into the body of a child. I have more energy than ever, can walk for miles, skip rope for hours. Unfortunately, there are also a few negatives to the process. I'm nearly always cold. My hands and feet especially turn icy and blue. I bruise very easily, and cuts and sores take months to heal. But these aren't such terrible sacrifices to make. I never get sick. I feel fine.

Liu, A. *Solitaire*. New York: Harper & Row, 1979, pp. 40–41. Reprinted by permission.

Bulimorexia or *bulimia*, a condition that takes the form of cyclical eating binges alternated with purging via self-induced vomiting or use of strong laxatives (and also indulged in by Miss Liu), is closely related to anorexia nervosa. Both are emotionally based perversions of normal eating habits and have similar outcomes. Because the anorexic or bulimic patient can go down to a weight of seventy pounds at an age when she should weigh a hundred and ten or more, the condition can be fatal. Physical education teachers might be among the first to observe a girl's unusual gauntness and call it to the attention of the school nurse or counselor, thus intervening before it is too late. Hospitalization is often required to avert possible death, which means that there will be an interruption (both physical and as part of the therapy) to the student's education.

Those with Behavioral Disorders

Those Who "Act Out"   Emotionally troubled youngsters may express their difficulties in several ways, some self-destructively (as in the cases just described) and some by turning against others. Take, for example, students who are hostile to everyone and everything. Perhaps they learned distrust rather than trust in infancy, were rejected or mistreated by their families in their early years, had negative experiences with authority figures, or simply imitated someone who seemed to accomplish a great deal by being negative in attitude and behavior. These students snarl and growl responses to questions, take a defiant "try me" attitude, reject friendly overtures, and may be physically aggressive or destructive as well—they *act out* their negative feelings.

Sometimes hostility is a defense against anxiety over whether the student will be accepted by others; in other instances, the negativism is genuine. When the wall of hostility does reduce acceptance, the hostile youngster becomes more negative, using the rejection as justification for her increased unpleasantness. The youngster who limits her hostility to verbal behavior can be unpleasant to be around, but she is mostly self-defeating. If she acts it out physically, however, she hurts others and thus becomes a threat to their emotional and physical health as well as her own.

Many children act out their problems in less serious ways. Finding it difficult to control their own feelings, they may indulge in temper tantrums, excessive crying, or other immature and excessive behavior. In some cases, they have never learned more mature and acceptable responses to frustration or anxiety, while in other instances they have learned that such behavior is a very effective means of getting what they want. Although lack of self-control initially poses problems for teachers and may warrant some supportive services by counselors or resource teachers, there are techniques by which such behavior can be changed, with the cooperation of the child's parents. Often the disturbing behavior is a bid for the teacher's attention, especially one who rarely reinforces the student's desirable behavior. Such attention-seeking behavior may also reflect an attempt to be noticed, if not accepted, by classmates.

Tracking the frequency of undesirable behavior is the first step in altering and controlling it. Figure 13.1 illustrates what can happen with an acting-out kindergartener. This particular nonconformist child rode tricycles when it was time to sing, sang when it was time to draw, and generally bothered both the teacher and his peers. Advised by the school psychologist that she was being manipulated by the child, the teacher kept a record for a week of his acceptable and nonconformist behavior (as well as her own responses to the latter, which were usually to give the boy attention). In the second week, the teacher stopped responding to

A youngster who has feelings of anxiety about peer acceptance or academic success may try to hide these feelings by acting as the "class clown." Perhaps funny at first, this form of acting out soon interferes with everyone's learning. They are aptly described as leaving behind a trail "reminiscent of the fallout from a Keystone Kops chase. They ignore rules, bang up against things, rarely do what anyone expects, and attract attention with their unkempt ways. . . . [They] use foolishness for frustrating and even gaining advantage over others. . . . They devise games with rules that seem to have been formulated by a Mad Hatter" (Fisher & Fisher, 1980, p. 64).

Such excessive bids for teacher and/or peer attention are inappropriate classroom behavior and call for intervention, though not generally for special classes (unless the behavior is so continuous that the class cannot proceed).

misbehavior unless it was threatening and concentrated on reinforcing acceptable behavior. The results are shown graphically for days six through ten.

"Inconsequential Children"　　Also among the children who have difficulty with self-control are those called "inconsequential children" by some of our British colleagues. These are the youngsters who act on impulse without regard for the consequences. A simple example is that of the youngster who chases a ball into the street, heedless of oncoming traffic. In the classroom, they may start an assignment before hearing all the directions, then tear up the paper when frustrated; they may strike out physically, despite rules against fighting that have severe penalties attached, or impulsively mix chemicals without thought for the possible incendiary or explosive consequences. Because they lack impulse control, these "inconsequential children" need special attention so that they can learn alternate, or more appropriate, ways of behaving.

"Model Children"　　There are emotionally troubled youngsters who, rather than disturb others or act self-destructively, are often perceived by teachers and parents as "model children." The model child sits quietly, does as she is told, never talks when she's not supposed to, and may be regarded as "a little shy, but so well behaved." The timidity and docile behavior may mask general anxiety, fear or feelings of rejection, a sense of

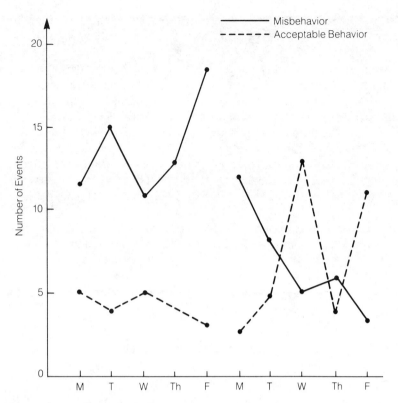

**Figure 13.1   Effects of behavior modification on classroom
behavior**

never doing the "right thing," or excessive feelings of guilt for real or
imagined actions. Rarely requiring special education, this youngster may
nonetheless need emotional support from the school counselor to help
develop more maturity, including the ability to act autonomously.

School "Phobics"   Students who hold themselves in low esteem are
also emotionally troubled, even if their self-perceptions are inaccurate.
The child who suffers chronic frustration at being a "low person" in
comparison with his classmates, or who is left out of group activities, may
be en route to *school phobia*. Frequent absences without legitimate cause,
frequent early morning or in-school headaches or stomach upsets, and
frequent requests for adjustment in school programs are all signals of
emotional problems that are at least partially related to school. The child
suffering from school phobia, who often exhibits these types of behavior,
may have separation anxiety related to a home situation (overdependence
on parents, a new baby in the family, death, divorce) or may be attempting

to withdraw from a classroom situation that he perceives as threatening (inappropriate class placement, an overdemanding teacher). The solution to a case of school phobia can be as varied as the causes of the condition.

Those Who Are Victims

Having parents who expect perfection from their children may contribute to anorexia; having alcoholic parents may lead to aggressiveness and/or alcoholism; other less than ideal family situations may lead to one or another of the behavior or personality disorders already described. In two other types of emotional problems, the child is literally the innocent victim of parental problems. These are the battered children and the children of divorced parents. In both cases, what happens at home can have very negative effects on what the child learns at school.

Victims of Child Abuse   Battered children may suffer from multiple broken limbs, burns, sexual abuse, and/or psychological abuse. They tend to hide their injuries (wearing long-sleeved clothing in warm weather, for instance) for fear that they will be separated from their parents, hurtful though they are, or that there will be repercussions at home if the school questions the parents (Schmitt, 1975). They may shrink away from any physical contact with an authority figure or possibly treat their peers and younger children as they have been raised at home. Some abused children become rigid and withdrawn, fearful of attracting attention, while others can barely focus on their schoolwork because of the physical or emotional pain they are experiencing. The age-inappropriate behavior they display may require some special handling in school, although they may not qualify for services under P.L. 94-142.

The teacher, counselor, school nurse, or principal who suspects a case of child abuse is advised to be certain of the facts before seeking police or welfare agency intervention. It is a legal obligation, however, in many states, to report suspected instances of child abuse to the local authorities, and school personnel should be aware of whether this is true in their district or state. Although prevention of further abuse is the aim of reporting such suspicions, it is difficult to remove a child from his parents' custody even under these circumstances. Historically and legally, parents have been entitled by judicially upheld "traditional family rights" to raise their children as they see fit, including using discipline techniques of their choice (although in some communities, abused children *are* being placed in foster home for their own protection). Physically or psychologically battered children, however, are victims of their parents' inability to exercise self-control and to respond appropriately to their children's behavior, whether it is "normal" or not. It is the responsibility of school

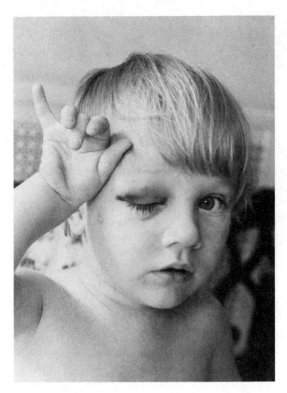

Abused children are frequently the victims of parents who were also abused as children. (James R. Holland/Stock, Boston)

personnel to do what they can for the abused child, both in school and, if necessary, at a hospital.

Children of Divorced Parents   Children whose parents are divorced may exhibit similar behavior that interferes with their learning because of an erroneous belief that they are the cause of the divorce, because they feel like a pawn in the divorce action, because they are unhappy with the custody and visitation arrangements, or because they are torn by the "loyalty dilemma" when forced to choose one parent over the other. Withdrawal, anxiety, and depression are common initial reactions when a youngster becomes aware of an impending divorce or just after it occurs. There are fears of parental rejection or abandonment, sometimes accompanied by denials of this threat. There is some variation, according to developmental level and the degree of anger and violence that preceded the parents' decision. Children and adolescents alike, however, initially become aware of their vulnerability in the situation, experience a rise in aggression, and worry about both their parents' and their own future welfare (Wallerstein & Kelly, 1980).

Wallerstein and Kelly followed one sample of children of divorced parents over a five-year period. A year after the divorce, the youngsters had adjusted somewhat to the situation, but many were still depressed and/or angry, and a sizable number exhibited manipulative behavior with their classmates and/or teachers. Those who were depressed tended to become underachievers at school. After five years, Wallerstein and Kelly found that the majority of their subjects had adjusted and were functioning academically as well as they had before the family was split. However, many of the 40 percent who were not doing well in school continued to be preoccupied with the divorce in one way or another (1980).

All emotionally disturbed students can obviously be a challenge to a teacher's patience and understanding. However, almost all of them can be helped to reduce their problems so that, instead of being emotionally (and therefore educationally) handicapped, they can function more appropriately and effectively in learning and other situations. Even in this time of tight school budgets, someone in the school needs to be available to intervene in a crisis, to support the classroom teacher's efforts, and to provide short- or long-term assistance to emotionally troubled students. The ways in which these steps can be put into operation are discussed in the next section.

EDUCATIONAL MODIFICATIONS

One of my professors used to say that "normal" persons exhibit adaptive, adequate, and appropriate behavior and are neither a threat, a nuisance, nor a liability to themselves or others. If we accept this definition, few of us are normal on all occasions throughout our lives. Emotionally troubled students, however, behave less normally too often. With them, therefore, we must work toward greater adequacy, adaptiveness, and appropriate behavior, by helping them put problem situations into perspective, understand reasons for their own and others' behavior, and acquire coping skills with which to handle threatening situations. Those emotionally troubled youngsters who begin to build up feelings of incompetence and nonacceptance during the elementary school years often progress at slower and slower rates until they give up and leave school physically, as well as emotionally, during adolescence. For this reason alone, teacher intervention and educational modifications are needed promptly, as soon as the problems become apparent.

Placement

The nature of modifications in education for emotionally troubled youngsters varies with the seriousness of their problems and the availability of special resources. In a large school district or through the pooled efforts of several small districts, there are usually a few classes for these students at both the elementary and secondary levels. In less populated and/or less affluent communities, the severely or moderately troubled child either may not be allowed to remain in the public schools (in which case the district would still have to pay for his schooling under P.L. 94-142) or may be placed in a catchall special education class that includes, among others, retarded and learning disabled students. Neither of these alternatives is satisfactory.

School placement must be based on student needs, not administrative convenience. In keeping with the mandate of P.L. 94-142 to place the exceptional student in the least restrictive environment, every possibility must be examined as to the appropriateness of the placement. For the most severely troubled, such as autistic or schizophrenic youths, residential placement is frequently necessary and most appropriate, with classes usually held within the institution.

More frequently, the emotionally troubled are placed in special classes. These usually have eight to twelve children at the elementary level and ten to fifteen students at the secondary level (the class size being set by each state's education code). The teacher is skilled both in working with troubled children and in remedial techniques, for often these students have fallen behind in their studies. As the child exhibits more appropriate behavior, her program can be adjusted so that she takes academic subjects under the special teacher and less ego-threatening activities with a regular class. The Madison Plan, suggested for children with learning disabilities, is also appropriate for the student with emotional problems (Blum, 1971).

At an even less restrictive level is the resource or crisis room. Here a special teacher helps youngsters to cope with their problem of the moment. The crisis room teacher may even work on academic assignments for a few hours or days with a youngster, until he has calmed down. The crisis teacher, if qualified, may also lead small groups of troubled students in counseling sessions.

The least restrictive environment is full mainstreaming, combined with a few special techniques on the part of the classroom teacher and support as needed from a resource teacher or counselor. This is entirely appropriate for the youngster with a mild chronic problem or behavior problems brought on by a family crisis. The classroom teacher may well find that a "time-out" room is all that is needed to control disruptive behavior. The time-out room is used when a student cannot control her impulses. This is not a punitive measure (in the sense that teachers years ago told a child to "go stand in the closet because you've been naughty"); rather, it puts the responsibility on the child to pull herself together. The time-out room usually has a chair and a light but is otherwise bare. The student takes nothing into the room. The first few times, it may take an hour or more for the youngster to calm down, but gradually she learns to come around in a matter of minutes and return to the work area as if nothing has happened. Nothing *has* happened, except that she has come to terms with herself and others. Most children learn that having something to do, even assignments, is more desirable than twiddling their thumbs in a bare room. For a few children, though, the time-out room is neither a successful nor a constructive alternative to other forms of special education.

Placing the youngster in a one-to-one situation is another alternative, but the disadvantage is that it may become an effective reinforcement for undesirable attention-getting behavior: The sole attention of the teacher may be just what the child wants. On the other hand, some children feel threatened by the presence of other children from time to time, and the one-to-one setting may be just what they need. Deciding which is the case in a specific instance is the teacher's delicate task.

Classroom Adjustments

Since psychotherapy is necessary for many troubled youngsters, scheduling adjustments may have to be made to allow for such sessions. The therapist and the teacher should be in contact with each other on a regular basis, exchanging nonconfidential information on the student's behavior and progress or changes in treatment. It is important that they not have conflicting goals, as can occur when the therapist does not want the child to experience frustration and the teacher is trying to have him reach for higher goals at the same time.

Teaching a child to handle frustration in constructive ways is basic to her learning. Emphasis should be placed on successes, no matter how small, and calm guidance should be given in correcting errors. The youngster needs to learn that she can be accepted even if her performance is less than perfect. She also needs to learn that she can benefit more from making an effort than she can from constantly withdrawing from activities to avoid the pain of failure. She must also acquire the ability to be patient, accepting the fact that the teacher cannot respond to her instantly every time she wants attention. Tolerance for frustration tends to develop slowly. As it gradually develops, positive reinforcement should be given for this increasingly appropriate behavior.

Behavior modification techniques have often been employed to encourage the emotionally troubled youngster to reduce strange or acting-out behavior and to conform more to the expectations of the real world. This not only means breaking down tasks into small steps, or ignoring undesired behavior and reinforcing desired behavior, but also setting up criterion levels of success and perhaps developing a "menu" of behavior patterns and reinforcers.

FOR EXAMPLE . . .

A "menu" lists desired behaviors, the number of points they earn, and the price in points that reinforcers or rewards "cost." Each menu has to be tailored to a specific child's behaviors and preferences if it is to be effective.

Behavior	Points	Reinforcement	Price
Sitting in seat for fifteen minutes	3	Ten minutes of puzzle time	5
Appropriate verbal response	10	Candy bar	3
Completing one workbook page	5	Drawing time	7
Not interrupting teacher for one hour	4	Use of tape recorder	10
Not fighting all day	10	Doing nothing for five minutes	10
Singing with class	3	Being teacher's helper	8
		New crayons	4

More points are awarded for behavior that is more difficult for the child to accomplish, and it costs more points to earn the really preferred "goodies" on the menu. Alterations can be made in expectations and their point values, as well as in the rewards and their prices, as the student's level of accomplishments rises or his interests change. (Even children tire of too much candy after a while!)

Teaching Adjustments

Communication is always a matter of primary concern. If the autistic child ignores the teacher, obviously little learning will take place. The first goal when working with autistic and other very withdrawn youngsters is to get them to attend to another person, and then to respond to that person. With autistic children, the progress may be painfully slow. Through very patient one-on-one efforts, Lovaas, Berberich, Perloff, and Schaeffer were able to use behavior modification to breach the walls with which these children surround themselves (1966). Nordoff and Robbins reported success in breaking through the barriers of autism with percussion instruments, rhythms, and special songs. As the child moved from unstable and disordered drum beating, for example, to a variety of ordered rhythms and singing, the authors found they could observe some connection between the changing musical self-portrait and the child's personality and problems. These connections were then utilized in therapy sessions (1971). In other instances, music has been used to relax the angry and stimulate a withdrawn child. As behavior becomes more acceptable, the child may be integrated into music activities or classes as a first step into a less restrictive environment.

Art and dancelike movement therapy are also helpful in establishing communication and as observable measures of emotional change. When a hostile youngster begins to use color in artwork or to create less warlike drawings, this should be carried over to therapy and eventually to the classroom. Body awareness through movement therapy, like the music therapy described above, can be used to reduce rigidity or to create ordered patterns, according to the individual's requirements.

In the case of school phobic children, there is a need to reintroduce the youngsters to school gradually. Most therapists use what is called a "desensitization" procedure: having the child approach the school neighborhood, then the school building (without entering), then walking up to the front door, and so on until he is integrated once again into the normal school routine. At each step, the child is encouraged to face and conquer the anxiety that he feels (Gordon & Young, 1976). A variation of this technique involves training in social skills, with real-life rehearsals in a therapeutic (or at least a nonschool) setting (Falloon, Lloyd, & Harpin, 1981). Originally designed for people who experience anxiety in social and interpersonal encounters, the training and rehearsal technique can be adapted to the needs of school phobic students.

If the root of the problem is within the school (as, for example, with a very sarcastic or hostile teacher), there are two alternatives: transfer to another school or transfer to another teacher. It is true that we all have to learn how to cope with a variety of people, some of them unpleasant, but if the teacher-student relationship is wholly negative, attitudes toward learning and toward the self may be established that will be more destructive in the long run than the change in environment and its implied "giving in" to the youngster. The anxiety reduction process and any placement decisions should be worked out by the therapist, parents, and school personnel (and the child, if mature enough) on a mutually cooperative and supportive basis.

Assuming that a special class is available for those who need it, the teacher does have some practical concerns. Bill is twelve, reads at a primer level, and tends to throw things when frustrated. Suzy, also twelve, is so fearful of failure that she cannot write down an answer to a simple question, despite having once been an above average student, and virtually hides under the desk whenever someone speaks to her. Johnny speaks to no one but nevertheless radiates hostility toward everyone. Karla whimpers and constantly jiggles her feet. Ned does nothing but look off into the distance. Wilma tears up her work as soon as she completes it. Group instruction is obviously inappropriate, if not impossible, in this classroom.

However, forming individualized, written and signed contracts with the students has been found effective in this type of situation. Obviously the teacher has to have a private session with each of these threatened youngsters in order to develop such a contract. Whether the contract is for academic work or behavioral change, the youngster is not placed in competition with anyone else. The threat of failure is removed, because the assignment is one that he has agreed he can complete in a reasonable amount of time. As progress occurs, the difficulty level of the assignments and the amount of time for completion can both be changed. In addition to the individualized instruction implicit in this approach, there is less potential for viewing the teacher as an authoritarian figure and greater potential for building a positive relationship with an adult who cares.

With less severely troubled students, the contract plan can also be used to good effect. It allows the student to work at her own pace to a degree, to compete with herself rather than others, and to experience a feeling of success on reaching her goal. There should also be external reinforcement of such success (praise rather than candy being preferred).

There are many emotionally troubled children who are given prescription drugs in an effort to reduce their aggressive behavior and thus make them more acceptable to others. The teacher should be alerted as to what is being given, how often, and possible side effects. If he observes that a tranquilizer is causing a child to be sleepy most of the day, the child's parents should be informed, for a drowsy youth is no more receptive to instruction than an aggressive one (and, of course, the drug may be too powerful).

One other possibility for aggressive youngsters is a practice used by one principal when fights break out in the schoolyard. The fighters are brought to the bench commonly found in front of the principal's office. Instead of sitting there for a specific period of time, the fighters are told to sit and stand alternately a certain number of times in fairly rapid succession. This activity soon tires them, and there are few repeaters.

When work on academic skills is threatening but necessary, content can be incorporated into seemingly nonacademic, and therefore nonthreatening, learning situations. For example, math fundamentals and fractions are easily integrated into sewing, cooking, and industrial arts courses. Reading ability is also necessary, of course, in order to follow the directions; however, most students are capable of following simple instructions and gain not only a feeling of competence from making a product but progress in basic skills and considerable pride in their achievement. Instructions can be given in an informal, linear format, so that the learners immediately recognize the results of their efforts. Of course, in such courses, teachers need to be alert to the potential dangers of boiling water, knives, scissors, or carpentry tools, should one of the disturbed youngsters lose control of his behavior.

There are many youngsters who can work well with books but not with people. Library privileges should be extended to those capable of using books without destroying them. (In residential settings or those where there are many emotionally troubled students, bookshelves should be bolted to the floor, in case of explosive behavior.) Books that deal with emotional problems similar to those a particular student has should also be considered for use as part of her therapy. Knowing that the problem is not unique may help to reduce her anxiety.

One experienced teacher of very troubled students set two rules for her classroom: (1) No child could hurt anyone else, and (2) every child was expected to put forth his or her best effort (Newman, 1980). The experiences of other teachers point to other important elements in managing the emotionally troubled in the classroom:

1. Avoid power struggles.
2. Be consistent in words and action.
3. Never threaten what you won't or can't do.
4. Be attuned to seating arrangements, in relation to students and teachers as well as sources of distraction.
5. Use scheduling to offset hyperactivity and aggression—quiet, structured tasks alternating with gym, recess, or lunch.
6. Be alert to the conditions that precede explosive behavior. (The teacher or an aide can track a student's behavior for several days and perhaps also talk with him about what "sets him off.")
7. Communicate frequently with each student (and with the students' parents), orally and in writing, to remind them of goals, praise their accomplishments, and maintain progress at school and at home.

Support Systems

The first line of support ought to be the parents. With neglectful, abusive, or absent parents, this will, of course, be very difficult. If her parents undo every weekend, or every night, what the teacher has accomplished at school, the progress of the student will be minimal. If the parents are hostile toward schools and authority figures, there will also be little progress. (Such persistent negativism should not transfer to the teacher, however.) Cooperative parents, on the other hand, can reinforce the teacher's efforts. They, too, might institute a point system, with menus or contracts for behavior control, and tasks to be done at home.

A second line of support is found at school. In a number of high schools, for example, the school counselor and/or psychologist leads small group counseling sessions with disturbed adolescents. Here the youths can discuss common problems, release pent-up feelings, and exchange suggestions for handling various situations. Such situations have been effective with children of divorced parents, among others.

With younger children, there is a trend toward class meetings that are intended to be preventive rather than interventive. These follow Glasser's proposal that class meetings be used to discuss feelings and ideas without evaluative judgments (1971). Everyone sits in a circle, listening to and interacting with the others. As they become involved in sharing experiences and reducing tensions, the class members discover that although each child is unique, his problems often are not. A mutual airing of feelings, without fear of recrimination, helps the children to see themselves as others do and as they would like to see themselves. A child whose inappropriate behavior creates problems in the classroom may be asked by a classmate to evaluate her behavior. The question "Is what you are doing helping you?" can be asked by the teacher in a private conference. Led skillfully by a teacher trained in this approach, class meetings can help reduce comparatively minor disturbances.

Others in the support network may be special education personnel, the principal, a psychotherapist, the school or agency social worker, and perhaps an empathetic relative who has good rapport with the troubled student. Uniting in the common effort to alleviate emotional problems and to restructure the youth's environment, when possible, they may be able to help him achieve more appropriate means of coping so that he can profit from education.

SUMMARY

This chapter deals with students with a variety of emotional problems: from those who cannot cope with any frustrations to those who frustrate all efforts to help them, from the immature to the autistic, and from the elective mute to the class clown. The primary source of the problem may be biological, environmental, psychological, or ecological, and the child may be the principal actor in the situation or an innocent victim of others' actions; these factors must be considered with respect to their effect on learning and behavior in the school setting.

After describing the types of troubles experienced by students who suffer personality disorders, behavioral disorders, and victimization, the emphasis shifts to educational modifications. Alternate types of placement, specific teacher and curriculum adjustments, and support networks are discussed. Often some form of behavior modification is appropriate, since before the student can learn, she must be able to attend and respond to the instructor. If you can't "reach" the youth, you can't teach her, nor can you help her to deal more adaptively with her problems.

SUGGESTED ADDITIONAL READINGS

Berger, A. M. The child abusing family: II. Child and child-rearing variables, environmental factors and typologies of abusing families. *American Journal of Family Therapy*, 1980, *8*, 53–66.

Bonvillian, J. D., Nelson, E. E., and Rhyne, J. M. Sign language and autism. *Journal of Autism and Developmental Disorders*, 1981, *11* (1), 125–137.

Bruch, H. Island in the river: The anorexic adolescent in treatment. In S. C. Feinstein and P. L. Giovacchini (Eds.), *Adolescent Psychiatry* (Vol. 7). Chicago: University of Chicago Press, 1979, pp. 26–40.

Cochrane, C. T., and Myers, D. V. *Children in crisis: A time for caring, a time for change.* Beverly Hills: Sage, 1980.

D'Ambrosio, R. *No language but a cry.* New York: Doubleday, 1970.

Dunlap, G., Koegel, R. L., and Egel, A. L. Autistic children in school. *Exceptional Children*, 1979, *45*, 552–558.

Fleming, D. C., Ritchie, B., and Fleming, E. R. Fostering the social adjustment of disturbed students. *Teaching Exceptional Children*, 1983, *15*, 172–175.

Guyer, M. J. Child abuse and neglect statutes: Legal and clinical implications. *American Journal of Orthopsychiatry*, 1982, *52*, 73–81.

Halpern, W. I., and Kessel, S. *Human resources for troubled children.* New York: John Wiley, 1976.

Harris, S. L., and Milch, R. E. Training parents as behavior therapists for their autistic children. *Clinical Psychology Review*, 1981, *1* (1), 49–63.

Hoover, T. A rural program for emotionally handicapped students: Democracy in action. *Teaching Exceptional Children*, 1978, *10*, 30–32.

Howlin, P. A. The effectiveness of operant language training with autistic children. *Journal of Autism and Developmental Disorders*, 1981, *11* (1), 89–105.

Kalman, R. *Child abuse: Perspectives on diagnosis, treatment and prevention.* Dubuque: Kendall/Hunt, 1977.

Kinard, E. M. The psychological consequences of abuse for the child. *Journal of Social Issues*, 1979, *35* (2), 82–100.

Lidz, C. S. Emotional disturbance in preschool children. *Teaching Exceptional Children*, 1983, *15*, 164–167.

Liem, J. H. Family studies of schizophrenia: An update and commentary. *Schizophrenia 1980.* Washington, D.C.: U.S. Department of Health and Human Services (Alcohol, Drug Abuse, and Mental Health Administration), 1980, pp. 82–108.

McDowell, R. L., Adamson, G. W., and Wood, F. H. *Teaching emotionally disturbed children.* Boston: Little, Brown, 1982.

Pfeffer, C. R. Suicidal behavior of children. *Exceptional Children*, 1981, *48*, 170–172.

Pines, M. The civilizing of Genie. *Psychology Today*, 1981, *15* (9), 28–34.

Rhodes, W. C., and Tracy, M. L., Eds. *A study of child variance, Volume I: Conceptual models*. Ann Arbor, Mich.: Institute for the Study of Mental Retardation and Related Disabilities, 1972.

Vacc, N. A. Long term effects of special class intervention for emotionally disturbed children. *Exceptional Children*, 1972, *39*, 15–22.

Vardin, P. A., and Brody, I. N., Eds. *Children's rights: Contemporary perspectives*. New York: Teachers College Press, 1979.

Wallerstein, J. S. Children of divorce: The psychological tasks of the child. *American Journal of Orthopsychiatry*, 1983, *53*, 230–243.

CHAPTER 14/
THE SOCIALLY
MALADJUSTED

S ocially maladjusted students have characteristics in common with many other exceptional students. Intellectually, some are gifted, but more function academically at a retarded level. Physically, illnesses and/or disabilities may have contributed to their handicapped functioning in society. Culturally, they may share some of the problems of minority children, but the socially maladjusted are also found increasingly among middle-class suburban families. Psychosocially, they share many of the difficulties of the emotionally troubled—feelings of hostility, rejection, and unresolved anxiety—but their response to these difficulties is negative involvement with the laws and customs of our society. What all these students have in common is nonconforming behavior that interferes with their academic progress and social development.

ROOTS OF SOCIAL MALADJUSTMENT
Society

We live in a society often torn between what is preached and what is practiced, where justice frequently seems to differentiate among socio-economic or ethnic groups, and where the guilty sometimes go unpunished. Young people observing these events are too easily convinced that laws are made to be broken. In recent years there has also been a spate of books focusing on the importance of looking out for oneself first and foremost. Small wonder then that so many young people put personal impulses above all other considerations—familial, legal, and rational.

Headlines almost daily inform us of shoplifters and pickpockets, some of whom, shockingly, aren't even old enough to attend school. Shoplifting, particularly, is not limited to the poor but has become an increasing source of thrills and "kicks" for youngsters from affluent families. These shoplifters are not sociopathic personalities; they are immoral (acting against moral or legal responsibilities) but not amoral (having no sense of moral responsibilities); they are not products of a criminal environment, nor are they unable to learn from their own or others' experiences. The more affluent shoplifters see their activity as "ripping off" a society to which they cannot or choose not to adjust, for whatever reason. Shoplifters from poverty-stricken families, on the other hand, may feel that they have been deprived of some of life's necessities by a hostile and powerful society. They want to have a share in some of the "goodies" they see daily, often on television, but which they cannot afford.

Youth gangs are prominent, too, in the news of large communities, whether fighting with other gangs or terrorizing innocent victims. Looked at objectively, the gang is a miniature and highly authoritarian society. The gang leader is often a youth with good intellectual potential that has been ignored, who has been submerged in the welter of emotional problems common to his environment or has otherwise gone astray. He has to be bright, to plan the activities of the gang, and a strong leader, to maintain group cohesion and see that his plans are carried out. His followers seek peer-group acceptance in the dominant group available to them. In this sense they are following a "normal" developmental pattern, but their goals don't conform to those of the larger society. They take opportunity—legal or not—where they find it.

A great deal of blame for youthful crime is placed on television, with its displays of aggression, abuse, terrorism, and crimes against property. Indeed, the influence of television was cited in cases where a preadolescent boy murdered his elderly female neighbor and a nine-year-old used a toy pistol to hold up a bank. These were unsuccessful defense ploys, but they nevertheless indicate an aspect of society that can be a contributing factor to delinquency and crime if other factors are also present. Those youths who are predisposed to antisocial behavior attend to different elements of television stories and identify with different characters than do youths who have no such predispositions.

The Family

Youths who try to "rip off" society for its real or imagined injuries to them have often learned the lesson well from their parents. A father who wouldn't think of stealing from a shop brags about "beating" a traffic ticket or "fudging" on his taxes. Or a mother may relate an incident where she was given too much change or an overcredit and let it pass, despite knowing that the person who made the error would have to pay for it.

In other families, crime is an accepted way of life. A parent or admired older sibling may be in jail—unjustly, of course, in the opinion of the family. Using weapons, particularly kitchen knives, to settle disagreements occurs so often that a youth may follow the example of her elders. As a result, many schools have weapons detection devices in use daily as students enter the building.

Children of drug addicts or alcoholics also learn by example. The parent who depends on drink or tranquilizers to face the day is giving permission, in effect, to indulge weaknesses (such as failure) by evading them (through the use of anxiety-reducing substances). Children can hardly be blamed for thinking that what is good for their parents is good for them, especially if there are no contrary examples.

Some youngsters have never been taught a clear set of values at home and view any such values expressed at school with suspicion. According to their experience, what they want is right and everyone else is wrong. Lacking a sense of what society views as moral, and also lacking parental supervision, such a youth feels no need to conform to the laws of an uncaring society, if, indeed, he is even aware of them.

Peers

The desire for peer acceptance and recognition is acknowledged as a normal component of development in middle childhood and adolescence. If the only peers available engage in asocial or antisocial acts, it would be the "abnormal" youth who acted differently. If she hesitates, there are shouts of "Don't be chicken!" as well as threats of rejection and/or physical harm.

Peer pressure accounts for much of the use of drugs and alcohol in groups and, later, alone. A successful shoplifting foray may be the initiation rite for acceptance by peers for whom shoplifting is a way of life.

Muggings and gang terrorism are the routine activities of some groups, and the youth seeking acceptance has to participate "or else." Extortion, arson, and rape are other crimes that are often stimulated by and committed in concert with peers.

WHO ARE THE SOCIALLY MALADJUSTED?

Among practically all of the socially maladjusted, there is a disregard for, almost an obliviousness to, what is acceptable to society at large. There is little concern for the long-range future or for the consequences (other than immediate gratification) of asocial behavior. Youngsters may feel little remorse or guilt even when apprehended or jailed. Probably because they felt powerless in nearly every sense during their early childhood, a sense of power assumes enormous importance in the minds of older socially maladjusted youths. Similarly, exaggerated significance may be attached to the source of power, whether it be physical strength, a weapon, or the peer group. Whatever the source, it will be used as long as it satisfies the need for even the most temporary and superficial dominance.

Delinquents

Crimes that are considered felonies for adults are usually regarded as delinquent acts when committed by minors. These include arson, looting, mugging, rape, extortion, terrorism, aggravated assault, burglary, and murder, among others. More than half of these serious crimes are committed by persons under eighteen years of age (Marohn, 1979). If a minor is considered mature enough in some of these cases, he (or less likely, she) may be tried in criminal court, but generally he will be tried in juvenile or family court. Since most states have too few facilities available for housing youthful offenders, the minor is frequently placed on probation, with strict orders to attend school (or work) as part of the judge's sentence. Affluent or influential parents are also often able to have their delinquent offspring placed on probation rather than in jail.

There are other acts that are considered delinquent in youths but would not be crimes for adults. These include truancy, running away from home, and pregnancy among the unwed. There are also "unmanageable" youths who cannot be controlled by their parents. They are placed either in foster homes or state institutions for "incorrigibles," usually as wards of the court.

There have been several studies of the backgrounds of delinquents in general (Cohen, 1955; Glueck & Glueck, 1956; A. M. Johnson, 1959; Offer, Marohn, & Ostrov, 1979), of extremely violent juvenile delinquents (D. O.

In the study by Gruber et al., the ninety juvenile fire setters identified were in a residential center that treated youngsters categorized as emotionally disturbed. The authors found that they tended to come from families characterized by "substantial social chaos, instability, and lower socioeconomic class." They also experienced heavy stress and had minimal problem-solving resources. When referred from the public schools, "approximately 57% were enrolled in *regular* classes. . . . Approximately 30% attended sporadically. As expected, most of the children were presenting marked behavior problems in school" (1981, pp. 485–486; italics added).

Two facts are important here. First, these arsonists have emotional problems as well as social ones. Second, while in regular classes, they should be taught (once the problems are in evidence) as emotionally troubled youngsters. Like many of the "inconsequential children" referred to in the previous chapter, young arsonists may not see all the possible results of the fires they set so cavalierly.

Lewis, Shanock, Pincus, & Glaser, 1979), of female delinquents (Benedek, 1979; Rosenthal, 1979), and of arsonists (Gruber, Heck, & Mintzer, 1981). Since many of the samples are obtained from among imprisoned delinquents, there is some bias in the characteristics and environmental variables, such as socioeconomic class, that are found (since many youths are not jailed).

Many delinquents are also drug addicts whose asocial acts were originally motivated by the need to obtain money to support their addiction. Whatever the underlying emotional or other conflicts may initially be, these acts are eventually performed almost autonomously—that is, for the thrill experienced rather than the original motive—regardless of risk or negative consequences.

Drug Addicts and Alcoholics

Drugs have become a monumental problem in the school-age population. Some of the addicts come to school so "stoned" that they can barely sit up at their desks. They certainly have little awareness of what is being said in the classroom. Marijuana is smoked by elementary school children and is as easy for them to obtain as chewing gum. Quaaludes are passed routinely among friends in middle and secondary schools. Amphetamines are often taken to start the day, resulting in hyperactivity. Those who use drugs may also sell them to others, sometimes giving "samples" to generate new business. Whether users or sellers, these youths are violating laws as well as being a threat to themselves and others, and are subject to arrest in or out of school.

Students who are alcoholics are also subject to arrest, as most of them are minors with respect to state laws regarding who may purchase alcoholic beverages (including beer). Juvenile alcoholics tend to come from families that are unstable and have members troubled by depression, alcoholism, and divorce (J. E. Mitchell, Hong, & Corman, 1979). Again, school officials report that these students exhibit a variety of behaviors that have a negative impact on learning, for themselves and sometimes their classmates. There are those who make it to school but sleep through classes, just as if they'd taken "downers." Others become mean and abusive, often behaving like the alcoholic parent who serves as their model. If the problem is severe enough, they may need detoxification in a hospital setting. Others may be helped in small counseling groups (some of which are sponsored by Alcoholics Anonymous, specifically for teenage drinkers) or in community rehabilitation settings.

Not illegal, but certainly harmful physically, is glue sniffing. Youngsters get "high" on the fumes and act accordingly. They become as addicted to this as others do to drugs.

The use of drugs, glue, and alcohol is not restricted to any particular socioeconomic class or neighborhood. It is a problem in inner-city public schools, suburban schools, and. exclusive boarding schools. Among the factors contributing to addiction are a need for peer acceptance, a low sense of self-esteem, a desire for "kicks," and a disdain for sociolegal conformity.

Teenage Parents

Being an unwed adolescent mother is rarely against the law today, but it is still perceived by many as being out of step with social norms. The girl presents no threat to others, except as a model of behavior unacceptable to the adult community. The problems of her unwed partner have been largely ignored until recently (Earls & Siegel, 1980). For both, the sexual activity may have been the only display of affection they have received from anyone, and the baby-to-come is regarded as someone they can love and be loved by without reservation. Sometimes the pregnancy is deliberately sought, for one or more of many reasons; more often it happens because no effort has been made to prevent it. It is estimated that about one million adolescent pregnancies occur annually, so this is not a small problem (Bolton, 1980).

Bolton has asserted that pregnancy influences almost every facet of the adolescent's life (1980). The normal developmental stages of adolescence are not completed, as she skips over them to fulfill the role of parent. Denial of the pregnancy in its early months may mean that there is little or no prenatal care during the first trimester, resulting is risks for her and her baby. Her family, and the boy's if he admits paternity, may be thrown into a state of crisis. And, as Bolton also noted, "educational and occupational aspirations are severely curtailed in many adolescent pregnancy experiences. This is a curtailment which may lead to an irrevocable path of dependency and reduced life expectations" (1980, p. 145). There is also a lower probability of success in future relationships.

These problems also contribute to child abusive environments. Too often, adolescent parents take out their frustrations on the baby, regardless of whether the child was wanted:

The adolescent reared in a dysfunctional family has sought another generation to love as her parents, in her perception, did not. The child is seen as the mechanism that will fulfill her and remove the hurts of the past. Unfortunately, in the midst of poverty, relationship stresses, the pressures of child rearing with an inadequate fund of child rearing knowledge, and isolation, the new mother does no better than her own. (Bolton, 1980, p. 169)

The link between teenage parenting and child abuse may not be causal, according to Kinard and Klerman, but may reflect instead "the association of both phenomena with impoverished backgrounds and disturbed family life. . . ." (1980, p. 487).

EDUCATIONAL MODIFICATIONS

The three groups of socially maladjusted students described in the past few pages frequently have overlapping populations. That is, the delinquent or pregnant teenager may also be an addict, and vice versa. All have emotional problems, and most are functioning as underachievers at school. On which aspect of their problems can or should educators focus? To some extent, the focus determines placement and the types of teaching techniques to be used.

The socially maladjusted student in the classroom poses a number of challenges to the teacher. Any pupil's actual or alleged asocial classroom or schoolground behavior is commonly referred to the school principal or the disciplinarian. Depending on the nature of the offense and/or the number of times the student has been referred to the office, he may be suspended or expelled from school, sent to a detention room during or after school hours, or warned of future penalties in the event of recurrence. Most of these practices at least temporarily reduce the pressure on the teacher but do little to assist the student's academic progress or change his behavior. It should be noted that suspension and expulsion require due process hearings at which the student's civil rights must be protected. (Referrals to mental health personnel for diagnostic testing or for therapy similarly must be made with respect for student and parental rights.)

There are alternatives to suspension that are more likely to be constructive, rather than merely punitive. These include "time-out" or "cooling off" rooms, which can be a kind of in-school suspension or a preventive measure; an in-school suspension center, where the student continues academic work under supervision; special counseling and guidance programs; pupil problem teams; school survival courses that teach students strategies for becoming better learners and staying out of trouble; work-study programs; and alternative schools (Garibaldi, 1979). Personnel costs may be high in periods of stringent budgeting, but the long-run costs are often lower than the costs of institutionalization.

Placement

Obviously, the most restrictive environment for socially maladjusted youths is institutionalization. Although incarceration may be an appropriate punishment for the crime or necessary for the safety of others, it is generally recognized that what the imprisoned youth frequently learns are new techniques of extortion, sadism, and thievery, both from his fellow inmates and from his treatment by some guards and attendants. Juvenile detention centers are, therefore, usually not sources of constructive reeducation or rehabilitation, and reformatories rarely reform.

Community halfway house for emotionally troubled and socially maladjusted youths. (Photo by Wendy Bishop)

Slightly less restrictive are halfway houses, which seek to provide a supportive environment within the larger community (Vachon, 1972). These are controversial, partly because of questions regarding their effectiveness in rehabilitation and partly because they are often viewed as unwelcome intruders in neighborhoods and around local schools. Citizens fear possible crimes against person or property, and the school administrators resist having to work with more "troublemakers."

Special schools, such as Philadelphia's "orthogenic disciplinary" schools and New York's "600" schools, represent a school district's last-ditch effort to cope with socially maladjusted pupils. They are the only public facilities where such students can be sent on an "outpatient" basis, but they do not necessarily provide a constructive environment. In fact, frequently the power goes to the strongest and biggest youths, and more crime than reading is learned. Attempts at counseling and therapy are rarely successful, principally because there are seldom enough skilled counselors in the district to perform this monumental task. Rigid rules and frequent demerits have not solved the problems of working with socially maladjusted youths in these or other settings. Should the youths then be sent to a more or less restrictive environment?

Special classes within regular school buildings are less restrictive, though they may be threatening to the staff and parents. These small units (as opposed to large special schools) do reduce anonymity and increase the probability of staff-student interaction. For some of the socially malad-

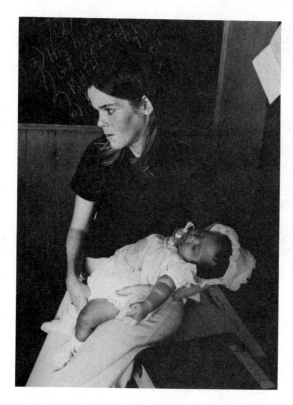

How *does* a teenage mother cope with her new baby and school? (Arthur Grace/Stock, Boston)

justed, this partial segregation from stresses in the regular classroom may be sufficient to reduce their undesirable behavior.

Among the special classes available in some districts are those for unwed pregnant girls. Part of the original purpose of these classes was to remove girls from their peers because they were "tainted" and unfit to be seen by their supposedly naive classmates. Most educators today are aware that it is this view that is naive. The continuing purpose of these classes, however, is to permit the girls to continue their studies up to delivery and, afterward, to resume them so that the young mother can eventually graduate from high school.

As a student is perceived as less threatening, he may be main-streamed, perhaps with visits as needed to a crisis room teacher or the school counselor. When class assignments are made, thought should be given to placing the student with teachers who can best establish a rapport with him. It is important that the student have confidence and trust in the teacher and that the teacher have a sincere interest in helping him readjust to social norms and also profit from class instruction. The selection of personnel to work with the socially maladjusted youngster is a critical factor in the success or failure of any program.

A crisis room teacher is a special resource teacher to whom a student can go when she cannot (or fears that she cannot) control her behavior acceptably. The crisis teacher is not a disciplinarian; he uses problem-solving techniques with the student who has a behavior problem or who is in a situation that is threatening in some way. Working with the classroom teachers and other school personnel, the crisis specialist can suggest and develop a number of ways to reduce the tensions and conflicts that plague the socially maladjusted.

A similar type of program can help disruptive elementary school students. The student who fights, throws things in the classroom, and verbally attacks the teacher or classmates frequently needs to be taken out of the room, both as a relief to others and to obtain remedial instruction. The principal and teachers can work together, for example, to choose the twenty to thirty most disruptive students in the school for the program. A special teacher with two aides (paraprofessionals or volunteers) can work with five or six students each hour. If the hour is divided into three twenty-minute segments, each child can have both remedial help in reading and arithmetic and affective education to help improve interpersonal relationships. The remedial instruction will reduce the frustration that undoubtedly contributes to the child's disruptive classroom behavior, while the affective instruction will help to modify his attitudes and behaviors. When a student improves enough to function satisfactorily in the classroom without the special educational and emotional support of the program, another child can become part of the daily program.

Some students respond well to a highly authoritarian teacher, since they cannot respect anyone who does not exhibit an aura of power. Others need a warmer, softer figure who can supply the nurturing they have apparently not received from parents. In any case, evaluation of the placement should ideally take place on a continuing basis, rather than merely as a response to a crisis.

In most cases, the socially maladjusted youth has difficulty establishing a positive relationship with any adult and will test it many times. This means that limits to the amount of acceptable deviant behavior that will be tolerated must be set in terms of age, type of behavior, facilities available, and staff-student ratio. Older socially maladjusted students may be guided toward more adaptive behavior if they are allowed to participate in setting the limits and dealing with violators. This also helps to teach them why rules and laws are needed for society to function.

Many of the delinquents and addicts are involved with the courts, and some of the mothers-to-be are involved with social welfare agencies. Whenever this is true, teachers, probation officers, case workers, and psychologists need to coordinate their efforts to plan appropriate placement and a consistent educational program. The constant quality of this effort is essential, as many youths have adopted socially deviant behavior as a means of coping with their chaotic home environment. With the older students, possible alternatives can be presented by the planning team for participation in and reaction to the possible programs.

Programming and Techniques

Once in a classroom, the socially maladjusted pupil tends to resist learning. Assessment may reveal that she is learning disabled. Often she has reading disabilities that cause frustration in learning situations (and therefore the likelihood of continued unacceptable behavior). Impulsivity or hyperactivity may interfere with learning. Truancy also often creates learning gaps with the same result. One obvious modification in the education of the socially maladjusted, then, is to provide a remedial reading program that will reduce frustrations in this area and thereby in learning generally. Through careful selection of high-interest materials, the reading program can be combined with therapy to alleviate or increase understanding of emotional problems and conflicts with others. Another approach, if the student is learning disabled, is to work with the resource teacher to develop appropriate remedial programs for specific areas of weakness.

Traditional approaches to teaching subject matter such as math, literature, or history are often useless in classes with several hostile, rebellious, or asocial youths. Creativity, variety, and flexibility are almost mandatory if these students are to be "turned on." Math can be taught in an applied rather than a theoretical mode or integrated into other subject matter. It can be broken into small units for mastery learning, with reinforcement for increases in competence and attention span. For literature and history, some of these students' abundant energy resources can be turned to acting out scenes in the text, either as written or as the students imagine they should or might have occurred.

Contracts, suggested earlier for other groups of exceptional students, can also be used with the socially maladjusted. They should move in the direction of greater student responsibility for both behavioral control and academic achievement. Reinforcement can include free time, the use of special equipment (such as computer terminals), "privileged" jobs (such as running errands for the teacher), being allowed to participate in sports or club activities, and the like, depending on the age and interests of the individual student.

In small special classes, where the ratio is eight to ten students per teacher, some variety in activities has been found to be effective. Changes of activities and/or teachers should follow a routine structure, however, as many socially maladjusted students have difficulty dealing with the unexpected. Some youngsters need almost constant support from the teacher in their efforts to accomplish anything, while others can function in a

Teenage junkies are problems to themselves, their families, and their schools. (Leonard Freed/Magnum Photos)

small group or work on their own for reasonable periods of time. For the former, the contract approach may reduce the total dependency over time.

Field trips of interest to the *students* can be worked gradually into the program. They should be treated both as a learning experience and as a privilege. The trips should be carefully planned on every level: duration, means of transportation, definition of acceptable (and unacceptable) behavior, goals, and so on. The teacher needs to establish reasonable limits for behavior, allowing for the usual playfulness on such trips, despite the students' antiauthoritarian attitudes. It may be the first time anyone has ever expressed enough concern for these youths to set limits, and the novelty can be very effective. As each field trip occurs without untoward incident, the students can be encouraged to help plan more ambitious projects. Apart from the formal learning aspects, field trips can introduce them to aspects of community life that may be unfamiliar and therefore could be threatening if encountered independently.

For the teenage mother, special class placement should provide a program that includes sessions dealing with prenatal and postnatal care, nutrition, and even principles of child development. After delivery, she should be encouraged to return to school, while her infant is cared for in the same building. There is no real need to modify the content of academic programs for these girls, except to recognize that they are now mothers and have new responsibilities to face. Exploring what these are and how to cope with them should be incorporated into the program. Other goals of such special programs are to teach proper infant care techniques, to provide medically accurate sex education (it's surprising how many of these girls have no idea of how they became pregnant!), and to enable the girls to complete high school with marketable skills, so that they can support themselves and their children (if they do not place them for adoption).

For drug and alcohol users, withdrawal programs may have to precede academic programs on the list of priorities. When the user, with counseling, becomes able to handle her problems without chemical supports, she may move into a halfway house and later return to school. It would be cruel and probably quite damaging if she were reminded at school of her past behavior or held up as a model of "what happens if you drink or take drugs." (The theory of self-fulfilling prophecies operates in this area, too.) Instead, she should receive constructive support in gaining coping abilities as well as academic and interpersonal competencies. Remediation for the work she has missed while a user can be arranged through tutors, self-paced workbooks, computer instruction, or a resource room teacher.

The institutionalized delinquent has frequently experienced school failure, but relatively little has been done to assess his abilities or needs. Whether this population qualifies for special education under P.L. 94-142, however, is subject to question (Brown & Robbins, 1979; J. L. Johnson, 1979). What services should be provided and by whom are also sources

---

FOR EXAMPLE . . .

At an experimental program at the Federal Detention Center in Washington, D.C., in the 1960s, behavior modification techniques were used quite effectively to induce the youths there to participate in learning sessions, do homework, and abide by the rules that were put into effect. In brief, where there had been ready access to recreation facilities, the youths now had to earn the privilege of access by completing study contracts. Assignment to "solitary" became a special privilege (because so few of them had ever had a bed or a room to themselves at home) instead of a punishment. Points earned could be converted to special dishes in the cafeteria or items from a mail-order catalog. The reinforcements, incidentally, were dispensed by the guard who had been most disliked in the center. The youths became very active learners, especially improving their extremely weak reading and math skills.

of controversy. That educational opportunities should be available and encouraged seems logical, though, if there is to be progress toward rehabilitation.

Institutional courses should emphasize basic skills and occupational training (with modern equipment). Those capable of pursuing high school courses should have the opportunity to do so. If there are too few youths to warrant hiring a teacher, correspondence or programmed materials should be used, along with (if possible) assistance from a volunteer tutor. In addition, there should be extensive occupational counseling to increase the probability of the youths' acceptance and success upon reentry to the community. The occupational counselor should also encourage local business operators to develop job opportunities for these youths so that they have less reason to resort to illegal behavior upon release.

SUMMARY

The socially maladjusted present difficulties to themselves and others. Typically they have emotional problems that contribute to their delinquent or asocial behavior, and they may have learning problems as well. The roots of these problems are found in contemporary social phenomena (such as high unemployment rates), in dysfunctional families, and in peer relationships.

Whether their problems are ultimately dealt with in school or a correctional institution, these youths do need special attention. Skills in basic subjects as well as in social interaction need to be taught. Behavior modification techniques appear to be effective with some of these students, particularly the use of academic and behavior contracts. For teenage mothers, the need is more in the direction of enabling them to continue their education, with supplementary courses or workshops in child care and sex education.

Psychotherapy and occupational counseling, too, are essential parts of rehabilitation programs, whether on a group or an individual basis. The absence of such help says to the socially maladjusted youth that he is perceived as both insignificant and incorrigible. The consequences of such perceptions are highly predictable.

SUGGESTED ADDITIONAL READINGS

Altbuch, P., and St. George, N. An educational alternative for delinquent offenders: Storms Street School. *Education*, 1981, *101*, 226–230.

Collingwood, T. R., and Genthner, R. W. Skills training as treatment for juvenile delinquents. *Professional Psychology*, 1980, *11*, 591–598.

Discipline and student rights. *Inequality in Education*, July 1975, No. 20.

Donnelly, P. Athletes and juvenile delinquents: A comparative analysis based on a review of literature. *Adolescence*, 1981, *16*, 425–432.

Gallas, H. B., Ed. Teenage parenting: Social determinants and consequences. *Journal of Social Issues*, 1980, *36* (1), entire issue.

Kelly, T. J., Bullock, L. M., and Dykes, M. K. Behavioral disorders: Teacher's perceptions. *Exceptional Children*, 1977, *43*, 316–318.

Lichtenstein, E. Suspension, expulsion, and the special education student. *Phi Delta Kappan*, 1980, *61*, 459–461.

Magrab, P. R., and Danielson-Murphy, J. Adolescent pregnancy: A review. *Journal of Clinical Child Psychology*, 1979, *8* (2), 121–125.

Rabkin, J. G. The epidemiology of forcible rape. *American Journal of Orthopsychiatry*, 1979, *49*, 634–647.

Sung, K-T. The role of day care for teenage mothers in a public school. *Child Care Quarterly*, 1981, *10* (2), 113–124.

Wasson, A. S. Susceptibility to boredom and deviant behavior at school. *Psychological Reports*, 1981, *48*, 901–902.

Wenk, E., and Harlow, N. *School crime and disruption: Prevention models.* Washington, D.C.: National Institute of Education, 1978.

PART SIX/
SPECIAL CONCERNS

T his final section is devoted to a consideration of
   the "significant others" who play a role in the
lives and education of exceptional students: their
teachers, school administrators, and families.

With regard to the teachers, we are concerned
with their attitudes and professional preparation. All
the positive changes in textbooks and curriculum
guides will be useless if teachers regard exceptional
students with rejection, hostility, and/or fear. Similarly, the educational modifications suggested in earlier chapters will be only so much window dressing
if teachers are inadequately prepared to implement them.

In examining the role of school administrators, we
must look at the lines of communication and organization, as well as at the ancillary personnel who have
important roles to play in the evaluation of and educational recommendations for exceptional students.
These include school psychologists, resource teachers, and school principals, as well as nonschool
physicians and therapists.

The families, being those most affected by and most important to exceptional students, deserve books, not merely a chapter, devoted to them. From the day that their child is labeled "exceptional" to the day he becomes independent or someone else's responsibility, their role is critical. How they respond to the child's needs, what barriers they choose to erect or to demolish, and the ways in which they interact with teachers will all be significant in the education of the exceptional student. At the same time, we must be aware that having an exceptional student, sibling, or grandchild is itself a significant factor in the life of the family member. The impact of these interactions is seen in the very fact that there is an "Education for All Handicapped Children Act," for it was family action on behalf of these children that ultimately resulted in this legislation.

CHAPTER 15/
TEACHER PREPARATION

The emphasis in special education, as it should be in all education, must be on the abilities rather than the disabilities of exceptional students. Most exceptional children *can* learn academics, sports, music, art, and vocational skills. To accomplish these things, a child must have (1) parents who encourage a positive self-concept and are willing to "fight" for their child and (2) teachers who approach their tasks with patience, imagination, adaptability, and an ability to juggle the realities of the present with the goals of the future. *Teachers have a marvelous power in their hands, for they can significantly affect a child's whole life.* Not only can they modify curriculum content as needed and control the model of instruction, but they also set the climate of the learning environment. To do this with exceptional students, teachers need exceptional preparation.

THE IMPACT OF MAINSTREAMING

Although we are principally concerned here with the preparation of special education teachers, the passage of P.L. 94-142 has increased the need for *all* teachers to have familiarity with the psychological and educational needs of the broad spectrum of exceptional children. Many classroom teachers have expressed their anxiety about teaching mildly retarded or gifted students. Certainly traditional teacher preparation programs did not prepare them for such heterogeneous classes. That situation is slowly beginning to change as mainstreaming increases.

General Teacher Education

In addition to providing in-service courses for those already teaching, several colleges of education have introduced a requirement that all students preparing for teacher certification take at least one course focused on exceptional children. Although this will not make them experts, they will at least acquire some basic information on the characteristics and needs of, and the available resources for, exceptional children. Byford, in a study of higher education institutions (1979), found that many in her sample of 128 colleges had increased their course offerings in diagnostic, remedial, and behavior management skill since 1970. Roberson did a similar survery in the southeastern United States. He found that larger colleges had already modified or were planning to modify their curricula, either by adding a separate, required course or by introducing modules on special education in other required courses (1980). Of course, until the state education agencies mandate such a course for certification, there is relatively little pressure on colleges to make any curriculum changes. Patton and Braithwaite found that, as of mid-1978, only ten states required special education courses for initial certification, with four others considering the requirement (1980). A year later, the same ten states required certification, but ten more were considering taking this step (Karnes & Collins, 1981).

It is a relatively simple matter to introduce the psychology and education of exceptional children into developmental and educational psychology courses, even where there is no requirement. When teaching the concepts of cognitive development, for example, the instructor can discuss rapid or slow development, as well as what is considered the average pace. In discussing motor or language development, reference can be made to hearing or visually handicapped children and the ways in which they differ from the norm. Additional means of integrating exceptionality into these courses are equally easy to devise.

At the student teaching level, an introduction to both exceptional students and mainstreaming can be integrated into the experience in several ways. McKinnon, Wine, Sires, and Bowser have suggested that local special education teachers work with college education faculty to provide information and guide the students' participation in introduction to teaching courses (1982). This is particularly needed at the secondary level, which has been too often overlooked with respect to special education. The team approach can be reinforced by tutoring or other activities involving exceptional students during the student teaching experience.

General Teachers' Attitudes

The key to successful mainstreaming is probably the attitude of the receiving teacher toward the child who is different. In addition to her own attitude, she is responsible for shaping appropriate peer attitudes in her classroom so that the exceptional child will be welcomed and not shunned. The more successful teachers not only welcome these youngsters but also set the stage for peer assistance to the exceptional child (Hendrickson, 1978).

W. M. Reynolds and Greco have developed a brief scale that might be useful in the selection of teachers who have the potential to integrate special students with positive results (1979). Such screening would not guarantee successful mainstreaming experiences, of course, but it would avoid placing a child with a nonreceptive teacher. Although placement is important at any grade level, it would seem to be more critical in the middle school years, where the "normal" youngsters have had little experience with "differences" but are very sensitive to them and, therefore, need the leadership of an empathetic teacher. Even at the college level, however, J. Newman found that only a slight majority of the faculty who responded (52 percent) "did not believe that there would be problems in the admission of handicapped students to their departments" (1976, p. 195). This was attributed to the faculty's lack of experience with such students, for relatively few handicapped students were able to attend colleges in the early 1970s. (Today, with modifications to facilities and the aid of both human and mechanical assistants, the number of handicapped college students has increased considerably.) The same lack of familiarity with disabled or retarded persons could be true for teachers at the kindergarten to twelfth-grade levels.

Exposure to the special Olympics, visits to special classes, and presentations by exceptional students should provide classroom teachers with information as to the students' levels of functioning, mobility, and social adjustment in a variety of settings. Meetings with colleagues who are already making mainstreaming work successfully would also be helpful. Well-designed in-service programs incorporate these and other activities in orienting the regular classroom teacher to the varied needs of exceptional students. If these opportunities could be made available to all education majors during the college years, as part of their preservice curriculum, clearly they would be less likely to face a crisis in the classroom when assigned an exceptional student.

At the "positive" end of the spectrum of exceptionality, in a study of experienced kindergarten and first-grade teachers, very few favored early admission to school for the intellectually gifted children, with the vast majority expressing concern about social and emotional maturity levels (Jackson, Famiglietti, & Robinson, 1981). Some had reservations about the long-term effects of removing these children from their age group, which would also suggest that they would be opposed to later acceleration of the gifted. There is concern, however, as to whether these same teachers would be able and/or willing to provide enrichment opportunities for gifted children in their regular classroom. Similar ambivalence is found with respect to nurturing creativity (Tan-Willman, 1981) and intellectual curiosity (R. S. Jones, 1980).

Where regular classroom teachers may feel threatened or flustered by students who are intellectually more able than they, they may be extremely anxious when retarded or disabled students are in their classes. There are at least three ways to reduce such anxiety. One, introducing the psychology of exceptional students into the teacher preparation curriculum, has already been suggested. A second method is to include simulation exercises in preservice (or in-service) teaching programs "to promote a better understanding of the difficulties exceptional children may experience in a classroom" (Glazzard, 1979, p. 101). A third approach is to have special education teachers prepare regular teachers in the adaptation of curricula to meet the special needs of disabled students as well as their regular students (Glazzard, 1980). Acquisition of specific techniques of adaptation removes the panic inherent in the unfamiliar. Teachers surveyed by Schultz, for example, indicated that planning for individual differences was their primary area of interest or concern in dealing with mainstreaming (1982). Support by the special educator would make that task easier.

Peer Attitudes

Once a classroom teacher has been informed that he will have one or more exceptional students in his class, he has a responsibility beyond self-

FOR EXAMPLE . . .

An elementary school teacher had two hearing impaired daughters who attended the school where she taught. To help the girls as well as their new classmates, she explained hearing disabilities to the second and third graders. When they responded with more questions about communications, she taught the youngsters the manual alphabet. Continuing interest in this new language led her to teach the classes the song "You Light up My Life" in sign language.

Other teachers became aware of their colleague's activities and asked that she and the classes she had taught share the new skill with the entire school. This was done at a school assembly. What had been a mother's effort to help her own children have a successful mainstreaming experience thus affected the entire student body and was eventually shown on local television news programs as well, reaching a large metropolitan audience.

preparation and academic concerns. How will peers respond to the "different" individual who has, possibly, special needs and who may need extra teacher attention? To begin with, if mainstreaming is to work for the exceptional student, acceptance by peers is very important. Children often follow the example of the adults around them, so if positive attitudes are wanted, the teacher must display a positive attitude toward *all* class members. In addition, it is the teacher's obligation to inform the class about the abilities and special needs of the exceptional student(s). For example, he should point out that they need not shout to their blind classmate, because she *can* hear, but that they should not stretch their legs out in the aisles, because she could be tripped. Where possible, simulation activities, special children's books about handicaps and "differences," and other resources should be employed to help in transmitting this information (Litton, Banbury, & Harris, 1980). That such instruction can be effective has been demonstrated in several studies throughout the 1970s (T. W. Jones, Sowell, J. K. Jones, & Butler, 1981). The ideal outcome of this information sharing is a student's question: "How can we help?"

The youngsters in the example readily accepted their hearing impaired classmates and became their aides in communicating with others as well as in classroom activities. Properly prepared, regular students can view pushing a wheelchair, assisting a blind classmate in fire drills, or coaching a less academically able peer as a privilege rather than a burden.

Since mainstreaming may occur at the opening of the school year as well as later on, there may not always be time to prepare students for their new classmates. In this case, the teacher must certainly set an example in attitude and behavior as well as plan ahead to meet the needs of exceptional students. If furniture and books need to be just so for the visually impaired student, or an escort is needed for changing classrooms, or some other peer participation is necessary, these situations should be included among the statements of class procedures on opening day. The teacher should also make the point that for some members of the class there may be more of a need for individualized attention than for others, but that no one will be ignored and no one will be favored. In order to be not "Pollyannish" but constructive in the classroom situation, teachers need to stress not only what exceptional students can do but also the ways in which they are like their classmates. Conversely, when a student responds with an emphasis on differences, the teacher can point out the uniqueness of each member of the class in one or more ways that does not override the similarities of those in the group.

THE CURRICULUM IN SPECIAL EDUCATION

The college course work for future teachers may pose few problems, but the realities of weeks of helping children to learn, frequently with only minute signs of progress, may not be sufficient reinforcement for otherwise well-intentioned special education teachers. Warmth and a sincere concern for the growth of special children are also not enough in themselves, but they are essential for a positive learning situation. Opportunities to put classroom learning plus personal factors to work in special education settings, early in the college career, offer the prospective special education teacher a chance to try out this combination to see whether the field is a personally appropriate and satisfying one.

Course Work

Typically, special education majors take about half their college credits in liberal arts courses and the remaining credits in specialized courses. The latter may vary somewhat, according to the criteria for certification in each state and/or college of education. In an increasing number of states, graduates are certified to teach the full range of exceptional children; in other states, the certification is specific to one or more fields within special education.

Basic to the professional curriculum are courses in introductory, developmental, and educational psychology; these provide a background for understanding how exceptional children differ from the "average" in development and learning style. Similarly, the introductory course to special education typically offers a broad perspective from which the

Education classes may be large or small. Here a teacher discusses elements of problem solving with her students.

prospective teacher can work toward specific areas of exceptionality. When we get to these specific areas, however, there are differing emphases in course content.

Teachers of the Retarded

Successful teachers of the retarded need to have patience with their students' slow learning pace, as well as enthusiasm, energy, flexibility, and a good measure of self-esteem. Those working with moderately or severely retarded preadolescents should have personal traits similar to those of a good nursery school or kindergarten teacher, for their students combine the chronological age of elementary school children with pre-school intellectual abilities.

The Board of Directors of the National Association for Retarded Citizens (NARC) in 1974 adopted standards for teacher certification programs that have already had some impact on preservice education in this field. They recommended that teachers of the retarded have a bachelor's degree that certifies competency in: "(1) a basic body of knowledge of mental retardation; (2) methods and techniques for teaching mentally retarded persons; (3) curriculum for mentally retarded students; and (4) demonstration of teaching competence with mentally retarded students" (National Association for Retarded Citizens, 1974). They also urged that standard minimal requirements be adopted throughout the country and that universal reciprocity (that is, interstate recognition) of the teaching certificate be instituted. This has not yet happened. The NARC recommendations also urged teachers to specialize in one or more areas of teaching the retarded.

Retardation is the type of exceptionality most frequently studied in college of education programs leading to a bachelor's level certification. Students in the preservice major take courses in identification and characteristics of the mentally retarded, curriculum adjustment, and special teaching techniques and materials, and they spend a practicum semester teaching retarded students. Those who plan to work with younger retarded children focus also on the study of early childhood development, while those who expect to work with retarded adolescents take course work in vocational and personal counseling, so that they can help prepare their students for adulthood (whether or not it will be totally independent). Experiences throughout the undergraduate program in activities for the retarded, whether academic, vocational, or recreational, provide realistic applications of course work as well as the opportunity to become increasingly familiar with the nature, needs, and challenges of retardation.

Not all who contribute to the education of the retarded have or need such extensive formal training. Paraprofessional personnel are prepared in programs at community colleges and other two-year institutions. Under the direction of certified teachers, these trained aides work closely with individual retarded students on specific tasks and lend general assistance throughout the school day or in residential settings. Their presence offers additional attention to individual youngsters that would otherwise not be available for reinforcement and encouragement as well as physical care.

Teachers of Children with Learning Disabilities

Certification of teachers for the learning disabled is not required in every state, even when one considers the variety of diagnostic labels attached to this type of exceptionality. There are, however, an increasing number of specific courses available at colleges of education that prepare teachers to diagnose strengths and weaknesses of students with learning disabilities and to teach them appropriately. Because of the widely varying combinations of disabilities and abilities, the teacher needs to be prepared for highly individualized instruction, in terms of curriculum adjustments and teaching techniques. According to M. C. Reynolds and Birch, "Teachers in high schools and elementary schools need freedom to seek out and use elements from any part of the entire school curriculum in working with children with learning disabilities" (1977a, p. 371). This implies that the teacher must be personally flexible and professionally competent in a wide range of subject matter at varying grade levels.

An appropriate preservice curriculum for teachers of the learning disabled includes diagnostic methods, diagnostic and developmental reading techniques, curriculum adjustment, and a practicum with learning disabled students. Other related learning experiences for the prospective teacher in this field include working with the emotionally troubled (recall that emotional and behavioral disturbances frequently follow the frustrations experienced by the learning disabled), gaining knowledge of effective guidance practices, and participating in the vocational rehabilitation counseling of learning disabled adolescents. Teachers who work with this type of exceptionality (as well as others) should also be prepared to work with parents and with therapists or colleagues in other teaching fields.

Teachers of the Exceptionally Able

In a survey of state support for education of the gifted, Laird found that only three states—Florida, Kansas, and Louisiana—had special requirements of professional preparation and experience for teachers of the gifted (1971). By 1980, there were still only nine that had special requirements, plus two others that were then developing certification criteria (B. M. Mitchell, 1980). Other surveys reveal that most programs focused on teaching the gifted are at the graduate level and often require prior teacher certification and/or teaching experience (M. Lindsey, 1980).

Teachers of the exceptionally able need not possess talents of the same magnitude as their students, but they do need to be sensitive to others, open-minded, adaptable, and resourceful. They must be able to guide without being authoritarian, to know where to seek answers that they don't have, and to provide access to human and material resources in the community and in the school. A group leader at the Creative Problem-Solving Institute once said that this means being "a guide by the side, not a sage on stage." The ideal teacher of the gifted and talented should also be able to rejoice in the successes of her students and, perhaps, learn from them as well. This requires a strong positive self-concept on the teacher's part and a continuing desire to learn and achieve.

Teachers of the exceptionally able need to be prepared to work differentially with their students. For those pupils who are self-motivated (any teacher's delight), the teacher should provide freedom for exploration and perhaps some guidance for coordinating multiple interests. For those who are able but not self-starters, the teacher must be more of a stimulant. Teachers soon discover that gifted youngsters vary in their self-confidence, desire to conform to authority, and willingness to function independently, much as other students do. Stimulation of the exceptionally able requires teachers who are able to focus on process as well as product, who are willing to be innovative and experimental, who emphasize both problem-solving procedures and varied strategies, and who respect the individuality and integrity of others (M. Lindsey, 1980). A sense of humor helps, too, as many gifted students, being both playful and creative, try to see in how many different ways they can bedevil their teachers without incurring penalties.

Typical certification or specialist programs for teachers of the exceptionally able include courses on "nature and nurture of the gifted and talented," curriculum adjustments, assessment techniques, creative studies, and specialized teaching materials and skills. Workshops and seminars more typically focus on techniques for teaching specific content areas to the gifted (such as language arts), the utilization of local resources (such as museums, urban parks, and architecture), or on guidance and counseling with the gifted and their parents. Apart from in-service programs provided by individual school districts, there are a number of summer institutes offered by the National/State Leadership Training Institute for the Gifted and Talented, Hunter College (New York City), Teachers College of Columbia University, Purdue University, the Creative Problem-Solving Institute (Buffalo), and other institutions that teach special skills and open new vistas to those teaching the exceptionally able.

Some thought is now being given also to certification of teachers for talented students. Seen as a subspecialty in certification for teachers of the gifted, teachers of the fine and performing arts would take several core courses in the gifted education program and special courses in methods of teaching the talented. They would also have to be recognized for their own artistic or creative accomplishments in their particular arts field.

Teachers of the Orthopedically Handicapped and Chronically Ill

There are several certification programs across the country that prepare people to teach the orthopedically handicapped but very few directed specifically toward teaching the chronically ill. Teachers of the latter group may be drawn from rosters of special education teachers in a district and simply reassigned, perhaps with an in-service workshop or two to help them adapt their knowledge and experience to this group of young people, who are homebound, hospitalized, or otherwise limited in their activity. For all teachers in this area, preparation should emphasize the modifications in facilities and instructional tools relevant to physical disabilities. Experience in recreation or camp programs for orthopedically handicapped, diabetic, or other chronically ill children is extremely useful for broadening the teacher's understanding of the physical and psychosocial needs of these youths.

Teachers need to be able to accept and be sensitive to, but not blinded by, physical limitations. They need to be warm, flexible, and not easily panicked by emergencies. Those working with terminally ill children or students with regressive diseases also need a quality that enables them to confront the reality of the situation without becoming emotionally overwhelmed and dysfunctional.

In recent years, educators have focused on the "whole child." For the handicapped and chronically ill, this means looking beyond the medical problem to view the child as a learner among other learners, a child among his peers. Of course, adjustments must be made to the medical problem, but this does not mean indulgence on the part of the regular or special teachers. One approach to finding balance in this situation is to have teachers who are better informed about the medical aspects of the children's conditions. Such a program has been introduced at one university, where pediatricians are invited as guest lecturers in a graduate special education course (Freund, Casey, & Bradley, 1982). A combination of physicians and special educators, an exchange of professional information, and diverse contacts with parents can lead to more successful academic programming for these children.

Teachers of the Hearing Impaired

Preparatory programs for teachers of hearing impaired children can be found in many colleges and universities. If combined in part with the training given to future speech therapists, the prospective teacher gains additional insight into the speech problems associated with hearing disabilities. Special teaching techniques are necessary, even for more basic school subjects, with special attention given to the teaching of reading to the prelingual deaf. Training in remedial speech methods further prepares the prospective teacher of the hearing impaired for the realities of the classroom.

The Council on Education of the Deaf formulated standards for teacher certification in this field, after a series of conferences in the 1960s and early 1970s. They determined that applicants for provisional certification had to complete a core program consisting of course work and experience equivalent to a minimum of thirty semester hours. Such a core program was to include: (1) foundations of education of the hearing impaired, (2) speech science and audiology, (3) language and communication for the hearing impaired, (4) curriculum and instruction modifications, and (5) a minimum of one full year of supervised student teacher experience (1974, pp. 244–245).

At Western Maryland College, where hearing and hearing impaired students study alongside each other to become teachers or social workers in this field, total communication is stressed to facilitate integration of the deaf into the hearing community (Wood, 1974). Gallaudet College also offers special opportunities for hearing and hearing impaired students to work together in learning to teach the deaf. Needless to say, an initial requirement for these prospective teachers is that they learn sign language, so that they can communicate effectively with their students. Extensive student teaching practicums have long been standard in these programs, because so many professional skills have to be modified. In practice, more than thirty semester hours are devoted to this branch of special education.

Since increasing numbers of hearing impaired students are being mainstreamed, the prospective teacher must understand and be familiar with the emotional and developmental problems of both the hearing impaired and normal children. These teachers also have to be prepared to work cooperatively with regular classroom teachers—coordinating goals and lessons, sharing special skills and information relevant to teaching the hearing impaired, and reducing possible sources of anxiety, irritation, or rejection by regular teachers.

Teachers of the Visually Impaired

Relatively few certification programs are offered by colleges of education that prepare people to teach the blind and partially sighted. There are, of course, single courses offered by many institutions that serve as an introduction to the needs and psychology of the visually impaired, but these need to be supplemented by in-depth seminars and practical experience.

The typical program includes course work in the anatomy, physiology, and hygiene of the eye; the principles of physiological optics; the study of eye diseases; Braille; and special methods that emphasize use of the auditory, kinesthetic, and tactile senses. These all contribute, it is believed, to a teacher's understanding of and ability to deal with the physical and educational problems of the visually impaired. Barraga, however, cites the complaints that there is too little applicability of several of these courses to meeting the classroom needs and that there is too much emphasis on blind learners and too little on partially sighted students (1981).

Training in music, art, and adaptive physical education is often included in these programs, to give the teachers added techniques for enriching their pupils' education and lives. However, there is a real need for these teachers to become skilled "in teaching the concepts necessary for movement, exploration, orientation, and, later, independent travel within the environment" (Barraga, 1981, p. 97). This is not always included in the curriculum. Indeed, there are very few professionally trained instructors available for the mobility training—crossing streets, using subways and buses, moving around buildings alone—that gives the blind individual freedom, independence, and self-assurance.

Frequent and prolonged contact with visually impaired people of all ages will greatly increase the prospective teacher's expertise and self-confidence; thus, extended practicums should also be included in a program. In addition, course work and (where possible) experience in dealing with the emotional concerns of the visually impaired and their parents are especially helpful. A blind or partially sighted youth is much more apt to achieve her goals if the teacher succeeds in gaining the cooperation and support of her parents. Similarly, experience in working with regular classroom teachers is important, because of the increase in mainstreaming of the visually impaired. Great frustration is in store for student and special teacher alike, if classroom procedures are undone or ignored at home or in regular classes.

One of the difficulties faced by teachers of the visually handicapped outside of large city school districts is that they may serve relatively few students as an itinerant teacher. Eighty-two such teachers surveyed in ten midwestern and western states cited "indifferent, uncooperative, undisciplined students" as their major source of dissatisfaction. A shortage of appropriate materials and texts and "poor communication with and cooperation from administrators" were two other problems for them (Bina, 1982). In general, teachers of the visually handicapped find great satisfaction in their students' progress but also feel the need for more support from colleagues and administrators and more challenge in their jobs. Recognition of potential sources of both satisfaction and dissatisfaction should be incorporated into the teacher education program, because a teacher's morale will ultimately affect his teaching effectiveness.

Teachers of the Multiply Handicapped

An examination of certification programs in colleges across the country revealed none specifically oriented to preparation for teaching the multiply handicapped (Vernon, 1969). In early 1982, there were still no such programs to the author's knowledge. There have been, however, a number of special teacher training programs for working with the deaf-blind, offered by the Perkins School for the Blind (Massachusetts), San Francisco State University, George Peabody College for Teachers (Nashville, Tennessee), and Michigan State University. The Center for Multiple Handicapped Children, operated by the New York City Board of Education, has also trained teachers of the handicapped, paraprofessionals (many of whom are themselves handicapped), and interns from the New York Hospital Medical Center.

In general, however, most of the preparation comes from on-the-job training and previous experiences with children who have only one disability. A teacher of the multiply handicapped probably needs more patience, versatility, resourcefulness, and compassion (but not pity) than is required of teachers of any other group of exceptional students. A strong academic and experiential background in early childhood development is a definite asset, too, since this is the level at which many multiply handicapped children function.

Teachers of the Speech Impaired

In public school systems, children with speech impairments usually work with a trained itinerant speech pathologist or therapist. This individual, to be certified, has participated in a college program that includes course work in anatomy and physiology (particularly of the speech and hearing apparatus), diagnostic methods, corrective techniques, and psychology (emphasizing problems of adjustment and mental health), plus supportive courses in education to help her work more effectively with the classroom teacher. Training in art, music, and the uses of instructional media gives the speech specialist additional techniques to use. It is important, too, that the teacher (regular or special) speak distinctly and correctly, as a model for both the speech impaired and non–speech impaired students. In some states, this is one of the qualifications necessary for teacher certification in any field. Increasingly, the program for certification in this field requires a fifth year of education.

In small school districts that have no speech therapist, the classroom teachers should be provided with in-service courses that teach them basic information on speech disorders, causes of speech problems, techniques for remedying at least the simpler problems, and the emotional by-products of speech disorders. If they are aware of these emotional by-products, they may be able, for example, to reduce the negative reactions of peers to the speech impaired child and thereby reduce possible sources of "acting-out" behavior and interference with learning.

Teachers of the Language Handicapped

The prospective teacher who wishes to specialize in teaching the language handicapped will find it difficult to locate regular college courses specifically designed to meet his interests and needs. A number of higher education institutions offer courses in teaching English as a second language (TESL) but, aside from this, expect the student to work toward the

Student teachers have many opportunities for individual contact with students in addition to classroom teaching. (Laimute Druskis/Jeroboam)

usual elementary- or secondary-level teaching certificate. Northern Arizona University prepares students to work with and teach AmerIndians in the Southwest, in part by requiring field experience on the reservations. The VISTA and Teacher Corps programs of the late 1960s and the 1970s similarly offered some on-the-job training with language instruction in Appalachia, inner-city urban neighborhoods, and the Southwest. Otherwise, there has been little effort to prepare teachers to meet these students' needs.

Solid preparation in language arts, music, arts and crafts, sociology, anthropology, and TESL is strongly emphasized for education majors hoping to work in this area. The child development courses usually found in teacher preparation curricula should be supplemented with cross-cultural studies to provide an understanding of varying child care practices and parental attitudes. There is a great need, when working with both the language handicapped and the culturally different, for positive and constructive interaction among teachers, parents, and the community; thus, these cross-cultural studies are vital if there is to be effective communication. Experience in working with staff members from other disciplines, such as social work, human relations, psychology, and anthropology, is also useful, for a team approach is frequently applied in working with language handicapped children and their parents.

In one survey of teachers working with bilingual/multicultural students, who were sometimes otherwise exceptional as well, the types of competency needed for effective teaching were rated for importance. High on the list were knowledge, interpretation, and use of assessment techniques and data; familiarity with the children's language or dialect; knowledge of specific teaching methods useful with bilingual/multicultural exceptional children; and being able to teach parents to work more effectively with their children (Prieto, Rueda, & Rodriguez, 1981).

In terms of personal characteristics, the teacher of the language handicapped needs a great deal of patience and the willingness to invest more time and effort than any teachers' manual calls for. In many cases, the teacher has to deal with hostility and resistance that is not common with other groups of exceptional children, so that these personal traits become important.

Teachers of the Culturally Different

As pride in our cultural diversity grows, teacher preparation programs have begun to incorporate approaches that increase the prospective teacher's exposure to different cultures and life-styles. These approaches include separate courses or modules, series of courses, experimental courses, and a general diffusion of information throughout the professional training program (Fuchigami, 1980). The last option implements the standard set for basic teacher education programs by the National Council for Accreditation of Teacher Education (NCATE), effective in 1979:

The institution gives evidence of planning for multicultural education in its teaching education curricula including both the general and professional studies component. (Carriker & Berdine, 1979, p. 66)

Subject matter and teaching techniques continue to be important, but the prospective regular or special teacher also needs to have a greater understanding of the urban poor, the realities of socioeconomic disadvantage, the bureaucratic and legislative intricacies of dealing with social problems, and the cultural mores and language difficulties of the children he is trying to teach. In particular, teachers "need to be trained not only in the overt aspects of cultural/linguistic differences, but will need to become familiar with culturally associated characteristics that may be directly related to educational attainment" (Rueda & Prieto, 1979, p. 9).

Courses in and field experience with cultural differences are essential to prepare teachers for dealing with culturally diverse students. The acquisition of foreign language competence (depending on where the education major expects to teach) or a course in linguistics that compares with nonstandard English dialects is also an asset, as these language skills make communication and rapport easier for both teacher and student. (Note: Bilingual teachers are "in demand" in many school districts; such competence thus increases the probability of obtaining a teaching position.) Those who want to work in a counseling/guidance capacity should have many of these same experiences, supplemented by courses in psychological testing of minorities and diagnostic and remedial techniques for culturally diverse students.

Teachers in any classroom must have respect for the cultural "baggage" that children bring with them to school. They must also be able to adapt to their unique characteristics and life-styles. However, there does not seem to be a simple list of traits of teachers who are successful with culturally diverse children. Rather, "effective teachers discover the techniques that work with particular children, not by matching techniques to observable characteristics, but rather by a search process, characterized by trial and error" (Murnane & Phillips, 1981, p. 99). Culturally effective counselors similarly need to meet their clients within the clients' cultural frame of reference and work from that point (Arredondo-Dowd & Gonsalves, 1980).

Teachers of the Emotionally Troubled

Like teachers of other exceptional children, the prospective teacher of the emotionally troubled should have a solid background in general and professional education, course work in the psychology and educational needs of exceptional students, and extensive experience in working directly with a variety of exceptional students, especially those with emotional problems. These practical experiences should ideally include interaction with other professionals who work with exceptional children, for the teacher of the emotionally troubled will have cause to work with these colleagues later. Many colleges offer an undergraduate curriculum, or sometimes only a graduate program, that prepares teachers for this field. Typically, more courses in psychology (especially clinical psychology) and classroom management techniques are included than in other special education programs, because they provide valuable insights and techniques relevant to working with emotionally troubled children.

A few studies have emphasized the levels of competency needed by the teacher of the emotionally troubled. Hewett, for example, described a hierarchy of such competencies. In descending order of importance, they were: objectivity, flexibility, structure (that is, the ability to set consistent and reasonable behavior limits that are maintained even when adapted to individual needs), resourcefulness, social reinforcement, curriculum expertise, and the ability to serve as an intellectual model (1966). This paragon among teachers should be able to leave the troubles of her students at the school door, but most have indicated that this was impossible.

Teachers of the Socially Maladjusted

Few, if any, undergraduate professional preparation programs are geared toward the teaching of socially maladjusted students. Instead, programs are generally focused on the emotionally troubled, with whom the socially maladjusted have much in common. To supplement the typical program, therefore, the prospective teacher of these youths should take courses dealing with delinquency and urban youth, social problems, and cultural differences, and perhaps even a few law courses dealing with children's rights, the legal system, and family law. Experience as a volunteer in the numerous tutoring programs, antigang projects, inner-city recreation programs, and court-sponsored rehabilitation efforts provides a vital dimension for enriching academic work and is strongly urged (if not required).

Teachers of the socially maladjusted should generally have experience with regular classes before attempting to work in this special field. That will provide a fuller perspective as well as self-confidence. Teachers will also need to be familiar with remedial teaching techniques and materials, as well as have an understanding of group dynamics. Sensitivity to the psychological needs of the socially maladjusted, imagination, a sense of humor, and the ability to be firm and consistent without rigidity or harshness are important personal attributes if a teacher is to be effective with this group of exceptional students. Finally, this teacher needs to be a positive thinker, able to transmit hope and optimism to his students.

SUMMARY

Mainstreaming has had an impact not only on exceptional students but also on the education of their teachers. This chapter has therefore focused on the ways in which regular teachers can be prepared to teach students in their classes and to introduce the needs of exceptional students to their nonexceptional classmates, on the importance of teacher and peer attitudes in the education of exceptional children, and on specific programs for teachers of different groups of exceptional children. Considerable emphasis has been placed on field experience with exceptional children during the undergraduate years, as this both tests the commitment of the prospective teacher to the chosen group and better prepares her for independent functioning in the field after graduation.

There is some question as to whether exceptional students should be added to class rolls as they are mainstreamed but based in a special homeroom, or whether they should be considered members of a regular homeroom (at the elementary level) and be excused for special instruction. If possible, the latter seems more desirable from the point of view of generating positive teacher attitudes toward the student. Both teachers and peers are more likely to be accepting of the student assigned regularly to the group than they might be of the student "added on" to the roster. In view of studies in which students assigned to regular or higher-level classes experienced successful personal and learning adjustments in those settings, placement in regular homerooms and classes also appears to contribute positively to a student's self-concept.

SUGGESTED ADDITIONAL READINGS

Benavides, A. Cultural awareness training for the exceptional teacher. *Teaching Exceptional Children*, 1980, *13*, 8–11.

Casso, H. J. *Bilingual/bicultural education and teacher training*. Washington, D.C.: National Education Association, 1976.

Frith, G. H., and Edwards, R. Misconceptions of regular classroom teachers about physically handicapped students. *Exceptional Children*, 1981, *48*, 182–184.

Golin, A. K., and Ducanis, A. J. Preparation for teamwork: A model of interdisciplinary education. *Teacher Education and Special Education*, 1981, *4* (1), 25–30.

Gonzales, E. Preparation for teaching the multicultural exceptional child. *Teacher Education and Special Education*, 1979, *2* (4), 12–18.

Heller, H. W., and Schillit, J. *Project RETOOL: Continuing education for teacher educators in special education*. University, Ala.: Project RETOOL and the Teacher Education Division, Council for Exceptional Children, 1979.

Maker, C. J. *Training teachers for the gifted and talented: A comparison of models*. Reston, Va.: Council for Exceptional Children, 1975.

McDaniel, L. Changing vocational teachers' attitudes toward the handicapped. *Exceptional Children*, 1982, *48*, 377–378.

Schloss, P., and Miller, S. R. Effects of the label "institutionalized" vs. "regular school student" on teacher expectations. *Exceptional Children*, 1981, *48*, 363–365.

Stainback, S., and Stainback, W. Influencing the attitudes of regular class teachers about the education of severely retarded students. *Education and Training of the Mentally Retarded*, 1982, *17*, 88–92.

Thompson, R. H., White, K. R., and Morgan, D. P. Teacher-student interaction patterns in classrooms with mainstreamed mildly handicapped students. *American Educational Research Journal*, 1982, *19*, 220–236.

Voeltz, L. M. Children's attitudes toward handicapped peers. *American Journal of Mental Deficiency*, 1980, *84*, 455–464.

Ysseldyke, J., Algozzine, B., and Allen, D. Participation of regular education teachers in special education team decision making. *Exceptional Children*, 1981, *48*, 365–367.

CHAPTER 16/
ADMINISTRATION
AND SPECIAL EDUCATION

Throughout this book, we have considered a number of modifications for the education of exceptional students. These have varied from segregated classes to placement in the regular classroom, with or without the support of resource teachers and resource centers—the whole range of "least restrictive environments." In any of these settings, there are administrative details that have to be worked out for teacher selection, student selection and assignment, curricula, scheduling, supplies, equipment, facilities, and staff support. Who has the responsibility for undertaking these tasks? What factors must they consider when making these decisions?

Basic to these questions are the responsibilities of the school board. These include financial concerns as a major element. To begin with, classrooms and programs must be made available to physically disabled and sensory impaired students to meet the requirements of Sections 503 and 504 of the Vocational Rehabilitation Act of 1973 (Stagich, 1980). Decisions about the costs of modifying building entrances, restrooms, and other restrictive physical barriers, about purchasing technological aids such as computers, and about hiring aides to accompany and assist some exceptional students rest finally with the school board, which acts on the recommendations of the superintendent's staff. The expense of in-service programs for regular classroom teachers who will implement the mainstreaming provision of P.L. 94-142 is also a matter for the school board. In most school districts, the initial decisions have already been made, but the continuing (and rising) costs of meeting these obligations have become a source of heated controversy between taxpayers and the boards. To this problem, there are no ready answers.

SCHOOL SYSTEM ORGANIZATION

The organizational chart of a school system shows who has authority over whom and who serves as an adviser to whom. The special education coordinator (or supervisor or director) can be placed either in a "line" position, as shown in Figure 16.1, or in a "staff" position, as shown in Figure 16.2. In the line position, the coordinator has responsibility for and authority over both the special education teachers and the special educa-

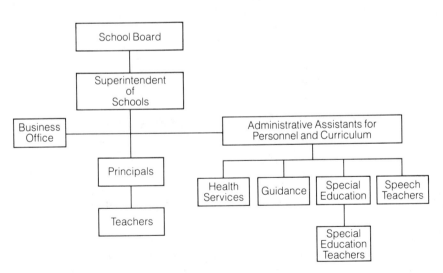

Figure 16.1   Special education as a line position

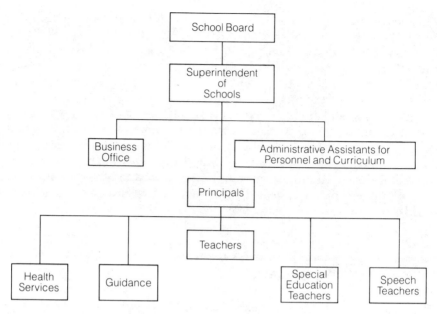

Figure 16.2   Special education as a staff position

tion program. Since the teachers are located in different buildings, the coordinator becomes a kind of principal without a building. In the staff position, on the other hand, the coordinator of special education is an adviser or consultant to the building principals and special education teachers but has little direct authority over the teachers and pupils assigned to a particular school building.

The administrative functions in special education can include:

1. Personnel selection
2. Personnel evaluation
3. Budget preparation for special education programs
4. Curriculum design
5. Selection of students for admission to special classes
6. Interaction with parents of exceptional students
7. Providing a supportive climate for innovation and research by special education teachers
8. Selection of materials for special education programs
9. Coordination of efforts with **ancillary personnel** (those who provide supportive services)

A number of advantages and disadvantages must be considered before deciding who has the primary responsibility for these and related tasks. In a line position, the coordinator has primary responsibility for all of these functions. This poses some problems in terms of the range of necessary capabilities and the amount of time required for effective supervision of each function. In a staff position, there is greater division of labor, with more specialists available for dealing with specific problems. A study in Indiana that included more than 250 senior administrators, directors of special education, elementary school principals, regular classroom teachers, and special education teachers found that these educators expected directors of special education to function primarily in boundary-spanning activities. That is, the directors should work with parents or other groups outside of the school building, with referral agencies, and as intermediaries between schools (Robson, 1981).

Personnel Selection

The school board is the legally constituted body responsible for the selection, employment, and dismissal of all school personnel. As a practical matter, the board generally follows the recommendations of the superintendent of schools, who is also hired by the board. The superintendent, in turn, tends to follow the recommendations of his assistant in charge of personnel. In the area of special education, one would expect that the assistant would consult with the special education coordinator about applicants' professional qualifications and with the building principal about their ability to fit into the specific school staff and program.

If the coordinator is in a line position, the building principal may participate minimally in personnel selection, but the coordinator has the primary authority, and the teacher's assignment to a specific school building is perceived only as a physical placement. On the other hand, if the coordinator is in a staff position, the building principal has greater responsibility for and authority over teacher selection and, therefore, participates more actively. In this latter situation, the special education teacher is perceived as an integral part of the staff of a particular school, not as someone with primary ties to the central administration.

Personnel Evaluation

Teachers, tenured or not, usually are subject to a formal (written) annual evaluation. This practice seems destined to continue, as demands for performance-based criteria and teacher accountability increase.

If the coordinator is in a line position, it is her responsibility to evaluate each special education teacher's competence and performance. If the coordinator is in a staff position, the responsibility for this goes to the building principal. Which of these administrators should be responsible? In Robson's survey, the participating educators felt that the principal should take major responsibility for all supervisory and evaluation functions regarding personnel (1981).

Logically, the evaluator should be the person who has the best opportunity to observe and interact with the special education teachers. Since these teachers are usually located in several schools, the coordinator can observe a specific teacher only periodically, while the building principal has opportunities to do so daily. The decision as to who is primarily responsible, then, has to be based on the set of observations and interactions that provides the more valid evaluation: periodic lengthy stays or brief but frequent visits. Ideally, whichever administrator has the task should consult with the other to obtain a fuller picture of the teacher's activities.

Budget Preparation

The usual pattern for transmission of budget requests is from the special education coordinator (after consultation with the teachers) to the administrative budget officer to the school superintendent and then to the school board. Modifications in the budget can, and usually do, occur anywhere along the way.

There should be little question that the entire special education staff knows, better than most other school personnel, which materials are best suited to the needs of exceptional students. On the basis of their information and experience, they should be able to recommend necessary and appropriate instructional and supporting materials, whether for short-term or long-term investment, and whether for segregated or main-streamed exceptional students. The remaining financial question then is whether such costs as custodial service for the special education classrooms, chalk, paper, audiovisual materials, texts, films, and records should be included in the special education or the building principal's budget.

Curriculum Design

Planning the curriculum for exceptional students must be a team effort. The development of an individualized education program (IEP), in keeping with the regulations of P.L. 94-142, requires the participation of the pupil's classroom teacher(s), a second academically qualified person (such as a special educator), the child's parents (unless they adamantly refuse), and the child himself, whenever possible. Other appropriate staff members to include in the planning sessions may be ophthalmologists,

Specialists and classroom teachers plan together in an IEP
conference. (Photo from H. Armstrong Roberts)

audiologists, psychologists, school counselors, psychiatrists, speech
therapists, social workers, orthopedists, and pediatricians, to name
several.

A critical reason for the existence of IEPs is to enforce a view of the
exceptional student as an individual rather than as a faceless member of
one of the groups we have considered. The attention given by teachers
and ancillary personnel contributes to such a view. To reach the goal of
planning optimally for the individual, however, non–special education
teachers and administrators alike should have in-service training in
the needs and abilities of exceptional students, as well as in the preparation of IEPs.

All IEPs must include

statements of the child's present levels of educational performance, annual goals,
short-term instructional objectives, the extent to which the child will participate
in regular programs, the dates during which the IEP will be applicable, and the
criteria and procedures that will be used in evaluating the program's effectiveness.
(National Advisory Committee on the Handicapped, 1977, pp. 7–8)

In creating the IEP, consultations might appropriately be held with the
special education coordinator and the building principal, who might have
suggestions regarding such practical matters as space availability, equipment or special facilities needed, and transportation requirements. An
especially "sticky" problem is scheduling needed special services (Lieberman, 1982). A balance needs to be struck between regular and special

educational services and demands so that there is minimum pressure on and conflict for the student as well as the staff. The effective implementation of the IEP will require the active support of a wide variety of personnel, so they should be involved in the planning as appropriate.

TEACHERS, STUDENTS, AND LEARNING

Supporting the Teachers

A classroom teacher may need several kinds of support: guidance in finding alternative instructional or classroom management techniques, new materials, resources for research, and opportunities to develop and test original ideas. In most cases, these can be supplied effectively by a competent and flexible special education coordinator. When a special class teacher becomes too involved with a child's problem or overwhelmed by difficulties in the classroom, to whom should she turn? Teacher "burnout," or stress, is a problem that has received increasing attention in recent years.

For short-term or immediate problems, the school principal tends to be "on the spot," so to speak, and the teacher may feel more comfortable and secure about taking a short walk to her office than about making a phone call to the coordinator in the central administration building. Even if the principal knows relatively little about special education itself, the teacher can expect her to have an understanding of both teacher-pupil relationships and classroom problems. If the coordinator and the teacher are physically miles apart, there is some question about whether a crisis can be handled or even reduced by a phone call. (This assumes that the teacher feels psychologically free to make the call and that the coordinator can be reached immediately.)

For the more chronic "burnout" problem, however, it is ultimately the responsibility of the coordinator to find the causes of stress and remove them if possible. The coordinator should investigate the environmental conditions, plan and implement appropriate intervention strategies, and then evaluate the effectiveness of the intervention in reducing stress (Dixon, Shaw, & Bensky, 1980). Possible strategies include placing a teacher aide (paid or volunteer) in the classroom, changing the teacher's assignment for a period of time, reducing the number of students with whom the teacher has to work, and providing emotional or academic support.

Selection of Students

There is no question that certain children need to be placed in a special education class on a full-time basis. The trainable mentally retarded and

Individual testing by a psychologist is often appropriate. (Photo from Stock, Boston)

the deaf-blind are two examples. In the case of other exceptional students, however—for example, the gifted, learning disabled, or psychosocially troubled—someone has to decide whether they will profit from special placement and, if so, whether this should be a short-term or long-term assignment.

Tucker has proposed a nineteen-step assessment system that involves personnel at the classroom, building, and district levels (1982). It begins with perceiving that a problem exists and involves subsequent consultation with specialists and parents. This proposal's virtue is that it is orderly and reduces confusion about what to do next.

Before a decision is reached, the special education teacher should have an opportunity both to observe the student and to review records of her past school performance, if she has attended school. The psychologist has the responsibility for examining the youngster to determine her levels of intellectual and social-emotional functioning and to diagnose, if possible, her particular strengths and weaknesses. Depending on the nature of the child's alleged exceptionality, the school counselor, a consulting psychiatrist, a reading specialist, or other personnel may also need to participate in the case study. If there are several students under consideration for a limited number of spaces in particular classes, the coordinator, in consultation with the reviewing team of teachers and specialists, will have to establish a placement priority list. Such a list would be based on a combination of entrance criteria for special programs, the children's individual needs and abilities, and each family's willingness to support the new placement.

In selecting students, it is necessary to avoid labeling them. It is much too easy to test children, using tests that may be biased, and to place them in "pigeonholes" on the basis of narrow assessment procedures. P.L. 94-142 is supposed to reduce such pigeonholing by its requirements, but in practice, unfortunately, the rules are not always followed. The victims of inadequate and/or inappropriate assessment are often members of minority groups or otherwise disadvantaged youngsters for whom the tests and other measures used are unrealistic.

These practices are in violation of the standards set by the American Psychological Association for testing (1981); the law, as defined in the Civil Rights Act of 1964 and various state statutes; and court decisions, such as *Griggs et al. v. Duke Power Co.* (1971), *Diana v. California State Board of Education* (1970), and *Larry P. v. Riles* (1972) (Oakland, 1977). Accordingly, efforts are being made (as noted earlier in this book) to design tests that are appropriate to culturally different children in language and content. The test results, together with other means of assessment, are then evaluated before proceeding with the development of an IEP, placing a student on a list for special education services, and seeking the least restrictive environment in which the child can profit from instruction. Selection criteria for mainstreaming exceptional students obviously must also conform to ethical practices and legal requirements.

Interaction with Parents

When the average school child has a problem, or when his parents have questions, concerns, or complaints about the classroom situation, the parents usually request an appointment with the school principal. It is no different with the parents of exceptional children. If, however, the special education coordinator is in a line position, the parents must go to her instead. This may pose practical problems for both parties. It may be difficult for the parents to get to the coordinator's office in the central administration building, and they may feel uncomfortable about going there. On the coordinator's part, travel to different locations for parent conferences takes up time that the busy coordinator can ill afford.

If the person responsible for all students in the school is the principal, there are fewer problems. It would be expected, however, that once the problem is presented by the parents, the principal would consult with the student's teacher(s) and, if warranted, with the special education coordinator. It should be noted here that it is difficult to divide a child into parts. Classroom performance and classroom behavior are two expressions of one individual. It is difficult for parents, particularly, to understand why one person is chiefly concerned with their child's learning and another with whether or not she is a disciplinary problem. Parental confusion on this point is justified: Most of the time, the two are intertwined.

Selection of Materials

Since the special education coordinator is assumed to be a specialist, one would expect that locating, evaluating, and selecting instructional materials for special classes and resource centers would be properly in her domain. Such selection must be done in consultation with those who teach exceptional students and, in some cases, with ancillary personnel. Competence and expertise in this area are clearly more common among special education coordinators than building principals; thus, selection should be primarily the responsibility of the coordinator.

COORDINATION OF EFFORTS

It seems fairly clear that the administrative aspects of special education require considerable interaction among all the staff involved—the special teachers, the coordinator, the principal, and other specialists in the school system. It is also clear that the geographical dispersion of special education teachers in multibuilding districts creates possibilities for jurisdictional disputes.

Scholl (1968), Calovini (1969), Roe and Drake (1974), and others maintain that the building principal has the final responsibility for all programs, students, and staff in his school. The feasibility of renewing a special class teacher's perspective, integrating both students and teachers into the total school picture, coordinating the programs of special and regular class teachers with respect to a particular student, ensuring acceptance of the special classes by others in the school, and working with the parents of exceptional students is greatest when the coordinator of these diverse activities is on the premises. This is even more true when special education services are provided by either itinerant or resource teachers. The principal is then the liaison between the special and regular teachers. Together, they have to make special education work for each student.

The principal also must decide whether the special class(es) will be isolated from or integrated with the rest of the school; arrange student and teacher schedules to accommodate class and therapy sessions, lunch periods, and transportation; and, if necessary, explain the special education program and the concept of mainstreaming to parents of other children in the school. First, of course, he must be willing to accept the special education program, teacher, and students into the school (although there may not be much choice under the law or in terms of district needs). More importantly, "the success of the special program depends upon the degree of leadership exercised by the principal" (Scholl, 1968, p. 25).

FOR EXAMPLE . . .

Studies of principals' attitudes toward exceptional students have been rare. One survey of 345 principals in Maine, however, revealed perceptions that could certainly have a significant impact on the support given to mainstreaming. These principals "apparently have little faith that mentally retarded pupils, regardless of degree of handicap, can be successfully integrated into regular classes, as compared with pupils with other handicaps. For example, of 21 handicapping conditions listed according to degree and type, 'mild mental retardation' was ranked #12. Only 46.4% of all principals viewed this category of pupils as having an 'excellent' or 'good' predictive success rate. . . . 65 respondents (representing 18.9% of the total sample) indicated that mildly retarded children have a 'poor' or 'very poor' chance to be successfully mainstreamed" (W. E. Davis, 1980, p. 176).

If the principal's attitude is negative, can a student's failure be blamed on inappropriate placement, the student himself, or the receiving teacher?

These added responsibilities of principals, combined with the pessimistic views of exceptional students that they may have, indicate that there should be some changes in the preparation of educational administrators. It seems appropriate that in graduate school or in special workshops they should be exposed to a basic course about exceptional students, just as regular classroom teachers are. In addition, it would be very helpful to them and others with whom they must interact if they were to learn directly from the various specialists how *they* perceive their roles and needs in the process of educating exceptional students. The combination of information and better communication should enable the principal to take a more positive attitude in what is a key role in this process.

Does the principal's role leave the special education coordinator with nothing to coordinate? Hardly. The coordinator is the key resource person in instructional matters, providing information to the special education and regular classroom teachers, as well as to other school personnel. She must coordinate the work of the teams involved in selection, placement, and programming of exceptional students. Her presence is often appropriate at IEP meetings with parents. Finally, she has important consulting responsibilities to the principals and the central administration, and she is the logical person to develop proposals for programs funded under the Education for All Handicapped Children Act.

SUMMARY

Special education programs reach into almost every part of the school system and necessitate a great deal of administrative effort. The advantages in having one person who is primarily responsible for all phases of the program are outweighed by considerations of the range of skills and expenditure of time required; these are too great for one person in most districts. It is suggested, therefore, that pupil selection and program development be the primary responsibilities of the special education coordinator, along with budget, and that all other matters involving special teachers and exceptional students, including supervision and evaluation, be the responsibility of the building principal. The coordinator would be a key consultant to the principal in all special education matters in his jurisdiction, as well as to the special education teachers themselves.

To increase the integration of special education with the total school program, the principal should arrange for the special teachers to participate in the professional activities of the school and to share in the usual faculty responsibilities and duties as much as possible. Such integration is personally and professionally valuable to the teachers and encourages acceptance of the program and the exceptional students by the entire school population.

In summary, the complexities of school organization and the expansion of information in special education are such that the special education coordinator is best viewed as a specialist in a staff position in the administrative hierarchy. The principal, a generalist in a line position, utilizes the expertise of the coordinator and other specialists in making decisions that affect the education of exceptional children. This arrangement, in the eyes of school principals, offers the most flexibility and effective lines of communication for the ultimate benefit of the students.

SUGGESTED ADDITIONAL READINGS

Christoplos, F. Keeping exceptional children in regular classes. *Exceptional Children*, 1973, *39*, 569–572.

Cline, R. Principals' attitudes and knowledge about handicapped children. *Exceptional Children*, 1981, *48*, 172–174.

Colella, H. V., and Foster, H. BOCES: A delivery system for special education. *Phi Delta Kappan*, 1974, *55*, 544–545.

Crossland, C. L., Fox, B. R., and Baker, R. Differential perceptions of role responsibilities among professionals in the public school. *Exceptional Children*, 1982, *48*, 536–538.

Gilliam, J. E., and Coleman, M. C. Who influences IEP committee decisions? *Exceptional Children*, 1981, *47*, 642–644.

Icabone, D. G., and Gallery, M. E. Caught in the mainstream: The severely and profoundly retarded learner and the least restrictive environment. *Rehabilitation Literature*, 1982, *43* (3/4), 66–71.

Krajewski, R. J., Martin, J. S., and Walden, J. C. *The elementary school principalship: Leadership for the 1980s*. New York: Holt, Rinehart & Winston, 1983.

Ottman, R. A. Before a handicapped student enters the classroom: What the special educator can do. *Teaching Exceptional Children*, 1981, *14* (1), 41–43.

Rocha, R. M., Wiley, D., and Watson, M. J. Special subject teachers and the special educator work to mainstream. *Teaching Exceptional Children*, 1982, *14*, 141–145.

Theimer, R. K., and Rupiper, O. J. Special education litigation and school psychology. *Journal of School Psychology*, 1975, *13*, 324–334.

Turnbull, A. P., Strickland, B., and Turnbull, H. R. Due process hearing officers: Characteristics, needs, and appointment criteria. *Exceptional Children*, 1981, *48*, 48–54.

Tymitz-Wolf, B. Guidelines for assessing IEP goals and objectives. *Teaching Exceptional Children*, 1982, *48*, 536–538.

CHAPTER 17/
FAMILIES OF
EXCEPTIONAL STUDENTS

From the time of identification and diagnosis of a child's exceptionality, which may be as early as shortly after birth, the family faces a challenge. What does having an exceptional child in the home mean to the parents? His siblings? His grandparents? How does having an exceptional child affect relationships with friends and neighbors? How do the parents respond to their child and his special needs? How do they view, and how are they viewed by, the professionals with whom they must interact? How do they view special education—as an opportunity or otherwise? Just as there really is no such thing as the "average" family, so there are no pat answers to these questions, but we can gain some idea of what having an exceptional child means to those closest to him. In individual cases, a clue to what may unfold in the future can be found in the family's perception of the exceptional child as a problem or as a challenge.

FAMILY RELATIONSHIPS

A child with either a gift or a disability obviously demands more time, attention, and financial expenditure than the average child. In some cases, the demands or needs may be so overwhelming as to interfere with normal family interaction. In other situations, the presence of an exceptional child may bring a special sense of purpose and commitment to the family. One thing is certain: There will be *some* reaction.

Parental Responses

There are a variety of possible parental reactions to having an exceptional child, ranging from overinvolvement to denial to realistic acceptance. In the case of a handicapping condition, the family initially experiences grief and disappointment that the child is not the wished-for and expected normal child. This is a perfectly normal reaction, and one that may recur at predictable points in the child's life.

Depending on the personal fantasies of the individual parent, these moments may occur during holidays, family reunions, birthdays, the wedding of their normal child, watching normal children play, or hearing mothers of normal children chat about their child's successes or failures. (Wikler, 1981, p. 283)

The family needs information about current and future care for their exceptional child, emotional support from other parents confronted with the same challenge, answers to questions about how to face social stigma, and ways to cope with their own chronic stress.

If a parent (usually the mother) becomes overinvolved with the child's needs, it can lead to neglect of the other children and the spouse. This can lead to emotional problems in those who are neglected and a strained relationship with the marital partner, possibly even divorce. Professionals involved with a family in this situation should urge the parents to find a relief caretaker, even for an hour a day. This brief respite may help them to realize that total preoccupation with the exceptional child is unfair to themselves, the child, and the rest of the family.

A second possible parental reaction to the exceptional child is denial of any exceptionality, a refusal to face or accept the fact that adjustments in the child's care are needed. This impedes the child's development and reduces the probability that special education programs will be beneficial. When the child is in special classes, the denying parents frequently undo at home any progress she has made in school. For example, they may deny enrichment opportunities to the gifted child, omit recommended exercises in the orthopedically handicapped child's daily routine, expect the hearing impaired child to respond to verbal directions, and reinforce the undesirable behavior of the emotionally troubled child. As a result, every

Strange as it may seem, some mothers of youngsters with acting talents are perfect examples of the overinvolved parent. They are called "stage mothers" (although the child may be a budding movie or television star rather than in live theater). All the mother's activities are focused on the child and his career. The mother tutors the child, sits for hours backstage, shops for costumes, argues with producers, travels with the cast, and has no life (nor has the child) apart from his acting career. A common outcome has been divorce from the husband/father and resentment on the child's part as he grows older.

Monday the special class teacher has to begin anew, attempting to overcome the problems created by the lack of parental cooperation over the weekend. In the extreme, denial can mean rejection of the child and abandonment of all responsibility for her welfare.

There is, of course, a third type of parental response: a realistic acceptance of the child's differences, combined with constructive efforts to work with him and with the professionals involved. These parents make special care and special education easier for everyone, particularly their exceptional child. This is not to say that they do not experience the same stresses as the parents who react in more extreme ways, only that they handle these stresses more effectively. Even they may not be able to avoid the strains on their mainstreamed exceptional child, however, when he becomes an adolescent (Chess, Fernandez, & Korn, 1980).

For all parents who try to help their exceptional children, there are tormenting questions: At what point do the family's sacrifices become too high a price to pay for keeping a profoundly retarded child at home? Where is the money to come from for psychotherapy and other care? What will happen to the physically or mentally dependent child when the parents die? Is it fair to place a lifelong burden on her siblings? Is the disability due to heredity? Should the retarded youngster or her siblings marry? If they marry, should they have children? What kinds of social interaction are available for the blind child? Although most of these questions face the parents of all but the exceptionally able, even they must be concerned about the quality of their child's education, the financial sacrifices, the time commitments, and the emotional involvement.

Siblings

Siblings of the exceptional child, as well as others, often take their cues from parental behavior and attitudes. They may accept or reject the "spe-

Sibling support is important if an exceptional youth is to have a better chance of leading an active life. (Bohdan Hrynswych/Stock, Boston)

cial person'' in the family, and they certainly might be resentful of overindulgence of the exceptional child by one or both parents. Trevino has asserted that the

prospects for the normal siblings appear to be worst for families in which (1) there are only two siblings, a normal and a handicapped child, (2) the normal sibling is close in age to or younger than the handicapped sibling, or is the oldest female child, (3) the normal and handicapped child are the same sex, or (4) the parents are unable to accept the handicap. (1979, p. 489)

Although this assertion is based on Trevino's research and experience, these factors do not hold true by any means in all families with exceptional children, except perhaps for the last one. Denial by the parents that a problem exists can cause many difficulties for their other children, ranging from neglect to inconsistency to delegation of responsibility to the siblings. There is also no question that it can be very hard for a young person to be outshone by a gifted younger sibling.

In contrast to Trevino's pessimistic, but also possibly valid, viewpoint, a study by F. K. Grossman with siblings of retarded children and youths suggests that many of their subjects (college students) benefited from their experience (1972). On the basis of tests and interviews, those who had benefited appeared

to be more tolerant, more compassionate, more knowing about prejudice and its consequences, and they were often, but not always, more certain about their own futures, about personal and vocational goals, than comparable young adults who had not had such experiences. (1972, p. 84)

There were also subjects for whom the experience had a negative impact. They had feelings of resentment, guilt, and anxiety. They indicated that they had often been "deprived of attention that they needed to help them develop, simply because so much of family time and energy had been given to the handicapped children" (1972, p. 84).

Realistic acceptance of and participation in caring for the handicapped child, with responsibilities geared to the abilities and maturity of the sibling(s), creates a happier family situation. Siblings cannot and should not be expected to devote all of their spare time to the exceptional brother or sister, but they can teach, play with, accompany, or "baby-sit" with their sibling occasionally and help with therapy. They should not always have to include the exceptional child in their peer-group activities, any more than an older brother should have to include a younger one in his activities.

Siblings may be confronted with taunts from other children, and this can be difficult at any age. How they respond to these and other unpleasant situations depends partly on their own maturity level and partly on their parents' attitudes and degree of support. As a result of their experiences, many siblings as college students enroll in the special education major or a related field, where they can enrich not only the lives of their future students but also those of their peers.

Grandparents

Grandparents, like the parents, tend to be initially disappointed at having a handicapped grandchild. Their hopes for posterity have been dashed, and, again like some parents, they perceive this as a negative reflection on themselves. However, grandparents can be a source of strong emotional support for the parents and provide extra pairs of hands in helping to care for the exceptional child. Much of their influence on the child and the family, of course, depends upon their physical proximity.

Even at a distance, however, grandparents can bring new information relevant to the child's condition or education to the parents' attention. They can, when with the family, give the child attention, love, stimulation, and reinforcement (Berns, 1980). They can be activists in advocacy or fund-raising organizations related to their grandchild's exceptionality. "If the problems of a handicapped child are never far from the parents' minds and hearts, grandparents may be needed to point out what is best not just for the child but for all members of the family as well" (Berns, 1980, p. 238). Indeed, they may be of greatest help to the siblings, if they are being neglected or overwhelmed because of the exceptional child, whether gifted or handicapped.

Friends and Neighbors

Friends and neighbors vary in their reactions to exceptional children and their families, just as members of the family vary. Some may be pitying, others sympathetic, and some will shun the family or keep their own children at a distance. If the exceptional child is in trouble with the law or poses a threat to personal safety, avoidance of the child is understandable. In other instances, however, ignorance and prejudice often underlie such negative behavior.

Often, however, children with learning disabilities, speech difficulties, mild retardation, and reduced motor coordination are accepted by neighborhood children and included in their after-school activities as "one of the gang."

FOR EXAMPLE . . .

Roger came into the neighborhood when he was five years old. He had a bad temper, almost unintelligible speech, and very good psychomotor coordination. A few years later, having fallen behind in his studies, he was diagnosed as a learning disabled student. His coordination and mechanical abilities turned out to be the keys to peer acceptance rather than rejection. His peers included him in backyard baseball games and went to him for repairs on their bicycles. They understood his speech, although their parents didn't, and so they undertook the task of being his interpreter to the local adults. By adolescence, with the aid of special education and therapy, Roger's temper had cooled and his speech and learning abilities had greatly improved. His parents believed that at least some of his social and emotional growth could be attributed to the friendship of his neighborly peers.

Supportive friends and neighbors can similarly be a source of strength for the parents. By being sensitive to the family's problems, assisting in therapeutic exercises, providing information, and occasionally staying with the exceptional child so that the parents can go out for an evening together, they perform acts of friendship that money can't buy.

PARENT-PROFESSIONAL RELATIONSHIPS

Parents and Nonteaching Professionals

Parents of exceptional children, even those who are themselves mental health professionals, have often found themselves being given bad advice or wrong diagnoses by the professionals they consult, according to Darling (1979) and Turnbull and Turnbull (1978). Conversely, they may be blessed with empathetic pediatricians and psychiatrists or psychologists. The parents do need support from these professionals, guidance that reflects an understanding of the family crisis and parental concerns and aid in coping with ambivalent emotional reactions to their exceptional child. Even pediatricians and psychologists who have worked with disabled and retarded children for years, however, are sometimes so overcome by their inability to "cure" that they develop an objective facade that is perceived by bewildered or grieving parents as lack of sympathy or understanding.

Clearly, what is needed is a better quality of professional-parent interaction, from the diagnostic stage on through all the years of care. Wolraich has presented some specific suggestions for training pediatricians for their roles as counselors to parents of exceptional children (1982). A similar program designed to improve relations between mental health specialists and other professionals involved with exceptional children and the parents of those children might be seen as equally appropriate and desirable.

Parents and Teachers

Not only do parents and teachers need to communicate with each other about the exceptional child's school placement and subsequent progress, but they also must try to understand each other's problems. Parents too often are perceived by teachers as neglectful when they are not. There is no need for teachers or other school personnel to create or increase parental feelings of guilt when the parents are doing all they can within their own resources and capabilities, however limited, to help the child.

Understanding is needed especially when the child is not identified as exceptional until after school entrance, as in the case of learning disabled students, for example. The youngster who appears to be bright and quick at home and who is found to need special services at school because of hearing or emotional problems is another case in point. The selection committee, homeroom teacher, or principal can explain to the parents that the classroom demands skills different from those expected or observed at home. Behavior that the parents may have tolerated or become accustomed to, such as perseveration or head-banging, may, together with other behavioral indicators, point to previously unsuspected minimal brain damage. Parents, of course, should inform school personnel if the child spoke or walked unusually late, for no apparent reason, or has exhibited other problems that could interfere with learning.

Rather than condemn culturally different parents for their seeming unwillingness to cooperate with the school, teachers should try to understand and respect their reluctance. Frequently these parents have had negative experiences with other government agencies or personnel, or with authority figures, and have strong anxiety feelings about the schools as a result. They may feel psychologically uncomfortable, perhaps inadequate, in the presence of the better-educated teacher. These feelings, the result of negative experiences, are unfortunately common, particularly to the culturally different and the poor. Their reluctance to confront, let alone cooperate with, school authorities need not mean lack of interest in their children's welfare.

Parents of culturally different handicapped and gifted students have a need for information about their rights and responsibilities with regard to their children's education. This information must be communicated in layman's terms so that even poorly educated parents can understand it. These parents want to feel that they are welcome in the school and in parent organizations and that the teachers are anxious to help them and their children, but often they don't know where to begin the relationship.

If parents are led to feel that they lack the qualifications necessary to meet the needs of their child, it can only serve to intimidate them. As a result, the parents' self-concept is further diminished and any additional attempts at communication are thwarted. Educators who are seeking to work effectively with parents of culturally diverse gifted and handicapped children have recognized that this outcome is in direct opposition to the intended goal of facilitating communication. (Marion, 1980, p. 621)

One way of reducing the apparent apathy or resistance of culturally different parents, as well as other parents of exceptional students, is to involve them actively in the education of their children. In one experimental project, the parents were taught to write contingency reinforcement contracts for their children, who were considered to be academically "at risk" by teachers. This intervention resulted in substantial improvement in the children's classwork performance (Blechman, Kotanchick, & Taylor, 1981). Another study of involvement programs with parents of learning disabled students yielded similarly positive results, obtained when the parents were actively participating in tutoring and reinforcement (Shapero & Forbes, 1981).

Involvement may also be the answer to the resistance of exceptionally able students. Some of these youngsters' parents attempt to downplay their child's abilities for a variety of reasons. Perhaps the father is afraid that artistic talent, encouraged in a special class placement, will make his son a "sissy." Or the parents of a very intelligent girl may believe that encouragement of her scientific curiosity and abilities will somehow defeminize her. Sometimes, too, parents anticipate that a brilliant or talented child will reject them. Reassurance by school personnel and participation in the implementation as well as the planning of the child's IEP may serve to alleviate their anxiety.

Although these interventions frequently mean extra work for the teachers of exceptional students, the effort is rewarded by more parental support and better student performance. Both parents and teachers need to "walk in the other's shoes"—that is to say, understand the difficulties and concerns of each other's living/working situations—if they are to cooperate with each other for the child's benefit.

PARENT ORGANIZATIONS

After a child's problem has been identified, his parents may be called, at the instigation of either the family physician or a mutual friend, by someone whose child shares a similar exceptionality. This can offer needed reassurance that the parents are neither alone nor unique in their situation. As this initially informal contact has recurred in recent years, parents of children with a common condition have created formal organizations to give each other moral support, provide recreation for their children, and serve other related needs.

As the organizations have become more sophisticated, and as society has become more attuned to the requirements of minority groups, the united parents have, in some instances, become action groups. A notable example is the Pennsylvania Association for Retarded Children, whose members brought suit to have their children educated at public expense under the "right-to-education" principle. In Colorado, a similar suit was filed by a parent organization on behalf of children who were retarded, perceptually handicapped, physically handicapped, autistic, and emotionally disturbed. Frustrated and angered by the inadequate education provided in some school systems for their gifted children, or angered by threatened budget cuts affecting enrichment programs, parents of the exceptionally able have organized in local, state, and national associations (Bennetts, 1980). The emotional bases for organizing are common to almost all the parent groups, for each has experienced inappropriate or inadequate handling of their children.

Once organized, the groups not only provide support networks but also mobilize to raise funds, for research on the one hand and to reach legislators on the other. The research they have sponsored has led to increases in medical, psychological, and educational information that has benefited many exceptional youngsters—if not their own, then those who came along a few years later. The groups' political efforts have resulted in finding sponsors for needed supportive legislation, leading ultimately to the passage of the Education for All Handicapped Children Act. (The amount of volunteer time given these causes by parents is staggering but usually worth it in the end.) In addition, as the local groups have joined together, annual national conventions have been scheduled. These bring together special educators, clinical specialists, and parents to exchange information and to learn from each other. Similar meetings are held at the local and state levels in some organizations.

Special educators ought to recognize the concern and dedication of these active parents and acknowledge the contributions and progress their organizations have brought about. They should also realize that more and more parents of exceptional children, through their experiences in these organizations, have gained sufficient expertise to qualify them as valuable resource persons.

OPEN-ENDED QUESTIONS

What difficulties do the special education laws and rulings create for the schools? Since most exceptional children should be in small classes of eight to fifteen children if they cannot be mainstreamed, there is a need for a large number of special education teachers and classrooms. The sad truth is that there are not nearly enough properly prepared teachers in some areas, nor enough classroom space, as underenrolled school districts shut down and sell school buildings. Nor are the funds available to pay so many specialists or to supply appropriate physical facilities.

Parents of exceptional children pay taxes to the school district, whether their children are average, bright, retarded, blind, or emotionally troubled. Relatively few of them can afford the tuition of special private schools, even with state subsidies and other financial aid. They rightfully feel that their children deserve an appropriate education, regardless of the family's income. What does the worker with a moderately retarded child, plus a few other children, and an annual income of under $15,000 do for her child if the public schools cannot provide that education? What about the family with a learning disabled child who is referred to psychotherapy at thirty-five to fifty dollars per session, plus special tutoring at ten dollars or more an hour? Must they go into debt, or should they expect that public funds should pay for these services as well as schooling? The uncertain status of P.L. 94-142 in the early 1980s does not provide the sure answers that these parents thought had been settled when the Act was passed.

Even if full public support continues, other questions remain. How much can the student be expected to gain from special education? Will the profoundly retarded child profit at all, or is it more practical to exempt them from the right-to-education laws? Furthermore, who will determine the point at which a child cannot profit? For that matter, what are the indicators of "profit"? Where will we find enough teachers for the homebound or hospitalized? How quickly are school districts moving to meet the requirements of the law and court decisions? How much is the taxpayer willing to pay to educate exceptional students?

Whether or not to provide special education for exceptional children is no longer a question. The question is, instead, how best to provide for the varied needs of unique individuals, within the limitations of financial and personnel resources and in keeping with the desires of a rapidly changing and highly mobile society. Too much may be attempted and too little accomplished when we try to please everyone. Too little may be attempted and nothing accomplished when we try to offend no one. Between these extremes there is a vast area in which much can be accomplished if there is cooperation and understanding among school personnel, legislators, nonteaching professionals, parents, and the students themselves.

SUMMARY

Whatever a child's exceptionality, we cannot look at it or her in a vacuum. The ripple effects of being "different" are felt most strongly within the family. The ways in which the parents respond affect both the child's perception of herself and the reactions of other family members, neighbors, and friends. To recognize that even parents who achieve optimal reactions to their child's needs also experience feelings of guilt, depression, frustration, and rejection at times is to acknowledge normal human responses to chronic stress. Therefore, professionals who interact with parents must be sensitive to and respect this reality. At the same time, parents must realize that professionals cannot always work "miracles," even with their cooperation, but that without it, their children are unlikely to progress.

The support network provided by organized parent groups is helpful in terms of both sharing the stress and mobilizing negative emotions in constructive ways. Without the persistent efforts of such groups, it is improbable that there would be any "right-to-education" laws for exceptional students.

SUGGESTED ADDITIONAL READINGS

Abrams, J. C., and Kaslow, F. W. Learning disabilities and family dynamics: A mutual interaction. *Journal of Clinical Child Psychology*, 1976, 5, 35–40.

Araoz, D. L. Marital problems and the exceptional child. *International Journal of Family Counseling*, 1977, 5 (1), 64–69.

Becker, L. D., Bender, N. N., and Kawabe, K. K. Exceptional parents: A survey of programs, services, and needs. *Academic Therapy*, 1980, 15, 523–538.

Cornell, D. G. Gifted children: The impact of positive labeling on the family system. *American Journal of Orthopsychiatry*, 1983, 53, 322–335.

Gath, A. The mental health of siblings of congenitally abnormal children. *Journal of Child Psychology and Psychiatry*, 1972, 13, 211–218.

Hicks, G. Parental attitudes toward blindness and developmental disabilities. *Visual Impairment and Blindness*, 1979, 73, 405–410.

Howard, J. The role of the pediatrician with young exceptional children and their families. *Exceptional Children*, 1982, 48, 316–322.

Huberty, C., and Huberty, D. J. Treating the parents of adolescent drug abusers. *Contemporary Drug Problems*, 1976, 5 (4), 573–592.

McKeever, P. Siblings of chronically ill children: A literature review with implications for research and practice. *American Journal of Orthopsychiatry*, 1983, 53, 209–218.

Moore, C. B., and Morton, K. G. *A reader's guide for parents of children with mental, physical, or emotional disabilities*. Rockville, Md.: U.S. Department of Health, Education, and Welfare, 1976.

Perske, R. *New directions for parents of persons who are retarded*. Nashville: Abingdon Press, 1973.

Schwartz, L. L. Are you a gifted parent of a gifted child? *Gifted Child Quarterly*, 1981, 25, 31–35.

Sinson, J. C. Down's infants: An interdisciplinary approach involving parents. *International Journal of Rehabilitation Research*, 1978, 1 (1), 59–69.

Strom, R., Ries, R., Slaughter, H., and Wurster, S. Role expectations of parents of intellectually handicapped children. *Exceptional Children*, 1980, 47, 144–147.

Wikler, L., Wasow, M., and Hatfield, E. Chronic sorrow revisited: Parent vs. professional depiction of the adjustment of parents of mentally retarded children. *American Journal of Orthopsychiatry*, 1981, 51, 63–70.

APPENDIX A/
LESSON PLANNING

Preparing lesson plans, which you will often be required to do both as a prospective and as an in-service teacher, involves nothing more than organizing on paper what you want to do in the classroom and how you are going to do it. Lesson plans are useful devices for you as a teacher, because they make you focus on your goals and techniques and on the special needs of your students. (They are also useful for substitute teachers, who can maintain a learning sequence for your students rather than merely "filling time.")

Ideally, you should have a master plan covering the semester or academic year that indicates your starting point in a course of study and the goals you hope to reach. This is then broken down into smaller units, such as historical periods, types of literature, types of skills, or groups of experiments, each including a few weeks of instruction. Each daily lesson plan is a subset of one of these units.

Rather than give a lesson plan for a specific topic, the approach here will be to outline a lesson plan format with questions relevant to each section of the plan. This should stimulate your thinking about ways in which to design any lesson you may teach. It is also a flexible format that can be adapted to specific models you may have to follow in different settings.

BASIC LESSON PLAN FORMAT

I. Subject Area
    Mathematics? Reading? Science? Art?
    Self-care? Physical education?

A. Unit

What is the general area of the subject matter?

B. Topic

What specific aspect of the unit are you teaching?

Can the content be taught in one lesson, or will it need more than one?

Is it part of a sequence (as in math or a foreign language)?

C. Content of Topic Lesson

What are the major points you want to stress?

Is 100% mastery essential for the students?

II. Techniques to Be Used (dependent upon objectives)

A. Activities (consider amount of time available)

Lecture

Discussion

Project

Worksheets

Experiment

Debate

Combination of two or more activities

(Note: Write out the sequence of activities and the approximate time needed for each.)

B. Materials Needed (dependent upon nature of activities)

Handouts

Chalkboard/chalk

Flannelboard/magnetic board

Filmstrips/films/slides/transparencies/opaque illustrations/overlays (Remember to have the correct projector available.)

Concrete objects (blocks, pennies, Cuisenaire rods, laboratory equipment)

Cassette tapes/phonograph recordings

Videotapes

Workbooks (assigned pages)

Textbooks (assigned pages)

Crayons/pens/pencils

C. Special Notes (needs of specific students)

Braille/large print materials

Amplification of sound

Pictures for nonreaders/diagrams

"Reminder" cards (for example, sequence of steps to be followed; alphabet)

III. Evaluation (success of the lesson)

Student responses to oral questions?

Quiz?

Application of content?

Mastery of content at a criterion level?

IV. Assignment for next lesson

Review?

Enrichment? (for those who do not need review)

Application of concepts?

New material?

You should be aware, of course, of the level of skill needed for each lesson prior to beginning the lesson (entry behavior). Have the prerequisite earlier steps been mastered satisfactorily? Do the students have the information needed to understand or apply the new material?

For some lessons with some students, you may need to do a careful task analysis, breaking the task down into a sequence of steps. This is often necessary for motor skills, whether they are tied to self-care, physical education, or music. An example was given in Chapter 2. To be certain that you include every step, you could:

1. Talk as you do the task, recording your commentary as you go

2. Observe someone else doing the task and tape-record your narrative

3. Have someone else observe you and do the narrative on tape

4. Videotape a person doing the task or film it in slow motion

As a class exercise, I've had students try to teach their peers how to tie shoelaces, a skill they all took for granted. They soon discovered that they had to define their terms fully (what are "rabbit ears" in terms of shoelaces?), consider whether their "student" was right- or left-handed, and decide whether to teach face-to-face or alongside the "student." Try it!

APPENDIX B/
SAMPLE INDIVIDUAL
EDUCATION
PROGRAMS (IEPS)

As noted several times in this book, P.L. 94-142, the Education for All Handicapped Children Act, requires that individual education programs, or IEPs, be developed for all handicapped children. In Pennsylvania and some other states, this includes exceptionally able students as well.

Two groups of IEPs are offered for your information. One group is for gifted children. "Anne Spears" is a fictitious third grader, and her IEP is a composite of those developed for several third-grade children. David Woodman was a real fifth grader, whose parents and teacher generously gave permission to use his IEP for 1978–79. The names of the school district and the director of special education have been changed, however. The second group of IEPs, for Roy and Robin, deals with the special needs of these two mentally retarded teenagers who are in EMR classes at the secondary level.

Note that in each of the short-term instructional activities, there is more than one evaluator. Sometimes it is the student and the teacher, and in others, the peers of the student and the teacher. In both sample IEPs, the participants in the planning conference included the student as well as parent(s) and professionals.

The format of IEPs is the same for all exceptional children: present status, long-term and short-term instructional goals, evaluation of activities designed to meet these goals, and a commitment to review the IEP a year later. As you can see, the activities and goals vary for students within a category as well as between categories of exceptionality. This emphasis on the individual rather than the exceptionality has long been sought.

INDIVIDUALIZED EDUCATION PROGRAM (IEP)

SCHOOL DISTRICT OF RESIDENCE: UPPER ASHLEY

Student's
Name: Anne Spears

Current Assignment: Round Meadow
Third Grade

Birthdate: 4/26/69

Date Written: 3/10/78

Participants in IEP Development & Writing:

Date of Annual Review: 3/10/79

Operating Agent: Upper Ashley Sch. Dist.

Name	Title

Mrs. Jacqueline Warren—Director of Special Education

Person responsible for Implementation of Program: Jacqueline Warren

Mr. Michael Rothstein—TEC Teacher

Mr. and Mrs. Spears—Parents

Date of IEP Planning Meeting: 3/3/78

Anne Spears—Student

PRIMARY ASSIGNMENT AND STATEMENT OF INTEGRATION	DATE OF INITIATION	EXPECTED DURATION OF SERVICES
Regular education	3/78	Ongoing
Gifted—Participation in the gifted		
program (TEC) with integration in		
regular education for all remaining		
areas of instruction.		

RELATED SERVICES:	DATE OF INITIATION	EXPECTED DURATION OF SERVICES
Physical education	3/78	Ongoing
Bus transportation	3/78	Ongoing

SPECIAL MEDIA OR MATERIALS: _____

Copies to:
- Teacher (Original)
- Parent
- Operating Agent
- District of Residence

STUDENT NAME ____Anne Spears____

DATE IEP WRITTEN ____3/3/78____

PRESENT EDUCATION LEVELS

Anne's intellectual functioning and classroom performance indicate
that she is eligible for and could benefit from participation in The
Enrichment Class (TEC) Program in the areas of Language Arts, Fine Arts,
Science, and Social Science.

Information from Anne's parents also suggests that she would benefit
from inclusion in such a program.

Anne's interests include reading, art, dramatics, and story telling.

STUDENT NAME ___Anne Spears___

DATE IEP WRITTEN _3/3/78_____

INSTRUCTIONAL AREAS & ANNUAL GOALS	SHORT TERM OBJECTIVES & EVALUATION PROCEDURES (INCLUDE TERMINAL BEHAVIOR, CONDITIONS, AND CRITERIA)
General: Student will expand her ability to use library efficiently.	1. Student will be able to write a resource survey card when working on or designing a project, citing information from books, and/or periodicals to teacher and librarian satisfaction. 2. Given a specific reference, student will be able to locate materials via the card catalogue to teacher and librarian satisfaction.

STUDENT NAME _____ Anne Spears

DATE IEP WRITTEN _3/3/78_

INSTRUCTIONAL AREAS & ANNUAL GOALS	SHORT TERM OBJECTIVES & EVALUATION PROCEDURES (INCLUDE TERMINAL BEHAVIOR, CONDITIONS, AND CRITERIA)
Language Arts: Student will explore folktales from countries of cultural origin.	1. Student will experience no less than five (5) folktales from countries of ancestral origin. 2. Using techniques of interviews and library skills, student will research specific aspects of cultural background to satisfaction of self and teacher. 3. Student will research customs of areas of cultural background as they relate to folktales to satisfaction of self and teacher. 4. Student will trace customs of her cultural background from past to present to the satisfaction of self and teacher. 5. Student will rewrite a folktale of her choosing, updating it to present day cultural level for presentation to her class.

STUDENT NAME   Anne Spears

DATE IEP WRITTEN 3/3/78

INSTRUCTIONAL AREAS & ANNUAL GOALS	SHORT TERM OBJECTIVES & EVALUATION PROCEDURES (INCLUDE TERMINAL BEHAVIOR, CONDITIONS, AND CRITERIA)
Fine Arts: Student will explore folk songs as expression of her cultural heritage.	1. Student will have experience with no less than ten (10) folk songs from countries of her ancestral origin and be able to relate each to its country to her and teacher satisfaction. 2. Student will be able to compare and contrast cultural aspects of American folk songs with those of her ancestral background to student and teacher satisfaction. 3. Using techniques of interview, active listening, and library research, student will be able to explain the part folk music of her ancestors played in the development of American folk music.

STUDENT NAME   Anne Spears

DATE IEP WRITTEN   3/3/78

INSTRUCTIONAL AREAS & ANNUAL GOALS	SHORT TERM OBJECTIVES & EVALUATION PROCEDURES (INCLUDE TERMINAL BEHAVIOR, CONDITIONS, AND CRITERIA)
Science: Student will explore principles of weather as determinants of culture.	1. Student will be able to interpret specific bodies of weather data and extrapolate information relating to effects of culture to her and teacher satisfaction. 2. Student will be able to compare and contrast modern techniques of weather data collecting with past folklore pertaining to weather to her and teacher satisfaction. 3. Student will be able to translate modern weather data into original folklore type stories for presentation to her peers. 4. Student will collect weather data from two different geographic regions and be able to hypothesize as to comparative effects on cultures to her and teacher satisfaction. 5. Working with a peer group, student will research, design, and construct a functioning weather station to her and peer satisfaction. 6. Using small test experiences within her school, student will compare differences in behaviors during a variety of weather conditions, i.e., rainy day/sunny day and present her data to class as part of group project to her and peer satisfaction. 7. Working within a peer group, student will develop and carry out a project studying the effects of weather on school children and possibly adults to satisfaction of self, teacher, and peers.

STUDENT NAME   Anne Spears

DATE IEP WRITTEN   3/3/78

INSTRUCTIONAL AREAS & ANNUAL GOALS	SHORT TERM OBJECTIVES & EVALUATION PROCEDURES (INCLUDE TERMINAL BEHAVIOR, CONDITIONS, AND CRITERIA)
Social Science: Student will expand her appreciation of music of foreign cultures.	1. Student will have experience with no less than two (2) of each of the following: folk songs, children's songs, and classical compositions from no less than five (5) foreign cultures to satisfaction of self and teacher. 2. Student will explore musical instruments native to specific cultures and design a presentation to self and peer satisfaction. 3. With the help of peers, teacher and outside resource people, student will attempt to construct a folk type musical instrument to her and teacher satisfaction. 4. When presented with folk song, children's song or classical composition experienced in number one of this page, student will be able to identify title and country of national origin with 80% accuracy.

INDIVIDUALIZED EDUCATION PROGRAM (IEP)

SCHOOL DISTRICT OF RESIDENCE: UPPER ASHLEY

Student's
Name: David Woodman

Current Assignment: Woodlawn
Fifth Grade

Birthdate: 8/30/67

Date Written: 4/26/78

Participants in IEP Development
& Writing:

Date of Annual Review 4/26/79

Name	Title

Operating Agent: Upper Ashley School
District

Jacqueline Warren—Director of
Special Education
Michael Rothstein—TEC Teacher

Person responsible for Implementation
of Program: Jacqueline Warren

Mrs. Lou Woodman—Mother

David Woodman—Student

Date of IEP Planning Meeting: 3/10/78

PRIMARY ASSIGNMENT AND STATEMENT OF INTEGRATION	DATE OF INITIATION	EXPECTED DURATION OF SERVICES
Regular Education	4/78	Ongoing
Gifted—Participation in the gifted		
program (TEC) with integration in		
regular education for all remaining		
areas of instruction.		

RELATED SERVICES:	DATE OF INITIATION	EXPECTED DURATION OF SERVICES
Physical education	4/78	Ongoing
Bus transportation	4/78	Ongoing

SPECIAL MEDIA OR MATERIALS: _____

Copies to:
— Teacher (Original)
— Parent
— Operating Agent
— District of Residence

STUDENT NAME___David Woodman___

DATE IEP WRITTEN ___4/26/78___

```
┌─────────────────────────────────────────────┐
│          PRESENT EDUCATION LEVELS             │
└─────────────────────────────────────────────┘
```

David's intellectual functioning and classroom performance
indicate that he is eligible and could benefit from participation in
The Enrichment Class (TEC) Program in the areas of Language Arts, Fine
Arts, Science, and Social Science.

Information from David's parents also suggests that he would benefit
from inclusion in such a program.

David's interests include reading, art, dramatics, and sports.

STUDENT NAME ___David Woodman___

DATE IEP WRITTEN ___4/26/78___

INSTRUCTIONAL AREAS & ANNUAL GOALS	SHORT TERM OBJECTIVES & EVALUATION PROCEDURES (INCLUDE TERMINAL BEHAVIOR, CONDITIONS, AND CRITERIA)
Language Arts: 1. Student will explore the field of debate as it relates to his areas of interest.	1. When given a specific topic, student will be able to find, interpret, and organize printed materials in order to present a debate, pro or con, to the satisfaction of peers and teacher. 2. Using information from his studies of science and/or social science, student will be able to build an argument to influence his classmates toward his viewpoint, to his and peer satisfaction.
2. Student will expand his abilities to use photography as a means of expressing his ideas.	1. Using a 35mm reflex camera, student will develop a photo essay as part of his ecology project (see Science) to his and peer satisfaction. 2. Using the movie camera, student will create film essay related to one or more of the areas of the TEC program to his and peer satisfaction.

STUDENT NAME ___David Woodman___

DATE IEP WRITTEN ___4/26/78___

INSTRUCTIONAL AREAS & ANNUAL GOALS	SHORT TERM OBJECTIVES & EVALUATION PROCEDURES (INCLUDE TERMINAL BEHAVIOR, CONDITIONS, AND CRITERIA)
Fine and Performing Arts: 1. David will extend his appreciation of the artist as a social commentator.	1. Using the facilities of the Philadelphia Museum of Art and slides belonging to the TEC program, David will look at the work of American and European artists who most closely reflect the events of their time to the satisfaction of his teacher. 2. Given a representative group of paintings, David will be able to differentiate Realism, Expressionism, and Abstraction to his and teacher satisfaction. 3. After reading representative works of William Shakespeare, David will explore the following question to his and teacher satisfaction: Why did this specific author's work survive centuries when the work of his contemporaries did not? 4. Working with Romeo and Juliet and West Side Story, David will compare and contrast the cultural conflicts to the satisfaction of his teacher.

STUDENT NAME _____ David Woodman _____

DATE IEP WRITTEN _____ 4/26/78 _____

INSTRUCTIONAL AREAS & ANNUAL GOALS	SHORT TERM OBJECTIVES & EVALUATION PROCEDURES (INCLUDE TERMINAL BEHAVIOR, CONDITIONS, AND CRITERIA)
Social Science: 1. David will expand his awareness of local political systems.	1. Using his ecology project (Science), David will study the impact of local government on his environment and design an effectiveness rating scale to his and teacher satisfaction. 2. David will design a questionnaire for a public opinion poll in order to assess community concern for the ecology problem he has selected. Evaluation to be made by peers and teacher. 3. David will compare and contrast political effectiveness of other communities in dealing with this problem with that of his own to his and teacher satisfaction.

STUDENT NAME   David Woodman

DATE IEP WRITTEN   4/26/78

INSTRUCTIONAL AREAS & ANNUAL GOALS	SHORT TERM OBJECTIVES & EVALUATION PROCEDURES (INCLUDE TERMINAL BEHAVIOR, CONDITIONS, AND CRITERIA)
Science: 1. David will extend his knowledge of solutions for environmental problems.	1. David will make a community survey of problems affecting local ecology with the aid of resource people from the Pennypack Watershed Association to his and teacher satisfaction. 2. David will be able to identify, define and research a specific local ecological problem, assessing possible solutions to his and teacher satisfaction. 3. David will formulate a theoretical model for his ecology project reflecting known principles and observations based on standard sources to the satisfaction of teacher. 4. David will use this model to evaluate the relationship between one or more hypotheses and observational evidence. Success will be measured by criteria on checklist designed by teacher and student. 5. David will use this theoretical model to deduce new hypotheses and to propose a plan for testing same. Performance will be assessed by student/teacher rating scale.
2. David will increase his knowledge of astronomy.	1. Working with a group of his peers, David will attempt to construct a telescope and be able to explain the principles of its functioning to his and peer group satisfaction. 2. Given a map of the heavens, David will be able to locate and identify each of the planets in our solar system to his and teacher satisfaction. 3. Using the telescope and/or the naked eye, David will be able to locate no less than six (6) constellations.

INDIVIDUALIZED EDUCATION PROGRAM
(IEP)

Student's name: *Roy —*

Address

Telephone

Pupil ID#

School	District	IEP Review Date	Today's Date	Birth Date
	8	6/83	6/9/82	7/16/67

Grade/Program
Sec. EMR

PRIMARY ASSIGNMENT(S) & STATEMENT OF INTEGRATION	Starting Date	Expected Duration of Service
Full time EMR class	9/82	1 yr.
0 Mainstreaming		

RELATED SERVICES

Speech Therapy		
Transportation – School Bus		
OT/PT service – 2x month direct and 2x month consultative with a		
review in 6 months of school starting	↓	↓

Reason for assignment(s):
     The CSET has determined that Roy's needs can best be met

     in the above placement.

Administrator/Supervisor responsible for program (name and title)

Address   Phone

The following persons have participated in the Educational Program Planning Conference:

School District Representative (name and title)

Teacher(s)
EMR Teacher

Others
Speech Therapist, Physical Therapist

Student   Parent(s)

_____ X _____

EDUCATIONAL LEVELS & OBJECTIVES

Assessment Procedures	Curricular Area	DESCRIPTION OF PRESENT EDUCATIONAL LEVELS	DATE	PROGRAM PLANNER
Teacher Made Tests	Life Skills	Roy can say the days of the week and months of the year in correct order, but has trouble spelling the days. He can tell time on the hour but has trouble with all quarter hours. He has some trouble making change from $1.00 and adding groups of coins to $1.00 value. He does not know the values of all coins.	5/4/82	

ANNUAL GOALS

Instructional Area				
Life Skills	Roy should increase his knowledge of functional information.			

SHORT TERM OBJECTIVES	Assessment Procedures	Pre-Test		Post-Test	
		Date	Score	Date	Score
Roy should spell the days of the week in their correct order – 100% accuracy	Teacher-made Tests				
Given a set of clocks without hands, Roy should draw hands with 100% accuracy –					
a. 4 clocks set at specific :15 times					
b. hands on 4 clocks to specific :30 times					
c. hands on 4 clocks to specific :45 times					
Given 10 amounts, Roy should make change from $1.00 with 100% accuracy					
Given 10 groups of coins, value to 50¢, Roy should add them with 90% accuracy to $1.00					

EDUCATIONAL LEVELS & OBJECTIVES

Assessment Procedures	Curricular Area	DESCRIPTION OF PRESENT EDUCATIONAL LEVELS	DATE	PROGRAM PLANNER

Instructional Area	ANNUAL GOALS
Life Skills, cont.	

SHORT TERM OBJECTIVES	Assessment Procedures	Pre-Test		Post-Test	
		Date	Score	Date	Score
Roy should tell the values of all coins with 100% accuracy					

326 APPENDIX B/SAMPLE INDIVIDUAL EDUCATION PROGRAMS (IEPS)

EDUCATIONAL LEVELS & OBJECTIVES

Assessment Procedures	Curricular Area	DESCRIPTION OF PRESENT EDUCATIONAL LEVELS	DATE	PROGRAM PLANNER
Silvaroli Reading Assessment	Reading	Independent level: Pre-Primer - 2 Instructional level - gr.3 Frustration level - gr.4 - 5	5/11/82	

ANNUAL GOALS

Instructional Area	
Reading	Roy should increase his comprehension skills to a level necessary for survival

SHORT TERM OBJECTIVES	Assessment Procedures	Pre-Test		Post-Test	
		Date	Score	Date	Score

Given a reading selection at his instructional level (standard & functional material) Roy should, with 90% accuracy answer:
  factual questions
  inferential questions
  vocabulary questions
  main idea questions
	Silvaroli Reading Assessment Teacher Made Tests				

EDUCATIONAL LEVELS & OBJECTIVES

Assessment Procedures	Curricular Area	DESCRIPTION OF PRESENT EDUCATIONAL LEVELS	DATE	PROGRAM PLANNER
Teacher Made Tests	Math	Addition - Roy knows his basic number facts 0-10 and most of those from 10-20. He can add 4 digits with no regrouping. He cannot add with regrouping. Subtraction - Roy knows his basic facts from 0-20. He can subtract 2 4-digit numbers without regrouping. He cannot subtract with regrouping. Multiplication - Roy knows some basic number facts. Division - Roy does not know his division facts.	5/24/82 5/24/82	B.Sloop

Instructional Area		ANNUAL GOALS
Math		Roy should increase his computational skills to a level necessary for survival.

SHORT TERM OBJECTIVES	Assessment Procedures	Pre-Test		Post-Test	
		Date	Score	Date	Score
Given 10 addition problems (2 digits + 2 digits) with regrouping, Roy should add with 90% accuracy					
Given 10 add. problems (3 digits + 1 digit with carrying), Roy should add with 90% accuracy					
Given 10 add. problems (3 digits + 2 digits)with carrying 1's and 10's, Roy should add with 90% accuracy					
Given 10 add. problems 3 dig. + 3 dig. with carrying 1's, 10's, and 100's, Roy should add with 90% accuracy					
Given 10 subtraction problems - 2 dig.- 1 dig. with borrowing, Roy should solve with 90% accuracy					

EDUCATIONAL LEVELS & OBJECTIVES

Assessment Procedures	Curricular Area	DESCRIPTION OF PRESENT EDUCATIONAL LEVELS	DATE	PROGRAM PLANNER

Instructional Area	ANNUAL GOALS
Math	

SHORT TERM OBJECTIVES	Assessment Procedures	Pre-Test		Post-Test	
		Date	Score	Date	Score
Given 10 subtr. problems - 2 dig. - 2 dig. with borrowing, Roy should solve with 90% accuracy					
Roy should learn his multiplication facts from 0-5 with 80% accuracy					
Roy should learn his division facts from 0-5 with 80% accuracy					

EDUCATIONAL LEVELS & OBJECTIVES

Assessment Procedures	Curricular Area	DESCRIPTION OF PRESENT EDUCATIONAL LEVELS	DATE	PROGRAM PLANNER
Oral Peripheral	Speech	Structure and function appear adequate for normal speech production. Wears braces on upper teeth. Vocal quality is very nasal with short gasping breaths.	5/26/82	Speech Therapist
Photo-Articulation Test	Speech	Correct pronunciation of all sounds except: CH and J sounds		Speech Therapist
Informal Conversation Speech Language Evaluation	Speech	Misarticulated sounds are apparent in words, sentences, and conversational speech. Good stimulability for speech sounds. Auditory discrimination of speech sounds is satisfactory.		Speech Therapist

ANNUAL GOALS

Instructional Area	
Speech	Improved production of misarticulated sounds in all positions (initial, medial, and final) in words, sentences, & conversational speech in the structured speech class

SHORT TERM OBJECTIVES	Assessment Procedures	Pre-Test Date	Pre-Test Score	Post-Test Date	Post-Test Score
1. Student will auditorily discriminate between correct and incorrect production of the misartic. sounds	1, 2, 3				
2. Student will produce the (CH,J) sounds in isolation, followed by nonsense syllables and vowel combinations	Student will achieve an accuracy level of 80% using specified materials				
3. Student will produce (CH,J) sounds in all positions (initial, medial, final) in words, sentences, and conversational speech.					
4. Student will practice at home with a parent on a daily basis (and complete homework assignments)	4 - Parent will sign speech book after each assignment				

EDUCATIONAL LEVELS & OBJECTIVES

Assessment Procedures	Curricular Area	DESCRIPTION OF PRESENT EDUCATIONAL LEVELS	DATE	PROGRAM PLANNER
Therapist Made Assessment	Motor ROM Sensory-motor ADL	Roy is a 14 y.o. with Down's Syndrome. Can dress himself independently. He is right foot and hand and eye dominant. Muscle tone and range of motion within normal limits. Sensory awareness is intact on either side.	6/11/82	Physical Therapist

ANNUAL GOALS

Instructional Area	
Gross Motor	A baseline of Roy's gross motor skills will be established.
Fine Motor	A baseline of Roy's fine motor skills will be established.

SHORT TERM OBJECTIVES	Assessment Procedures	Pre-Test		Post-Test	
		Date	Score	Date	Score
1. Using standardized tests of motor performance, Roy's gross motor abilities as per developmental age level of performance will be established	Standardized tests	6/22/81			
2. Roy's performance will be compared to others gross motor program and results tabulated	Observation	6/22/81			
3. ADL independence will be documented as to rate of motor performance	Observation	6/22/81			
4. Using standardized tests, Roy's fine motor performance will be tabulated	Standardized tests	6/22/81			

DIVISION OF SPECIAL EDUCATION

INDIVIDUALIZED EDUCATION PROGRAM
(IEP)

Student's Name: _Robin_ — _ _ _ _

Address

Telephone | Pupil ID #

School	District 8	IEP Review Date 6/83	Today's Date 6/10/82	Birth Date 3/6/64
			Grade/Program _Sec. EMR_	

PRIMARY ASSIGNMENT(S) & STATEMENT OF INTEGRATION	Starting Date	Expected Duration of Service
Secondary EMR	9/82	1 yr.
0 Mainstreaming	9/82	1 yr.

RELATED SERVICES		
Music, Phys. Ed.	9/82	1 yr.
Pre-Vocational Ed.	9/82	1 yr.
Transportation: Bus Tokens	9/82	1 yr.

Reason for Assignment(s):
   Child Study Evaluation Team (CSET) has determined that psychological,
   intellectual, and educational assessments indicate that Robin may best be
   served in the above assignments.

Administrator/Supervisor responsible for program (name and title)

Address | Phone

The Following Persons have participated in the Educational Program Planning Conference:

School District Representative (name and title)

Teacher(s): _EMR Teacher_

Others _Music Teacher, Phys. Ed. Teacher_

Student | Parent(s)
| X

EDUCATIONAL LEVELS & OBJECTIVES

Assessment Procedures	Curricular Area	DESCRIPTION OF PRESENT EDUCATIONAL LEVELS	DATE	PROGRAM PLANNER
Informal Math Inventory (IMI)	Math	Robin uses addition and subtraction of 4 & 5 digit numbers in columns and w/regrouping. She uses multiplication and division with a two digit multiplier and divisor. But, with division she is inconsistent. She uses linear and liquid measurement but needs continued reinforcement of this concept. Robin uses the classroom cash register to "make change" up to and including one dollar. She can tell time to the minute, write checks, and carry a balance. Robin does use fractions. But with unlike denominators there is a weakness.	6/4/82	C.B.G.

ANNUAL GOALS

Increase math skills in division and in using fractions with unlike denominators.

Instructional Area
MATH

SHORT TERM OBJECTIVES	Assessment Procedures	Pre-Test		Post-Test	
		Date	Score	Date	Score
1. Review/reteach division as the inverse of multiplication (a) solve at least ten division problems a day using a two digit divisor without remainders with an accuracy of 95-100% for five consecutive days. (b) after Robin has mastered the above, she will repeat the process, this time using remainders. 2. Review/reteach addition and subtraction of fractions using like and unlike denominators. (a) solve at least five addition & subtraction of fractions w/a common denominator, w/an accuracy of 95-100% for five consecutive days	Teacher-constructed materials				

EDUCATIONAL LEVELS & OBJECTIVES

Assessment Procedures	Curricular Area	DESCRIPTION OF PRESENT EDUCATIONAL LEVELS	DATE	PROGRAM PLANNER

ANNUAL GOALS

Instructional Area

MATH

SHORT TERM OBJECTIVES	Assessment Procedures	Pre-Test		Post-Test	
		Date	Score	Date	Score

(b) after the above has been mastered, repeat this process using unlike denominators for five consecutive days w/an accuracy of 80–85%.

EDUCATIONAL LEVELS & OBJECTIVES

Assessment Procedures	Curricular Area	DESCRIPTION OF PRESENT EDUCATIONAL LEVELS	DATE	PROGRAM PLANNER
Informal Reading Inventory (IRI)	Reading	Robin uses consonants, digraphs, and blends in all positions. She understands and uses nouns (common & proper), pronouns, verbs, and adjectives. She uses vowels, short and long, and vowel digraphs. Robin uses irregular plurals and other variant endings, understands organization of a book, alphabetizes word lists and uses the classroom dictionary. Weak area at this level (6.2 word rec., 4.5 comprehension) is word recognition and comprehension.	6/11/82	

ANNUAL GOALS

Instructional Area				
READING	Increase word recognition and comprehension skills			

SHORT TERM OBJECTIVES	Assessment Procedures	Pre-Test		Post-Test	
		Date	Score	Date	Score
1. To increase her word recognition skills, Robin will alphabetize, write, and spell all new words with an accuracy of 95-100% for five consecutive days	Teacher-constructed materials				
2. Robin will begin making a simple 3 point outline: (a) Name of the main character(s) in a story (b) Problems of the character(s) (c) Solution to the problem(s)					
3. Robin will use skills learned to give a written or oral book report once a month relating the main idea of the report to the class with an accuracy of 95-100%.					

APPENDIX C/
RESOURCE AGENCIES

Alexander Graham Bell Association for the Deaf
3417 Volta Place, N.W.
Washington, D.C. 20007
Informational

American Association for the Education of the Severely/Profoundly Handicapped
1600 West Armory Way
Garden View Suite
Seattle, Washington 98119
Informational

American Association for the Gifted
15 Gramercy Park
New York, New York 10003
Informational; advocacy

American Association of Instructors of the Blind
711 Fourteenth Street, N.W.
Washington, D.C. 20005
Professional

American Association on Mental Deficiency
5201 Connecticut Avenue, N.W.
Washington, D.C. 20015
Professional

American Foundation for the Blind
15 West Sixteenth Street
New York, New York 10011
Information; distributes aids and appliances for the blind

American Printing House for the Blind
1839 Frankfort Avenue
Louisville, Kentucky 40206
Provides educational and other publications in Braille, large print, and recorded form to the blind

American Speech and Hearing Association
10801 Rockville Pike
Rockville, Maryland 20852
Professional

Association for Children and Adults with Learning Disabilities
4156 Library Road
Pittsburgh, Pennsylvania 15234
Advocacy

Canadian National Institute for the Blind
1929 Bayview Avenue
Toronto, Ontario
Informational; provides materials and supportive services for visually impaired persons in Canada

Closer Look
Box 1492
Washington, D.C. 20013
A National Information Center for parents and professionals, operated by the Parents' Campaign for Handicapped Children and Youth.

Council for Exceptional Children
1920 Association Drive
Reston, Virginia 22091
Primarily a professional organization for teachers and teacher educators, with several divisions that each focus on a different exceptionality

Epilepsy Foundation of America
1828 L Street, N.W.
Washington, D.C. 20036
Informational

Muscular Dystrophy Assocation of America
1790 Broadway
New York, New York 10019
Informational; fund raising for research

National Association for Gifted Children
2070 County Road H
St. Paul, Minnesota 55112
Advocacy; professional

National Association for Retarded Citizens
2709 Avenue E East
Arlington, Texas 76011
Advocacy (There are also state and local chapters in most states.)

National Easter Seal Society for Crippled Children and Adults
800 Second Avenue
New York, New York 10016
Advocacy

National Federation of the Blind
218 Randolph Hotel Building
Des Moines, Iowa 50309
Organization of blind people

The Orton Society
8415 Bellona Lane
Towson, Maryland 21204
Professional (learning disabilities)

United Cerebral Palsy Association, Inc.
66 East Thirty-fourth Street
New York, New York 10016
Informational; service; fund raising for research

United States Government Agencies:

Division for the Blind and Physically Handicapped
The Library of Congress
Washington, D.C. 20542

Media Services and Captioned Film Branch
Bureau of Education for the Handicapped
Seventh and D Streets, S.W.
Washington, D.C. 20202
Free loan of captioned films and other materials to schools and organizations serving the hearing impaired

National Institute of Child Health and Human Development
9000 Rockville Pike
Bethesda, Maryland 20014

National Institute of Mental Health
5454 Wisconsin Avenue
Chevy Chase, Maryland 20015

APPENDIX D/
LITERARY REFERENCES

The books and short stories listed below are examples of biographical and fictional readings in which the exceptional individual is a leading character. Many of them are available in paperback or as part of collections.

Exceptionally Able
Clark, Ronald W.: *Einstein: The Life and Times*
Curie, Eve: *Madame Curie*
Duncan, Isadora: *My Life*
Goertzel, Mildred G., Goertzel, Victor, and Goertzel, Ted G.:
   Three Hundred Eminent Personalities
Hersey, John: *The Child Buyer*
Miller, Alice: *Prisoners of Childhood*

Mentally Retarded
Buck, Pearl S.: *The Child Who Never Grew*
Faulkner, William: *The Sound and the Fury*
Keyes, Daniel: "Flowers for Algernon"
Kosinski, Jerzy: *Being There*
Nichols, Peter: *Joe Egg*
Sharp, Margery: *The Innocents*
Spencer, Elizabeth: *The Light in the Piazza*
Steinbeck, John: *Johnny Bear*

Orthopedically Handicapped and Chronically Ill
Berg, Margaret: *Wednesday's Child*
Killalea, Marie: *Karen*
O'Connor, Flannery: *Good Country People*
Segal, Erich: *Love Story*
Sheed, Wilfred: *People Will Always Be Kind*
Valens, Evans G.: *A Long Way Up: The Story of Jill Kinmont*

Hearing Impaired
Fields, Rachel: *And Now Tomorrow*
McCullers, Carson: *The Heart Is a Lonely Hunter*

Visually Impaired
Chevigny, Hector: *My Eyes Have a Cold Nose*
Husing, Ted: *My Eyes Are in My Heart*

Multiply Handicapped
Monsarrat, Nicholas: *The Story of Ester Costello*
Peare, Catherine Owens: *The Hellen Keller Story*

Speech and Language Impaired
Caldwell, Erskine: *Tobacco Road*
Huxley, Aldous: *Eyeless in Gaza*
Shaw, George Bernard: *Pygmalion*

Culturally Different
Gambino, Richard: *Blood of My Blood*
                              Vendetta
Haley, Arthur: *Roots*
Howe, Irving: *World of Our Fathers*
Kingston, Maxine Hong: *China Men*
                                    The Woman Warrior
Rodriguez, Richard: *Hunger of Memory*
Schwarz-bart, Andre: *A Woman Named Solitude*
Wheeler, Thomas C., Ed.: *The Immigrant Experience*

Emotionally Troubled and Socially Maladjusted
Aiken, Conrad: *Silent Snow, Secret Snow*
Axline, Virginia M.: *Dibs: In Search of Self*
Beers, Clifford: *A Mind That Found Itself*
Braithwaite, E. R.: *To Sir with Love*
Cather, Willa: "Paul's Case"
Craig, Eleanor: *P.S. Your Not Listening*
D'Ambrosio, Richard: *No Language but a Cry*
Daudet, Alphonse: "The Arlesian Girl"
Greenberg, Joanne: *I Never Promised You a Rose Garden*
Greenfeld, Josh: *A Child Called Noah: A Family Journey*
Kesey, Ken: *One Flew Over the Cuckoo's Nest*
Lindner, Robert: *Rebel Without a Cause*
Rothman, Esther P.: *The Angel Inside Went Sour*
Rubin, Theodore: *David and Lisa*
Stevenson, Robert Louis: "The Strange Case of Dr. Jekyll and Mr. Hyde"

GLOSSARY

Achievement test A measure of what has been learned.

Ancillary personnel People who provide supportive services in education, such as speech therapy, psychological services, counseling, school health services, social work, and medical services.

Aphasia A condition in which the ability to use language is partially or completely lost, usually due to cerebral damage.

Aptitude test A measure of the individual's probable ability to profit from instruction; a predictor of future achievement.

Autism A condition in children characterized by extreme preoccupation with one's own thoughts and wishes and living in a world of one's own fantasies, with thoughts governed by personal needs and focused on the self.

Barrio The name given to neighborhoods in the Southwest that are lived in principally by Mexican-Americans.

Cerebral palsy A paralytic condition caused by injury to the brain, usually during pregnancy.

Chronic condition A condition that is persistent over an extended period of time (such as cerebral palsy or deafness) with little expectation of cure.

Cleft palate A fissure or opening in the roof (palate) of the mouth that is present at birth.

Cognates: Two or more words in different languages that have the same derivation or root.

Convergent thinking A type of productive thinking in which the resources of information, experiences, and flexibility are combined to derive a single correct answer to a question or problem.

Cranmer abacus An adaptation of an ancient Japanese calculating device that is used by visually handicapped children to do arithmetic.

Criterion-referenced evaluation Assessment of a person's performance with respect to specific criteria or standards (rather than in competition with someone else).

Cued speech A speech-based method of communication that combines hand locations and shapes around the mouth area with lip movements to differentiate the forty sounds of English.

Decibel (dB) A measurement unit of the intensity of sound.

340

Developmental aphasia   Inappropriate use of language or poor speech due to problems in processing language in children of adequate intelligence and functioning speech and hearing systems.

Divergent thinking   A type of productive thinking in which the resources of information, experience, and flexibility are combined to find as many possible correct responses to a problem as one can.

Itinerant teacher   Usually a specialist (such as a speech, art, or remedial reading teacher) who is assigned to work with students at more than one location.

Language bifurcation   An inadequate command of two or more languages.

Magnet schools   Schools with specialized programs, often requiring special skills or talents for admission, that are designed to attract students from an entire school district rather than from the immediate neighborhood only (for example, a school for the performing arts).

Muscular dystrophy   A progressively degenerative disease in which there is increasing weakness and atrophy of the skeletal muscles.

Neurosis   A mental disorder in which there is partial impairment of the personality and in which the victim is beset by anxiety, conflicts, and an inability to gain complete insight into the nature of difficulties; is sometimes irrationally afraid (phobic); and may exhibit other behavioral symptoms.

Patois   A dialect, provincial speech, or jargon.

Perinatal   Refers to events occurring at the time of birth or very shortly after birth.

Phenylketonuria (PKU)   An inherited error in metabolism in which there is a deficiency in the production of phenylalanine hydroxylase (an amino acid). If not corrected by changes in diet, mental retardation usually results.

Psychosis   A severe mental disorder characterized by disorientation of time, space, and person; disorganization of thought processes; and disturbances of emotional behavior. Often the person is "out of touch" with reality.

Reliability   The consistency of the results of assessments (e.g., test-retest scores, agreement of observers, agreement among observation data or scores over a period of time).

Resource rooms   Central locations in schools, equipped with special learning materials used to help exceptional students acquire or develop specific skills.

Schizophrenia   A group of psychotic reactions that include withdrawal, disturbances in emotional life, and (depending on the type) hallucinations, delusions, negativistic behavior, inappropriate emotional responses, and gradual deterioration.

Selective attention   Attending to a limited number of sounds, sights, or other stimuli, while being unaffected by other stimuli.

Spina bifida   A birth defect in which the spinal cord is not completely covered by vertebrae, usually resulting in loss of sensation below the point at which the spine is "open."

Standard deviation   A statistical unit expressing the measure of variation from the mean or average.

Validity   The degree to which a test measures what its authors say it will measure.

REFERENCES

American Psychological Association. Ethical standards of psychologists. *American Psychologist*, 1981, *36*, 633–638.

Anastasi, A., and Cordova, F. A. Some effects of bilingualism upon the intelligence test performance of Puerto Rican children in New York City. *Journal of Educational Psychology*, 1953, *44*, 1–19.

Anders, F. M. If you can teach an ape to read, can you do something for my retarded child? *The New York Times Magazine*, June 1, 1975, *14*, 47–59.

Arredondo-Dowd, P. M., and Gonsalves, J. Preparing culturally effective counselors. *Personnel and Guidance Journal*, 1980, *58*, 657–661.

At 12, he's looking forward to June and a college degree. *New York Times*, May 2, 1982.

Baca, L. Issues in the education of culturally diverse exceptional children. *Exceptional Children*, 1980, *46*, 583.

Bailey, D. B., Jr., and Harbin, G. L. Nondiscriminatory evaluation. *Exceptional Children*, 1980, *46*, 590–596.

Baller, W. R., Charles, D. C., and Miller, E. L. Mid-life attainment of the mentally retarded: A longitudinal study. *Genetic Psychology Monographs*, 1967, *75*, 235–329.

Barraga, N. C. Innovations in teacher education. *Visual Impairment and Blindness*, 1981, *75* (3), 96–100.

Battle, J. Enhancing self-esteem: A new challenge to teachers. *Academic Therapy*, 1981, *16*, 541–550.

Battle, J., and Blowers, T. A longitudinal comparative study of the self-esteem of students in regular and special education classes. *Journal of Learning Disabilities*, 1982, *15*, 100–102.

Bayley, N. *Bayley's Scales of Infant Development*. New York: The Psychological Corporation, 1969.

Bellamy, E. *Looking backward*. Boston: Ticknor and Co., 1888.

Benedek, E. Female delinquency: Fantasies, facts, and future. In S. C. Feinstein and P. L. Giovacchini (Eds.), *Adolescent psychiatry* (Vol. 7). Chicago: University of Chicago Press, 1979, pp. 524–539.

Bennetts, L. Organizing to overcome the pain of being different. *New York Times*, April 14, 1980.

Bereiter, C., and Engelmann, S. *Teaching disadvantaged children in the preschool*. Englewood Cliffs, N.J.: Prentice-Hall, 1966.

Berger, A., and Kautz, C. The Braille informal reading inventory. *The Reading Teacher*, 1967, *21* (2), 149–152.

Berns, J. H. Grandparents of handicapped children. *Social Work*, 1980, *25*, 238–240.

Bettelheim, B. *The empty fortress*. New York: Free Press, 1967.

Biklen, D., and Bodgan, R. Media portrayals of disabled people: A study in stereotypes. *Interracial Books for Children Bulletin*, 1977, *8* (6–7), 4–9.

Bilingual preschool program teaches ways of two worlds. *TC Today*, Spring 1980, *8* (2), 4–5.

Bina, M. J. Morale of teachers of the visually handicapped: Implications for administrators. *Journal of Visual Impairment and Blindness*, 1982, *76* (4), 121–128.

Blechman, E. A., Kotanchik, N. L., and Taylor, C. J. Families and schools together: Early behavioral intervention with high risk children. *Behavior Therapy*, 1981, *12*, 308–319.

Block grant bill submitted to Congress. *Insight*, 1981, *12* (5), 5–6.

Bloom, B. S., Ed. *Taxonomy of educational objectives, Handbook I: Cognitive domain*. New York: David McKay, 1956.

Blum, E. R. The Madison Plan as an alternative to special class placement: An interview with Frank Hewett. *Education and Training of the Mentally Retarded*, 1971, *6* (1), 29–42.

Bolton, F. G., Jr. *The pregnant adolescent: Problems of premature parenthood*. Beverly Hills, Calif.: Sage Publications, 1980.

Borman, C., Nash, W., and Colson, S. Career guidance for gifted and talented students. *The Vocational Guidance Quarterly*, 1978, *27* (1), 72–76.

Brinich, P. M. Relationship between intellectual functioning and communicative competence in deaf children. *Journal of Communication Disorders*, 1981, *14*, 429–434.

Bronfenbrenner, U. Is early intervention effective? In B. Z. Friedlander, G. M. Steritt, and G. E. Kirk (Eds.), *Exceptional Infant* (Vol. 3). New York: Brunner/Mazel, 1975, pp. 449–475.

Brooks, R. Gifted delinquents. *Educational Research*, 1980, *22*, 212–220.

Brown, S. M., and Robbins, M. J. Serving the special education needs of students in correctional institutions. *Exceptional Children*, 1979, *45*, 574–579.

Bryan, T. H., and Pearl, R. A. Self-concepts and locus of control of learning disabled children. *Journal of Clinical Child Psychology*, 1979, *8*, 223–226.

Bryant, B., and Meadow, A. School related problems of Mexican-American adolescents. *Journal of School Psychology*, 1976, *14* (2), 139–150.

Buriel, R., and Saenz, E. Psychocultural characteristics of college-bound and non–college bound Chicanas. *Journal of Social Psychology*, 1980, *110*, 245–251.

Byford, E. M. Mainstreaming: The effect on regular teacher training programs. *Journal of Teacher Education*, 1979, *30* (6), 23–24.

Calovini, G. *The principal looks at classes for the physically handicapped*. Arlington. Va.: Council for Exceptional Children, 1969.

Calvert, D. R., Redell, R. C., Jacobs, U., and Baltzer, S. Experiences with preschool deaf-blind children. *Exceptional Children*, 1972, *38*, 415–421.

Carriker, W. R., and Berdine, W. H. Multiculture and special education teacher education and accreditation. *Teacher Education and Special Education*, 1979, *2* (4), 65–68.

Cassivi, D. Special programs for the gifted: A critique of some arguments. *McGill Journal of Education*, 1979, *14*, 189–198.

Castle, N. A group experience with physically handicapped children. *Child Welfare*, 1980, *59*, 235–241.

Cathey, M. L., and Jansma, P. Mainstreaming orthopedically disabled individuals in various physical activities—Part 2. *The Directive Teacher*, 1980, *2* (3), 16, 27. (a)

Cathey, M. L., and Jansma, P. Mainstreaming orthopedically disabled individuals in various physical activities—Part 4. *The Directive Teacher*, 1980, *2* (5), 20. (b)

Chambers, J. A., and Barron, F. The culturally different gifted student: Identifying the ablest. *Journal of Creative Behavior*, 1978, *12*, 72–75.

Chance, P. The remedial thinker. *Psychology Today*, 1981, *15* (10), 62–73.

Charles, C. M., and Malian, I. M. *The special student: Practical help for the classroom teacher*. St. Louis: C.V. Mosby, 1980.

Charnofsky, S. *Educating the powerless*. Belmont, Calif.: Wadsworth, 1971.

Chase, J. C. A retrospective study of retrolental fibroplasia. *New Outlook for the Blind*, 1974, *68*, 61–71.

Chess, S., and Fernandez, P. Do deaf children have a typical personality? *Journal of the American Academy of Child Psychiatry*, 1980, *19*, 654–664.

Chess, S., Fernandez, P., and Korn, S. The handicapped child and his family: Consonance and dissonance. *Journal of the American Academy of Child Psychiatry*, 1980, *19*, 56–67.

Cleary, M. E. Helping children understand the child with special needs. *Children Today*, 1976, *5* (4), 6–10.

Cline, S. *A practical guide to independent study*. New York: Trillium Press, 1980.

Cohen, A. K. *Delinquent boys*. New York: Free Press, 1955.

Congressional Record, October 10, 1978, H-12179.

Connor, L. E. New directions in infant programs for the deaf. *Volta Review*, 1976, *78*, 8–15.

Conroy, P. *The water is wide*. Boston: Houghton Mifflin, 1972.

Cook-Clampert, D. The development of self-concept in blind children. *Visual Impairment and Blindness*, 1981, *75*, 233–238.

Coopersmith, S. *The antecedents of self-esteem*. San Francisco: W. H. Freeman, 1967.

Council on Education of the Deaf. Standards for the certification of teachers of the hearing impaired. *Volta Review*, 1974, *76*, 239–249.

Cox, A. Teaching gifted students in regular classrooms. *Teacher*, November/December 1979, *97*, 75–76.

Crowe, T. A., and Walton, J. H. Teacher attitudes toward stuttering. *Journal of Fluency Disorders*, 1981, *6*, 163–174.

Culatta, R., and Culatta, B. K. Communication disorders. In A. E. Blackhurst and W. H. Berdine (Eds.), *An introduction to special education*. Boston: Little, Brown, 1981, pp. 108–148.

Cuniberti, B. Profile: Annie Glenn savors victory over stuttering. *Philadelphia Inquirer*, July 10, 1982, 1-C, 3-C.

Dardig, J. C. Helping teachers integrate handicapped students into the regular classroom. *Educational Horizons*, 1981, *59*, 124–130.

Darling, R. B. *Families against society: A study of reactions to children with birth defects*. Beverly Hills, Calif.: Sage Publications, 1979.

Davis, J. M., Shepard, N. T., Stelmachowicz, P. G., and Gorga, M. P. Characteristics of hearing-impaired children in the public schools: Part II—psychoeducational data. *Journal of Speech and Hearing Disorders*, 1981, *46*, 130–137.

Davis, W. E. Public school principals' attitudes toward mainstreaming retarded pupils. *Education and Training of the Mentally Retarded*, 1980, *15*, 174–178.

Dearman, N. B., and Plisko, V. W. *The condition of education* (1980 ed.). Washington, D.C.: National Center for Education Statistics, 1980, p. 69.

Deich, R. F., and Hodges, P. M. Learning from Sarah. *Human Behavior*, 1975, *4* (5), 40–42.

Dettman, D. F., and Colangelo, N. A functional model for counseling parents of gifted students. *Gifted Child Quarterly*, 1980, *24*, 158–161.

Dillard, J. M., and Perrin, D. W. Puerto Rican, Black, and Anglo adolescents' career aspirations, expectations, and maturity. *Vocational Guidance Quarterly*, 1980, *28*, 313–321.

Dixon, B., Shaw, S. F., and Bensky, J. M. Administrator's role in fostering the mental health of special services personnel. *Exceptional Children*, 1980, *47*, 30–36.

Doll, E. A. *Vineland Social Maturity Scale*. Circle Pines, Minn.: American Guidance Service, 1965.

Doob, D. An intensive speech and language program in the rehabilitation process of multihandicapped children. *Rehabilitation Literature*, 1968, *29*, 8–10.

Dormady, B. Teaching employers how to communicate with deaf multiply handicapped persons. *Visual Impairment and Blindness*, 1980, *74*, 391–394.

Duffey, J. B., Salvia, J., Tucker, J., and Ysseldyke, J. Nonbiased assessment: A need for operationalism. *Exceptional Children*, 1981, *47*, 427–434.

Earls, F., and Siegel, B. Precocious fathers. *American Journal of Orthopsychiatry*, 1980, *50*, 469–480.

Edmonson, B. Sociosexual education for the handicapped. *Exceptional Education Quarterly*, 1980, *1* (2), 67–73.

Educational Testing Service. Handicapped meet challenges: ETS expanding test services. *ETS Developments*, 1979, *26* (1), 1, 7–8.

Fair, D. T., and Birch, J. W. Effect of rest on test scores of physically handicapped and nonhandicapped children. *Exceptional Children*, 1971, *38*, 335–336.

Falloon, I. R. H., Lloyd, G. G., and Harpin, R. E. The treatment of social phobia: Real-life rehearsal with nonprofessional therapists. *Journal of Nervous and Mental Disease*, 1981, *169*, 180–184.

Feldhusen, J., and Sokol. L. Extra-school programming to meet the needs of gifted youth: Super Saturday. *Gifted Child Quarterly*, 1982, *26*, 51–56.

Feldhusen, J. F., and Wyman, A. R. Super Saturday: Design and implementation of Purdue's special program for gifted children. *Gifted Child Quarterly*, 1980, *24*, 15–21.

Fisher, S., and Fisher, R. L. Schlemiel children. *Psychology Today*, 1980, *14* (4), 64–73.

Fraiberg, S. *Insights from the blind*. Ann Arbor: University of Michigan Press, 1977.

Franklin Institute News (Philadelphia) Spring/Summer 1972, pp. 12–16.

Fremstad, L. The immigrants: Is California the end of the rainbow? *California Business*, August 1981, 54–62.

Freund, J. H., Casey, P. H., and Bradley, R. H. A special education course with pediatric components. *Exceptional Children*, 1982, *48*, 348–351.

Frey, R. M., and Krause, I. B. The incidence of color-blindness among deaf children. *Exceptional Children*, 1971, *37*, 373–394.

Frick, E. Adjusting to integration: Some difficulties hearing impaired children have in public schools. *Volta Review*, 1973, *75*, 36–46.

Fuchigami, R. Y. Teacher education for culturally diverse exceptional children. *Exceptional Children*, 1980, *46*, 634–641.

Gajar, A. H. Characteristics across exceptional categories: EMR, LD, and ED. *Journal of Special Education*, 1980, *14*, 165–173.

Gallagher, J. J. *Teaching the gifted child* (2nd ed.). Boston: Allyn & Bacon, 1975.

Gallagher, J. J., and Lucito, L. J. Intellectual patterns of gifted compared with average and retarded. *Exceptional Children*, 1961, *27*, 479–482.

Garcia, E. E. Bilingualism in early childhood. *Young Children*, 1980, *35* (4), 52–66.

Gardner, D. C., and Gardner, P. L. Goal-setting and learning in the high school resource room. *Adolescence*, 1978, *13*, 489–493.

Garibaldi, A. M., Ed. *In-school alternatives to suspension: Conference report*. Washington, D.C.: National Institute of Education, 1979.

Gearheart, B. R., and Weishahn, M. W. *The handicapped child in the regular classroom*. St. Louis: C. V. Mosby, 1976.

Gesell, A., et al. *Gesell Developmental Schedules*. New York: The Psychological Corporation, 1940.

Glass, R. M., Christiansen, J., and Christiansen, J. L. *Teaching exceptional students in the regular classroom*. Boston: Little, Brown, 1982.

Glasser, W. *The effect of school failure on the life of a child*. Washington, D. C.: National Education Association, 1971.

Glazzard, P. Simulation of handicaps as a teaching strategy for preservice and inservice training. *Teaching Exceptional Children*, 1979, *11*, 101–104.

Glazzard, P. Adaptations for mainstreaming. *Teaching Exceptional Children*, 1980, *13*, 26–29.

Glueck, S., and Glueck, E. *Physique and delinquency*. New York: Harper, 1956.

Goddard, H. H. *The Kallikak family: A study in the heredity of feeble-mindedness*. New York: Macmillan, 1927 (originally pub. 1912).

Gold, M. W., and Rittenhouse, R. K. Task analysis for teaching 8 practical signs to deaf-blind individuals. *Teaching Exceptional Children*, 1978, *10*, 34–37.

Goldberg, L. M. Creative use of media in schools and programs for the hearing impaired. *Volta Review*, 1980, *82*, 440–446.

Goleman, D. 1,528 little geniuses and how they grew. *Psychology Today*, 1980, *13* (9), 28–53.

Gordon, D. A., and Young, R. D. School phobia: A discussion of etiology, treatment, and evaluation. *Psychological Reports*, 1976, *39*, 783–804.

Gordon, I. J. A home learning center approach to early stimulation. Gainesville: Institute for Development of Human Resources, University of Florida, 1972.

Gottlieb, J. Mainstreaming: Fulfilling the promise? *American Journal of Mental Deficiency*, 1981, *86*, 115–126.

Gould, H. M., Jr. For gifted, summer school that's all business. *Philadelphia Inquirer*, July 16, 1981, 7-C.

Gowan, J. C. The organization of guidance for the able. *Personnel and Guidance Journal*, 1960, *39*, 275–279.

Gray, D. J., and Orrick, A. H. *Designs of famous utopias*. New York: Rinehart & Company, 1959.

Gregory, S. *The deaf child and his family*. New York: Halsted Press, 1976.

Gresham, F. M. Misguided mainstreaming: The case for social skills training with handicapped children. *Exceptional Children*, 1982, *48*, 422–433.

Grossman, F. K. Brothers and sisters of retarded children. *Psychology Today*, 1972, *5* (11), 83–84, 102–104.

Grossman, H. J., Ed. *Manual on terminology and classification in mental retardation*. Washington, D.C.: American Association on Mental Deficiency, 1973.

Gruber, A. R., Heck, E. T., and Mintzer, E. Children who set fires: Some background and behavioral characteristics. *American Journal of Orthopsychiatry*, 1981, *51*, 484–488.

Hadary, D. E., Cohen, S. H., and Haushalter, R. M. Out of darkness and silence. *Science and Children*, 1979, *16* (6), 40–41.

Hallahan, D. P., and Kaufman, J. M. *Exceptional children: Introduction to special education*. Englewood Cliffs, N.J.: Prentice-Hall, 1978.

Hammill, D. Improving spelling skills. In D. D. Hammill and N. R. Bartel (Eds.), *Teaching children with learning and behavior problems* (2nd ed.). Boston: Allyn & Bacon, 1978, pp. 147–171.

Haraguchi, R. S. Developing programs meeting the special needs of physically disabled adolescents. *Rehabilitation Literature*, 1981, *42* (3–4), 75–78.

Harasymin, S. J., and Horne, M. D. Teacher attitudes toward handicapped children and regular class integration. *Journal of Special Education*, 1976, *10*, 393–400.

Hardman, M. L., Egan, M. W., and Landau, E. D., Eds. *What will we do in the morning? The exceptional student in the regular classroom*. Dubuque: Wm. C. Brown, 1981.

Hayes, D., and Grether, L. *The school year and vacation: When do students learn?* Paper presented at a meeting of the Eastern Sociological Association, New York, 1969 (cited in Bronfenbrenner, 1975).

Hayes, M. L. Giving handicapped students the least restrictive alternative. *Educational Horizons*, 1981, *59*, 119–123.

Heber, R., and Garber, H. The Milwaukee Project: A study of the use of family intervention to prevent cultural-familial retardation. In B. Z. Friedlander, G. M. Steritt, and G. E. Kirk (Eds.), *Exceptional infant* (Vol. 3). New York: Brunner/Mazel, 1975, pp. 399–433.

Hedberg, S. Integrating LD students into a regular high school. *Academic Therapy*, 1981, *16*, 559–562.

Hedrick, V. Applying technology to special education. *American Education*, 1972, *8* (1), 22–25.

Hendrickson, B. Teachers make mainstreaming work. *Learning*, October 1978, 104–110.

Herbers, J. Census data show gains in housing and in education. *New York Times*, April 20, 1982, pp. 1, B-6.

Heward, W. L., and Orlansky, M. D. *Exceptional children: An introductory survey to special education*. Columbus, Ohio: Charles E. Merrill, 1980.

Hewett, F. M. A hierarchy of competencies for teachers of emotionally handicapped children. *Exceptional Children*, 1966, *33*, 7–11.

Hickman, M. R., and Anderson, C. R. Evaluating instructional materials for learning disabled children. *Journal of Learning Disabilities*, 1979, *12*, 355–359.

Highland, A. C. Depression in adolescents: A developmental view. *Child Welfare*, 1979, *58*, 577–585.

Hobbs, N. *The futures of children*. San Francisco: Jossey-Bass, 1976.

Holden, C. A new visibility for gifted children. *Science*, November 21, 1980, *210*, 879–882.

Holmes, L. How fathers can cause the Down syndrome. *Human Nature*, 1978, *1* (10), 70–72.

Huber, J., Treffinger, D., Tracy, D., and Rand, D. Self-instructional use of programmed creativity-training materials with gifted and regular students. *Journal of Educational Psychology*, 1979, *71*, 303–309.

Hunter, B. Policy issues in special education for migrant students. *Exceptional Children*, 1982, *48*, 469–472.

Huxley, A. *Brave new world*. New York: Harper, 1932.

Implementing the IEP concept. *American Education*, 1977, *13* (7), 6–8.

Interpreter not required for deaf student. *Chronicle of Higher Education*, July 7, 1982.

Isaacs, J., and McElroy, M. R. Psychosocial aspects of chronic illness in children. *Journal of School Health*, 1980, *50*, 318–321.

Jackson, N. E., Famiglietti, J., and Robinson, H. B. Kindergarten and first grade teachers' attitudes toward early entrants, intellectually advanced students, and average students. *Journal for the Education of the Gifted*, 1981, *4*, 132–142.

Johnson, A. M. Juvenile delinquency. In S. Arieti (Ed.), *American handbook of psychiatry* (Vol. 1). New York: Basic Books, 1959, pp. 840–856.

Johnson, C. LD adults: The inside story. *Academic Therapy*, 1981, *16*, 435–442.

Johnson, J. L. An essay on incarcerated youth: An oppressed group. *Exceptional Children*, 1979, *45*, 566–571.

Johnson, W. *Toward understanding stuttering*. Chicago: National Society for Crippled Children and Adults, 1958.

Jones, R. S. Teachers who stimulate curiosity. *Education*, 1980, *101*, 158–165.

Jones, T. W., Sowell, V. M., Jones, J. K., and Butler, L. G. Changing children's perceptions of handicapped people. *Exceptional Children*, 1981, *47*, 365–368.

Kandel, D. B., Kessler, R. C., and Margulies, R. Z. Antecedents of adolescent initiation into stages of drug use: A developmental analysis. In S. Chess and A. Thomas (Eds.), *Annual progress in child psychiatry and child development* (Vol. 12). New York: Brunner/Mazel, 1979.

Karmel, C. A. "Rubella bulge" of the '60s reaches the college. *New York Times*, April 26, 1982, *12*, 29.

Karnes, F. A., and Collins, E. C. Teacher certification in the education of the gifted: An update. *Journal for the Education of the Gifted*, 1981, *4*, 123–131.

Kaslow, F. W. The use of creative arts therapy in special education. In L. L. Schwartz (Ed.), *The exceptional child: A primer* (2nd ed.). Belmont, Calif.: Wadsworth, 1979, pp. 179–187.

Kelly, J. A., Wildman, B. G., and Berler, E. S. Small group behavioural training to improve the job interview skills repertoire of mildly retarded adolescents. *Journal of Applied Behavior Analysis*, 1980, *13*, 461–471.

Kinard, E. M., and Klerman, L. V. Teenage parenting and child abuse: Are they related? *American Journal of Orthopsychiatry*, 1980, *50*, 481–488.

Koch, R., and Koch, J. H. We can do more to prevent the tragedy of retarded children. *Psychology Today*, 1976, *10* (7), 88–93, 108.

Kolvin, I., and Fundudis, T. Elective mute children: Psychological development and background factors. *Journal of Child Psychology and Psychiatry*, 1981, *22*, 219–232.

Kutsick, K. Remedial strategies for learning disabled adolescents. *Academic Therapy*, 1982, *17*, 329–335.

La Greca, A. M., and Mesibov, G. B. *Social intervention with learning disabled children*. Paper presented at the annual meeting of the American Psychological Association, New York, 1979.

Laird, A. W. The fifty states' educational provisions for gifted children. *Gifted Child Quarterly*, 1971, *15*, 205–216.

Landman, J. B. *The computer as a tool in gifted education*. Paper presented at the annual meeting of the National Association for Gifted Children, Minneapolis, 1980.

Lavallee, E. Genius burns young in Mass. *Philadelphia Bulletin*, September 22, 1980, 2.

Laycock, V. K. Prescriptive programming in the mainstream. In J. W. Schifani, R. M. Anderson, and S. J. Odle (Eds.), *Implementing learning in the least restrictive environment*. Baltimore: University Park Press, 1980, pp. 285–319.

Leff, S. L., and Leff, R. B. *Talking pictures: A kit for people with communication difficulties*. Milwaukee: Crestwood Company, 1982.

Levitt, H. Computer applications in audiology and rehabilitation of the hearing impaired. *Journal of Communication Disorders*, 1980, *13*, 471–481.

Levy, H. B. *Square pegs in round holes: The learning disabled child in the classroom and at home*. Boston: Little, Brown, 1973.

Levy, P. S. The story of Marie, David, Richard, Jane, and John: Teaching gifted children in the regular classroom. *Teaching Exceptional Children*, 1981, *13*, 136–142.

Lewis, C. City of the future. *G/C/T*, March/April 1979, *7*, 21–29.

Lewis, D. O., Shanock, S. S., Pincus, J. H., and Glaser, G. H. Violent juvenile delinquents: Psychiatric, neurological, psychological, and abuse factors. *Journal of the American Academy of Child Psychiatry*, 1979, *2*, 307–319.

Lieberman, L. M. The nightmare of scheduling. *Journal of Learning Disabilities*, 1982, *15*, 57–58.

Lindsey, J. D., and Kerlin, M. A. Learning disabilities and reading disorders: A brief review of the secondary level literature. *Journal of Learning Disabilities*, 1979, *12*, 408–415.

Lindsey, M. *Training teachers of the gifted and talented*. New York: Teachers College Press, 1980.

Litton, F. W., Banbury, M. M., and Harris, K. Materials for educating nonhandicapped students about their handicapped peers. *Teaching Exceptional Children*, 1980, *13*, 39–43.

Liu, A. *Solitaire*. New York: Harper & Row, 1979.

Locks, N. A., Pletcher, B. A., and Reynolds, D. F. *Language assessment instruments for limited English-speaking students: A needs analysis*. Washington, D.C.: National Institute of Education, 1978.

Longstreth, L. E. Revisiting Skeels' final study: A critique. *Developmental Psychology*, 1981, *17*, 620–625.

Lovaas, O. I., Berberich, J. P., Perloff, B. F., and Schaeffer, B. Acquisition of imitative speech in schizophrenic children. *Science*, 1966, *151*, 705–707.

Luick, A. H., Kirk, S. A., Agranowitz, A., and Busby, R. Profiles of children with severe oral language disorders. *Journal of Speech and Hearing Disorders*, 1982, *47*, 88–92.

Luxenberg, S. Easing into English. *American Education*, 1981, *17* (1), 31–36.

Macdonald, R. Future education for the multiply handicapped. *American Annals of the Deaf*, 1979, *124*, 594–597.

MacMillan, D. L. *Mental retardation in school and society* (2nd ed.). Boston: Little, Brown, 1982.

Mann, P. H., and Suiter, P. *Handbook in diagnostic teaching: A learning disabilities approach.* Boston: Allyn & Bacon, 1974.

Marion, R. L. Communicating with parents of culturally diverse exceptional children. *Exceptional Children*, 1980, *46*, 616–623.

Markel, G. Improving test-taking skills of LD adolescents. *Academic Therapy*, 1981, *16*, 333–342.

Marland, S. P., Jr. The gifted child and the library. *Top of the News*, 1971, *28* (1), 27–28 (American Library Association).

Marohn, R. C. A psychiatric overview of juvenile delinquency. In S. C. Feinstein and P. L. Giovacchini (Eds.), *Adolescent Psychiatry.* (Vol. 7). Chicago: University of Chicago Press, 1979, pp. 425–432.

Maron, S. S., and Martinez, D. H. Environmental alternatives for the visually handicapped. In J. W. Schifani, R. M. Anderson, and S. J. Odle (Eds.), *Implementing learning in the least restrictive environment.* Baltimore: University Park Press, 1980, pp. 149–198.

McKinnon, A., Wine, A., Sires, M., and Bowser, G. Introducing secondary education university students to mainstreaming. *The Directive Teacher*, 1982, *4* (1), 26.

McNett, I. KEEP Early Education Project . . . From research to evaluation to success. *APA Monitor*, 1981, *12* (12), 8–9, 33.

Mehren, E. He's not your average 12-year-old—or your average genius. *Philadelphia Inquirer*, January 29, 1981, 3-B.

Mental retardation and developmental disabilities. Washington, D.C.: U.S. Department of Health and Human Services, Research Programs of the National Institute of Child Health and Human Development, 1981.

Mercer, J. R. *Labeling the mentally retarded: Clinical and social system perspectives on mental retardation.* Berkeley: University of California Press, 1973.

Mercer, J. R., and Lewis, J. F. *System of multicultural pluralistic assessment: Technical manual.* New York: The Psychological Corporation, 1979.

Meyen, E. L., and Lehr, D. H. Mainstreaming: An instructional perspective. *Educational Horizons*, 1981, *59*, 113–118.

Milne, N. M. Music and art activities for the physically or health impaired student. *Teaching Exceptional Children*, 1981, *14*, 73–74.

Minde, K., Lewin, D., Weiss, G., Lavigeur, L., Douglas, V., and Sykes, E. The hyperactive child in elementary school: A 5-year, controlled followup. *Exceptional Children*, 1971, *38*, 215–221.

Mitchell, B. M. What's happening to gifted education in the United States today? *Phi Delta Kappan*, 1980, *61*, 563–564.

Mitchell, J. E., Hong, K. M., and Corman, C. Childhood onset of alcohol abuse. *American Journal of Orthopsychiatry*, 1979, *49*, 511–513.

Moorefield, S. Alaskan journal. *American Education*, 1976, *12* (7), 15–22.

Moores, D. F. *Educating the deaf: Psychology, principles, and practices.* Boston: Houghton Mifflin, 1978.

Mullins, D., and Hays, J. R. Personality characteristics and employability of mentally retarded adults. *Psychological Reports*, 1980, *47*, 1063–1067.

Murnane, R. J., and Phillips, B. R. What do effective teachers of inner-city children have in common? *Social Science Research*, 1981, *10*, 83–100.

Nasca, D. Teacher nomination of intellectually gifted students. *G/C/T*, 1979, *7*, 38–41.

National Advisory Committee on the Handicapped. *The individualized education program: Key to an appropriate education for the handicapped child. 1977 Annual Report.* Washington, D.C.: Bureau of Education for the Handicapped, Office of Education, Department of Health, Education, and Welfare, 1977.

National Association for Retarded Citizens. *Mental Retardation News*, 1974, *23* (1).

Nazzaro, J. N. *Exceptional timetables: Historic events affecting the handicapped and gifted.* Reston, Va.: Council for Exceptional Children, 1977.

Newman, J. Faculty attitudes toward handicapped students. *Rehabilitation Literature*, 1976, *37*, 194–197.

Newman, D. J. Salvaging a gem from a "garbage" classroom. *Philadelphia Inquirer*, May 25, 1980, 1-2-G.

Newsnotes. Cambridge, Mass.: Center for Law and Education, Inc., March/April 1982, *27*.

Nihira, K., Foster, R., Shelhaas, M., and Leland, H. *AAMD Adaptive*

Behavior Scale (rev. ed.). Washington, D.C.: American Association on Mental Deficiency, 1974.

Norden. K. Learning processes and personality development in deaf children. *American Annals of the Deaf*, 1981, *126*, 404–410.

Nordoff, P., and Robbins, C. *Music therapy in special education*. New York: John Day, 1971.

Oakland, T. *Psychological and educational assessment of minority children*. New York: Brunner/Mazel, 1977.

Offenberger, D. M. Science for Jann: A blind pupil in a sighted class. *Journal of Visual Impairment and Blindness*, 1981, *75* (1), 13–16.

Offer, D., Marohn, R. C., and Ostrov, E. *The psychological world of the juvenile delinquent*. New York: Basic Books, 1979.

Orwell, G. *Nineteen eighty-four*. New York: Signet Classics, 1961 (originally pub. 1938).

Page, E. B., and Grandon, G. M. Massive intervention and child intelligence: The Milwaukee Project in critical perspective. *Journal of Special Education*, 1981, *15*, 239–256.

Pang, H. Undistinguished school experiences of distinguished persons. *Adolescence*, 1968, *3*, 319–326.

Patton, J. M., and Braithwaite, R. L. P.L. 94-142 and the changing status of teacher certification/recertification. *Teacher Education and Special Education*, 1980, *3* (2), 43–47.

Pegnato, C. W., and Birch, J. W. Locating gifted children in junior high schools: A comparison of methods. *Exceptional Children*, 1959, *25*, 300–304.

Pittenger, J. C., and Kuriloff, P. Educating the handicapped: Reforming a radical law. *The Public Interest*, 1982, *66*, 72–96.

Polis, J. E. Observation at the school for the deaf in Luxembourg. Private communication, 1973.

Porter, G. The missing vital dimension in successful integration. *Volta Review*, 1975, *77*, 416–422.

Prieto, A. G., Rueda, R. S., and Rodriguez, R. Teaching competencies for bilingual/multicultural exceptional children. *Teacher Education and Special Education*, 1981, *4* (4), 35–39.

Rabkin, B. *Growing up dead*. Nashville: Abingdon Press, 1978.

Reed, S. Chicago's early focus on learning problems. *New York Times Winter Survey of Education*, January 10, 1982, 36–37.

Renzulli, J. S., and Hartman, R. K. Scale for rating behavioral characteristics of superior students. *Exceptional Children*, 1971, *38*, 243–248.

Reynolds, M. C., and Birch, J. W. *Teaching exceptional children in all America's schools*. Reston, Va.: Council for Exceptional Children, 1977. (a)

Reynolds, M. C., and Birch, J. W. The interface between regular and special education. *Teacher Education and Special Education*, 1977, *1*, 12–27. (b)

Reynolds, M. C., and Birch, J. W. *Teaching exceptional children in all America's schools* (rev. ed.). Reston, Va.: Council for Exceptional Children, 1982.

Reynolds, W. M., and Greco, V. T. *Development of a scale to measure teachers' attitudes toward mainstreaming*. Paper presented at the annual meeting of the American Psychological Association, New York, 1979.

Rist, R. C., and Harrell, J. E. Labeling the learning disabled child: The social ecology of educational practice. *American Journal of Ortho-psychiatry*, 1982, *52*, 146–160.

Roberson, J. B. Preservice changes in teacher education relative to mainstreaming. *Teacher Education and Special Education*, 1980, *3* (2), 48–51.

Robson, D. L. Administering educational services for the handicapped: Role expectations and perceptions. *Exceptional Children*, 1981, *47*, 377–378.

Rock, M. A. Keyboard symbols enable retarded children to "speak." *Smithsonian*, 1979, *10* (1), 90–96.

Rodriguez, R. *Hunger of memory: The education of Richard Rodriguez*. Boston: Godine, 1981.

Roe, W. H., and Drake, T. H. *The principalship*. New York: Macmillan, 1974.

Rosenthal, P. A. Delinquency in adolescent girls: Developmental aspects. In S. C. Feinstein and P. L. Giovacchini (Eds.), *Adolescent psychiatry* (Volume 7). Chicago: University of Chicago Press, 1979, pp. 503–515.

Rosenthal, R., and Jacobsen, L. *Pygmalion in the classroom*. New York: Holt, Rinehart & Winston, 1968.

Ross, A. O. *Psychological aspects of learning disabilities and reading disorders*. New York: McGraw-Hill, 1976.

Roth, E. B. Education for performance. *American Education*, 1981, *17* (3), 6–15.

Rubin, R. A., and Balow, B. Prevalence of teacher identified behavior problems: A longitudinal study. *Exceptional Children*, 1978, *45*, 102–111.

Rueda, R., and Prieto, A. G. Cultural pluralism: Implications for teacher education. *Teacher Education and Special Education*, 1979, *2* (4), 4–11.

Russell, T., and Hardin, P. Sex education for the mentally retarded. *Education and Training of the Mentally Retarded*, 1980, *15*, 312–314.

Sabatino, D. A., Miller, P. F., and Schmidt, C. Can intelligence be altered through cognitive training? *Journal of Special Education*, 1981, *15*, 125–144.

Schifani, J. W., Anderson, R. M., and Odle, S. J., Eds. *Implementing learning in the least restrictive environment*. Baltimore: University Park Press, 1980.

Schmitt, B. D. What teachers need to know about child abuse and neglect. *Childhood Education*, November/December 1975, *52*, 58–62.

Scholl, G. T. *The principal works with the visually impaired*. Washington, D.C.: Council for Exceptional Children, 1968.

Schultz, L. R. Educating the special needs student in the regular classroom. *Exceptional Children*, 1982, *48*, 366–368.

Schwartz, L. L. Advocacy for the neglected gifted: Females. *Gifted Child Quarterly*, 1980, *24*, 113–117. (a)

Schwartz, L. L. *A program for pre-college gifted*. Paper presented at the annual meeting of the National Association for Gifted Children, Minneapolis, 1980. (b)

Schwartz, L. L., and Isser, N. Forgotten minorities, self-concept, and the schools. *The Social Studies*, 1978, *69*, 187–190.

Shapero, S., and Forbes, C. R. A review of involvement programs for parents of learning disabled children. *Journal of Learning Disabilities*, 1981, *14*, 499–504.

Singh, V., and Ling, G. M. Amphetamines in the management of children's kinesis. *Contemporary Drug Problems*, 1980, *9*, 227–240.

Skeels, H. M. Adult status of children with contrasting early life experiences. *Monographs of the Society for Research in Child Development*, 1966, *31*.

Smith, D. F. Adolescent suicides: A problem for teachers? *Phi Delta Kappan*, 1976, *57*, 539–542.

Smith, S. L. *No easy answers: The learning disabled child*. Rockville, Md.: National Institute for Mental Health, 1978.

Spanish 'not needed' by students in Texas. *Philadelphia Inquirer*, July 13, 1982.

Spaulding, R. L. *Effects of a five-year compensatory education program on social, intellectual, linguistic, and academic development*. Paper presented at the annual meeting of the Eastern Psychological Association, Boston, 1972.

Stagich, T. M. Mainstreaming in education: Rights, barriers, and administrative alternatives. *Educational Horizons*, 1980, *58*, 217–221.

Stanley, J. C. Accelerating the educational progress of intellectually gifted youth. *Educational Psychologist*, 1973, *10*, 133–146.

Starting points: Futuring. *Learning*, 1974, *2* (6), 41–56.

Stroud, J. G. The handicapped in adolescent fiction. *Journal of Reading*, 1981, *24*, 519–522.

Swallow, R-M. Fifty assessment instruments commonly used with blind and partially sighted individuals. *Journal of Visual Impairment and Blindness*, 1981, *75* (2), 65–72.

Swap, S. M., Prieto, A. G., and Harth, R. Ecological perspectives of the emotionally disturbed child. In R. L. McDowell, G. W. Adamson, and F. H. Wood (Eds.), *Teaching emotionally disturbed children*. Boston: Little, Brown, 1982, pp. 70–98.

Swenson, E. V. Teacher assessment of creative behavior in disadvantaged children. *Gifted Child Quarterly*, 1978, *22*, 338–343.

Tan-Willman, C. Canadian student teachers' attitudes about creativity. *Psychological Reports*, 1981, *48*, 49–50.

Tawney, J. W. Programmed language instruction for the severely developmentally retarded. *The Directive Teacher*, 1980, *2* (3), 11–12.

Taylor, H. M. Learning to listen to English. *TESOL Quarterly*, 1981, *15* (1), 41–50.

Telzrow, C. F., and Hartlage, L. C. *Behavioral characteristics of learning disabled children*. Paper presented at the annual meeting of the American Psychological Association, Los Angeles, 1981.

Thernstrom, A. M. E Pluribus Plura—Congress and bilingual education. *The Public Interest*, 1980, *60*, 3–22.

Torrance, E. P. *The Torrance Tests of Creative Thinking: Norms and technical manual*. Princeton, N.J.: Personnel Press, 1966.

Torrance, E. P. *Discovery and nurturance of giftedness in the culturally different*. Reston Va.: Council for Exceptional Children, 1977.

Trevino, F. Siblings of handicapped children: Identifying those at risk. *Social Casework*, 1979, *60*, 488–493.

Trotter, R. Environment and behavior. *APA Monitor*, 1976, *7* (7, 10), 4–5, 19, 46.

Tucker, J. A. Issues and considerations when screening and assessing handicapped pupils. *Measurement and Evaluation in Guidance*, 1982, *15*, 117–127.

Tuckman, B. W., and Bierman, M. *Beyond Pygmalion: Galatea in the schools*. Paper presented at the annual meeting of the American Educational Research Association, 1971.

Turnbull, A. P., and Schulz, J. B. *Mainstreaming handicapped students: A guide for the classroom teacher*. Boston: Allyn & Bacon, 1979.

Turnbull, A. P., and Turnbull, H. R. III. *Parents speak out: Views from the other side of the two-way mirror*. Columbus, Ohio: Charles E. Merrill, 1978.

Tweedie, D., and Baud, H. Future directions in the education of deaf-blind multihandicapped children and youth. *American Annals of the Deaf*, 1981, *126*, 829–834.

U.S. Department of Labor. *Dictionary of occupational titles.* Washington, D.C.: U.S. Government Printing Office, 1976.

Vachon, B. Hey man, what did you learn in reform school? Well, uh, like how to disconnect a burglar alarm. *Saturday Review*, September 16, 1972, 69–76.

Vernon, McC. *Multiply handicapped deaf children: Medical, educational and psychological considerations.* Washington, D.C.: Council for Exceptional Children, 1969.

Vernon, McC. Education's "Three Mile Island": P.L. 94-142. *Peabody Journal of Education*, 1981, *59*, 24–29.

Wagner, J. Spanish on Friday, Japanese on Saturday. *American Education*, 1980, *16* (8), 49–57.

Wallbrown, J. D. The occupational implications of learning patterns. *School Psychology Digest*, 1979, *8*, 240–244.

Wallerstein, J. S., and Kelly, J. B. *Surviving the breakup: How children and parents cope with divorce.* New York: Basic Books, 1980.

Weber, J. L., Kushnir, W. V., and Weber, S. E. A comprehensive approach to assessment and treatment of severe developmental speech and language disorders. *Journal of Learning Disabilities*, 1982, *15*, 8–14.

Wechsler, D. *Manual for the Wechsler Intelligence Scale for Children — Revised.* New York: The Psychological Corporation, 1974.

Weener, P. On comparing learning disabled and regular classroom children. *Journal of Learning Disabilities*, 1981, *14*, 227–232.

Weikart, D. P., Ed. *Preschool intervention: A preliminary report of the Perry Preschool Project.* Ann Arbor, Mich.: Campus Publishers, 1967.

Weisz, J. R., and Zigler, E. Cognitive development in retarded and nonretarded persons: Piagetian tests of the similar sequence hypothesis. *Psychological Bulletin*, 1979, *86*, 831–851.

Wencil, L. A prevocational program for multiply handicapped blind adolescents. *Journal of Visual Impairment and Blindness*, 1980, *74*, 351–353.

Wexler, H. Rescuing trapped minds. *American Education*, 1980, *16* (6), 38. (a)

Wexler, H. Access to learning for handicapped children. *American Education*, 1980, *16* (10), 29. (b)

Wikler, L. Chronic stresses of families of mentally retarded children. *Family Relations*, 1981, *30*, 281–288.

Wilson, J. J. Notetaking: A necessary support service for hearing-impaired students. *Teaching Exceptional Children*, 1981, *14* (1), 38–40.

Winer, M. Job opportunities for the visually impaired—A self-help concept. *Visual Impairment and Blindness*, 1980, *74*, 232–237.

Wingate, M. E. *Stuttering: Theory and treatment*. New York: Irvington Publishers (Halsted Press), 1976.

Winslow, R. College for the learning disabled. *The New York Times Magazine*, February 21, 1982, 80, 87–91.

Wolraich, M. L. Communication between physicians and parents of handicapped children. *Exceptional Children*, 1982, *48*, 324–329.

Wood, W. By the deaf, for the deaf. *American Education*, 1974, *10* (1), 18–24.

Yarnall, G. D. Teaching geometric sameness to a deaf-blind child. *Journal of Rehabilitation for the Deaf*, 1981, *15* (1), 1–6.

Zaffran, R. T., and Colangelo, N. Counseling with gifted and talented students. *Gifted Child Quarterly*, 1977, *21*, 305–321.

NAME INDEX

Goleman, D., 84
Gonsalves, J., 279
Gordon, D. A., 239
Gordon, I. J, 204
Gorga, M. P., 127
Gottlieb, J., 42
Gould, H. M., 100
Gowan, J. C., 101
Grandon, G. M., 202
Gray, D. J., 96
Greco, V. T., 265
Gresham, F. M., 17
Grossman, F. K., 299
Grossman, H. J., 29
Gruber, A. R., 249
Guilford, 81

Hadary, D. E., 87
Hallahan, D. P., 144
Haraguchi, R. S., 119
Harasymin, S. J., 13
Harbin, G. L., 210
Hardin, P., 49
Hardman, M. L., 136
Harpin, R. E., 239
Harrell, J. E., 57
Harris, K., 267
Harth, R., 224
Hartlage, L. C., 61
Haushalter, R. M., 87
Hayes, M. L., 12
Hays, J. R., 53
Heber, R., 33, 201
Heck, E. T., 249
Hedberg, S., 75
Hedrick, V., 156
Hendrickson, B., 265
Herbers, J., 218
Heward, W. L., 146
Hewett, F. M., 280
Hickman, M. R., 69
Highland, A. C., 227
Holden, C., 89
Holmes, L., 31
Hong, K. M., 250
Horne, M. D., 13
Howe, S. G., 148
Huber, J., 97
Hunder, B., 199
Huxley, A., 96

Isaacs, J., 111
Isser, N., 214, 217

Jackson, N. E., 266
Jacobs, U., 158
Jacobson, L., 211
Jansma, P., 116
Johnson, A. M., 248
Johnson, C., 75

Johnson, J. L., 258
Johnson, W., 168
Jones, J. K., 267
Jones, R. S., 266
Jones, T. W., 267

Kandall, D. B., 250
Karmel, C. A., 160
Karnes, F. A., 264
Kaslow, F. W., 74
Kaufman, J. M., 144
Kautz, C., 148
Kelley, J. A., 53
Kelly, J. B., 234–235
Kerlin, M. A., 72
Kessler, R. C., 250
Kinard, E. M., 251
Kirk, S. A., 169
Klerman, L. V., 251
Koch, J. H., 31
Koch, R., 31
Kolvin, I., 227
Korn, S., 297
Kotanchick, N. L., 302
Krause, I. B., 155
Kuriloff, P., 17
Kushnir, M. V., 169
Kutsick, K., 73

LaGreca, A. M., 75
Laird, A. W., 89, 271
Landau, E. D., 136
Landman, J. B., 98
Lavallee, E., 89
Lavigeur, L., 65
Laycock, V. K., 47
Leff, R. B., 172
Leff, S. L., 172
Lehr, D. H., 12
Leland, H., 39
Levitt, H., 136
Levy, H. B., 56
Levy, P. S., 96
Lewin, D., 65
Lewis, C., 96, 184
Lewis, D. O., 249
Lieberman, L. M., 287
Lindsey, J. D., 72
Lindsey, M., 271–272
Ling, G. M., 65
Litton, F. W., 267
Lloyd, G. G., 239
Locks, N. A., 184
Lovass, O. I., 238
Lucito, L. J., 26
Luick, A. H., 169
Luxenberg, S., 190

MacMillan, D. L., 43, 45
Macdonald, R., 161

Malian, I. M., 171
Margulies, R. Z., 250
Marion, R. L., 302
Markel, G., 73
Marland, S., 6
Marland, S. P., 81
Marohn, R. C., 248
Maron, S. S., 148, 150
Martinez, D. H., 148, 150
McElroy, M. R., 111
McKinnon, A., 265
McNett, I., 200
Meadow, A., 213
Mehren, E., 89
Meisbov, G. B., 75
Mercer, J. R., 184, 210
Meyen, E. L., 12
Miller, E. L., 36
Miller, P. F., 46
Milne, N. M., 116
Minde, K., 65
Mintzer, E., 249
Mitchell, B. M., 271
Mitchell, J. E., 250
Montessori, M., 70
Moores, D. F., 123, 126, 131
Mullins, D., 53
Murnane, R. J., 279

Nasca, D., 81
Nash, W., 102
National Advisory
   Committee on the
   Handicapped, 287
National Association for
   Retarded Citizens,
   270
Nazzaro, J. N., 112, 131
Newman, D. J., 241
Newman, J., 265
Newsnotes, 178
Nihira, K., 39
Norden, K., 128
Nordoff, P., 238

Offenberger, D. M., 150
Orlansky, M. D., 146
Orrick, A. H., 96
Orwell, G., 96
Ostrov, E., 248

Page, E. B., 202
Pang, H., 89
Parnes, 81
Patton, J. M., 264
Pearl, R. A., 66
Pegnato, C. W., 81
Perloff, B. F., 238
Perrin, D. W., 216
Phillips, B. R., 279

SUBJECT INDEX

Evaluation. *See* Assessment
Exceptional students:
  categories of, 2–3
  families of, 295–306
  federal legislation, 5–18
  friends of, 300–301
  grandparents of, 299–300
  local school districts and, 19–20
  optimal conditions for, 263
  parent organizations, 303–304
  parental reactions to, 296–297
  peer response, 13–14
  prevalence of, 3–4
  professional-parent interaction, 301–303
  regular class integration, 15
  state laws and, 18–19
Exceptionally able students, 79–104
  academic counseling, 100–101
  acceleration of, 91, 93
  career guidance, 101–102
  educational modifications, 89–100
  educational options, 90–95
  enrichment for, 94–95
  ESEA provisions, 6
  exceptionally gifted, 88–89
  gifted disadvantaged students, 87–88
  gifted handicapped students, 85
  girls, 95, 102
  independent study for, 96–97
  magnet schools, 90
  mainstreaming of, 93–99
  programmed materials for, 97
  segregation of, 90–91
  socially gifted, 87
  special programs for, 99–100
  testing patterns of, 9
  teacher preparation, 271–272
  WISC results, 26–27
See also Intellectually gifted students;
    Creative students; Talented students
Expressive psychomotor dysfunction, 62
Eye-hand coordination:
  activities for, 69
  deficits, 62, 65

Federal legislation:
  bilingual education, 178
  exceptional students, 5–18
  government role and responsibility, 17–18
  for physically impaired, 106
  See also Education for All Handicapped
    Children Act of 1975
Finger spelling, 134

Gates-McKillop Reading Diagnostic Test, 8
Genetics, mental retardation and, 30–31
Geniuses, 88–89
Gesell Developmental Schedules, 39
Get Set, 199, 202–203

Gifted students. *See* Exceptionally able
  students
Gifted and Talented Children's Act of 1978
  (Public Law 95–561), 80
Goodenough-Harris Draw-a-Man Test, 60, 81
Grand mal seizure, 111
Griggs et al. v. *Duke Power Co.*, 290
Group tests, 26

Hearing impaired students, 122–139
  categories of, 125–126
  Computer Assisted Instruction, 136
  communication methods, 134–135
  communication techniques controversy,
    134–135
  cued speech, 135
  educational difficulties, 127–128
  educational modifications for, 129–137
  emotional adjustments, 128–129
  instructional equipment, 130–131
  intelligence test and, 127–128
  lipreading, 134–135
  mainstreaming, 132–134
  manual alphabet, 134–135
  nonverbal tests and, 127–128
  Phonic Ear, 130
  personal-social difficulties, 128–129
  physical facilities for, 129–130
  placement of, 131–134
  prelingual deaf, 131
  segregated day schools, 132
  "signed English," 134
  TTY, 129
  teacher preparation, 273–274
  teaching strategies, 135–137
  vocational planning for, 137
Hearing impairment:
  causes of, 123–124
  degrees of impairment, 125–126
  early diagnosis, 123–124
  premature birth and, 123
Hygiene, instruction for mentally retarded,
  49
Hyperactivity:
  dance and music for, 74
  learning disabled and, 65
  stimulant drug therapy, 65
Hyperdistractability, 57
  academic activities and, 70

IEP. *See* Individualized Education Program
IQ tests:
  assessment of mentally retarded, 39–40
  use as aptitude test, 39
Illinois Test of Psycholinguistic Abilities,
  60, 169
Inconsequential children, 231
Individualized Education Program (IEP), 7,
  10–11

Psychomotor skills, instruction for mentally retarded, 47–48
Psychosocially troubled students, 221–222. *See also* Emotionally troubled students; Socially maladjusted students
Public Law 94–142. *See* Education for All Handicapped Children Act of 1975
Public Law 95–561 (Title IX, Education Amendments of 1978), 6
Pygmalion in the Classroom (Rosenthal and Jacobson), 211

Rapid advancement, 91
Reading:
 comprehension activity, 71
 instruction for mentally retarded, 51–52
 learning disabled and, 65
Receptive psychomotor dysfunction, 61–62
Regular class placement, PARC decision, 6
Rehabilitation Act of 1973, 6, 19, 106–112
Renzulli-Hartman scales, 80
Resource agencies, 336–337
Retinitis pigmentosa, 141
Retrolental fibroplasia (RLF), 142
Rubella (German Measles), 31
 blindness and, 142
 epidemic of 1964–65, 156
 hearing impairment and, 123

Schizophrenics, 226
School phobia, 232–233
Selective attention, 57
Sensory impairments, multiple, 155
Severely and profoundly retarded, 34, 38
 personal-social skills, 48
 psychomotor skills, 47–48
Severely hearing impaired, 127
 average IQ, 127
 mainstreaming, 132
 TTY, 129
Sex education:
 mentally retarded, instruction, 49
 physically disabled, 118
Siblings, of exceptional children, 297–299
Sign language, 134
"Signed English," 134
"Six-hour retardates," 36
Skill level, assessment of, 8
Snellen eye chart, false results, 9
Socially gifted students, 87
Socially maladjusted students, 245–260
 arsonists, 249
 behavior modification program, 258
 delinquents, 248–249
 family influences on, 246–247
 institutionalized delinquents, 252, 258–259
 orthogenic disciplinary schools, 253
 peer influences on, 247–248

placement for, 252–256
 societal influences on, 246–247
 substance abusers, 249–251
 teacher preparation, 279–280
 teaching strategies, 256–259
 teenage parents, 251
Sound discrimination, remediation of, 70
Spasticity, 109–110
Special education:
 administration and, 282–294
 administrator/parent interaction, 290
 budget preparation, 286
 coordinator as line/staff position, 283–285
 course work, 268–269
 curriculum design, 286–288
 developing IEPs, 286–288
 general description, 2
 materials selection, 291
 personnel evaluation and selection, 285–286
 principal's role, 291–292
 student selection for, 288–290
 teacher "burnout," 288
 teachers of the exceptionally able, 271–272
 teachers of the learning disabled, 270–271
 teachers of the retarded, 269–270
Speech impaired students, 165–175
 classroom support and, 174
 emotional factors, 169
 psychotherapy, 173
 remedial techniques, 171–173
 resource teachers and, 169–171
 stuttering therapy program, 167, 172–173
 teacher preparation, 276–277
Speech impairments:
 articulation difficulties, 166–168
 causes of, 166–167
 lack of fluency, 168
 severe disorders, 169
 vocal disorders, 166, 168
Speech pathologist, 276
Spelling disability, remediation techniques, 72
Spina bifida, 109
Standard deviation, 38
Stanford-Binet, 8
State legislation, for exceptional students, 18–19
State level, services for physically impaired, 106
Statistical approach, to evaluation, 37–38
Stimulants, drug therapy, 65
Stuttering:
 remediation approaches, 167, 172–173
Substance abuse:
 predictors of, 250
 programs for, 258
Suicidal students, 228